"Navy Blue and Gold"
History of Navy Midshipmen Football

College Football History Books available at www.stevesfootballbible.com

Introduction

My love of College Football began in 1966. As a 7-year-old kid I remember watching the Notre Dame-Michigan State "Game of the Century". Next, I remember the 1967 USC-UCLA game and O.J. Simpson weaving through the UCLA defense for the winning touchdown with 6 minutes left in the game. I remember the 1968 Rose Bowl, Indiana vs USC. Who was this Indiana team that went to the Rose Bowl over my beloved Minnesota Golden Gopher's?   I attended my first college football game in 1971. Michigan vs Minnesota at Memorial Stadium on the Campus of the University of Minnesota. My Aunt Roberta took me. I was hooked after that. The Golden Gophers were defeated that day 35-7 by the Wolverines. George Honza of the Golden Gophers scored the only touchdown that day on a pass from Craig Curry. Ironically, I met Mr. Honza in January of 2017 while officiating a basketball game. Growing up in a rural farming town (Alden) in southern Minnesota, as a youth I spent a lot of my Saturday's in the fall watching ABC Sports College game of the week.

This book is for all the College Football fans, casual or diehard, historians or those who just plain love the College game. I hope everyone enjoys it.

Steve Fulton

Contents

College Football History Books are available at www.stevesfootballbible.com

Brief History of Navy Football
Navy Midshipmen

The Naval Academy completed its final season as an FBS independent school (not in a conference) in 2014 and became a single-sport member of the American Athletic Conference beginning in the 2015 season. Navy has 19 players and three coaches in the College Football Hall of Fame and won the college football national championship in 1926 according to the Boand and Houlgate poll systems. The 1910 team also was undefeated and unscored upon (the lone tie was a 0–0 game). The mascot is Bill the Goat. The three major service academies—Air Force, Army, and Navy—compete for the Commander-in-Chief's Trophy, which is awarded to the academy that defeats the others in football that year (or retained by the previous winner in the event of a three-way tie).

Early History

The Naval Academy's football program is one of the nation's oldest, with its history dating back to 1879. There were two separate efforts to establish a Naval Academy football team in 1879. The first was guided by first-classman J.H. Robinson, who developed it as a training regimen to help keep the school's baseball team in shape. The team played the sport under rules that made it much closer to soccer, where the players were permitted only to kick the ball to advance it. The second effort, headed by first-classman William John Maxwell was more successful in its efforts. Maxwell met with two of his friends, Tunstall Smith and Henry Woods, who played for the Baltimore Athletic Club and officially challenged their team to a game with the Naval Academy. A team was formed from academy first-classmen, which Maxwell led as a manager, trainer, and captain. The team would wake up and practice before reveille and following drill and meals. The squad received encouragement from some of the faculty, who allowed them to eat a late dinner and skip final drill for additional practice. This was against the direct orders of the school superintendent, who had banned football and similar activities.

The year's sole contest was played on December 11 against the Baltimore Athletic Club. The opposition's team was reportedly composed of players from Princeton, Yale, Pennsylvania, and Johns Hopkins. The Naval Academy hosted the Baltimore team on a temporary field drawn on part of the superintendent's cow pasture. Rules decided upon between the teams established that the game was to be played under rugby rules. The Baltimore American and Chronicle, which covered the contest, described it as such: The game, played under rugby rules, was a battle from beginning to end—a regular knock down and drag out fight. Both sides became immediately excited, and the audience was aroused to the highest pitch of enthusiasm by the spirited contest. The ball oscillated backward and forward over the ground without any material result.

The scrimmages were something awful to witness—living, kicking, scrambling masses of humanity surging to and fro, everyone after the leather oval. If a Baltimorean got the ball and started for a run, he was unfailingly caught by one of the brawny Cadets and dashed to earth with five or six men falling on him. The game was closely fought and was finally declared a scoreless tie by the referee about an hour after it began. Navy reportedly never gained possession of the ball. However, the Naval Academy managed to keep the Baltimore Athletic Club from ever being in a scoring position. On three separate occasions, Navy forced Baltimore back into its own end zone for a safety; these were not worth any points until 1882, however, so they offered Navy no benefit. The American and Chronicle reported that Maxwell, Craven, and Sample of Navy gave the strongest performances, but were also reckless in their play and were repeatedly penalized for jumping offside or kicking the ball out of play, a form of delay of game.

Sometime after the game, Walter Camp, known as the "Father of American Football", credited Maxwell as the inventor of the first football uniform. After he was informed that the Baltimore team, he was playing outweighed his by an average of ten pounds, Maxwell looked for a way to make the teams more evenly matched. Using his knowledge of sailing, he decided to design a sleeveless canvas jacket which would make his players "difficult to grasp when they begin to sweat". He presented the design to the academy's tailor, who created the double-lined jackets which "were laced down the front and drawn tightly to fit snugly around a player's body". The weighted suits were worn by the team, which was confused by the "strangle, heavy, newfangled getups".

The Naval Academy would not produce another football team until the 1882 season. The 1882 team would be the first with a coach, being supported by Academy officials. The 1879 season was the last time that a Navy squad would play the Baltimore Athletic Club. Navy would finish the 1880s with four winning seasons, and an overall record of 14–12–2, with one of those ties being the game against the Baltimore Athletic Club. Navy would outscore their opponents 292–231 and would finish the 19th century with an overall record of 54–19–3. The lack of a coach for the 1879 season was one of the two times the Naval Academy squad lacked one, the other time being from 1883 through 1891.

Frank Berrien served as Navy's head football coach from 1908 to 1910, compiling a record of 21–5–3. He was the thirteenth head coach of the Naval Academy's football program, and, under his tutelage, the Midshipmen compiled an undefeated 8–0–1 mark in 1910.

Three undefeated teams with nearly identical records would cause a stir among fans and pollsters today, but this was the case when Navy earned its lone national championship in 1926, as the Midshipmen shared the honor with Stanford and Alabama. A 7–7 tie between Alabama and Stanford in the 1926 Rose Bowl gave Stanford a 10–0–1 mark, while the Crimson Tide and the Midshipmen each had identical 9–0–1 records.

The Midshipmen opened the '26 season with a new coach, Bill Ingram. A Navy football standout from 1916 through 1918, Ingram took over a Navy team that had only won seven games in the previous two seasons combined. One of the keys to Navy's 1926 squad was a potent offense led by All-America tackle and team captain Frank Wickhorst, who proved to be a punishing blocker for the Navy offense. One member of the Navy offense that appreciated the blocking of Wickhorst was Tom Hamilton. The quarterback and kicker had a pair of 100 yard rushing games en route to All-America honors.

Navy's biggest win that year was against Michigan in front of 80,000 fans in Baltimore. The Midshipmen scored 10 second half points to upset the Wolverines, 10–0. Navy's offense tallied 165 yards behind the powering attack of Hamilton and Henry Caldwell who scored Navy's lone touchdown on a one yard plunge. Jubilation from the victory continued after the game, as the Midshipmen tore down the goal post at each end of the field and carried away all the markers that lined both sides of the field.

Navy headed into its season finale against Army with a 9–0 record. The game was to be played in Chicago at Soldier Field, which had been built as a memorial to the men killed in World War I. It was only natural Army and Navy would be invited to play the inaugural contest there. James R. Harrison of the New York Times described the game as "the greatest of its time and as a national spectacle." Over 110,000 people witnessed the Midshipmen open a 14–0 lead on the Cadets, only to see Army fight back to take a 21-14 lead early in the third quarter. The Navy offense responded behind its strong ground game led by running back Alan Shapley. On fourth down and three yards to go, Shapley ran eight yards for a touchdown to tie the game at 21. As the final quarter concluded, Army mounted a brief threat only to miss a 25 yard field goal.

The tie gave the Midshipmen a share of the national championship based on retroactive rankings by both the William Boand and Deke Houlgate mathematical poll systems.

Navy was one of the very few programs to field a football team during World War II, with John Whelchel leading the Midshipmen from 1942 to 1943 and Oscar Hagberg serving as head coach from 1944 to 1945. During those years, three of the four Navy teams finished ranked in the top 10 of the final AP poll.

George Sauer left his post as Kansas head coach and took over in Annapolis from 1948 to 1949. The Midshipmen struggled under Sauer's tutelage, posting a 3–13–2 record which included a winless 1948 season.

Traditions
Anchors Aweigh
"Anchors Aweigh" was written by Lt. Charles Zimmermann, Musical Director of the Naval Academy in 1906, with the lyrics provided by Alfred H. Miles of the Class of 1906, as a fight song for the 1907 graduating class instead of the usual class march Zimmermann had composed for previous classes. The song made its debut at the 1906 Army-Navy game, and when the Midshipmen won the game, the song became traditional at this game. It gained national exposure in the 1920s and 1930s when it was heard on the radio and was in several popular movies.

Bill the Goat
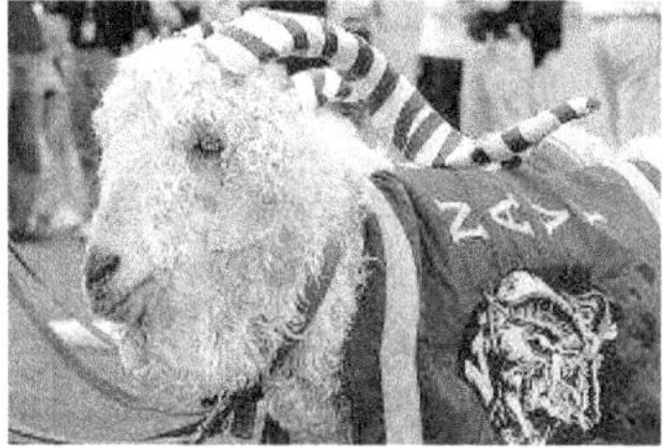
The first recorded use of a goat mascot for Navy athletic teams was in 1893 when an animal named El Cid (The Chief) was turned over to the Brigade by young officers of the USS New York. El Cid helped Navy to a 6-4 triumph over Army that year. Two cats, a dog, and a carrier pigeon have also enjoyed brief reigns as the Navy mascot, but goats have served without interruption since 1904.

Bill XXXVI (36) and Bill XXXVII (37) are the current mascots. A group of midshipmen from the 8th company, known as Team Bill, are trained as goat handlers to ensure the goats' safety, security and comfort on the sidelines during football games.

Enterprise Bell
From the bridge of the famed World War II aircraft carrier, it has been a part of the Naval Academy tradition since 1950. The late Admiral Harry W. Hill, then Superintendent, was instrumental in bringing the "E" Bell to Annapolis. It rings during special ceremonies honoring the sports teams that won the N-Star against Army. The bell is stationed in front of Bancroft Hall.

Midshipman
The word midshipman first appeared in English in the 17th century in the form of the word midshipman to designate those men who were stationed "amidships," i.e. in the waist or middle portion of the vessel, while on duty. By 1687, however, the second's' had been dropped to give the current form of the word. Midshipmen were originally boys, sometimes as young as seven or eight, who were apprenticed to sea captains to learn the sailor's trade.

In the early days of the American Navy, midshipmen trained aboard ship until they were eventually commissioned as ensigns. With the founding of the Naval Academy in 1845, it became possible, as it still is, for a midshipman to enter the Navy directly from civilian life. The name of students at the Naval Academy changed several times between 1870 and 1902, when Congress restored the original title of Midshipman, and it has remained unchanged since.

Tecumseh
The familiar Native American figurehead facing Bancroft Hall and Tecumseh Court has been an Annapolis resident since 1866. Originally, the figurehead of the USS Delaware was meant to portray Tamanend, the great chief of the Delawares. It developed that Tamanend was a lover of peace and did not strike the fancy of the Brigade. Looking for another name, Midshipmen referred to the figurehead as Powhatan and King Philip before finally settling on Tecumseh, the fierce Shawnee chieftain who lived from 1768-1813. The original wooden statue was replaced after some 50 years in the open weather by a durable bronze replica, presented by the Class of 1891. It is considered a good luck "mascot" for the midshipmen, who in times past would throw pennies at it and offer left-handed salutes whenever they wanted a 'favor', such as a sports win over West Point, or spiritual help for examinations. These days it receives a fresh coat of war paint and is often decorated in various themes during football weeks and other special occasions such as Commissioning Week.

National championships

Season	Coach	Selector	Record
1926	Bill Ingram	Boand System, Houlgate System	9–0–1

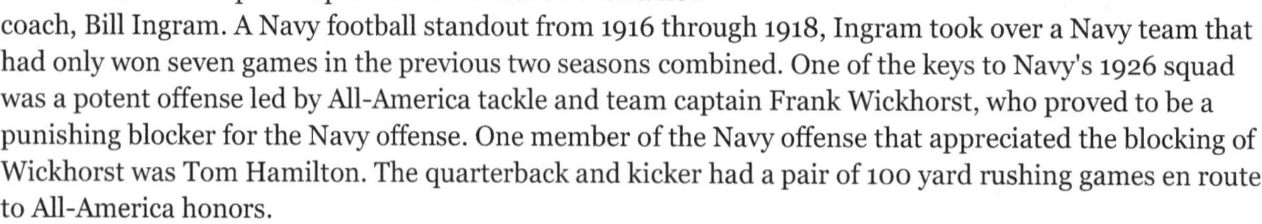

Three undefeated teams with nearly identical records would cause a stir among fans and pollsters today, but this was the case when Navy earned its lone national championship in 1926, as the Midshipmen shared the honor with Stanford and Alabama. A 7–7 tie between Alabama and Stanford in the 1927 Rose Bowl gave Stanford a 10–0–1 mark, while the Crimson Tide and the Mids each had identical 9–0–1 records.

The Midshipmen opened the '26 season with a new coach, Bill Ingram. A Navy football standout from 1916 through 1918, Ingram took over a Navy team that had only won seven games in the previous two seasons combined. One of the keys to Navy's 1926 squad was a potent offense led by All-America tackle and team captain Frank Wickhorst, who proved to be a punishing blocker for the Navy offense. One member of the Navy offense that appreciated the blocking of Wickhorst was Tom Hamilton. The quarterback and kicker had a pair of 100 yard rushing games en route to All-America honors.

Navy's biggest win that year was against Michigan in front of 80,000 fans in Baltimore. The Mids scored 10 second half points to upset the Wolverines, 10–0. Navy's offense tallied 165 yards behind the powering attack of Hamilton and Henry Caldwell who scored Navy's lone touchdown on a one yard plunge. Jubilation from the victory continued after the game, as the Midshipmen tore down the goal post at each end of the field and carried away all the markers that lined both sides of the field.

Navy headed into its season finale against Army with a 9–0 record. The game was to be played in Chicago at Soldier Field, which had been built as a memorial to the men killed in World War I. It was only natural Army and Navy would be invited to play the inaugural contest there. James R. Harrison of the New York Times described the game as "the greatest of its time and as a national spectacle." Over 110,000 people witnessed the Midshipmen open a 14–0 lead on the Cadets, only to see Army fight back to take a 21–14 lead early in the third quarter. The Navy offense responded behind its strong ground game led by running back Alan Shapley. On fourth down and three yards to go, Shapley ran eight yards for a touchdown to tie the game at 21. As the final quarter concluded, Army mounted a brief threat only to miss a 25 yard field goal.

The tie gave the Midshipmen a share of the national championship based on retroactive rankings by both the William Boand and Deke Houlgate mathematical poll systems.

Lambert Trophy

The Lambert-Meadowlands Trophy (known as the Lambert Trophy), established in 1936, is an annual award given to the best team in the East in Division I FBS (formerly I-A) college football and is presented by the Metropolitan New York Football Writers. Navy has won the Lambert Trophy five times.

Year	Coach	Record	Final AP Rank
1943	John Whelchel	8-1	#4
1957	Eddie Erdelatz	9-1-1	#5
1960	Wayne Hardin	9-2	#4
1963	Wayne Hardin	9-2	#2
2015	Ken Niumatalolo	11-2	#18
2019	Ken Niumatalolo	11-2	#20

Commander-In-Chief Trophy

The Commander-in-Chief's Trophy is awarded to each season's winner of the American college football series among the teams of the U.S. Military Academy (Army Black Knights), the U.S. Naval Academy (Navy Midshipmen), and the U.S. Air Force Academy (Air Force Falcons). The Navy–Air Force game is normally played on the first Saturday in October, the Army–Air Force game on the first Saturday in November, and the Army–Navy Game on the second Saturday in December. In the event of a tie, the award is shared, but the previous winner retains physical possession of the trophy. The Commander-in-Chief's Trophy and the Michigan MAC Trophy are the only NCAA Division I FBS triangular rivalry trophies awarded annually. A few others, such as the Florida Cup and the Beehive Boot, are contested sporadically. Through 2022, the Air Force Falcons hold the most trophy victories with 21. The Navy Midshipmen have won 16. The Army Black Knights trail with 9. The trophy has been shared on five occasions, most recently in 2021.

The Commander-in-Chief's trophy was the brainchild of Air Force General George B. Simler, a former Air Force Academy athletic director who envisioned the trophy to create an annual series of football games for the Air Force Academy against the Military Academy and the Naval Academy. First awarded in 1972 by President Richard Nixon, the trophy itself is jointly sponsored by the alumni associations of the three academies. The trophy is named for the U.S. President, who is the Commander-in-Chief of all U.S. military services under the U.S. Constitution. The President has personally awarded the trophy on several occasions. During the 1980s, for instance, President Ronald Reagan presented the award in an annual White House ceremony. In 1996, President Bill Clinton presented the trophy to the Army team at Veterans Stadium after the Army–Navy Game. From 2003 to 2007, President George W. Bush presented the trophy to Navy teams at ceremonies in the White House.

Years Navy has won the CIC

1973	1975
1978	1979
1981	2003
2004	2005
2006	2007
2008	2009
2012	2013
2015	2019
2024	2025

Heisman Trophy Winners
Joe Bellino {1960}

Joe Bellino, the "Winchester Rifle" is the first Naval Academy football player to win the Heisman Trophy. Born and raised in Winchester, Mass., Bellino was a three-sport star for Winchester High. He was good enough in baseball to be offered a contract out of high school by the Pittsburgh Pirates, but he chose to play football for Navy despite offers from Notre Dame and several Big Ten schools. After a year in prep school, Bellino became an instant star for the Midshipmen. In his three years at Navy, he scored 31 touchdowns, rushed for 1,664 yards on 330 carries, returned 37 kicks for 833 more yards and altogether set 15 Naval Academy football records.

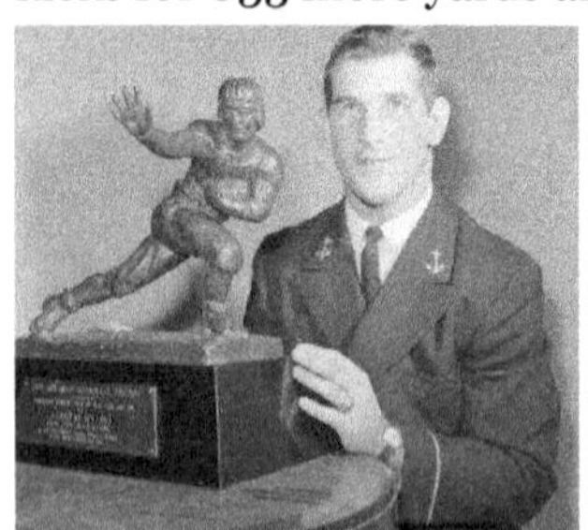

In 1960, Bellino rushed for 834 yards and 17 touchdowns and added 17 receptions for another 280 yards and scored another three TDs via pass receptions, while leading Navy to a 9-2 record. After beating archrival Army 17-12, Navy earned an invitation to the prestigious Orange Bowl – losing 21-14 to Missouri on Jan. 2 in Miami. Bellino also inspired a 14-7 win over Notre Dame and had four touchdowns and a 90 yard run against Virginia that season. He was a unanimous All-America selection and the winner of the Maxwell Award. He won the Heisman handily over Richie Lucas of Penn State, totaling 1,929 points to Lucas' 613. Bellino's number 27 jersey was retired after the 1960 season. He had a three-year stint with the Boston Patriots after he had completed his four-year service obligation. He then stayed in the Navy Reserves and reached the rank of Captain. Bellino was a 1977 inductee into the National Football Foundation and Hall of Fame and was a charter inductee into the Maryland Football Shrine in 1984.

Roger Staubach {1963}

In 1963, Staubach became the second Naval Academy football player in four years to win the Heisman Trophy. Known as "Roger the Dodger," all he did as a junior quarterback was lead Navy to a ranking of second in the country and a berth in the Cotton Bowl, where he set Bowl records for pass completions (21-of-31) and yards passing (228). The Midshipmen posted wins over West Virginia, Michigan, Notre Dame and Maryland that season. He completed 106 passes in 161 attempts for 1,474 yards, while earning consensus All-America honors, as well as the Maxwell Trophy and Walter Camp Memorial Trophy.

At one time, Staubach, who was hampered by injuries in his senior season of 1964, had set 28 Naval Academy records in football. He also had some outstanding performances as a varsity baseball player and a brief but significant moment as a varsity basketball player. He lettered in baseball three-straight years (1963-65) as an outfielder and pitcher. In 1963, he hit .420, and in 1965 he was the team captain. He also won a letter in basketball in 1962-63. Staubach was the recipient of the Thompson Trophy Cup at the Academy for three-consecutive years and was the 1965 winner of the Naval Academy Athletic Association Sword. He was the first sophomore to win the Thompson Trophy Cup and is its only three-time winner. He was only the fourth midshipman since 1900 to win both the Thompson Trophy Cup and NAAA Sword.

After four years in the U. S. Navy, including a tour in Vietnam, Staubach joined the Dallas Cowboys and led that team to unprecedented heights. Again, displaying the daring play he had shown at Navy, Staubach directed the Cowboys to 23 fourth-quarter comeback wins, 14 in the final two minutes of a game or in overtime. He played 11 season with the Cowboys and led them to the Super Bowl four times, including world championships in 1972 and 1978. The Cowboys were 90-31 with Staubach as their starting quarterback. Among his awards were the NFL Players Association Most Valuable Player and The Sporting News NFL Player of the Year in 1971, Most Valuable Player of Super Bowl VI (1972), Washington Touchdown Club NFC Player of the Year in 1976 and 1978, NFC Pro Bowl selection five times, the Vince Lombardi Sportsman of the Year Award in 1975, NFL Players' Association NFC Offensive Player of the Year (1978), and the Byron "Whizzer" White Humanitarian Award in 1979. Staubach was named Walter Camp Foundation Man of the Year in 1985, was selected to the Pro Football Hall of Fame in 1985, his first year of eligibility. The football locker room in Ricketts Hall was named in his honor in 1996 and in 2008, Staubach received the National Football Foundation's Gold Medal, the highest honor one can receive from that organization. Staubach has also been honored as a "Distinguished Graduate" of the United States Naval Academy. He recently was named to the Walter Camp All-Century Team, was elected to the Cotton Bowl Hall of Fame, spearheaded a successful movement to land North Texas and the Dallas Cowboys the Super Bowl in 2011 and was named to the Navy-Marine Corps Memorial Stadium All-Stadium Team.

College Football Hall of Fame

Players	Years	Inducted
Ron Beagle {End}	1953–55	1986
Joe Bellino {RB}	1958–60	1977
Buzz Borries {HB}	1932–34	1960
George Brown {G}	1942–43	1947
John Brown {G / T}	1910–13	1951
Slade Cutter {T}	1932–34	1967
John Dalton {HB}	1908–11	1970
Dick Duden {End}	1943–45	2001
Steve Eisenhauer {T / G}	1951–53	1994
Tom Hamilton {HB}	1924–26	1965
Jonas H. Ingram {FB}	1904-1906	1906
Napoleon McCallum {RB}	1981–85	2002
Skip Minisi {HB}	1944–47	1985
Chet Moeller {S}	1973–75	2010
Bob Reifsnyder {T}	1956–58	1997
Clyde Scott {HB}	1944–48	1971
Dick Scott {C}	1945–47	1987
Roger Staubach {QB}	1962–64	1981
Don Whitmire {T}	1941–44	1956
Frank Wickhorst {T}	1924–26	1970

Coaches	Inducted
Gil Dobie	1951
Bill Ingram	1973
George Welsh	2004
Wayne Hardin	2013

Retired numbers

Number	Player	Position	Tenure
12	Roger Staubach	QB	1961–63
19	Keenan Reynolds	QB	2012–15
27	Joe Bellino	HB	1958–60
30	Napoleon McCallum	RB	1981–85

Bowl Games

Date	Team		Opponent				Bowl
1/2/2026	#23 NAVY {11-2}	vs	CINCINNATI {8-5}	35	13	W	Liberty Bowl
12/27/2024	NAVY (10-3)	vs	OKLAHOMA (6-7)	21	20	W	Armed Forces Bowl
12/31/2019	#21 NAVY (11-2)	vs	KANSAS STATE (8-5)	20	17	W	Liberty Bowl
12/28/2017	NAVY (7-6)	vs	VIRGINIA (6-7)	49	7	W	Military Bowl
12/22/2016	#25 NAVY (9-5)	vs	LOUISIANA TECH (9-5)	45	48	L	Armed Forces Bowl
12/28/2015	#21 NAVY (11-2)	vs	PITTSBURGH (8-5)	44	28	W	Military Bowl
12/23/2014	NAVY (8-5)	vs	SAN DIEGO STATE (7-6)	17	16	W	Poinsettia Bowl
12/30/2013	NAVY (9-4)	vs	MIDDLE TENNESSEE (8-5)	24	6	W	Armed Forces Bowl
12/29/2012	NAVY (8-5)	vs	ARIZONA STATE (8-5)	28	62	L	Kraft Fight Hunger Bowl
12/23/2010	NAVY (9-4)	vs	SAN DIEGO STATE (9-4)	14	35	L	Poinsettia Bowl
12/31/2009	NAVY (10-4)	vs	MISSOURI (8-5)	35	13	W	Texas Bowl
12/20/2008	NAVY (8-5)	vs	WAKE FOREST (8-5)	19	29	L	EagleBank Bowl
12/20/2007	NAVY (8-5)	vs	UTAH (9-4)	32	35	L	Poinsettia Bowl
12/30/2006	NAVY (9-4)	vs	#23 BOSTON COLLEGE (10-3)	24	25	L	Meineke Car Care Bowl
12/22/2005	NAVY (8-4)	vs	COLORADO STATE (6-6)	51	30	W	Poinsettia Bowl
12/30/2004	#24 NAVY (10-2)	vs	NEW MEXICO (7-5)	34	19	W	Emerald Bowl
12/30/2003	NAVY (8-5)	vs	TEXAS TECH (8-5)	14	38	L	Houston Bowl
12/25/1996	NAVY (9-3)	vs	CALIFORNIA (6-6)	42	38	W	Aloha Bowl
12/30/1981	NAVY (7-4-1)	vs	#15 OHIO STATE (9-3)	28	31	L	Liberty Bowl
12/14/1980	NAVY (8-4)	vs	HOUSTON (7-5)	0	35	L	Garden State Bowl
12/22/1978	NAVY (9-3)	vs	BYU (9-4)	23	16	W	Holiday Bowl
1/1/1964	#2 NAVY (9-2)	vs	#1 TEXAS (11-0)	6	28	L	Cotton Bowl
1/2/1961	#4 NAVY (9-2)	vs	#5 MISSOURI (10-1)	14	21	L	Orange Bowl
1/1/1958	#8 NAVY (9-1-1)	vs	#9 RICE (7-4)	20	7	W	Cotton Bowl
1/1/1955	#5 NAVY (8-2)	vs	#6 MISSISSIPPI (9-2)	21	0	W	Sugar Bowl
1/1/1924	NAVY (5-1-3)	vs	WASHINGTON (10-1-1)	14	14	T	Rose Bowl

Rivalries
ARMY

The Army–Navy game is one of the most traditional and enduring rivalries in college football. It has been frequently attended by sitting U.S. presidents. The game has been nationally televised each year since 1945 on either ABC, CBS or NBC. CBS has televised the game since 1996 and has the rights to the broadcast through 2018. Instant replay made its American debut in the 1963 Army–Navy game. Since 2009, the game has been held the Saturday following FBS conference championship weekend. The game has been held in multiple locations, but outside the 1926 game in Chicago and 1983 game in Pasadena, California, it has been along the East Coast, most frequently in Philadelphia, followed by the New York City area and Baltimore. The series has been marked by several periods of domination by one team or the other, with Navy's 14 game winning streak from 2002 through 2015 being the longest for either side.

The **Thompson Cup** is between the Army West Point Black Knights of the United States Military Academy (USMA) at West Point, New York, and the Navy Midshipmen from the United States Naval Academy (USNA) at Annapolis, Maryland. The Black Knights (formerly the "Army Cadets" and "Army Black Knights") and Midshipmen each represent their service's oldest officer commissioning sources. As such, the game has come to embody the spirit of the inter service rivalry of the United States Armed Forces. The game marks the end of the college football regular season and the third and final game of the season's Commander-in-Chief's Trophy series, which also includes the Air Force Falcons of the United States Air Force Academy (USAFA) near Colorado Springs, Colorado.

Series history - Army and Navy first met on the football field on November 29, 1890. The series has been renewed annually since 1899, except for 1909, 1917, 1918 and 1929. It has been held at several locations throughout its history, including Baltimore and New York City, but has most frequently been played in Philadelphia, roughly equidistant from the two academies. Historically played on the Saturday after Thanksgiving (a date on which most other major college football teams end their regular seasons), the game is now played on the second Saturday in December and is traditionally the last game of the season for both teams and the last regular-season game played in College football. With the permanent expansion of the regular season to 12 games starting in 2006, several conference championship games joined the Army–Navy Game on its then-current date of the first weekend of December. In 2009, the game was moved from the first Saturday in December to the second Saturday; this means that it no longer conflicts with conference championship games and once again is the last non-bowl contest in college football. This game has inter-service "bragging rights" at stake. For much of the first half of the 20th century, both Army and Navy were often national powers, and the game occasionally had national championship implications. However, as the level of play in college football improved nationally and became fueled by prospects of playing in the National Football League (NFL), the high academic entrance requirements, height and weight limits, and the five-year military commitment required has reduced the overall competitiveness of both academies. Since 1963, only the 1996, 2010, and 2016 games have seen both teams enter with winning records. Nonetheless, the game is considered a college football institution. It has aired nationally on radio since the late 1920s and has been nationally televised every year since 1945. The tradition associated with the game assures that it remains nationally broadcast to this day. Arguably, one of the reasons this game has maintained its appeal is that the players are playing solely for the love of the game. Most players are required to fulfill a post-graduation active duty military commitment and, by the time this ends, many players are deemed too old to consider playing competitively again. Nevertheless, some participants in the Army–Navy Game have gone on to professional football careers. Quarterback Roger Staubach (Navy, 1965) went on to a Hall of Fame career with the Dallas Cowboys that included starting at quarterback in two Super Bowls including being named the Most Valuable Player of Super Bowl VI. Wide receiver and Return Specialist Phil McConkey (Navy,

1979) was a popular player on the New York Giants squad that won Super Bowl XXI. Running back Napoleon McCallum (Navy, 1985) was able to complete his commitment to the Navy and play for the then-Los Angeles Raiders in 1986. After satisfying his Navy commitment, he joined the Raiders full-time.

The game is especially emotional for the seniors, called "first classmen" by both academies, since it is typically the last competitive regular season football game they will ever play (though they sometimes play in a subsequent bowl game). During wartime the game is even more emotional, as some seniors will make the ultimate sacrifice once they are deployed. Recognition of those who share the uniform and are deployed overseas is an important part of the day. At the end of the game, both teams alma maters are played and sung. The winning team stands alongside the losing team and faces the losing academy's students; then the losing team accompanies the winning team, facing their students. This is done in a show of mutual respect and solidarity. Since the winning team's alma mater is always played last, the phrase "to sing second" has become synonymous with winning the rivalry game. The rivalry between Annapolis and West Point, while friendly, is intense. Even the mascots (the Navy Goat and Army Mule) have been known to play pranks on each other. The cadets live and breathe the phrase "Beat Navy!" while for midshipmen the opposite phrase, "Beat Army!" is ingrained. They have become a symbol of competitiveness, not just in the Army–Navy Game, but in the service of their country, and are often used at the close of (informal) letters by graduates of both academies. A long-standing tradition at the Army-Navy football game is to conduct a formal "prisoner exchange" as part of the pre-game activities. The prisoners are the cadets and midshipmen currently spending the semester studying at the sister academy. After the exchange, students have a brief reprieve to enjoy the game with their comrades.

The game is the last of three contests in the annual Commander-in-Chief's Trophy series, awarded to each season's winner of the triangular series between Army, Navy, and Air Force since 1972. In years when Navy and Army have each beaten Air Force before the Army-Navy Game (1972, 1977, 1978, 1996, 2005 & 2012) the Army-Navy game has also determined whether Army or Navy would win this trophy. In years when Air Force has split its two games, the Army-Navy game determines whether the trophy is shared or won outright by the winner of the game. The rivalries Army and Navy have with Air Force are much less intense than the Army–Navy rivalry, primarily due to the relative youth of the USAFA, established in 1954, and the physical distance between the USAFA and the other two schools. The Army–Air Force and Navy–Air Force games are usually played at the academies' regular home fields, although on occasion they have been held at a neutral field. Navy won 14 Army-Navy games in a row from 2002 to 2015, the longest winning streak in the history of the series. On December 10, 2016, Army snapped its 14 game losing streak against Navy with a 21–17 victory.

Traditionally, the game is played in Philadelphia, due to the historic nature of the city and the fact that it is approximately halfway between West Point and Annapolis. Additionally, Philadelphia has always had a stadium large enough to accommodate the crowds. Philadelphia's John F. Kennedy Stadium (JFK) hosted the game from 1936 to 1979 (except for three years in World War II) – more than any other venue in the history of the series. It even hosted the game for several years after the 1971 construction of nearby Veterans Stadium, which finally became the game's host in 1980. The Pennsylvania Railroad and its successors offered game-day service to all Army–Navy games (except several during WWII) at John F. Kennedy Stadium, using a sprawling temporary station constructed each year on the railroad's nearby Greenwich freight yard. The service, with 40-odd trains serving as many as 30,000 attendees, was the single largest concentrated passenger rail movement in the country. Franklin Field, on the campus of the University of Pennsylvania, hosted the game in the early twentieth century before it was moved to JFK. New York's Polo Grounds holds the record for most games hosted outside of Philadelphia, even though the last time it hosted one was 1925. The city of Baltimore has hosted a number of games throughout the history of the series as well, even though Baltimore is closer to Annapolis. The Rose Bowl is the only site west of the Mississippi River to host the Army–Navy game; it did so in 1983. The city of Pasadena, California, paid for the travel expenses of all the students and supporters of both academies – 9,437 in all. A substitute, however, for Bill XXII – the Navy mascot – and four rented Army mules were brought in. The attendance was 81,000. The game was held at the Rose Bowl that year because there are many military installations and servicemen and women, along with many retired military personnel, on the West Coast. The game has been held one other time in a non-East Coast venue, at Chicago's Soldier Field, which played host to the 1926 game.

Currently the game is played primarily at Lincoln Financial Field in Philadelphia, the home of the Philadelphia Eagles. Since the 1980s, the game has been held roughly once every three or four years at a site other than Philadelphia. These sites have included Giants Stadium in East Rutherford, New Jersey (replaced in 2010 by MetLife Stadium, which has yet to host the game), M&T Bank Stadium in Baltimore and FedEx Field in Landover, Maryland. These are still considered neutral site games but provide locations that are closer to one academy or the other.

Historical facts of the Army-Navy game

The first Army-Navy game occurred in 1890 when Army Cadet Dennis Mahan Michie agreed to play the Naval Academy after the Midshipmen issued the challenge. The Army team was new, and the game was played at West Point with Navy blanking Army 24-0. Three years later, Navy defeated Army at Annapolis and a post-game argument between a Navy rear admiral and an Army brigadier general almost ended in a duel. President Grover Cleveland called a cabinet meeting that resulted in the Secretary of the Navy and the Secretary of War declaring that each team was restricted from playing one another at home and may not play each other. In fact, a Navy Midshipman wore what is regarded by many as the first ever football helmet, the same game that almost resulted in a duel. His name was Joseph Mason Reeves, and he went on to become an admiral and a major lead of the Navy's aircraft carrier fleet. He had been advised by a Navy doctor that any further trauma to his head would result in "instant insanity" or even death. He asked a local shoemaker to make him a helmet out of leather and the football helmet was born.

- Cadets and midshipmen played the first Army-Navy football game on Nov. 29, 1890 on "The Plain" at West Point. Navy had been playing organized football since 1879 and defeated the newly established Army team, 24-0.
- The 271 members of the Corps of Cadets each contributed 52 cents to pay half of the Navy's traveling costs for the 1890 game.
- Although today we know the game as an annual tradition (and it has been such since 1930), there have been 10 times when the Army-Navy game was not played. It's said that the longest interruption, which lasted from 1894 to 1898, came about after an argument between an Army general and a Navy admiral almost resulted in a duel following the 1893 game. The game also wasn't played in 1909. That year, Army canceled its remaining games after Cadet Eugene Byrne died from an injury sustained in an October game against Harvard. Twice during World War I, in 1917 and 1918, games were canceled on orders from the War Department. And in 1928 and 1929, the academies could not reconcile player eligibility standards.
- On Nov. 27, 1926, the game was held in Chicago for the formal dedication of Soldier Field in honor of the American servicemen who had fought in World War I.
- Going into both the 1944 and 1945 games, Army and Navy were ranked #1 and #2, respectively. Army won both games.
- The tradition of mules as mascots for Army dates to 1899, when a quartermaster officer decided the team needed a mascot to counter the Navy goat and chose a white mule used to pull an ice wagon. However, the first "official" mule was a former U.S. Army pack mule named "Mr. Jackson" that arrived at West Point in 1936. Since Mr. Jackson, there have been 17 "official" Army mules. "Buckshot," the only female of the bunch, arrived at West Point in 1964, a gift from the Air Force Academy. Today, three mules serve as Army mascots: Raider, Ranger II and General Scott.
- Instant replay made its American debut in the 1963 Army-Navy game.
- A 1973 episode of "M*A*S*H" referenced a fictional Army-Navy game that ended 42-36 Navy. To this day, no Army-Navy game has ended with that score. The radio announcer in the episode says the game is the 53rd Army-Navy game. That game was played in 1952; Navy won, 7-0.

- The Rose Bowl is the only site west of the Mississippi River to host the Army-Navy game -- it did so in 1983. Only six Army-Navy games have been held on the campus of either academy. Two of those games were during World War II, one in 1942 and the other in 1943.
- New York's Polo Grounds holds the record for the most games hosted outside of Philadelphia, although the last game played there was in the 1920s.
- Following each game, players sing both teams' alma maters. The winning team joins the losing team and sings facing the losing team's students. Then the losing team joins the victors on their side of the field and sings the winner's alma mater to its students. This act is a show of mutual respect and solidarity.

NOTRE DAME

The **Rip Miller Trophy** is played between the Navy Midshipmen and Notre Dame Fighting Irish. It has been played annually since 1927, making it the longest uninterrupted intersectional rivalry in college football. **Notre Dame leads the series 84–13–1 through the 2025 season.** The trophy is named in honor of Edgar "Rip" Miller, one of Notre Dame's famed "Seven Mules," who served the Naval Academy for 48 years as a coach and athletic administrator. Before Navy won a 46–44 triple-overtime contest in 2007, Notre Dame had a 43-game

winning streak that was the longest series win streak between two annual opponents in the history of Division I FBS football. Navy's previous win came in 1963, 35–14 with future Heisman Trophy winner and NFL QB Roger Staubach at the helm. Navy had come close to winning on numerous occasions before 2007. The Midshipmen subsequently won again in 2009, 2010 and 2016. Though the game is often played at Notre Dame Stadium in South Bend, it has never been played at Navy–Marine Corps Memorial Stadium, due to its relatively small size. Instead, Navy usually hosts the game at larger facilities such as Baltimore's old Memorial Stadium or current M&T Bank Stadium, FedEx Field in Landover, Maryland, or at Giants Stadium in East Rutherford, New Jersey. From 1960 to 1970, the Midshipmen hosted the game at John F. Kennedy Stadium in Philadelphia, and they hosted the 1972, 1974 and 1993 games at Philadelphia's Veterans Stadium. The game has been played twice in Dublin, Ireland—in 1996 at Croke Park and 2012 at Aviva Stadium. The game was also occasionally played at old Cleveland Stadium. The 2016 game was held at EverBank Field in Jacksonville, Florida. Navy's 2018 home game will be played at Qualcomm Stadium in San Diego, California (the first time the teams will have played each other west of the Eastern Time Zone), and the 2020 game will be at MetLife Stadium in East Rutherford, New Jersey (where it also was played in 2010).

History - Despite the one-sided result of the last few decades, most Notre Dame and Navy fans consider the series a sacred tradition for historical reasons. Both schools have strong football traditions going back to the beginnings of the sport. Notre Dame, like many colleges, faced severe financial difficulties during World War II, which were exacerbated by the fact that it was then still an all-male institution. The US Navy made Notre Dame a training center for V-12 candidates and paid enough for usage of the facilities to keep the University afloat. Notre Dame has since extended an open invitation for Navy to play the Fighting Irish in football and considers the game annual repayment on a debt of honor. The series is marked by mutual respect, as evidenced by each team standing at attention during the playing of the other's alma mater after the game, a tradition that started in 2005. Navy's athletic director, on renewing the series through 2016, remarked "...it is of great interest to our collective national audience of Fighting Irish fans, Naval Academy alumni, and the Navy family at large." The series is scheduled to continue indefinitely; renewals are a mere formality.

MARYLAND

The **Crab Bowl Classic**, also known as the **Crab Bowl** or the **Maryland–Navy rivalry**, is between the Maryland Terrapins and the Navy Midshipmen. The two institutions, located in proximity in the state of Maryland, first met for a football game in 1905. Since then, the series has often been marked by controversy, with incidents by players and supporters occurring both on and off the field. The winner of the game is awarded the **Crab Bowl Trophy**. Navy dominated the series early by winning the first eight games, between 1905 and 1930, which remains the longest streak. Maryland secured its first win in 1931 at a neutral site in Washington, D.C. After two more meetings, the series was suspended in 1934 when the

Maryland administration protested a play. The teams met again in 1950 when Navy had a last-minute opening in its schedule. The Terrapins won three consecutive games from 1950 to 1952, and the Midshipmen won three from 1958 to 1963. During the 1964 game, a Maryland player twice flashed an obscene gesture, which prompted Navy to cancel the series again. After contractual obligations were fulfilled with the following year's game, the series was put on hiatus for 40 years. Maryland and Navy finally resumed the rivalry in 2005 and again in 2010, with the Terps winning both contests. **Navy leads the series 14-7** with the last meeting in 2010.

The Naval Academy and the University of Maryland are separated by about 30 miles in the state of Maryland. The schools by their nature, a Federal service academy and a public university, differ radically in terms of culture and lifestyle. For many years, the University of Maryland possessed the reputation of a blue-collar, working-class school. Some students viewed the Naval Academy, with its strictly regimented culture, as elitist. A former Terrapins linebacker, Jerry Fishman, believed that many Midshipmen "thought they were far superior to the Maryland redneck coal miners." A former Navy fullback, Pat Donnelly, said that compared to a "public institution, [the Naval Academy] was night and day. I think there was a feeling of mutual dislike, but it wasn't personal, it was more institutional." According to former Maryland head coach (and former Maryland player) Ralph Friedgen, the sentiment at Navy has been that beating their archrival "Army is a must, but Maryland is a necessity." Darryl Hill, who attended both schools and broke the color barrier on each team, said that the Midshipmen "had a saying that beating Army is great, but beating Maryland is a must." Despite a lopsided start in the early 20th century, the Terps and Midshipmen were evenly matched for most of the history of the series. Between 1931 and 1965, Navy won six and Maryland five games. In the 2005 season opener, Navy was coming off one of its best seasons in history with a 10–2 record the previous year. Maryland struggled later in 2005 but proved a competitive match for Navy and achieved a last-minute win, 23–20. In addition to proximity and competitiveness, the rivalry was fueled by controversial incidents both on and off the field. Maryland supporters long held that Navy players used unnecessary roughness during play, a charge counter-accused by the Academy after the 1963 game. Some Midshipmen would travel to College Park to meet female students, which served to aggravate the ill feelings. Pranks and vandalism were commonplace on both campuses and exacerbated the already tense situation between Maryland and Navy

Trophy - In 2010, the Touchdown Club of Annapolis commissioned the Crab Bowl Trophy, with underwriting by the D'Camera group. The trophy is a large "pewter bowl overflowing with pewter crabs", meant to be replicas of the Chesapeake Bay blue crab. The bowl rests atop a mahogony base, engraved with "the results of the twenty previous Maryland-Navy games", which reach back to the rivalry's origin in 1905. It was designed by Tilghman Company, a family-owned jewelry store in Annapolis, Maryland. The Touchdown Club, founded in 1954, has been associated with both teams for a long time, and annually hosts a dinner honoring both teams. The trophy has been well received; the Terrapins' *Testudo Times* newspaper said that having the trophy "awarded by a third party" rather than "having a trophy dreamed up by the administrations at each school to create a more 'rivalry-y' feel" makes the award seem "more legitimate and less cheesy". Sports Illustrated included the award in its list of the 40 most "Unusual Trophies in College Football".

SMU

The **Ganz Trophy** was created in 2009 through a collaboration between the athletic departments of the United States Naval Academy and Southern Methodist University. The trophy is named for Frank Ganz who played linebacker at the Naval Academy from 1957 through 1959. Ganz later served on the coaching staffs at Colgate, Oklahoma State, SMU, Army, UCLA, Air Force and Navy. **Navy leads the overall series 13-12** through the 2025 season.

Stadiums
Worden Field {1890-1923}

The field is named for Admiral John Lorimer Worden (pictured at right), who joined the navy in 1834. He was captured by the South at the start of the Civil War but was freed in 1862. He became captain of the ironclad USS Monitor and received considerable fame after its battle with the CSS Virginia at the Battle of Hampton Roads. Worden suffered eye injuries in the battle and gave up his command; he supervised ship construction for the rest of the war. He was the superintendent of the academy for five years (1869–1874), and died in 1897, a few years after the field was named after him. The field served as the home stadium for the academy's Midshipmen football team from that year through 1923, replaced by Thompson Stadium in 1924. Since the early 1900s, the field has hosted all the academy's various yearly parades and many of its drills. It has progressively grown smaller, due to the addition of buildings and roads within the academy. The Navy football team played its first game against the Baltimore Athletic Club in 1879 and it ended in a scoreless tie. From that year throughout the 1880s, Navy played all but one of their games at home. Writers Taylor Baldwin Kiland and Jamie Howren stated that all the games played at Annapolis were likely hosted on an unused parade or drill field. During that period, the team amassed a record of thirteen wins, twelve losses, and two ties, including a 6–3 lead over rival Johns Hopkins. Sometime around 1890, Worden Field began operation as the football team's home field. In that year, Navy went 4–1–1 at home, ending its season with a shutout victory of Army in the first annual Army-Navy Game, held at West Point. The following year, the team played its entire seven-game schedule at home, winning the first five games and dropping the final two, including a 32–16 loss to Army.

In 1892, Coach Ben Crosby led Navy to a 4–2 record in games played on the field. The following year's team, coached by John A. Hartwell, hosted its entire season on the field, amassing a record of 5–3. The final game of that season, the fourth Army-Navy Game, made national news at the time because of the events which took place. During the game, numerous violent fistfights occurred in the field's stands, and after the contest finished, President Grover Cleveland banned further playing of the competition. It was not reinstated until 1899, at the insisting of Theodore Roosevelt, the former Assistant Secretary of the Navy and new Governor of New York. The game did not return to Annapolis, except for special reasons in 1942 during World War II.

Thompson Field {1924-1958}

Robert Means Thompson Stadium Constructed in 1914, it was the home stadium of the Navy Midshipmen from 1924 through 1958 and was named after alumnus Robert Means Thompson (1849–1930). He created or led several athletically based organizations at the academy until his death. It was succeeded by the larger Navy–Marine Corps Memorial Stadium in 1959, the current venue of Navy football. Before its conversion to a football stadium, the Thompson Stadium site was an unused area on the south end campus, near the water of Annapolis Harbor. Work on the stadium began in 1914 and was finished later the same year. The seating capacity was 12,000, and it underwent few changes during its entire use. It was surrounded by a regulation quarter mile (402 m) running track, and only had a single seating section, along the southwest sideline. The field had a northwest-southeast alignment, at an elevation slightly above sea level. During the 1940s, the Naval Academy began to look for options to construct a new, larger football stadium. The school's directors collected money to build the stadium, for which much support was given by the public, due to the lack of seating at Thompson Stadium. Construction on the new stadium began in 1958 and it opened in September 1959. Use of Thompson Stadium ended for varsity games, but it remained until the early 1980s, when it was replaced by Lejeune Hall.

Navy-Marine Corp Memorial Stadium {1959-present}

Navy–Marine Corps Memorial Stadium opened in 1959 and serves as the home stadium of the Navy Midshipmen college football and lacrosse teams, and the professional Chesapeake Bayhawks of Major League Lacrosse. The stadium is also the host of the Military Bowl. The stadium's opener was a 29–2 win over William & Mary on September 26, 1959, and its current seating capacity is 34,000. The attendance record is 38,792, set in 2017 during Navy's 48–45 defeat of Air Force on October 7. The stadium serves as a memorial to the Navy and Marine Corps; it is dedicated to those who have served (and will serve) as upholders of the traditions and renown of the Navy and Marine Corps of the United States. The thousands of memorial bench-back and wall plaques are a constant reminder, as well as the list of numerous battles involving the Naval and Marine Corps forces since the early 1900s.

For its first 46 years, the stadium's playing field was natural grass. Prior to the 2005 football season, the grass field was replaced with FieldTurf, a next generation infilled synthetic turf. The field runs northwest to southeast, with the press box along the southwest sideline, and the elevation of the field is approximately 45 feet above sea level. The field at Navy–Marine Corps Memorial Stadium is named "Jack Stephens Field", for Jackson T. Stephens (Class of 1947), whose gift aided the renovation of the stadium, the Class of 1947 Legacy project to benefit the Academy's Museum, and other Academy projects.

1879 Navy Midshipmen

The team was the first intercollegiate football squad to represent the United States Naval Academy. The team had no coach, as it was entirely student-operated; however, it was captained by squad member Bill Maxwell. The team played just a single game, which was a scoreless tie with the Baltimore Athletic Club. The team was entirely student operated and was not supported by the Naval Academy's faculty. The school would not have another football squad until 1882.

The birth of football at the Naval Academy is debated among historians. The most accepted occurrence was in 1869, when a midshipman (a student) returned from his leave with a football. While throwing the ball with a friend, it was dropped, and a group of fellow midshipmen attempted to take it. A contest was eventually organized, which ended abruptly when the ball was kicked into the Severn River. However, biographer C. Douglas Kroll stated that the first evidence of a form of football at the United States Naval Academy came in 1857, but the school's cadets lost interest in the game shortly afterward, a theory supported by journalist Jack Clary. Regardless, the sport had been banned for several years prior to 1879.

There were two separate efforts to establish a Naval Academy football team in 1879. The first was guided by first-classman J.H. Robinson, who developed it as a training Regiment to help keep the school's baseball team in shape. The team played the sport under rules that made it much closer to soccer, where the players were permitted only to kick the ball to advance it. The second effort, headed by first-classman William John Maxwell was more successful in its efforts. Maxwell met with two of his friends, Tunstall Smith and Henry Woods, who played for the Baltimore Athletic Club and officially challenged their team to a game with the Naval Academy. A team was formed from academy first-classmen, which Maxwell led as a manager, trainer, and captain. The team would wake up and practice before reveille and following drill and meals. The squad received encouragement from some of the faculty, who allowed them to eat a late dinner and skip final drill for additional practicing. This was against the direct orders of the school superintendent, who had banned football and similar activities.

Home games were played Western King Field

12/11/1879	NAVY	vs	BALTIMORE AC	0	0	**T**
Coach: NO COACH			**Season Record >>**	0	0	**0-0-1**

Schedule Source: Steve's Football Bible LLC

Selected game(s) highlights

BALTIMORE ATHLETIC CLUB

The year's sole contest was played on December 11 against the Baltimore Athletic Club. The opposition's team was reportedly composed of players from Princeton, Yale, Pennsylvania, and Johns Hopkins. The Naval Academy hosted the Baltimore team on a temporary field drawn on part of the superintendent's cow pasture. Rules decided upon between the teams established that the game was to be played under rugby rules. The game was closely fought and was finally declared a scoreless tie by the referee about an hour after it began. Navy reportedly never gained possession of the ball. However, the Naval Academy managed to keep the Baltimore Athletic Club from ever being in a scoring position. On three separate occasions, Navy forced Baltimore back into its own end zone for a safety; these were not worth any points until 1882, however, so they offered Navy no benefit. The American and Chronicle reported that Maxwell, Craven, and Sample of Navy gave the strongest performances, but were also reckless in their play and were repeatedly penalized for jumping offside or kicking the ball out of play, a form of delay of game.

1882 Navy Midshipmen

The team was the second intercollegiate football squad to represent the United States Naval Academy, and the first since 1879. The team was coached by player-coach Vaulx Carter and was entirely student-operated. It was captained by squad member Alex Jackson. The team played just a single game, an 8 to 0 (8–0) shutout of Johns Hopkins, which was the school's first ever win. The squad was entirely student operated and was not supported by the Naval Academy's faculty. The season would mark the beginning of eight season rivalry between the Midshipmen and Johns Hopkins.

Home games were played Western King Field

11/30/1881	NAVY	vs	JOHNS HOPKINS	8	0	W
Coach: Vauix Carter			Season Record >>	**8**	**0**	**1-0**

Schedule Source: Steve's Football Bible LLC

Selected game(s) highlights

JOHNS HOPKINS

The 1882 season began when second-year cadet Vaulx Carter formed a team, which he led as both a player and the coach. Alex Jackson was appointed captain of the squad. Carter scheduled a single game for the season, which was played on Thanksgiving Day against the Baltimore-based Clifton Football Club. The Clifton team was made up of players from Johns Hopkins University, who were unable to play for their school due to their administrator's negative views towards the sport. Navy's team itself played without official permission; the first year the team received approval was in 1885, when, according to Morris Allison Bealle, "some of the faculty actually gave in and admitted that football might, at that, be or become an interesting diversion".

It snowed heavily before the game, to the point where players for both teams had to clear layers of snow off the field, making large piles of snow along the sides of the playing ground. The field was 110 yards by 53 yards, with goalposts 25 feet apart and 20 feet high. The first half of the game went scoreless; the Baltimore American reported that "the visitors pushed Navy every place but over the goal line in the first half". During play, the ball was kicked over the seawall several times, once going so far out it had to be retrieved by boat before play could continue. The American described the second half in detail:

After ten minutes interval the ball was again put in play, this time being kicked off by the Cliftons. The rest period had apparently stiffened the Cliftons, for the Academy making a vigorous spurt got the ball through them, and Street, following it up well, scored a touchdown for the Academy. The try at goal failed, but the ball, instead of going to the Cliftons behind the line, fell into the field and into the hands of one of the Academy team. By a quick decisive run, he again got the ball over the Cliftons goal line and scored a touchdown.

Cadet George Washington Street, of Wisconsin, was identified as the first person ever to score a touchdown for the Naval Academy. The Baltimore Sun stated that William Abrose O'Malley, of Pennsylvania, was the cadet who caught Street's blocked kick and scored the second touchdown. The Sun also covered, in detail, the uniforms the squads wore; Johns Hopkins sported blue, black, and white striped uniforms, while the Naval Academy wore maroon and white uniforms. Both teams also nailed strips of leather to the bottom of their shoes to help deal with slipping.

1883 Navy Midshipmen

The team was the third intercollegiate football squad to represent the United States Naval Academy, and the first time the school participated in consecutive seasons. The squad was captained by member Frank Hill. The team played just a single game, a 2 to 0 (2−0) shutout loss to Johns Hopkins, which was the school's first ever loss. The squad was the first to have the approval of the academy's staff and is regarded as the first official game played by the Midshipmen. The season continued a seven-season, eight game rivalry between the Naval Academy and Johns Hopkins.

Home games were played Western King Field

11/29/1883	NAVY	vs	JOHNS HOPKINS	0	2	L
Coach: NO COACH			**Season Record >>**	**0**	**2**	**0-1**

Schedule Source: Steve's Football Bible LLC

Selected game(s) highlights

JOHNS HOPKINS

The Naval Academy team played its only game of the 1883 season against a squad from Johns Hopkins University. It was captained by Frank Hill and was the first squad to receive approval from Naval Academy faculty. Previously, the squad was operated entirely by students. The game was played at the Naval Academy on November 29, 1883, Thanksgiving Day, most likely on an unused drill field or parade field. The game "began in heat and discussion", with the "skillful and lightweight" Johns Hopkins controlling the "endurance and muscle" of the Naval Academy's team. However, tensions in the game quickly escalated. During the middle of the game, "matters grew so hot" that Johns Hopkins players were preparing to stop playing. Johns Hopkins scored two single-point safeties and shutout Navy, winning 2−0. The game "ended in quarrel and wrangle".

1884 Navy Midshipmen

The team was the fourth intercollegiate football squad to represent the United States Naval Academy and was the final time the school played a single-game season. The squad was captained by rusher Jim Kittrell. The team's single game was a 9 to 6 (9–6) defeat of rival-school Johns Hopkins. The season continued a seven-season, eight game rivalry between the Naval Academy and Johns Hopkins. It was the final season that a Naval Academy team would go unbeaten and untied.

Home games were played Western King Field

11/27/1884	NAVY	vs	JOHNS HOPKINS	9	6	W
Coach: NO COACH			**Season Record >>**	**9**	**6**	**1-0**

Schedule Source: Steve's Football Bible LLC

Selected game(s) highlights

JOHNS HOPKINS

The sole game of Navy's 1884 season was the annual competition against rival Johns Hopkins, the third consecutive playing of the series. In what was the final season where the rivalry was the only game of the year, Navy defeated Johns Hopkins 9–6. The game, played on November 27, was hosted by the Academy, likely on an unused drill or parade field. In an unusual agreement between the two schools, the contest was played entirely under rugby rules. In the first half, Hopkins scored twice, on a touchdown from Mr. Bonsall and on a two point safety. Navy scored twice in the second half of the game, when halfback Julius Dashiell, brother of Hopkins' Paul Dashiell, kicked a five-point goal and rusher David W. Taylor scored a touchdown to secure a victory. The game was somewhat marred by one of the players suffering a broken collarbone and another spraining an ankle.

1885 Navy Midshipmen

The team was the fifth intercollegiate football squad to represent the United States Naval Academy and marked the first time that the school played a multiple-game season. The squad was captained by halfback Cornelius Billings. The year began with a blowout victory over St. John's College but was followed by close losses to Johns Hopkins University and the Princeton Tigers reserves squad. The season continued a seven-season, eight game rivalry between the Naval Academy and Johns Hopkins, and began a ten-game, seven-year rivalry with St. John's. The Naval Academy scheduled three games for the 1885 season, breaking from the tradition of playing only Johns Hopkins. According to Morris Allison Bealle, "Football at Annapolis had shed its swaddling clothes when the autumn of 1885 rolled around. Some of the faculty gave in and admitted that football might, at that, be or become an interesting diversion" so the squad was allowed to schedule three games.

Home games were played Western King Field

11/14/1885	NAVY	vs	ST. JOHN'S (Maryland)	46	10	**W**
11/26/1885	NAVY	vs	JOHNS HOPKINS	8	12	**L**
11/28/1885	NAVY	vs	PRINCETON JV	0	10	**L**
Coach: NO COACH			**Season Record >>**	**54**	**32**	**1-2**

Schedule Source: Steve's Football Bible LLC

Selected game(s) highlights

ST. JOHN'S {Maryland}

The first was played against St. John's College, also located in Annapolis. The game kicked off a brief rivalry with St. John's, which would conclude in 1911 with Navy winning eighteen of twenty-one contests. The 1885 match was a 46–10 blowout victory over St. John's.

JOHNS HOPKINS

The second game of the season was the annual Thanksgiving Day match against Johns Hopkins. After winning the previous year, Navy fell to Johns Hopkins 12–8.

PRINCETON JV

The season concluded with the Naval Academy challenging the Princeton freshman team, a game which ended in a 10–0 shutout loss for Navy.

1886 Navy Midshipmen

The team marked the second time that the school played a multiple-game season. The squad was captained by halfback Clarence Stone. The year began with consecutive wins over rivals St. John's College and Johns Hopkins, but then regressed with a loss to the former and a close victory over the latter. The year concluded with shutout losses to the Princeton reserve squad and Gallaudet. The season was the programs longest until 1890, when that year's team played seven games.

Home games were played Western King Field

11/10/1886	NAVY	vs	ST. JOHN'S (Maryland)	12	0	W
11/13/1886	NAVY	vs	JOHNS HOPKINS	6	0	W
11/20/1886	NAVY	vs	ST. JOHN'S (Maryland)	0	4	L
11/25/1886	NAVY	vs	JOHNS HOPKINS	15	14	W
11/27/1886	NAVY	vs	PRINCETON JV	0	30	L
12/4/1886	NAVY	vs	GALLAUDET	0	16	L
Coach: NO COACH			**Season Record >>**	**33**	**64**	**3-3**

Schedule Source: Steve's Football Bible LLC

Selected game(s) highlights

ST. JOHN'S {Maryland}

The season began with a game against St. Johns, one of the first contests in what would become a heated rivalry. Navy won the game with relative ease, 12–0.

JOHNS HOPKINS

The following game was against Johns Hopkins, played on November 13. The contest was an irregularity in the schools' rivalry; all previous and most following games were played on Thanksgiving Day, as a part of the Naval Academy's Thanksgiving athletic carnival. Although the score was close, a 6–0 win for the Naval Academy, Hopkins was never a threat to the cadets.

JOHNS HOPKINS

They barely defeated Johns Hopkins in a 15–14 contest, played as a part of the athletic carnival. Early in the first half, by much rushing, forcing, snapbacks and vigorous bully-ragging Riggs, the huge Hopkins quarterback, crashed over the goal line for 4 points. Paul Dashiell converted. Riggs repeated his performance, but Dashiell missed conversion. Navy then adopted the Hopkins rushing tactics and Stone went over for the first score. With Hopkins backed up against her own goal line, Dashiell broke through the entire Navy team for a touchdown. Goal was missed and the score was 14 to 6 against Navy. With the game fast ending The Tars formed a closely knit ball with the halfback in center. Navy hit pay-dirt but the referee found something illegal and called the ball back, much to the consternation of the Cadet rooters. But on the next play, George Hayward kicked a field goal, making the score 14 to 11. Just before the game ended, a double pass, Bill Cloke to captain Clarence Stone, carried to ball over the Hopkins goal for the 4 points that won the game.

PRINCETON JV

Just two days after the second Hopkins game, on November 27, the Naval Academy challenged the Princeton Tigers reserve squad and was easily shutout, 30–0. The Academy never came close to scoring on the reserves.

GALLAUDET

The Naval Academy hosted Gallaudet in its final game of the season sometime in December, a contest that the visitors won in a shutout, 16–0.

1887 Navy Midshipmen

The team compiled a 3–1 record and outscored its opponents 41 to 22. The Midshipmen shut out their first three opponents, including an 8–0 victory in the seventh installment of the Johns Hopkins–Navy football rivalry. The Johns Hopkins game was played at the Academy grounds in Annapolis, Maryland, and was described by The Sun (New York) as "a veritable slugging match" and "one of the roughest games of football" ever seen there. In the final game of the 1887 season, the Midshipmen lost to the Princeton Tigers "B" team in the final game of the season. The team captain was George Hayward.

Home games were played Western King Field

11/5/1887	NAVY	vs	ST. JOHN'S (Maryland)	4	0	**W**
11/12/1887	NAVY	vs	ST. JOHN'S (Maryland)	24	0	**W**
11/24/1887	NAVY	vs	JOHNS HOPKINS	8	0	**W**
12/3/1887	NAVY	vs	PRINCETON JV	5	22	**L**
Coach: NO COACH			**Season Record >>**	**41**	**22**	**3-1**

Schedule Source: Steve's Football Bible LLC

Selected game(s) highlights

JOHNS HOPKINS

The Naval Cadets and Johns Hopkins University team played one of the roughest games of football on the Academy grounds today that was ever seen there. The Cadets won by a score of eight points to nothing. From beginning to end it was a veritable slugging match on both sides the Cadets heavy weight and strength telling in their favor. Much fighting and kicking and grumbling were probably never seen in a game of football. Soon after the ball was kicked off by Hayward of the Cadets, Ashill, the captain of Johns Hopkins was severely injured by a kick in the stomach. Fermier of the Cadets was next hurt by someone sitting on his nose and Ulldersliove of Hopkins had hls ankle sprained. Coats of the same team was also hurt by being struck accidentally in the face by a Cadets elbow.

1888 Navy Midshipmen

The team compiled a 1–4 record and were outscored by its opponents 73 to 35. In the eighth installment of the Johns Hopkins–Navy football rivalry, Navy lost by a 25 to 12 score. In the final game of the 1888 season, the Midshipmen lost to St. John's College by a 22–6 score, with a brawl breaking out at the end of the game. The team captain was George Hayward.

Home games were played Western King Field

11/3/1888	NAVY	vs	GALLAUDET	4	0	**W**
11/10/1888	NAVY	vs	ST. JOHN'S (Maryland)	4	6	**L**
11/29/1888	NAVY	vs	JOHNS HOPKINS	12	25	**L**
12/1/1888	NAVY	vs	PENNSYLVANIA	9	20	**L**
12/9/1888	NAVY	vs	ST. JOHN'S (Maryland)	6	22	**L**
Coach: NO COACH			**Season Record >>**	**35**	**73**	**1-4**

Schedule Source: Steve's Football Bible LLC

Selected game(s) highlights

JOHNS HOPKINS

The Johns Hopkins university football team of Baltimore came to Annapolis and defeated the naval cadets by a score of 26 to 14. The game was witnessed by an immense crowd, nearly all the students at Johns Hopkins were present and went wild at the defeat of the "Kidets".

ST. JOHN'S {Maryland}

The football game at the Naval Academy this afternoon between the Naval Cadets and the St. John College team was played with much excitement, but at its close a very unusual scene occurred. About thirty college boys, ranging in age from twelve to twenty, grouped together and showed their delight at the second defeat that their club had given the Cadets this season. The Cadets were angered by the same result and maddened by the college cries and taunts of the opponents. About 100 of the former, formed in a solid phalanx and marched down on the St. Johns backers. The college boys were rushed about twenty yards, 5 when they made a stand and one threw off his coat and a regular set-to began, in which eyes were blackened, heads knocked, teeth went down the throat {and little boys were picked up and thrown pell-mell into the struggling mass of their comrades.

1889 Navy Midshipmen

The team compiled a 4–1–1 record and outscored opponents 112 to 42. This was a good enough record to take the title "Champions of the South". In the ninth installment of the Johns Hopkins–Navy football rivalry, Navy won by a 36 to 0 score. The team captain was Albertus Catlin.

Home games were played Western King Field

10/26/1889	NAVY	vs	ST. JOHN'S (Maryland)	20	10	**W**
11/2/1889	NAVY	vs	JOHNS HOPKINS	36	0	**W**
11/9/1889	NAVY	vs	DICKINSON	0	0	**T**
11/28/1889	NAVY	vs	LEHIGH	6	26	**L**
12/7/1889	NAVY	vs	VIRGINIA	22	12	**W**
12/25/1889	NAVY	vs	WASHINGTON STARS	24	0	**W**
Coach: NO COACH			**Season Record >>**	**108**	**48**	**4-1-1**

Schedule Source: Steve's Football Bible LLC

Selected game(s) highlights

JOHNS HOPKINS

That year's game ended in a 36–0 shutout victory for the Naval Academy and wound up being the breaking point for Johns Hopkins. Hopkins decided to terminate the series following that game. However, Hopkins' students returned to the Naval Academy the following year, yet again to root against Navy, this time supporting Lehigh.

1890 Navy Midshipmen

The team compiled a 5–1–1 record and outscored its opponents 204 to 49. The season featured the inaugural meeting in the Army–Navy Game, which ended in a 24–0 victory for Navy. After the victory, Navy cadets in Annapolis "fired twenty-four great guns, and then paraded the streets with horns." Charles Emrich was the Navy team captain in 1890.

Home games were played at Worden Field

10/25/1890	NAVY	vs	ST. JOHN'S (Maryland)	45	0	**W**
11/1/1890	NAVY	vs	GEORGETOWN	70	4	**W**
11/8/1890	NAVY	vs	DICKINSON	32	6	**W**
11/12/1890	NAVY	vs	COLUMBIA AC	6	6	**T**
11/19/1890	NAVY	vs	KENDALL	24	0	**W**
11/27/1890	NAVY	vs	LEHIGH	4	24	**L**
11/29/1890	NAVY	@	Army	24	0	**W**
Coach: NO COACH			**Season Record >>**	**205**	**40**	**5-1-1**

Schedule Source: Steve's Football Bible LLC

Selected game(s) highlights

Army

November 29, 1890, marked the beginning of the greatest rivalry in all American sports: Army-Navy football, which came about primarily because of the efforts of Dennis Mahan Michie.

The Midshipmen arrived by special ferry on game day. Looking for a mascot, the Navy players spotted a feisty goat tired up outside an Army NCO's quarters. The invaders "borrowed" the goat, thus acquiring their mascot which lasts to this day. The

game was played on a gridiron marked off on the Plain, the main parade ground at West Point and the site of annual summer camp until 1922. A good crowd of 500 spectators was on hand to see the competition. The "competition" quickly turned into a rout.

Veteran Red Emerich scored 20 of Navy's 24 points in its series-opening shutout of the host Cadets. Moulton Johnson added the other touchdown (touchdowns were worth four points), as the Mids served as Army's first college football opponent.

1891 Navy Midshipmen

The team compiled a 5–2 record and outscored its opponents 205 to 40. To be noted the Western King Field was tore down to be replaced by Worden Field. In the second installment of the Army–Navy Game, Army prevailed by a 32–16 score. Charles Macklin was the Navy team captain in 1891.

Home games were played at Worden Field

10/24/1891	NAVY	vs	ST. JOHN'S (Maryland)	28	6	W
10/31/1891	NAVY	vs	RUTGERS (8-6)	21	12	W
11/7/1891	NAVY	vs	GALLAUDET	6	0	W
11/11/1891	NAVY	vs	GEORGETOWN	16	4	W
11/14/1891	NAVY	vs	DICKINSON (2-2-1)	34	4	W
11/21/1891	NAVY	vs	LAFAYETTE (2-9-1)	0	4	L
11/28/1891	NAVY	vs	ARMY (4-1-1)	16	32	L
Coach: Edgar A. Poe			**Season Record >>**	121	62	**5-2**

Schedule Source: Steve's Football Bible LLC

Selected game(s) highlights

Army

Army avenged its series-opening loss to Navy by doubling up the Midshipmen, 32-16, in Annapolis. The Cadets overpowered the Midshipmen on the ground, scoring three first-half touchdowns to take an 18-6 lead at intermission. Elmer Clark scored on two touchdown runs, while plebe Fine Smith blocked Worth Bagley's punt and returned it for a touchdown. Navy was not to be embarrassed on its home field and answered with touchdowns from C.F. Maclin and Henry Pearson to open the second half. Nonetheless, the Cadets padded their lead with two more touchdowns to provide the 16-point difference.

1892 Navy Midshipmen

In their first and only season under head coach Ben Crosby (pictured at right), the Midshipmen compiled a 5–2 record and outscored their opponents by a combined score of 121 to 62. Team Captain was Martin Trench.

Home games were played at Worden Field

10/12/1892	NAVY	vs	PENNSYLVANIA (15-1)	0	16	L
10/15/1892	NAVY	vs	PRINCETON (13-2)	0	28	L
10/22/1892	NAVY	vs	LAFAYETTE (5-7)	22	4	W
10/29/1892	NAVY	vs	FRANKLIN & MARSHALL	24	0	W
11/5/1892	NAVY	vs	RUTGERS (3-5-1)	48	12	W
11/19/1892	NAVY	vs	GEORGETOWN	40	0	W
11/26/1892	NAVY	@	ARMY (3-1-1)	12	4	W
Coach: Ben Crosby			**Season Record >>**	**146**	**64**	**5-2**

Schedule Source: Steve's Football Bible LLC

Selected game(s) highlights

Army

Worth Bagley proved to be quite valuable to Navy, accounting for eight of the team's 12 points in a 12-4 win over Army. All the scoring came in the second half. Walter Izard had Navy's first touchdown run, and Bagley added the conversion. Army's Thomas Carson answered with a touchdown for the Cadets, but Bagley put the game away with six more points late in the half.

1893 Navy Midshipmen

In their first and only season under head coach John A. Hartwell (pictured at right), the Midshipmen compiled a 5–3 record, shut out two opponents, and outscored all opponents by a combined score of 122 to 78. Team Captain was Art Kavanagh.

Joseph Mason Reeves became the first football player to wear a helmet in 1893. 18 years after the first confirmed use of a glove on the diamond, Navy's Joseph Mason Reeves flashed the leather on the gridiron. Injuries prompted the Admiral to enlist the help of an Annapolis shoemaker for his football career to continue. In doing so, he becomes the first player to use a football helmet

Home games were played at Worden Field

10/11/1893	NAVY	vs	PENNSYLVANIA	0	34	L
10/14/1893	NAVY	vs	DICKINSON	26	0	W
10/21/1893	NAVY	vs	VIRGINIA	28	0	W
10/28/1893	NAVY	vs	LEHIGH	6	12	L
11/4/1893	NAVY	vs	GEORGETOWN	22	10	W
11/18/1893	NAVY	vs	FRANKLIN & MARSHALL	34	6	W
11/22/1893	NAVY	vs	VIRGINIA	0	12	L
12/2/1893	NAVY	vs	ARMY	6	4	W
Coach: Josh Hartwell			**Season Record >>**	122	76	**5-3**

Schedule Source: Steve's Football Bible LLC

Selected game(s) highlights

ARMY

Henry Kimball's one yard touchdown run, and two point conversion was all Navy needed in a 6-4 victory over Army. The Cadets' Thomas Carson responded with his second touchdown in as many years against Navy, but the two point conversion was unsuccessful.

1894 Navy Midshipmen

In their first and only season under head coach William Wurtenburg (pictured at right), the Midshipmen compiled a 4–1–2 record, shut out three opponents, and outscored all opponents by a combined score of 72 to 30. The Army–Navy Game was canceled due to Presidential cabinet order. Team Captain was Mike McCormick.

Home games were played at Worden Field

10/6/1894	NAVY	vs	ELIZABETH AC	6	6	T
10/21/1894	NAVY	vs	GEORGETOWN	12	0	W
10/24/1894	NAVY	vs	PENNSYLVANIA	0	12	L
10/27/1894	NAVY	vs	CARLISLE	8	0	W
11/3/1894	NAVY	vs	LEHIGH	10	0	W
11/10/1894	NAVY	vs	PENN STATE	6	6	T
11/24/1894	NAVY	vs	BALTIMORE CITY COLLEGE	30	6	W
Coach: Bill Wurtenburg			**Season Record >>**	72	30	4-1-2

Schedule Source: Steve's Football Bible LLC

1895 Navy Midshipmen

In their first and only season under head coach Matthew McClung (pictured at right), the Midshipmen compiled a 5–2 record and outscored their opponents by a combined score of 152 to 16. The Army–Navy Game was canceled due to Presidential cabinet order. Team Captain was Ed Macauley.

Home games were played at Worden Field

10/5/1895	NAVY	vs	ELIZABETH AC	6	0	W
10/12/1895	NAVY	vs	NEW JERSEY AC	34	0	W
10/19/1895	NAVY	vs	FRANKLIN & MARSHALL	68	0	W
10/26/1895	NAVY	vs	CARLISLE	34	0	W
11/2/1895	NAVY	vs	VIRGINIA COLLEGE	1	0	W
11/9/1895	NAVY	vs	ORAGNE AC	6	10	L
11/16/1895	NAVY	vs	LEHIGH	4	6	L
Coach: Matt McClung			**Season Record >>**	152	16	5-2

Schedule Source: Steve's Football Bible LLC

1896 Navy Midshipmen

In their first and only season under head coach Johnny Poe (pictured at right), the Midshipmen compiled a 5–3 record and outscored their opponents by a combined score of 180 to 53. The Army–Navy Game was canceled due to Presidential cabinet order. Team Captain was Joe Powell.

Home games were played at Worden Field

10/7/1896	NAVY	vs	PENNSYLVANIA (14-1)	0	8	L
10/10/1896	NAVY	vs	FRANKLIN & MARSHALL (3-4-2)	49	0	W
10/17/1896	NAVY	vs	ST. JOHN'S (Maryland)	50	0	W
10/24/1896	NAVY	vs	PENNSYLVANIA Reserves	0	6	L
10/31/1896	NAVY	vs	RUTGERS	40	6	W
11/7/1896	NAVY	vs	LEHIGH (2-5)	24	10	W
11/23/1896	NAVY	vs	WHITE SQUADRON	11	5	W
11/26/1896	NAVY	vs	LAFAYETTE (11-0-1)	6	18	L
Coach: Johnny Poe			**Season Record >>**	180	53	5-3

Schedule Source: Steve's Football Bible LLC

1897 Navy Midshipmen

In their first season under head coach Bill Armstrong (pictured at right), the Midshipmen compiled an 8–1 record, shut out seven opponents, and outscored all opponents by a combined score of 111 to 34. The Army–Navy Game was canceled due to Presidential cabinet order. Team Captain was Johnny Calligan.

Home games were played at Worden Field

10/9/1897	NAVY	vs	PRINCETON (10-1)	0	28	L
10/13/1897	NAVY	vs	PENNSYLVANIA Reserves	22	0	W
10/16/1897	NAVY	vs	PRINCETON AC	6	0	W
10/23/1897	NAVY	vs	PENN STATE (3-6)	4	0	W
11/6/1897	NAVY	vs	VIRGINIA	4	0	W
11/13/1897	NAVY	vs	MARYLAND-Baltimore	38	0	W
11/20/1897	NAVY	vs	LEHIGH (3-7)	28	6	W
11/25/1897	NAVY	vs	WHITE SQUADRON	8	0	W
Coach: Bill Armstrong			**Season Record >>**	110	34	7-1

Schedule Source: Steve's Football Bible LLC

1898 Navy Midshipmen

In their second season under head coach Bill Armstrong, the Midshipmen compiled a 7–1 record, shut out three opponents, and outscored all opponents by a combined score of 130 to 56. The Army–Navy Game was canceled due to Presidential cabinet order. Team Captain was Charlie Fischer.

Home games were played at Worden Field

10/8/1898	NAVY	vs	BUCKNELL (4-4-3)	11	0	W
10/15/1898	NAVY	vs	PRINCETON (11-0-1)	0	30	L
10/22/1898	NAVY	vs	PENN STATE (6-4)	16	11	W
10/29/1898	NAVY	vs	LAFAYETTE (3-8)	18	0	W
11/5/1898	NAVY	vs	COLUMBIA AC	52	5	W
11/12/1898	NAVY	vs	LEHIGH (3-6-1)	6	5	W
11/19/1898	NAVY	@	Virginia	6	0	W
11/24/1898	NAVY	vs	VMI	21	5	W
Coach: Bill Armstrong			**Season Record >>**	130	56	7-1

Schedule Source: Steve's Football Bible LLC

Selected game(s) highlights

COLUMBIA AC

The Naval Cadets had an easy time defeating the Columbian University at the Naval Academy this afternoon. The score was 52 to 5 in the middies favor. In the first half the Navy scored 18 and the visitors 5. Wortman, of the home eleven, had his nose broken in the first half.

1899 Navy Midshipmen

In their third season under head coach Bill Armstrong, the Midshipmen compiled a 5–3 record, shut out five opponents, and outscored all opponents by a combined score of 94 to 27. Team Captain was Ward Wortman.

Home games were played at Worden Field

10/7/1899	NAVY	vs	PRINCETON (12-1)	0	5	L
10/14/1899	NAVY	vs	GEORGETOWN	12	0	W
10/21/1899	NAVY	vs	PENN STATE (4-6-1)	6	0	W
10/28/1899	NAVY	vs	LAFAYETTE (12-1)	0	5	L
11/4/1899	NAVY	vs	NORTH CAROLINA	12	0	W
11/11/1899	NAVY	vs	TRINITY (Connecticut) (3-5-1)	35	0	W
11/18/1899	NAVY	vs	LEHIGH (2-9)	24	0	W
12/2/1899	NAVY	vs	ARMY (4-5)	5	17	L
Coach: Bill Armstrong			**Season Record >>**	94	27	5-3

Schedule Source: Steve's Football Bible LLC

Selected game(s) highlights

Army {@ Franklin Field – Philadelphia, PA}

In the first Army-Navy game held at Franklin Field, Army's Verne Rockwell and Bob Jackson combined to score three touchdowns in the Cadets' 17-5 victory. Considering Navy had shut out its previous three opponents — North Carolina, Trinity and Lehigh — by a combined 71-0 score, this game was termed an upset of sorts. After Jackson started the scoring in the first half with a short run, Navy drove to the Army nine yard line before time ran out in the half. Rockwell and Jackson tallied second-half scores, as the Cadets took a commanding 17-0 lead. The Midshipmen avoided a shutout when Ward Wortman scored with just seconds left in the game.

1900 Navy Midshipmen

Under first-year head coach Garrett Cochran (pictured at right), the team compiled a 6–3 record, outscored its opponents 106 to 51, and shut out five of its nine opponents. Their losses were to Columbia, Pennsylvania and Princeton. Penn would lose only one game that season, but the Midshipmen ended the season on a high note by beating rival Army, 11-7. Team Captain was Orie Fowler.

Home games were played at Worden Field

10/6/1900	NAVY	vs	MARYLAND-Baltimore	6	0	W
10/13/1900	NAVY	vs	PRINCETON (8-3)	0	5	L
10/20/1900	NAVY	vs	GEORGETOWN	6	0	W
10/24/1900	NAVY	vs	LEHIGH (5-6)	15	0	W
11/3/1900	NAVY	vs	WASHINGTON & JEFFERSON	18	0	W
11/10/1900	NAVY	vs	PENN STATE (4-6-1)	44	0	W
11/17/1900	NAVY	vs	COLUMBIA (7-3-1)	0	11	L
11/21/1900	NAVY	vs	PENNSYLVANIA (12-1)	6	28	L
12/1/1900	NAVY	vs	ARMY (7-3-1)	11	7	W
Coach: Garrett Cochran			Season Record >>	106	51	6-3

Schedule Source: Steve's Football Bible LLC

Selected game(s) highlights

PRINCETON

The Naval Cadets were defeated by the Princeton Tigers today by a score of 5 to 0. In the first half, the Cadets kicked off and Duncan ran the ball for ten yards. Princeton, making heavy gains through the left end of the Cadets' line, brought the ball within five yards of the Cadets goal. Here, through hard work by the Cadets, the Tigers lost the ball on downs. Freyer punted for fifty yards, Princeton brought it back to the 25 yard line, and Hodgman tried a drop kick, but failed. The ball was brought out to the 25 yard line and Freyer again punted. Time was called, near the middle of the field, with the ball in the Tigers' possession. In the second half Princeton kicked off and Fowler brought the ball back for fifteen yards. Freyer again punted down the field. In this half Hodgman ran twenty yards, being the longest run of the game. Here the Cadets played hard, and the Tigers were compelled to kick. Mattis kicked the ball from the middle of the field to the Cadets 3 yard line. While the Cadets waited for the ball to roll behind the line. Roper fell on it. McClave was then sent through the line for a touchdown. Mattis failed at goal.

Army {@ Franklin Field – Philadelphia, PA}

Navy's Bryon Long may have hit the game-tying field goal in the first half, but his recovery of a blocked punt in the end zone proved more valuable in the Midshipmen's 11-7 win over Army. Emory Land's touchdown run early in the second half snapped a 5-5 tie and made the score 11-5 after Orie Fowler's extra point. Then, with 10 seconds left in the game, the Cadets' Quinn Gray blocked Charles Belknap's punt into the Navy end zone. If Gray recovers the punt, it's an Army touchdown. But if Long recovers it, it's a safety. Fortunately for the Midshipmen, Long pounced on the ball in the end zone, and Navy had itself an 11-7 triumph.

1901 Navy Midshipmen

In its first season under head coach Art Hillebrand (pictured at right), the team compiled a 6–4–1 record and outscored opponents by a total of 113 to 81.
President Theodore Roosevelt attended the Army–Navy Game in Philadelphia on December 1. A newspaper account noted: "For the first time in the history of football a President of the United States added dignity to a noted contest by his presence." Team Captain was Neil Nichols.

Home games were played at Worden Field

10/5/1901	NAVY	vs	GEORGETOWN	0	0	**T**
10/9/1901	NAVY	vs	ST. JOHN'S (Maryland)	28	2	W
10/12/1901	NAVY	vs	YALE (11-1-1)	0	24	L
10/19/1901	NAVY	vs	LEHIGH (1-11)	18	0	W
10/21/1901	NAVY	vs	PENNSYLVANIA (10-5)	6	5	W
10/26/1901	NAVY	vs	PENN STATE (5-3)	6	11	L
11/2/1901	NAVY	vs	DICKINSON (4-6)	12	6	W
11/9/1901	NAVY	vs	CARLISLE (5-7-1)	16	5	W
11/16/1901	NAVY	vs	WASHINGTON & JEFFERSON	17	11	W
11/22/1901	NAVY	vs	COLUMBIA (8-5)	5	6	L
11/30/1901	NAVY	vs	ARMY (5-1-2)	5	11	L
Coach: Doc Hillebrand			**Season Record >>**	113	81	6-4-1

Schedule Source: Steve's Football Bible LLC

Selected game(s) highlights

WASHINGTON & JEFFERSON

One of the most Interesting games of the season was played here this afternoon when the naval cadets defeated the football team of Washington & Jefferson College by a score of 17 to 11. The first half was marked by good defensive work on the part of the visitors and the Navy scored a goal and a touchdown only after the Pennsylvanians had made two fumbles on kicks and lost the ball. The first part of the second half was a walkover for Washington & Jefferson and it scored a touchdown, goal and field goal In the first ten minutes. At this point Nicholls went into the game and in the remaining fifteen minutes the navy lads played their opponents off their feet and scored two touchdowns, on one of which a goal was kicked.

Army {@ Franklin Field – Philadelphia, PA}

Vice President Theodore Roosevelt, who was sworn in as chief executive right after William McKinley was assassinated, became the first president to watch an Army-Navy game. He saw Army quarterback Charles Daly turn in a fine individual performance, leading the Cadets past Navy, 11-5.

Daly opened the scoring with a first-half field goal, only to have Navy's Newton Nichols tie the score with a touchdown just before intermission. The multi-talented Daly then took the wind out of Navy's sails with a 95 yard kickoff return for a touchdown to open the second half and clinch the 11-5 victory.

1902 Navy Midshipmen

In their second season under head coach Art Hillebrand, the Midshipmen compiled a 2–7–1 record and were outscored by opponents by a combined score of 99 to 35. Team Captain was Charles Belknap.

Home games were played at Worden Field

9/27/1902	NAVY	vs	GEORGETOWN (7-3)	0	4	L
10/4/1902	NAVY	vs	PRINCETON (8-1)	0	11	L
10/15/1902	NAVY	vs	LEHIGH (7-3-1)	5	5	T
10/22/1902	NAVY	vs	PENNSYLVANIA (9-4)	10	6	W
10/25/1902	NAVY	vs	DICKINSON (4-6)	0	6	L
11/1/1902	NAVY	vs	PENN STATE (7-3)	0	6	L
11/8/1902	NAVY	vs	LAFAYETTE (8-3)	12	11	W
11/15/1902	NAVY	vs	BUCKNELL (6-4)	0	23	L
11/19/1902	NAVY	vs	COLUMBIA (6-4-1)	0	5	L
11/29/1902	NAVY	vs	ARMY (6-1-1)	8	22	L
Coach: Doc Hillebrand			**Season Record >>**	**35**	**99**	**2-7-1**

Schedule Source: Steve's Football Bible LLC

Selected game(s) highlights

LEHIGH

In the presence of about 2,500 spectators Lehigh and the Navy played each other to a standstill. The score was 5 to 5, and the feature of the game was a 100 yard run by A. Farabaugh and the kicking of Coach Newton and his men over a decision of Professor Dashiell, the umpire. The game was thereby delayed at least a half-hour, and loud murmurs of dissatisfaction were heard. Lehigh's score was made on a play almost exactly similar to that of Daly at Philadelphia last November, when he executed a 100 yard dash through the entire Navy line for a touchdown. . The first half, notwithstanding the run and other flue plays, was tame in comparison with the second. Smith made a beautiful dash of 35 yards through the entire Lehigh team before he was thrown. Right here the trouble commenced. Amid admonitions to ginger up, both teams went at it. Belknap again essayed a field goal from the 35 yard line, but missed it, and the whole mass of players scrambled after the ball. One of the Lehigh men grabbed it, but the wary leather bounced from his outstretched arms and rolled down the hill, with several players in pursuit. Whiting, with Soule interfering for him, distanced the rest and fell on-the ball way back of Lehigh's goal for a touchdown. The Lehigh men, led by Coach Newton, set up a tremendous howl, claiming that none of their players had touched the ball, but Mr. Dashiell allowed the touchdown. Lehigh protested in great heat. Amid threats on the part of Lehigh to leave the field and warnings of the umpire to declare the game forfeited and to have Coach Newton escorted off the field 30 minutes or more elapsed. When quiet had been restored Belknap kicked out to Smith for the position to kick goal, but he was tackled before he could get it down.

Army {@ Franklin Field – Philadelphia, PA}

Offense, defense and special teams each had a hand in Army's 22-8 victory over Navy. Paul Bunker and quarterback Charles Daly each had rushing touchdowns for the Cadets, while Navy's Ralph Strassburger tackled Daly in the end zone for a safety. Navy cut Army's lead to 10-8 just before halftime when Strassburger returned a punt 55 yards for a touchdown. The Cadets held off the furious Navy comeback with a pair of second-half touchdowns. Bunker reached the end zone for the second time that afternoon, while Daly scored a touchdown and added the extra point.

1903 Navy Midshipmen

In their first and only season under head coach Burr Chamberlain (pictured at right), the Midshipmen compiled a 4–7–1 record, shut out four opponents (including a scoreless tie with Baltimore Medical College), and were outscored by all opponents by a combined score of 130 to 77. Team Captain was Charles Soule.

Home games were played at Worden Field

10/10/1903	NAVY	vs	GALLAUDET	18	0	**W**
10/14/1903	NAVY	vs	VIRGINIA (7-2-1)	6	5	**W**
10/17/1903	NAVY	vs	DICKINSON (7-5)	5	0	**W**
10/21/1903	NAVY	vs	BALTIMORE MEDICAL COLLEGE	0	0	**T**
10/24/1903	NAVY	vs	LAFAYETTE (7-3)	5	6	**L**
10/28/1903	NAVY	vs	GEORGETOWN (7-3)	5	12	**L**
10/31/1903	NAVY	vs	PENN STATE (5-3)	0	17	**L**
11/4/1903	NAVY	vs	NEW YORK Naval Militia	28	0	**W**
11/7/1903	NAVY	vs	WASHINGTON & JEFFERSON	0	16	**L**
11/14/1903	NAVY	vs	BUCKNELL (4-5)	5	23	**L**
11/21/1903	NAVY	vs	VIRGINIA TECH (5-1)	0	11	**L**
11/28/1903	NAVY	vs	ARMY (6-2-1)	5	40	**L**
Coach: Burr Chamberlain			**Season Record >>**	77	130	**4-7-1**

Schedule Source: Steve's Football Bible LLC

Selected game(s) highlights

Army {@ Franklin Field – Philadelphia, PA}

Army used two Navy fumbles and a blocked field goal attempt to overcome a five-point deficit and overwhelm the Midshipmen, 40-5. Navy took a 5-0 lead on an H.L. Chambers field goal in the first half, but that was the extent of the Midshipmen' offensive output. They mustered just three first downs the rest of the day. Army, on the other hand, boasted a balanced scoring attack. Fred Prince had 15 points, Ray Hill added 10, Tom Doe seven, Russell Davis five, while Ernest Graves, Charles Davis and Horatio Hackett had one point each.

1904 Navy Midshipmen

In their first season under head coach Paul Dashiell (pictured at right), the Midshipmen compiled a 7–2–1 record, shut out six opponents, and outscored all opponents by a combined score of 149 to 38. Team Captain was Lou Farley.

Home games were played at Worden Field

10/8/1904	NAVY	vs	VMI (3-5-1)	12	0	**W**
10/12/1904	NAVY	vs	MARINE OFFICERS	68	0	**W**
10/15/1904	NAVY	vs	PRINCETON (8-2)	10	9	**W**
10/19/1904	NAVY	vs	ST. JOHN'S (Maryland)	23	0	**W**
10/22/1904	NAVY	vs	DICKINSON (8-3-1)	0	0	**T**
10/29/1904	NAVY	vs	SWARTHMORE (6-3)	0	9	**L**
11/5/1904	NAVY	vs	PENN STATE (6-4)	20	9	**W**
11/12/1904	NAVY	@	Virginia (6-3)	5	0	**W**
11/19/1904	NAVY	vs	VIRGINIA TECH (5-3)	11	0	**W**
11/26/1904	NAVY	vs	ARMY (7-2)	0	11	**L**
Coach: Paul Dashiell			**Season Record >>**	**149**	**38**	**7-2-1**

Schedule Source: Steve's Football Bible LLC

Selected game(s) highlights

Army {@ Franklin Field – Philadelphia, PA}

Midway through the first half, Navy lined up to accept Army's punt at the 50 yard line. The ball apparently touched Navy's Homer Norton, and the Cadets' Art Tipton, racing down the field, kicked the ball ahead of him. The game had suddenly transformed into a modern day soccer match, with Tipton kicking the ball once again toward the Navy goal line. When the ball reached the end zone, Tipton fell on top of it for Army's first touchdown.

Despite the controversy surrounding this incident, it was ruled a touchdown and set the tone for Army's 11-0 triumph. This was the Cadets' fourth win in a row over Navy and Army's first shutout in series history.

1905 Navy Midshipmen

In their second season under head coach Paul Dashiell, the Midshipmen compiled a 10–1–1 record, shut out eight opponents, and outscored all opponents by a combined score of 243 to 23. Team Captain was Douglas Legate Howard.

Navy lost by 1 point to Swarthmore, and they tied Army in their finale. They gave Virginia Tech their only loss, and they beat Penn State.

Home games were played at Worden Field

10/7/1905	NAVY	vs	VMI	34	0	W
10/11/1905	NAVY	vs	ST. JOHN'S (Maryland)	29	0	W
10/14/1905	NAVY	vs	DICKINSON (4-4)	6	0	W
10/18/1905	NAVY	vs	MCDANIEL	29	0	W
10/21/1905	NAVY	vs	NORTH CAROLINA (4-3-1)	38	0	W
10/25/1905	NAVY	vs	MARYLAND	17	0	W
10/28/1905	NAVY	vs	SWARTHMORE (7-1)	5	6	L
11/4/1905	NAVY	vs	PENN STATE (8-3)	11	5	W
11/11/1905	NAVY	vs	BUCKNELL (5-5)	34	0	W
11/18/1905	NAVY	vs	VIRGINIA (5-4)	22	0	W
11/25/1905	NAVY	vs	VIRGINIA TECH (9-1)	12	6	W
12/2/1905	NAVY	vs	ARMY (4-4-1)	6	6	T
Coach: Paul Dashiell			**Season Record >>**	243	23	10-1-1

Schedule Source: Steve's Football Bible LLC

Selected game(s) highlights

Army {@ University Field – Princeton, NJ}

Princeton President Woodrow Wilson convinced West Point and Annapolis officials to play the 1905 Army-Navy game at Princeton, where the two service academies battled to a 6-6 tie.

It was immediately obvious that Princeton was ill-equipped to handle the large crowd in attendance, as a huge traffic jam made both teams late for kickoff. As a result, the game was suspended with four minutes left due to darkness. Henry Torney scored Navy's touchdown early in the first half, while Archibald Douglas tallied Army's touchdown.

1906 Navy Midshipmen

In their third season under Paul Dashiell, the Midshipmen compiled an 8–2–2 record, shut out nine opponents (including a scoreless tie with Bucknell), and outscored all opponents by a combined score of 149 to 14. They lost to Princeton and Penn State by identical 5-0 scores in addition to the 0-0 ties with Dickinson and Bucknell. Team Captain was Herbert Spencer.

Home games were played at Worden Field

10/6/1906	NAVY	vs	DICKINSON (3-4-2)	0	0	**T**
10/10/1906	NAVY	vs	MARYLAND	12	0	W
10/13/1906	NAVY	vs	PRINCETON (9-0-1)	0	5	L
10/17/1906	NAVY	vs	ST. JOHN'S (Maryland)	34	0	W
10/20/1906	NAVY	vs	LEHIGH (5-5-1)	12	0	W
10/24/1906	NAVY	vs	MCDANIEL	31	0	W
10/27/1906	NAVY	vs	BUCKNELL (3-4-1)	0	0	**T**
11/3/1906	NAVY	vs	PENN STATE (8-1-1)	0	5	L
11/10/1906	NAVY	vs	SWARTHMORE (7-2)	5	4	W
11/17/1906	NAVY	vs	NORTH CAROLINA (1-4-2)	40	0	W
11/24/1906	NAVY	vs	VIRGINIA TECH (5-2-2)	5	0	W
12/1/1906	NAVY	vs	ARMY (3-5-1)	10	0	W
Coach: Paul Dashiell			**Season Record >>**	149	14	**8-2-2**

Schedule Source: Steve's Football Bible LLC

Selected game(s) highlights

Army {@ Franklin Field – Philadelphia, PA}

"Anchors Aweigh" made its debut at the 1906 Army-Navy game, and the Midshipmen took the song to heart in defeating the Cadets, 10-0. The win over Army was Navy's first since 1900.

The 1906 football season was memorable nationwide, as it marked the debut of the forward pass. Navy coach Paul Dashiell added a twist to this new rule to help his team to victory. Thanks to a long field goal by Percy Northcroft, Navy led 4-0 in the second half. On the Midshipmen's next possession, Navy's Homer Norton dropped back in punt formation. Yet, when the ball was snapped, he threw a 25 yard touchdown pass to Jonas Ingram to give Navy the 10-0 victory.

"Anchors Aweigh" premiered at an Army-Navy game in 1906. Former Naval Academy Band bandmaster Lt. Charles Zimmermann wrote the song's famous tune, while the lyrics were written by Alfred Hart Miles, a midshipman, according to the band's website.

1907 Navy Midshipmen

In their first and only season under Joseph M. Reeves (pictured at right), the Midshipmen compiled a 9–2–1 record, shut out eight opponents, and outscored all opponents by a combined score of 118 to 34. A. H. Douglas made Walter Camp's third-team All-America, the second Southerner ever to have done so. Team Captain was A.H. Douglas.

End Bill Dague and quarterback Homer Norton were consensus All Americans this season.

Home games were played at Worden Field

10/2/1907	NAVY	vs	ST. JOHN'S (Maryland)	26	0	**W**
10/5/1907	NAVY	vs	DICKINSON (3-6-1)	15	0	**W**
10/9/1907	NAVY	vs	MARYLAND	12	0	**W**
10/12/1907	NAVY	vs	VANDERBILT (5-1-1)	6	6	**T**
10/16/1907	NAVY	vs	ST. JOHN'S (Maryland)	12	0	**W**
10/19/1907	NAVY	vs	HARVARD (7-3)	0	6	**L**
10/26/1907	NAVY	vs	LAFAYETTE (7-2-1)	17	0	**W**
11/2/1907	NAVY	vs	WEST VIRGINIA	6	0	**W**
11/9/1907	NAVY	vs	SWARTHMORE (6-2)	0	18	**L**
11/16/1907	NAVY	vs	PENN STATE (6-4)	6	4	**W**
11/23/1907	NAVY	vs	VIRGINIA TECH (7-2)	12	0	**W**
11/30/1907	NAVY	vs	ARMY (6-2-1)	6	0	**W**
Coach: Joe Reeves			**Season Record >>**	118	34	**9-2-1**

Schedule Source: Steve's Football Bible LLC

Selected game(s) highlights

VANDERBILT

The Commodores held the Navy team to a 6–6 tie in one of the highlights of the season. McGugin proved prophetic; before the game he said, "We have an even chance with the Navy." The Nashville papers said Vandy should've won, and Grantland Rice criticized the officiating, as did coach McGugin. Navy's captain Tootsie Douglas called the tie "the bitterest pill I have ever had to swallow."

Army {@ Franklin Field – Philadelphia, PA}

Navy combined an early Army turnover with a solid defensive outing to turn back the Cadets, 6-0. The Midshipmen's Percy Wright recovered Frederick Montiford's punt at the Army 25 yard line. It took Navy six plays to score, as Archibald Douglas plowed through from the one yard line to give Navy all the points it would need in its second-straight shutout over Army.

1908 Navy Midshipmen

In their first season under Frank Berrien, the Midshipmen compiled a 9–2–1 record, shut out seven opponents, and outscored all opponents by a combined score of 218 to 38. They lost the year end rivalry game to Army, 6-4. Team Captain was Percy Northcroft.

Ed Lange {RB} and Northcroft {OL} were selected as consensus All-Americans.

Home games were played at Worden Field

10/3/1908	NAVY	vs	RUTGERS	18	0	**W**
10/4/1908	NAVY	vs	ST. JOHN'S (Maryland)	22	0	**W**
10/10/1908	NAVY	vs	DICKINSON (5-4)	22	0	**W**
10/14/1908	NAVY	@	Maryland	57	0	**W**
10/17/1908	NAVY	vs	LEHIGH (4-3)	16	0	**W**
10/24/1908	NAVY	vs	HARVARD (9-0-1)	6	6	**T**
10/28/1908	NAVY	vs	GEORGE WASHINGTON (8-1-1)	17	0	**W**
10/31/1908	NAVY	vs	CARLISLE (10-2-1)	6	16	**L**
11/7/1908	NAVY	vs	VILLANOVA (1-6)	30	6	**W**
11/14/1908	NAVY	vs	PENN STATE (5-5)	5	0	**W**
11/21/1908	NAVY	vs	VIRGINIA TECH (5-4)	15	4	**W**
11/28/1908	NAVY	vs	ARMY (6-1-2)	4	6	**L**
Coach: Frank Berrien			Season Record >>	218	38	**9-2-1**

Schedule Source: Steve's Football Bible LLC

Selected game(s) highlights

Army {@ Franklin Field – Philadelphia, PA}

Ed Lange's fumble on the opening kickoff proved costly to Navy, as Army's Henry Chamberlain retrieved the loose ball and raced all the way to the Navy one yard line. From there, Bill Dean crossed the goal line for the touchdown (worth five points). He kicked the extra point himself to account for all six points in the 6-4 Army win. Lange somewhat redeemed himself by kicking a second-half field goal (worth four points), but it wasn't enough to upend the Cadets.

1909 Navy Midshipmen

In their second season under Frank Berrien, the Midshipmen compiled a 4–3–1 record and outscored their opponents by a combined score of 99 to 42. Team Captain was George Meyer.

Home games were played at Worden Field

10/6/1909	NAVY	vs	ST. JOHN'S (Maryland)	16	6	**W**
10/9/1909	NAVY	vs	RUTGERS	12	3	**W**
10/16/1909	NAVY	vs	VILLANOVA (3-2)	6	11	**L**
10/23/1909	NAVY	vs	VIRGINIA (7-1)	0	5	**L**
10/30/1909	NAVY	vs	PRINCETON (6-2-1)	3	5	**L**
11/6/1909	NAVY	vs	WASHINGTON & JEFFERSON (8-1-1)	0	0	**T**
11/13/1909	NAVY	vs	WESTERN RESERVE	17	6	**W**
11/20/1909	NAVY	vs	DAVIDSON (3-4-2)	45	6	**W**
Coach: Frank Berrien			**Season Record >>**	99	42	**4-3-1**

Schedule Source: Steve's Football Bible LLC

Selected game(s) highlights

None

1910 Navy Midshipmen

The team compiled an undefeated 8–0–1 record and were not scored upon, having defeated all nine opponents by a combined score of 99 to 0. The annual Army–Navy Game was played on November 26, 1910, at Franklin Field in Philadelphia. After initially missing seven attempts at field goal, Navy won by a 3 to 0 score on a kick by Jack Dalton. Two players from the 1910 Navy team received first-team honors on the 1910 College Football All-America Team. Guard John Brown received first-team honors from The New York Sun, New York Herald, and Pittsburgh Leader. Jack Dalton received first-team honors from The New York Times. Brown and Dalton were both later inducted into the College Football Hall of Fame.

The 1910 season was Navy's third with Lt. Frank D. Berrien as head coach. Despite the undefeated season, the Navy announced on December 2 that Berrien would be assigned to duties outside the Naval Academy and would not return as the head football coach for 1911. At the end of the 1910 season, Jack Dalton, the halfback who scored Navy's only points against Army, was selected to serve as captain of the 1911 team. Team Captain for the 1910 season was T. Starr King.

Home games were played at Worden Field

10/1/1910	NAVY	vs	ST. JOHN'S (Maryland)	16	0	**W**
10/8/1910	NAVY	vs	RUTGERS	0	0	**T**
10/15/1910	NAVY	vs	WASHINGTON & JEFFERSON (3-3-1)	15	0	**W**
10/22/1910	NAVY	vs	VIRGINIA TECH (6-2)	3	0	**W**
10/29/1910	NAVY	vs	WESTERN RESERVE	17	0	**W**
11/5/1910	NAVY	vs	LEHIGH (2-6-1)	30	0	**W**
11/12/1910	NAVY	vs	CARLISLE (8-6)	6	0	**W**
11/19/1910	NAVY	vs	NEW YORK UNIVERSITY	9	0	**W**
11/26/1910	NAVY	vs	ARMY (6-2)	3	0	**W**
Coach: Frank Berrien			Season Record >>	99	0	**8-0-1**

Schedule Source: Steve's Football Bible LLC

Selected game(s) highlights

LEHIGH

Showing by far its best form of the season, the Navy football team this afternoon rolled up the big score of 30 points on Lehigh University. The visitors were hopelessly outclassed and at no stage of the contest did they endanger the Annapolis goal line.

Army {@ Franklin Field – Philadelphia, PA}

Seven proved to be a lucky number for both Jack Dalton and his Midshipmen teammates. After missing his first-six field goal attempts in the 1910 Army-Navy game, Dalton connected on his seventh, which was all Navy needed in a 3-0 triumph. This field goal was also valuable in that it capped the Midshipmen's first undefeated season, a year that saw them outscore all nine opponents, 99-0. Dalton's field goal was the lone offensive highlight in a game that saw both clubs combine to punt 40 times.

1911 Navy Midshipmen

The team compiled an undefeated 6–0–3 record, shut out seven opponents, and defeated its opponents by a combined score of 116 to 11. The annual Army–Navy Game was played on November 25 at Franklin Field in Philadelphia. For the second consecutive year, the game was a low-scoring affair; Navy won 3–0 on a field goal by Jack Dalton.

Fullback Jack Dalton was the team captain and was a consensus first-team selection for the All-America team. Three other Navy player received first-team honors from one or more selectors: tackle John Brown received first-team honors from Ted Coy; guard Ray Wakeman received first-team honors from Henry L. Williams; and guard George Howe received first-team honors from The New York Globe. Brown and Dalton were both later inducted into the College Football Hall of Fame.

Home games were played at Worden Field

10/7/1911	NAVY	vs	JOHNS HOPKINS	27	5	**W**
10/11/1911	NAVY	vs	ST. JOHN'S (Maryland)	21	0	**W**
10/14/1911	NAVY	vs	WASHINGTON & JEFFERSON (6-4)	16	0	**W**
10/21/1911	NAVY	vs	PRINCETON (8-0-2)	0	0	**T**
10/28/1911	NAVY	vs	WESTERN RESERVE	0	0	**T**
11/4/1911	NAVY	vs	NC STATE (5-3)	17	6	**W**
11/11/1911	NAVY	vs	WEST VIRGINIA	32	0	**W**
11/18/1911	NAVY	vs	PENN STATE (8-0-1)	0	0	**T**
11/24/1911	NAVY	vs	ARMY (6-1-1)	3	0	**W**
Coach: Doug Howard			**Season Record >>**	116	11	**6-0-3**

Schedule Source: Steve's Football Bible LLC

Selected game(s) highlights

Army {@ Franklin Field – Philadelphia, PA}

On paper, the 1911 Army-Navy game was slated to be an even matchup. Army entered the season finale 6-0-1, while Navy was 5-0-3. Each team had surrendered less than two points per contest, while averaging two touchdowns per outing. The game lived up to its billing, with Jack Dalton's second-quarter field goal proving to be the difference in a 3-0 win. Dalton did much more than kick a field goal, however. He had a pair of 15 yard runs on the Mids' scoring drive and recorded a 72 yard punt.

1912 Navy Midshipmen

In their second season under head coach Douglas Legate Howard, the team compiled a 6–3 record, shut out four opponents, and defeated its opponents by a combined score of 126 to 61. Team Captain was Pete Rodes

The annual Army–Navy Game was played on November 30 at Franklin Field in Philadelphia; Navy won 6–0.

Home games were played at Worden Field

10/5/1912	NAVY	vs	JOHNS HOPKINS	7	3	W
10/12/1912	NAVY	vs	LEHIGH (9-2)	0	14	L
10/19/1912	NAVY	vs	SWARTHMORE (7-1-1)	6	21	L
10/26/1912	NAVY	vs	PITTSBURGH (3-6)	13	6	W
11/1/1912	NAVY	vs	WESTERN RESERVE	7	0	W
11/9/1912	NAVY	vs	BUCKNELL (6-3-1)	7	17	L
11/16/1912	NAVY	vs	NC STATE (4-3)	41	0	W
11/23/1912	NAVY	vs	NEW YORK UNIVERSITY	39	0	W
11/30/1912	NAVY	vs	ARMY (5-3)	6	0	W
Coach: Doug Howard			**Season Record >>**	126	61	6-3

Schedule Source: Steve's Football Bible LLC

Selected game(s) highlights

PITTSBURGH

Early in the first period Navy advanced the ball deep into Pitt territory and Carl Hockensmith was injured and had to be replaced by John Blair. Navy halfback Ingram took the ball to the five. The Pitt defense held for three downs and Pitt recovered a Navy fumble on fourth down. Wagner boomed a punt that Navy halfback Nichols fumbled, and Pitt end Francis Joyce pounced on the ball in the end zone for a touchdown. Frank Carboy missed the point after. The Navy offense then advanced the ball, with Ingram and Nichols doing the bulk of the ground gains, to the Pitt 5 yard line. "Nichols carried the ball over for the touchdown." The point after failed and the score was tied at 6-6. Pitt quarterback William McEllroy was injured on the touchdown play and replaced by Harry Shof.

After an exchange of punts, an interception, and another exchange of punts the Midshipman had the ball on the Pitt forty yard line. Four plays later they were on the Pitt ten yard line. "Ingram tore through the Pitt defense like a bull and shaking off three or four tacklers, scored Navy's second touchdown. Brown kicked goal." The halftime score read Navy 13 – Pitt 6. The second half was a defensive struggle as both teams dealt with fumbles, penalties and incomplete passes. Navy lined up for a field goal early in the third quarter but fumbled the snap and Pitt recovered. The Pitt offense could not sustain a scoring drive and lost their third straight game. "The game showed ragged spots in both teams, but was exceptionally clean, and the 3,000 spectators seemed to enjoy every minute of it."

Army {@ Franklin Field – Philadelphia, PA}

At 6-2, 228 pounds, Navy's John "Babe" Brown was not your typical placekicker. In fact, he used his imposing frame to his advantage in the 1912 Army game, and the result benefited all the Midshipmen. With five minutes left in the game, he lined up to attempt a field goal. But rather than dropkick the ball when it was snapped to him, he took off running before the Cadets tackled him at the five yard line. He booted a 12 yard field goal two plays later and tacked on a 35 yarder with less than a minute left to give Navy a 6-0 victory. The triumph was Navy's sixth in nine decisions and dropped Army's final record to 5-3.

1913 Navy Midshipmen

In their third season under head coach Douglas Legate Howard (pictured at right), the team compiled a 7–1–1 record, shut out seven opponents, and defeated its opponents by a combined score of 304 to 29. The team's sole loss came in the annual Army–Navy Game, played on November 29 at the Polo Grounds in New York City; Army won 22–9. Team Captain was K.P. Gilchrist. John Brown {OL} was selected as a consensus All-American.

Home games were played at Worden Field

10/4/1913	NAVY	vs	PITTSBURGH (6-2-1)	0	0	**T**
10/11/1913	NAVY	vs	GEORGETOWN (4-4)	23	0	W
10/18/1913	NAVY	vs	DICKINSON	29	0	W
10/25/1913	NAVY	vs	MARYLAND	76	0	W
11/1/1913	NAVY	vs	LEHIGH (5-3)	39	0	W
11/8/1913	NAVY	vs	BUCKNELL (6-4)	70	7	W
11/15/1913	NAVY	vs	PENN STATE (2-6)	10	0	W
11/22/1913	NAVY	vs	NEW YORK UNIVERSITY	48	0	W
11/29/1913	NAVY	vs	ARMY (8-1)	9	22	L
Coach: Doug Howard			**Season Record >>**	304	29	**7-1-1**

Schedule Source: Steve's Football Bible LLC

Selected game(s) highlights

PITTSBURGH

On Navy's second possession, they advanced the ball to the Pitt 35 yard line. On first down Navy guard Brown faked a field goal and was tackled for a loss. On second down he attempted a field goal "which was smeared by several Pitt linemen." Early in the second quarter, the Navy offense again advanced to the Pitt 25 yard line. "Brown again tried a field goal from placement, but it was blocked." The Pittsburgh defense kept the Midshipmen out of scoring range for the remainder of the first half. "The Pitt squad went wild in the third quarter when after advancing the ball to the Navy 20 yard line, Heil shot a forward pass to Wagner which the latter grabbed on the bound and carried over the Navy line." The officials claimed another Pitt player had touched the ball and did not allow the touchdown. "Coach Duff was in evidence on the field, vigorously protesting the decision which spoiled a victory for Pittsburgh." Navy then blocked Heil's field goal attempt and regained possession. The remainder of the game was a punting duel with penalties and interceptions stalling both team's offensive drives.

NEW YORK UNIVERSITY

Playing with five of the regular men out of the line-up, Navy closed its local football season here this afternoon by easily disposing of the eleven of New York University. The score was 48 to 0. The game was the most ragged exhibition of football that has been witnessed on the Academy gridiron this fall. Both teams were frequently penalized for holding and offside, although the Middies suffered the loss of almost twice as many yards as the visitors in this respect. The New Yorkers were lamentably weak on the defensive. Their forwards not only did not play low enough but also charged slowly. As a result, the Navy backs found little difficulty plunging through tackle and guard for substantial gains.

Army {@ Franklin Field – Philadelphia, PA}

Navy coach Doug Howard could look at the 1913 season from two perspectives. His defense allowed a total of 29 points in nine games, which is quite impressive. But when you consider the Midshipmen allowed 22 in one game, and it was the game against Army, Howard's club did not end the year on a solid note. Indeed, Navy would need more than three Babe Brown field goals to overcome the Cadets. Vernon Prichard and Louis Merrilat caught the Midshipmen defense off-guard with two touchdown passes, and Merrilat's 60 yard run set up West Point's other score in the 13-point victory.

1914 Navy Midshipmen

In its fourth season under head coach Douglas Legate Howard, the team compiled a 6–3 record, shut out three opponents, and defeated its opponents by a combined score of 174 to 83. The annual Army–Navy Game was played on November 28 at Franklin Field in Philadelphia; Army won 20–0. Team Captain was Harvey Overesch.

Home games were played at Worden Field

10/3/1914	NAVY	vs	GEORGETOWN (2-4-2)	13	0	W
10/10/1914	NAVY	vs	PITTSBURGH (8-1)	6	13	L
10/17/1914	NAVY	@	Pennsylvania (4-4-1)	6	13	L
10/24/1914	NAVY	vs	WESTERN RESERVE	48	0	W
10/31/1914	NAVY	vs	NC STATE (2-3-1)	16	14	W
11/7/1914	NAVY	vs	FORDHAM	21	0	W
11/14/1914	NAVY	vs	COLBY	31	21	W
11/21/1914	NAVY	vs	URSINUS	33	2	W
11/28/1914	NAVY	vs	ARMY (9-0)	0	20	L
Coach: Doug Howard			**Season Record >>**	**174**	**83**	**6-3**

Schedule Source: Steve's Football Bible LLC

Selected game(s) highlights

PITTSBURGH

For the third year in a row the Pitt contingent traveled to Annapolis, MD to battle the Midshipmen of Navy. Near the end of the first quarter, Pitt secured possession on Navy's 45 yard line. "On first down Miller sprinted around end for 20 yards before he was thrown." Another first down advanced the ball to the 15 yard line. "Williamson passed to Herron for a 12 yard gain landing the ball on the Middies 3 yard line." On second down "Williamson fell across the line between tackle and guard." Hastings kicked the goal and Pitt led 7-0. Early in the second quarter, the Navy offense advanced the ball to the Pitt 3 yard line but turned it over on downs. A few plays later Pitt quarterback Guy Williamson hurt his leg trying to scamper around the Navy end. Roy Heil replaced him for the remainder of the first half. Pitt led at halftime 7-0.

At the start of the third quarter Navy punted to Pitt. "Williamson, (back in the game) charging in on Blodgett's punt, juggled the ball and Overesch recovered for Navy on the visitor's 45 yard line." "Navy carried the ball to Pittsburgh's 30 yard mark. Here the visitors braced, and it was at this juncture that Mitchell essayed a beautiful forward pass to Overesch. The Navy Captain was on a dead run, and turning, caught the fast sailing pigskin under his left arm. He was directly in front of the goal line and almost instantaneously was brought to earth. In the fall he went across the mark." The goal after failed and Pitt led 7-6. DeHart replaced a limping Williamson. After a Pitt punt, Navy lined up to punt it back. "The whole Pitt line charged through and blocked Blodgett's attempted punt on Navy's first play and Peck taking the ball from the air cleared the crowd and registered Pitt's second touchdown." Hastings missed the goal after, and Pitt led 13-6. "Throughout the fourth and last period Navy made tremendous but futile efforts to crush Pitt's defense, finally advancing the ball to the Varsity's 12 yard line. Here the line held, and Vail's pass to Overesch was intercepted by Miller." Pitt beat the Midshipmen 13-6

Army {@ Franklin Field – Philadelphia, PA}

Army capped its first undefeated season (9-0) with a "textbook perfect" 20-0 triumph over Navy. The Cadets took advantage of a blocked punt and two Navy fumbles to score their first 14 points. After forcing Navy to punt on its opening possession, Louis Merrilat blocked the punt in the end zone for a safety. The Mids' H.C. Blodgett fumbled a second-quarter punt that Robert Neyland picked up at the Navy 20 yard line. One play later, Merrilat was in the end zone after catching a 20 yard touchdown pass from Vernon Pritchard. Finally, Blodgett fumbled a second punt that quarter which resulted in a Paul Hodgson one yard touchdown run.

1915 Navy Midshipmen

In its first season under head coach Jonas Ingram (pictured at right), the team compiled a 3–5–1 record and was outscored by a combined score of 118 to 99. The annual Army–Navy Game was played on November 27 at the Polo Grounds in New York City; Army won 14–0. Team Captain was Arthur Miles.

Home games were played at Worden Field

10/2/1915	NAVY	**vs**	GEORGETOWN (7-2)	0	9	**L**
10/9/1915	NAVY	**vs**	PITTSBURGH (8-0)	12	47	**L**
10/16/1915	NAVY	**vs**	PENNSYLVANIA (3-5-2)	7	7	**T**
10/23/1915	NAVY	**vs**	VIRGINIA TECH (4-4)	20	0	**W**
10/30/1915	NAVY	**vs**	NC STATE (3-3-1)	12	14	**L**
11/6/1915	NAVY	**vs**	BUCKNELL (2-6-3)	13	3	**W**
11/13/1915	NAVY	**vs**	COLBY	28	14	**W**
11/20/1915	NAVY	**vs**	URSINUS	7	10	**L**
11/27/1915	NAVY	**vs**	ARMY (5-3-1)	0	14	**L**
Coach: Jonas Ingram			**Season Record >>**	**99**	**118**	**3-5-1**

Schedule Source: Steve's Football Bible LLC

Selected game(s) highlights

PITTSBURGH

"Pittsburgh invaded the Navy goal line on seven occasions and five of the attempts at goal were successful." The touchdowns were scored by George McLaren (2), Andy Hastings, Guy Williamson, Whitey Miller, Leonard Hilty and Jimmy DeHart. George Fry kicked 3 goals and Andy Hastings and Bob Peck added one each. "The most sensational affair of the whole game was staged when "Jimmie" DeHart caught a kickoff five yards behind his own goal line and with perfect interference streaked the entire length of the field for a touchdown." "The first touchdown of the opposition was registered by Martin, the Navy right end, when he pulled Fry's uncovered pass out of the sky on his own ten yard line and raced ninety yards for the score. "Navy's second score was hung up in the final quarter, when Williamson, standing for a kick formation 13 yards from his goal line, fumbled and Navy recovered the ball. The Middies made a mighty effort here. Four plunges through the line were successful, Vail finally going over for the touchdown."

"Though outplayed and outmaneuvered at every stage, Navy lived up to its traditions and went down fighting. Even at the end of the match with Pitt 35 points ahead, the sailors fought back the visitors' approach and recovered a fumble in the very last seconds of play on their one yard line."

Army {@ Polo Grounds – New York, NY}

The 1915 Army-Navy game marked the first time each team wore numbered jerseys for identification. However, the Navy offense finished with the same number it had a year ago, 0, as Army blanked the Midshipmen, 14-0. Elmer "Ollie" Oliphant certainly left his impression on the Navy defense, accounting for 130 of his team's 196 total offensive yards, along with 11 punt returns for 114 yards. The contest once again fell victim to bad weather, which factored into a combined 30 punts and 10 turnovers between the two teams.

1916 Navy Midshipmen

In their second season under head coach Jonas Ingram, the Midshipmen compiled a 6–3–1 record and outscored their opponents by a combined score of 199 to 76. The annual Army–Navy Game was played on November 25 at the Polo Grounds in New York City; Army won 15–7. Team Captain was Clarence Ward.

Home games were played at Worden Field

9/30/1916	NAVY	vs	DICKINSON	0	0	**T**
10/7/1916	NAVY	vs	GEORGETOWN (8-1)	13	7	W
10/11/1916	NAVY	@	Maryland	14	7	W
10/14/1916	NAVY	vs	PITTSBURGH (8-0)	19	20	L
10/21/1916	NAVY	vs	WEST VIRGINIA (5-2-2)	12	7	W
10/28/1916	NAVY	vs	GEORGIA (6-3)	27	3	W
11/4/1916	NAVY	vs	WASHINGTON & LEE (5-2-2)	0	10	L
11/11/1916	NAVY	vs	NC STATE (2-5)	50	0	W
11/18/1916	NAVY	vs	VILLANOVA	57	7	W
11/25/1916	NAVY	vs	ARMY (9-0)	7	15	L
Coach: Jonas Ingram			**Season Record >>**	199	76	**6-3-1**

Schedule Source: Steve's Football Bible LLC

Selected game(s) highlights

PITTSBURGH

The Middies drew first blood early in the opening period when (Eric) Meadows fumbled a punt on his own five yard line. Jackson recovered for Navy and darted across the goal line. The try for goal failed." Pitt then proceeded to advance the ball down the field and Hastings' touchdown tied the game. He was successful on the goal after to put Pitt ahead 7–6 at the end of the first quarter. George McLaren scored his touchdown in the second quarter and Hastings again added the point after to make the score 14–6 at halftime.

Early in the third quarter, "a 48 yard sprint by Welcher after receiving one of Hastings' punts was a hair-raising incident. He finally was tackled inside of Pittsburgh's five yard line. Three line plunges and Ingram shot through the visitor's left side for a touchdown." Holtman kicked the goal and Pitt led 14 to 13. Pitt again retaliated with a long drive. It ended when "McLaren double passed to DeHart, who went around the Navy right flank for touchdown. Hastings missed goal." Pitt led 20 to 13. Late in the fourth quarter, Davis of Navy recovered a Pitt fumble on the Pitt 20 yard line. "The Middies came through with a touchdown as the result of the forward pass from Hanafee to Welcher that caught the Pitt boys napping. The Navy rooters literally held their breath as Holtman steadied himself for the try at goal and there was keen dismay when his toe proved untrue." Final score Pitt 20 – Navy 19.

Army {@ Polo Grounds – New York, NY}

Through 103 Army-Navy games, there has been one constant — neither team can afford to miss an extra point. Of course, there are exceptions to this standard. Take 1916, when Ollie Oliphant missed the extra point on Army's first score of the afternoon. Army coach Charles Daly could not have been that upset, considering Oliphant had carried the ball three times for 89 yards during that drive. It was just a sign of things to come for Navy, which suffered a 15-7 defeat at the hands of the Cadets. Oliphant added a field goal late in the first quarter, and the Cadets used a trick play for their final score of the day. Army was attempting a field goal when holder Charles Gerhardt took the snap and threw to fullback Eugene Vidal for the touchdown. Navy scored its first series touchdown since 1907 when Harry Goodstein blocked a punt and returned it for a touchdown.

1917 Navy Midshipmen

In their first season under head coach Gil Dobie (pictured at right), the Midshipmen compiled a 7–1 record, shut out four opponents, and outscored all opponents by a combined score of 442 to 23. The annual Army–Navy Game was not played this season or the next due to World War I. Team Captain was Earnest von Heimburg.

Home games were played at Worden Field

9/29/1917	NAVY	vs	DAVIDSON (6-4)	27	6	W
10/6/1917	NAVY	vs	WEST VIRGINIA (6-3-1)	0	7	L
10/13/1917	NAVY	vs	MARYLAND (4-3-1)	62	0	W
10/20/1917	NAVY	vs	CARLISLE (3-6)	62	0	W
10/27/1917	NAVY	vs	HAVERFORD	89	0	W
11/3/1917	NAVY	vs	WESTERN RESERVE	95	0	W
11/10/1917	NAVY	vs	GEORGETOWN (7-1)	28	7	W
11/17/1917	NAVY	vs	VILLANOVA	80	3	W
Coach: Gil Dobie			**Season Record >>**	**443**	**23**	**7-1**

Schedule Source: Steve's Football Bible LLC

Selected game(s) highlights

CARLISLE

Outplayed in every department of the game, and meeting a team which uncovered just the type of football their own predecessors at Carlisle used to hand its opponents in the days of Glenn Warner, the Indians this afternoon walloped by the Midshipmen. The final score was 62-0 in favor of the Middies. While the Indians were utterly helpless, the sailors uncorked every variety of football, with the exception of field goal kicking.

1918 Navy Midshipmen

In their second season under head coach Gil Dobie, the Midshipmen compiled a 4–1 record, shut out two opponents, and outscored all opponents by a combined score of 283 to 20. Team Captain was Bill Ingram. Wolcott Roberts {RB} and Lyman Perry {OL} were selected as consensus All-Americans.

The Spanish Flu outbreak ravaged the World. The flu, which came in multiple waves from 1918-1919, killed more than 675,000 in the United States. Not only was there a deadly pandemic in 1918, but World War I was still winding down. According to a report in the Charleston (S.C.) Post and Courier, 18 schools did not play football in 1918 because of the flu and the war. While there were some who felt college football should completely shut down because of the pandemic, President Woodrow Wilson felt that football added to the overall morale of the country. As a result, football teams were created at various military posts around the country and actually played against established college teams.

The annual Army–Navy Game was not played during the 1918 season due to World War I.

Home games were played at Worden Field

10/26/1918	NAVY	**vs**	NEWPORT NTS	47	7	**W**
11/2/1918	NAVY	**vs**	ST. HELENA NTS	66	0	**W**
11/9/1918	NAVY	**vs**	NORFOLK NAVY	37	6	**W**
11/16/1918	NAVY	**vs**	URSINUS	127	0	**W**
11/23/1918	NAVY	**vs**	GREAT LAKES NAVY (6-0-2)	6	7	**L**
Coach: Gil Dobie			**Season Record >>**	**283**	**20**	**4-1**

Schedule Source: Steve's Football Bible LLC

Selected game(s) highlights

GREAT LAKES NAVY

Navy was leading 6–0 late in the game. Bill Ingram fumbled at the 10 yard line, and Great Lakes Harry Eielson picked up the ball and ran for the goal. He crossed midfield, and Gil Dobie muttered "Tackle him" to nobody. An obedient Bill Saunders bolted from the Navy sideline and tackled Eielson at the 25. In the ensuing mayhem, Bluejackets halfback George Halas took a swing at Saunders and an admiral brandished a sword to try to restore order.

1919 Navy Midshipmen

In their third season under head coach Gil Dobie, the Midshipmen compiled a 7–1 record, shut out five opponents, and outscored all opponents by a combined score of 298 to 18. Team Captain was Eddie Ewen.

After cancellation in 1917 and 1918 due to World War I, the annual Army–Navy Game was played on November 29 at the Polo Grounds in New York City; Navy won 6–0.

Home games were played at Worden Field

10/4/1919	NAVY	vs	NC STATE (7-2)	49	0	**W**
10/11/1919	NAVY	vs	JOHNS HOPKINS	66	0	**W**
10/25/1919	NAVY	vs	BUCKNELL (5-4-1)	21	6	**W**
11/1/1919	NAVY	vs	WEST VIRGINIA Wesleyan	20	6	**W**
11/8/1919	NAVY	vs	GEORGETOWN (7-3)	0	6	**L**
11/15/1919	NAVY	vs	COLBY	121	0	**W**
11/29/1919	NAVY	vs	ARMY (6-3)	6	0	**W**
12/5/1919	NAVY	vs	USS UTAH	15	0	**W**
Coach: Gil Dobie			**Season Record >>**	**298**	**18**	**7-1**

Schedule Source: Steve's Football Bible LLC

Selected game(s) highlights

Army {@ Polo Grounds – New York, NY}

After a two-year series hiatus due to World War I, Army and Navy renewed their heated rivalry in 1919. Despite posting seven times as much total offensive yardage as the Cadets, Navy could only manage a pair of Clyde King field goals. Fortunately for Naval Academy fans, that was enough for a 6-0 win. The victory marked the fourth time in 10 years that Navy had beaten Army strictly by kicking field goals. Although the game was played in a steady downpour, neither team lost a fumble nor committed a turnover. The Midshipmen finished the year 6-1, while the Cadets were 6-3.

1920 Navy Midshipmen

In their first season under head coach Bob Folwell (pictured at right), the Midshipmen compiled a 6–2 record, shut out three opponents, and outscored all opponents by a combined score of 164 to 43. Team Captain was Eddie Ewen.

The annual Army–Navy Game was played on November 27 at the Polo Grounds in New York City; Navy won 7–0.

Home games were played at Worden Field

10/2/1920	NAVY	vs	NC STATE (7-3)	7	14	L
10/9/1920	NAVY	vs	LAFAYETTE (5-3)	12	7	W
10/16/1920	NAVY	vs	BUCKNELL	7	2	W
10/23/1920	NAVY	@	Princeton (6-0-1)	0	14	L
10/30/1920	NAVY	vs	WESTERN RESERVE	47	0	W
11/6/1920	NAVY	vs	GEORGETOWN	21	6	W
11/13/1920	NAVY	vs	SOUTH CAROLINA (5-4)	63	0	W
11/27/1920	NAVY	vs	ARMY	7	0	W
Coach: Bob Folwell			**Season Record >>**	164	43	6-2

Schedule Source: Steve's Football Bible LLC

Selected game(s) highlights

Army {@ Polo Grounds – New York, NY}

Navy's first offensive touchdown in 10 Army-Navy games proved to be a big one, handing the Cadets a 7-0 defeat. This also evened the all-time series mark at 11-11-2. Army was unable to convert on any of its three first-half field goal attempts, forcing the teams into halftime deadlocked in a scoreless tie. This remained until Vic Noyes tossed a seven yard touchdown to Ben Koehler for the score. The Midshipmen nullified any hopes of an Army comeback with an interception at midfield to end the game.

1921 Navy Midshipmen

In their second season under head coach Bob Folwell, the Midshipmen compiled a 6–1 record, shut out six opponents, and outscored all opponents by a combined score of 147–13. Team Captain was Emery Lawson.

The annual Army–Navy Game was played on November 26 at the Polo Grounds in New York City; Navy won 7–0.

Home games were played at Worden Field

10/1/1921	NAVY	vs	NC STATE (3-3-3)	40	0	**W**
10/8/1921	NAVY	vs	WESTERN RESERVE	53	0	**W**
10/15/1921	NAVY	vs	PRINCETON (4-3)	13	0	**W**
10/29/1921	NAVY	vs	BETHANY (West Virginia)	21	0	**W**
11/5/1921	NAVY	vs	BUCKNELL	6	0	**W**
11/12/1921	NAVY	@	Penn State (8-0-2)	7	13	**L**
11/26/1921	NAVY	vs	ARMY	7	0	**W**
Coach: Bob Folwell			**Season Record >>**	147	13	**6-1**

Schedule Source: Steve's Football Bible LLC

Selected game(s) highlights

Army {@ Polo Grounds – New York, NY}

Allowing just 124 yards of total offense, Navy posted its sixth shutout in its last seven wins with a 7-0 victory over Army. Vince Conroy gave Navy all the points it needed with a short touchdown run midway through the first quarter. The Midshipmen defense sealed the deal with a superb effort, halting the Cadets on two key occasions. Army had driven to the Navy 33 yard line in the fourth quarter, as Denis Mulligan's field goal attempt fell short. The Midshipmen's Ira McKee spoiled Army's next hope with an interception at the Navy eight yard line.

This win was Navy's third-straight victory over its archrival. In addition to outscoring Army 20-0 in the last three quarters, Navy had a 40-13 advantage in first downs and had outgained the Cadets, 683-230.

1922 Navy Midshipmen

In their third season under head coach Bob Folwell, the Midshipmen compiled a 5–2 record, shut out four opponents, and outscored all opponents by a combined score of 185 to 37. Team Captain was Vincent Conroy (pictured at right). The annual Army–Navy Game was played on November 25 at Franklin Field in Philadelphia; Army won 17–14.

Wendell Taylor {E} was selected as a consensus All-American.

Home games were played at Worden Field

10/7/1922	NAVY	vs	WESTERN RESERVE	71	0	W
10/14/1922	NAVY	vs	BUCKNELL	14	7	W
10/21/1922	NAVY	vs	GEORGIA TECH (7-2)	13	0	W
10/28/1922	NAVY	@	Pennsylvania (6-3)	7	13	L
11/3/1922	NAVY	vs	PENN STATE (6-4-1)	14	0	W
11/11/1922	NAVY	vs	XAVIER	52	0	W
11/25/1922	NAVY	vs	ARMY (8-0-2)	14	17	L
Coach: Bob Folwell			**Season Record >>**	**185**	**37**	**5-2**

Schedule Source: Steve's Football Bible LLC

Selected game(s) highlights

Army {@ Franklin Field – Philadelphia, PA}

Army's George Smythe proved to be a thorn in Navy's side, as his 47 yard punt return set up his seven yard touchdown pass to Fran Dodd and gave the Cadets a 17-14 win before 55,000 fans at Philadelphia's Franklin Field.

Trailing 10-7, momentum swung to Navy's side as Vince Conroy's one yard touchdown run gave the Midshipmen a 14-10 lead at the start of the fourth quarter. However, the excitement shifted back to the Army sideline, as Smythe's punt return and touchdown pass gave the Cadets a lead they would not relinquish. The Army defense clinched the victory by stopping Navy at the Cadet 22 yard line late in the game. Despite the outcome, the Midshipmen won the statistical battle, outgaining Army, 283-154.

1923 Navy Midshipmen

In their fourth season under head coach Bob Folwell, the Midshipmen compiled a 5–1–3 record, shut out three opponents, and outscored all opponents by a combined score of 168 to 62. Team Captain was Arthur Carney.

The annual Army–Navy Game was played on November 25 at the Polo Grounds in New York City and the teams played to a scoreless tie. Navy was invited to play in the Rose Bowl on New Year's Day and played Washington to a 14–14 tie.

Home games were played at Worden Field

9/29/1923	NAVY	vs	WILLIAM & MARY (7-3)	39	10	W	
10/6/1923	NAVY	vs	DICKINSON	13	7	W	
10/13/1923	NAVY	vs	WEST VIRGINIA Wesleyan	26	7	W	
10/20/1923	NAVY	@	Penn State (6-2-1)	3	21	L	
10/27/1923	NAVY	vs	PRINCETON (3-3-1)	3	3	T	
11/3/1923	NAVY	vs	COLGATE (6-2-1)	9	0	W	
11/10/1923	NAVY	vs	XAVIER	61	0	W	
11/24/1923	NAVY	vs	ARMY (6-2-1)	0	0	T	
1/1/1924	**NAVY**	**vs**	**Washington (10-1-1)**	**14**	**14**	**T**	**Rose Bowl**
Coach: Bob Folwell			**Season Record >>**	**168**	**62**	**5-1-3**	

Schedule Source: Steve's Football Bible LLC

Selected game(s) highlights

Army {@ Polo Grounds – New York, NY}

The 1923 Army-Navy game may have resulted in a scoreless tie, but that doesn't mean the afternoon was lacking in excitement. After all, when the two teams combine to punt 26 times, something is bound to happen — maybe even more than once. On the first play of the fourth quarter, Army's Henry Baxter blocked Navy punter Carl Cullen's kick. The alert Cullen scrambled to recover the punt inside his own 10 yard line, which under the rules allowed Navy to retain possession. Although this was long before instant replay existed, the 65,000 fans were treated to the same incident on Navy's next punt. Again, the Mids were inside their own 10 yard line as August Farwick got a hand on Cullen's kick, which the Navy punter also recovered.

Navy closed its season with a 14-14 tie against Washington in the Rose Bowl to finish 5-1-3 on the year.

1924 ROSE BOWL

The game began at the rescheduled time, with a temperature of 52 °F and the field still wet. Because of the playing conditions, running plays were ineffective, which caused problems for the Washington offense. Navy instead used passing plays, which the Washington defense had trouble stopping. Navy was driving down to the 22 yard line of Washington when the first quarter ended. Navy controlled the first quarter, completing all six passing attempts and holding  the Washington offense to under 100 yards gained. On their first play of the second quarter, Navy scored a touchdown on a pass play from Ira McKee to Carl Cullen. McKee kicked the extra point for Navy, giving them a 7–0 lead. To trick Washington, Navy tried an onside kick on the next play, but Washington recovered the ball. After two short running plays, Washington quarterback Fred Abel completed a 23 yard pass to running back Kinsley Dubois, bringing Washington inside the 25 yard line. On the next play, running back George Wilson ran the ball 23 yards for a touchdown. Washington's kicker converted the extra point to tie the game at 7–7. After several drives from each team that did not result in further scoring, Navy completed a 57 yard pass down to the Washington eight yard line. Two plays later, Ira

McKee ran the ball in from two yards out for a touchdown, then afterward converted the extra point. The first half ended with Navy leading by 14–7, having completed all 11 passes they attempted.

Both teams' defenses controlled the third quarter, allowing no points to be scored. Navy's McKee completed three more pass plays before his first incompletion, which came on his fourteenth attempt. Washington's offense had little success in the third quarter, being held to only a few yards gained and turning the ball over once. In the fourth quarter, after several unsuccessful drives by each team, Navy made a major error. After being stopped on their own 26 yard line, Navy improperly lined up in a punt formation, and the center snapped the ball over the punter's head. The ball was recovered by Washington on the Navy ten yard line. Washington lost two yards in three plays and faced a fourth down from the Navy 12 yard line. Washington stacked their offensive line, allowing their left guard, James Bryan, to become an eligible receiver. Fred Abel passed the ball to Bryan, who caught it just short of the goal line and walked into the end zone for the touchdown. Washington's kicker then converted the extra point, tying the game at 14. Navy received the ball from Washington and began to throw it erratically. After gaining several yards, Ira McKee threw an interception near midfield. On the next play, Fred Abel threw a long pass to George Wilson, who was tackled on the Navy 20 yard line after gaining 30 yards. Washington brought out their placekicker, Leonard Ziel, to kick a 32 yard field goal, which would have won them the game. Ziel kicked the ball about a yard short of the right upright, giving the ball back to Navy with the game still tied. A few plays later the game ended in a 14–14 tie.

1924 Navy Midshipmen

In their fifth season under head coach Bob Folwell, the Midshipmen compiled a 2–6 record and outscored opponents by a combined score of 84 to 69. Team Captain was Edmund Taylor

The annual Army–Navy Game was played on November 29 in Baltimore, Maryland; Army won 12–0. The Midshipmen defeated Vermont 53–0 but were outscored 69–31 in their other seven games.

Home games were played Thompson Field

10/4/1924	NAVY	vs	WILLIAM & MARY (6-2-1)	14	7	**W**
10/11/1924	NAVY	vs	MARQUETTE	3	21	**L**
10/18/1924	NAVY	@	Princeton (4-2-1)	14	17	**L**
10/25/1924	NAVY	vs	WEST VIRGINIA Wesleyan	7	10	**L**
11/1/1924	NAVY	vs	PENN STATE (6-3-1)	0	6	**L**
11/8/1924	NAVY	vs	VERMONT	53	0	**W**
11/15/1924	NAVY	vs	BUCKNELL	0	6	**L**
11/29/1924	NAVY	vs	ARMY (5-1-2)	0	12	**L**
Coach: Bob Folwell			**Season Record >>**	**91**	**79**	**2-6**

Schedule Source: Steve's Football Bible LLC

Selected game(s) highlights

VERMONT

A revamped Navy backfield, that showed all kinds of speed and dash, buried the lighter but plucky fighting team of the University of Vermont under an avalanche of touchdowns on Farragut Field at the Naval Academy this afternoon. When the final whistle sounded the Middies had piled up a total of 50 points to their opponents 0. The game offered fine opportunity for the Middies to experiment with their crop of forward-pass plays and they got off some fine ones for great gains.

Army {@ Memorial Stadium – Baltimore, MD}

Given the choice of where to play the 1924 Army-Navy game, Annapolis officials chose Baltimore's 80,000-seat stadium. But this supposed home field advantage did not pay the dividends the Midshipmen had hoped, as Edgar Garbisch booted four field goals to give Army a 12-0 win.

He may have accounted for all 12 points, but Garbisch had the opportunity to score 21 against the Mids. Army's opening drive ended with Garbisch attempting a 30 yard dropkick field goal, however, it was blocked. Garbisch recovered the block, but his 40 yard attempt four downs later fell short. He also had a 45 yard attempt midway through the second quarter that sailed wide. Navy may not have reached the end zone, but it wasn't due to a lack of effort. The Midshipmen set a then series record by completing 12-of-22 passes for 50 yards. The Army victory gave the Cadets a 13-12-2 series advantage, a lead it would not relinquish for 56 years.

1925 Navy Midshipmen

In its first season under head coach Jack Owsley (pictured at right), the team compiled a 5–2–1 record, shut out four opponents, and outscored all opponents by a total of 134 to 81. Team Captain was August Lentz.

The annual Army–Navy Game was played on November 28 at the Polo Grounds in New York City; Army won 10–3.

Home games were played Thompson Field

10/3/1925	NAVY	vs	WILLIAM & MARY (7-4)	25	0	W
10/10/1925	NAVY	vs	MARQUETTE	19	0	W
10/17/1925	NAVY	vs	PRINCETON (5-1-1)	10	10	**T**
10/24/1925	NAVY	vs	WASHINGTON (MARYLAND)	37	0	W
10/31/1925	NAVY	@	Michigan (7-1)	0	54	L
11/7/1925	NAVY	vs	MCDANIEL	27	0	W
11/14/1925	NAVY	vs	BUCKNELL	13	7	W
11/28/1925	NAVY	vs	ARMY (7-2)	3	10	L
Coach: Jack Owsley			Season Record >>	134	81	**5-2-1**

Schedule Source: Steve's Football Bible LLC

Selected game(s) highlights

MARQUETTE

Showing great alertness in following the ball and taking full advantage of the opportunities when they came their way, the Annapolis Midshipmen triumphed over Marquette University on Farragut Field today, 19 to 0. Revenge was sweet for the Middies, who last year were forced to bow to their intersectional opponents, 21 to 3, as a maze of forward passes swept them off their feet.

PRINCETON

A characteristic Navy-Princeton gridiron struggle ensued while history was being repeated yesterday afternoon at Baltimore Stadium. And when the final whistle came, with Navy clinging to the ball on its own 22 yard line, while Princeton, with Jake Slagle and Sammy Ewing again in the backfield and just itching for a final opportunity to try for a decisive coup, the score was deadlocked at 10 all.

Michigan

The game was the first meeting between the two traditional football powers. The 1925 Navy team came into the game undefeated, averaging almost 23 points a game, and featuring two players (Tom Hamilton and Frank Wickhorst) who were later inducted into the College Football Hall of Fame. The defeat was the worst suffered by a Navy football team up to that time. On

Michigan's second play from scrimmage, quarterback Benny Friedman completed a pass to Bruce Gregory for a 20 yard gain, and Bo Molenda then ran 18 yards for a touchdown. Michigan scored its second touchdown when William Flora blocked a punt and recovered the ball in the end zone. According to one account, Flora broke through the line so quickly that he was able to snatch the ball as it dropped from the punter's hand to his foot. On the next scoring drive, Friedman passed to Sammy Babcock and then threw an 18 yard touchdown pass to Molenda. Michigan led 21–0 at the end of the first quarter. In the third quarter, Friedman passed 22 yards to Oosterbaan for the fourth touchdown. On the next drive, Friedman completed two passes to Oosterbaan, with Oosterbaan running out of bounds at the Navy one-foot line after the second pass. Molenda ran for the touchdown from there. In the fourth quarter, Michigan played its second-string backfield. William Herrnstein returned a punt 50 yard and then scored on a run from the

11 yard line. James Miller intercepted a pass and returned it 35 yards for a touchdown. And Leo Hoffman ran for a final touchdown just before the game ended. Friedman kicked five extra points in the game, and Miller added one.

MCDANIEL

Western Maryland College played a surprisingly strong game against the Navy here today, and instead of the sailor lads rolling up something like half a hundred points, as had been expected, they had to fight their hardest to come through on the long end of a 27-to-0 count. Fortune began to work against the Methodists immediately after the first kickoff. Hamilton booted the ball to Chambers, who was thrown on his 25 yard line. On the first lineup, a fumble was recovered by Navy on the Green Terrors' 15 yard line and, despite a 5 yard penalty for offside, the Middies hammered their way through the line for the objective. Caldwell made the touchdown on a 2 yard dive off tackle. Shapley added a point via placement goal and the rout was on.

Army {@ Polo Grounds – New York, NY}

Six turnovers proved to be Navy's demise, as Army held on for a 10-3 triumph before 60,000 fans at the Polo Grounds. After driving to the Army three yard line early in the second quarter, Navy had to settle for a 12 yard field goal by Tom Hamilton. The Cadets, on the other hand, were able to capitalize upon a fourth down situation just before halftime. On fourth-and-four from the nine, Neil Harding hit Henry Baxter for the touchdown and the 7-3 win. Russell Reeder tacked on a field goal in the fourth quarter for the victory.

1926 Navy Midshipmen {National Champions}

The Midshipmen were coached by Bill Ingram in his first year and finished the season undefeated with a record of nine wins, zero losses and one tie (9–0–1). Team Captain was Frank Wickhorst. Although Alabama and Stanford have been named the 1926 national champion by most selectors, the 1926 Navy team was named as the national champion under Boand and Houlgate Systems.

Wickhorst {OL} was selected as a consensus All-American.

NATIONAL CHAMPIONS
Home games were played Thompson Field

10/2/1926	NAVY	vs	PURDUE (5-2-1)	17	13	W
10/9/1926	NAVY	vs	DRAKE (2-6)	24	7	W
10/9/1926	NAVY	vs	RICHMOND	26	0	W
10/16/1926	NAVY	@	Princeton (5-1-1)	27	13	W
10/23/1926	NAVY	vs	COLGATE (5-2-2)	13	7	W
10/30/1926	NAVY	vs	MICHIGAN (7-1)	10	0	W
11/6/1926	NAVY	vs	WEST VIRGINIA Wesleyan	53	7	W
11/13/1926	NAVY	vs	GEORGETOWN	10	7	W
11/20/1926	NAVY	vs	LOYOLA (Baltimore)	35	13	W
11/27/1926	NAVY	vs	ARMY (7-1-1)	21	21	T
Coach: Bill Ingram			Season Record >>	236	88	9-0-1

Schedule Source: Steve's Football Bible LLC

Selected game(s) highlights

PURDUE

Tom Hamilton missed a field goal, then hit one from 30 yards out for a 3-0 lead. In the 2nd quarter, Purdue tossed a touchdown pass, but Navy halfback Ned Hannegan responded with a 25 yard touchdown run for a 10-7 halftime lead. Purdue threw another touchdown pass in the 3rd quarter, but Navy again responded, this time on two passes from Hamilton to end Russell "Whitey" Lloyd, the second going into the end zone. Purdue advanced 2 more scoring threats in the 4th quarter, but they got no points, and Navy held on for the 17-13 win.

Princeton

Navy traveled to Princeton in week 4. Princeton led 13-10 at the half, but Navy's line dominated the second half, opening gaping holes that turned simple line plunges into big gains, and Navy won 27-13.

COLGATE

Navy dominated the 1st quarter and scored a touchdown for a 6-0 lead. Colgate dominated the 2nd quarter and scored a touchdown, adding the extra point for a 7-6 halftime lead. It was Navy's turn to dominate the 3rd quarter, making 6 first downs to none for Colgate, but they were unable to score, losing the ball once on downs at the Colgate 6. Colgate then seized control of the game in the 4th quarter, making 8 first downs to none for Navy. With 2 minutes to play, Colgate had the ball 4th down and inches away from the Navy goal line. The game appeared to be all but over as Colgate fullback Clark Shaughnessy slammed into the line. But they did stop Shaughnessy in a huge pile-up at the goal line. And then suddenly, Navy end Russell Lloyd came out of the pile with the ball. Colgate didn't notice or pursue him until too late. Lloyd was the fastest man on Navy's team, and he had been a 4th-quarter substitute, so he had fresh legs. Colgate had only substituted once all game. Lloyd took it 99 yards for a touchdown, delivering a miraculous 13-7 win.

MICHIGAN {Memorial Stadium – Baltimore, MD}

Michigan lost to Navy by a 10-0 score at Baltimore, Maryland. Navy's Howard Caldwell ran for a touchdown against the Wolverines. Caldwell's touchdown was the first scored against Michigan since the 1924 season. Navy smothered Michigan's running game, and they used a new pass defense that held Michigan's powerful air attack to just 6 completions in 27 attempts. Michigan's only signs of offensive life came in the 2nd quarter, but they were unable to score when they had the chances. First, Michigan quarterback Benny Friedman attempted a field goal that was blocked by Navy tackle Tom Eddy. Later, Michigan drove to the Navy 10, where a 3rd down pass from Benny Friedman to Bennie Oosterbaan was knocked down by Navy halfback Tom Hamilton. On 4th down, Friedman hit Oosterbaan with a short pass, but Oosterbaan was tackled at the Navy 2 yard line, snuffing out Michigan's last threat of the game. In the 3rd quarter, Tom Hamilton threw a 25 yard pass to halfback Maurice Goudge, then Goudge ripped an 18 yard run to set up a Hamilton field goal from the 28 yard line, finally breaking the scoreless tie.

After the game, the Navy midshipmen stormed the field, tore down the goalposts and broke them into splinters to be kept as souvenirs. The game was played before approximately 50,000 spectators.

GEORGETOWN

Georgetown's line dominated Navy badly in the first half, but they didn't get quite enough points out of it. They missed a long field goal in the opening quarter, then blocked a punt at the Navy 18 to set up a touchdown and a 7-0 halftime lead. But Navy was far better in the 2nd half, thanks to the insertion of fullback Alan Shapley into the game. He had been injured early in the season, but his return came just in time for Navy. In the 3rd quarter, Shapley returned an interception 23 yards to the Georgetown 40 yard line, and from there he caught a touchdown pass from Tom Hamilton to tie the game up 7-7.
In the 4th quarter, Georgetown mounted a drive, but they lost the ball on downs at the Navy 25. With time running out and still on their own end of the field, Navy went for it on 4th down, Tom Hamilton throwing to Ned Hannegan for just enough to get the first down. Then Hamilton hit Russell Lloyd for 40 yards to the Georgetown 18. Shapley carried for 8 yards, and then Hamilton kicked the field goal that gave Navy a 10-7 win in the closing seconds.

Army {@ Soldiers Field – Chicago, IL}

In his first season as head coach at his alma mater, West Point graduate Biff Jones used an intriguing strategy for the Army-Navy game. By starting his second-team units against the Midshipmen, he hoped to give Navy a false sense of confidence. The Mids took full advantage of the "mismatch," as touchdown runs by Henry Caldwell and James Schuber handed Army an early deficit.

The Cadets responded with three touchdowns, the last a 44 yard run by Chris Cagle, to take the lead by the end of the third quarter. Nonetheless, an eight yard touchdown run by Alan Shapley in the fourth quarter salvaged a 21-21 tie for Navy. Army may have spoiled the Midshipmen's bid for a 10-0 record, but Coach Bill Ingram's club still laid claim to the national title.

1927 Navy Midshipmen

In their second season under head coach Bill Ingram (pictured at right), the Midshipmen compiled a 6–3 record, shut out two opponents, and outscored all opponents by a combined score of 192 to 84. Team Captain was Ned Hannegan.

The annual Army–Navy Game was played on November 26 at the Polo Grounds in New York City; Army won 14–9.

Home games were played Thompson Field

10/1/1927	NAVY	vs	DAVIS & ELKINS	27	0	W
10/8/1927	NAVY	vs	DRAKE (3-6)	35	6	W
10/15/1927	NAVY	vs	NOTRE DAME (7-1-1)	6	19	L
10/22/1927	NAVY	vs	DUKE (4-5)	32	6	W
10/29/1927	NAVY	@	Pennsylvania (6-4)	12	6	W
11/5/1927	NAVY	vs	WEST VIRGINIA Wesleyan	26	0	W
11/12/1927	NAVY	@	Michigan (6-2)	12	27	L
11/19/1927	NAVY	vs	LOYOLA (Baltimore)	33	6	W
11/26/1927	NAVY	vs	ARMY (9-1)	9	14	L
Coach: Bill Ingram			**Season Record >>**	192	84	**6-3**

Schedule Source: Steve's Football Bible LLC

Selected game(s) highlights

Michigan

Michigan defeated Navy by a 27-12 score at Michigan Stadium. Fullback George Rich scored two touchdowns for Michigan. Quarterback Jim Miller ran for 117 yards on 17 carries and scored a touchdown. The final Michigan touchdown was scored by Bennie Oosterbaan. Louis Gilbert kicked three points after touchdown. Navy's touchdowns were scored by Whitey Lloyd and Shag Ransford.

Army {@ Polo Grounds – New York, NY}

In the last Army-Navy game played at the Polo Grounds, the Cadets overcame a pesky Midshipmen club to claim a 14-9 victory.

Navy held a 2-0 lead at halftime, but it could have just as easily been 16-0. On its first possession, Navy reached the Army eight yard line but came away without a point. Midway through the second quarter, the Mids' Carl Giese blocked a punt out of the end zone to give Navy a 2-0 lead. Navy had another chance to reach the end zone just before halftime, but Army stopped Joe Clifton on a fourth-and-goal from the one yard line.

A two yard run by Lighthorse Harry Wilson gave the Cadets a 7-2 advantage early in the third quarter. Army added another touchdown to its lead when Chris Cagle intercepted an Ed Hannegan pass and returned it 41 yards to the Navy four yard line. Wilson scored again, and Army was on its way to the win. Navy scored its touchdown when Russell Lloyd hit Ted Sloane on a 28 yard touchdown, but it wasn't enough.

1928 Navy Midshipmen

In their third season under head coach Bill Ingram, the Midshipmen compiled a 5–3–1 record, shut out five opponents, and outscored all opponents by a combined score of 121 to 21. Team Captain was Ed Burke. Burke {OL} was selected as a consensus All-American.

The annual Army–Navy Game was canceled due to disagreement over player eligibility standards.

Home games were played Thompson Field

9/29/1928	NAVY	vs	DAVIS & ELKINS	0	2	L
10/6/1928	NAVY	vs	BOSTON COLLEGE	0	6	L
10/13/1928	NAVY	@	Notre Dame (5-4)	0	7	L
10/20/1928	NAVY	vs	DUKE (5-5)	6	0	W
10/27/1928	NAVY	@	Pennsylvania (8-1)	6	0	W
11/3/1928	NAVY	vs	WEST VIRGINIA Wesleyan	37	0	W
11/10/1928	NAVY	vs	MICHIGAN (3-4-1)	6	6	T
11/17/1928	NAVY	vs	LOYOLA (Baltimore)	57	0	W
11/24/1928	NAVY	vs	PRINCETON (5-1-2)	9	0	W
Coach: Bill Ingram			**Season Record >>**	**121**	**21**	**5-3-1**

Schedule Source: Steve's Football Bible LLC

Selected game(s) highlights

Michigan {@ Memorial Stadium – Baltimore, MD}

Michigan played Navy to a 6–6 tie before a crowd of approximately 35,000 at Municipal Stadium in Baltimore. After a scoreless first half, Johnny Gannon of Navy returned the second-half kickoff for 72 yards to Michigan's eight yard line. Gannon then ran for the touchdown on third down. Gannon's kick for extra point went wide. Michigan fullback Joe Gembis was injured prior to the game and was unavailable to play against Navy. Michigan tied the game in the fourth quarter when backup fullback Stanley Hozer led a 50 yard drive culminating with a short touchdown run. Michigan's kick for extra point was blocked. As time ran out, Navy attempted a field goal that went wide of the goal post.

1929 Navy Midshipmen

In their fourth season under head coach Bill Ingram, the Midshipmen compiled a 6–2–2 record, shut out four opponents, and outscored all opponents by a combined score of 233 to 59. Team Captain was Lyle Koepke.

The annual Army–Navy Game was not played in 1929 due to disagreement over player eligibility standards.

Home games were played Thompson Field

9/28/1929	NAVY	vs	DENISON	47	0	**W**
10/5/1929	NAVY	vs	WILLIAM & MARY	15	0	**W**
10/12/1929	NAVY	vs	NOTRE DAME (9-0)	7	14	**L**
10/19/1929	NAVY	vs	DUKE (4-6)	45	13	**W**
10/26/1929	NAVY	@	Princeton (2-4-1)	13	13	**T**
11/2/1929	NAVY	@	Pennsylvania (7-2)	2	7	**L**
11/9/1929	NAVY	vs	GEORGETOWN (5-2-2)	0	0	**T**
11/16/1929	NAVY	vs	WAKE FOREST (6-5-1)	61	0	**W**
11/23/1929	NAVY	vs	WEST VIRGINIA Wesleyan	30	6	**W**
11/30/1929	NAVY	vs	Dartmouth (7-2)	13	6	**W**
Coach: Bill Ingram			**Season Record >>**	233	59	**6-2-2**

Schedule Source: Steve's Football Bible LLC

Selected game(s) highlights

NOTRE DAME {@ Memorial Stadium – Baltimore, MD}

Navy, with all but two regulars back from the team that had held Notre Dame to a seven-point victory in 1928, was confident of victory. When the Midshipmen rushed the shock troops off their feet to score in the first quarter, their swagger seemed to be justified. Frank Carideo tossed a sleight-of-hand pass to Elder for a touchdown and later tied the score with his placekick. Carideo intercepted a Navy pass in the third quarter. Larry Mullins scored the game winning touchdown for the Irish.

1930 Navy Midshipmen

In their fifth season under head coach Bill Ingram, the Midshipmen compiled a 6–5 record, shut out four opponents, and outscored all opponents by a combined score of 148 to 117. Team Captain was Bob Bowstrom. The annual Army–Navy Game was played on December 13 at the Polo Grounds in New York City; Army won 6-0.

Home games were played Thompson Field

10/4/1930	NAVY	vs	WILLIAM & MARY	19	6	**W**
10/11/1930	NAVY	@	Notre Dame (10-0)	2	26	**L**
10/18/1930	NAVY	vs	DUKE (8-1-2)	0	18	**L**
10/25/1930	NAVY	@	Princeton (1-5-1)	31	0	**W**
11/1/1930	NAVY	vs	WEST VIRGINIA Wesleyan	37	14	**W**
11/8/1930	NAVY	vs	OHIO STATE (5-2-1)	0	27	**L**
11/15/1930	NAVY	vs	SMU (6-3-1)	7	20	**L**
11/22/1930	NAVY	vs	MARYLAND (7-5)	6	0	**W**
11/29/1930	NAVY	vs	GEORGE WASHINGTON	20	0	**W**
12/6/1930	NAVY	@	Pennsylvania (5-4)	26	0	**W**
12/13/1930	NAVY	vs	ARMY (9-1-1)	0	6	**L**
Coach: Bill Ingram			**Season Record >>**	**148**	**117**	**6-5**

Schedule Source: Steve's Football Bible LLC

Selected game(s) highlights

OHIO STATE {Memorial Stadium – Baltimore, MD}

This home-and-home series was scheduled to start in 1929. However, Navy asked for a one-year delay. The extra year did not help the Midshipmen against the Wes Fesler led Buckeyes. The senior do-everything sensation played fullback and end, threw a touchdown to Dick Larkins, was a beast on defense and pinned Navy with his punting skills. Fesler's efforts gave Ohio State a 27-0 victory in the school's first game against Navy.

GEORGE WASHINGTON

Navy second and third team men were held scoreless for two periods by George Washington University today but the Capital eleven could not withstand the assault of regulars who went into the fray long enough to score three touchdowns and a 20 to 0 victory in the last Middy home game of the season With Penn and Army in the offing on the next two Saturdays Rip Miller assistant coach started a team of reserves in the absence of Bill Ingram head coach who watched the Notre Dame-Army game at Chicago They failed to score in the first half though within the 20 yard line twice At the start of the second half Middy regulars went in and marched for a touchdown from the kickoff Hurley playing Bullet Lou Kirn's position smashed over from the one yard line Navy repeated after the next kick off Hagber scoring from the ten yard line after Gannon Intercepted a George Washington pass Early in the final period Tschrigi and Hurley took the ball 40 yards to the one yard line and Hurley plunged across and then the burden was given back to the substitutes

Army {@ Yankee Stadium – Bronx, NY}

A disagreement regarding eligibility policies may have cancelled the 1928 and '29 Army-Navy games, but a capacity crowd at Yankee Stadium welcomed the rivalry's return Dec. 13, 1930. Unfortunately for Navy, Army retained its recent series dominance with a 6-0 victory. The final score certainly doesn't reflect Army's commanding performance, as the Cadets finished the afternoon with 265 yards of total offense, compared to 63 for the Midshipmen. Yet, Navy was able to keep Army off the scoreboard until the fourth quarter, when Ray Stecker ran 56 yards for the game's lone score. Navy had a chance to win the game on its final possession. Army's Wendell Bowman fumbled a punt on his own 37 yard line, and the Midshipmen's John Byng recovered. The Midshipmen drove 12 yards but were stopped on downs. The Cadets took over and advanced to the Navy seven yard line as time ran out.

1931 Navy Midshipmen

In their first season under head coach Edgar "Rip" Miller (pictured at right), the Midshipmen compiled a 5–5–1 record, shut out three opponents, but outscored all opponents by a combined score of 95 to 78. Team Captain was Magruder Tuttle.

The annual Army–Navy Game was played on December 12 at Yankee Stadium in the Bronx, NY; Army won 17-7.

Home games were played Thompson Field

10/3/1931	NAVY	vs	WILLIAM & MARY	13	6	W
10/10/1931	NAVY	vs	Maryland (8-1-1)	0	6	L
10/17/1931	NAVY	vs	DELAWARE	12	7	W
10/24/1931	NAVY	@	Princeton (1-7)	15	0	W
10/31/1931	NAVY	vs	WEST VIRGINIA Wesleyan	0	0	T
11/7/1931	NAVY	@	Ohio State (6-3)	0	20	L
11/14/1931	NAVY	vs	NOTRE DAME (6-2-1)	0	20	L
11/21/1931	NAVY	@	Smu (9-1-1)	6	13	L
11/28/1931	NAVY	vs	WOOSTER	19	6	W
12/5/1931	NAVY	@	Pennsylvania (6-3)	6	0	W
12/12/1931	NAVY	vs	ARMY (8-2-1)	7	17	L
Coach: Rip Miller			**Season Record >>**	78	95	**5-5-1**

Schedule Source: Steve's Football Bible LLC

Selected game(s) highlights

Ohio State

The night before the game, pranksters struck. A handful of Ohio State students were able to grab the Midshipmen's mascot, a dingy gray goat, and they proceeded to dye half of Bill the Goat scarlet prior to the game. The students owned the mascot Friday night, while the players owned the field on Saturday afternoon, winning 20-0. Playing in a constant downpour of rain and sleet, the Buckeyes used the "uncommon play" to score all three touchdowns. In the second period, with the ball at the Navy 35, a pass from OSU's Carl Cramer was deflected by Navy end Larry Smith–the ball ended-up squarely in the hands of Sid Gillman, who raced to the end zone for touchdown number one. Near halftime Martin Varner blocked a Navy punt, which was returned 32 yards by Junius Ferrall for OSU's second score. Ferrall also scored the final TD with a 20 yard interception return in the third period.

Army {@ Yankee Stadium – Bronx, NY}

The running of Ed Herb and Ray Stecker paced Army to a 17-7 win over Navy at Yankee Stadium. The first of Herb's touchdown runs and a Travis Brown 25 yard field goal gave the Cadets a 10-0 halftime lead. Navy cut the deficit to 10-7 in the third quarter when Lou Kirn and Harvey Tschirgi connected on a 55 yard scoring strike. Herb then erased any hopes of a Navy triumph when he went up and over from the one yard line late in the final stanza. By reaching the end zone twice, Herb certainly garnered most of the headlines. However, the real hero was Stecker, who turned in a workman-like 141 yards on 29 carries.

1932 Navy Midshipmen

In their second season under head coach Edgar Miller, the Midshipmen compiled a 2–6 record and were outscored by opponents by a combined score of 80 to 67. Team Captain was Jim Reedy.

The annual Army–Navy Game was played on December 3 at Franklin Field in Philadelphia, PA. Army won 20-0.

Home games were played Thompson Field

10/1/1932	NAVY	vs	WILLIAM & MARY (8-4)	0	6	L
10/8/1932	NAVY	vs	WASHINGTON & LEE (1-9)	33	0	W
10/15/1932	NAVY	vs	OHIO	0	14	L
10/22/1932	NAVY	@	Princeton (2-2-3)	0	0	T
10/29/1932	NAVY	@	Pennsylvania (6-2)	0	14	L
11/5/1932	NAVY	vs	COLUMBIA (7-1-1)	6	7	L
11/12/1932	NAVY	vs	Maryland (5-6)	28	7	W
11/19/1932	NAVY	vs	Notre Dame (7-2)	0	12	L
12/3/1932	NAVY	vs	ARMY (8-2)	0	20	L
Coach: Rip Miller			**Season Record >>**	67	80	**2-6-1**

Schedule Source: Steve's Football Bible LLC

Selected game(s) highlights

Princeton

A scrapping Navy eleven, which hasn't been doing so well this season, made up for any previous lapses by playing Princeton's well-liked Tigers to a scoreless tie before 40,000 spectators at Palmer stadium today. Not only did Coach Rip Miller's Middies avert what the experts had predicted was certain defeat, but they roundly outplayed the Tigers most of the way and contributed to what few scoring threats were offered in a dull contest. Once In the initial quarter the Midshipmen carried the ball within seven yards of a touchdown; again, they were only 13 yards away and on another occasion 16 yards separated them from victory. Princeton, on the other hand, gave Its supporters real hope only the one time, when they drove down within the Navy five yard stripe, only to be set back and thwarted by a five yard penalty for off-side. They never had another real opportunity to score.

Pennsylvania

The Quakers of Penn lashed themselves into a Red rage yesterday afternoon on Franklin Field and sent their guests back to Annapolis very Blue Indeed to contemplate a 14 to 0 defeat. Approximately 50,000 football fanatics roared with approval as Penn pounded out a touchdown early in the second quarter after an unbroken march of 67 yards an advance climaxed by a forward pass, Munger to Pennypacker. Two thousand blue-coated Midshipmen, banked in the north stand, groaned with dismay as their foemen scored again early in the fourth period when Munger got away for a brilliant 15 yard scamper.

Army {@ Franklin Field – Philadelphia, PA}

Thanks in large part to a Navy offense that mustered just 15 yards on the ground and turned the ball over seven times, Army rolled to a 20-0 win over the Midshipmen. Rip Miller's club had an early indication this may not be its day when its opening drive was halted by an interception at the Army six yard line. On first down, the Cadets' Kenneth Field "quick-kicked" the ball 85 yards to the Navy 15 yard line. Peck Vidal opened the scoring with a two yard touchdown run in the first quarter, and Army added two more scores in the final half. Jack Buckler scored one on a short run and took a lateral from Tom Kilday and passed 43 yards to Bill Frentzer for the other touchdown.

1933 Navy Midshipmen

In their third season under head coach Edgar Miller, the Midshipmen compiled a 5–4 record and outscored their opponents by a combined score of 90 to 86. Team Captain was Hugh Murray.

The annual Army–Navy Game was played on November 25 at Franklin Field in Philadelphia, PA. Army won 12-7.

Home games were played Thompson Field

9/30/1933	NAVY	vs	WILLIAM & MARY (6-5)	12	0	**W**
10/7/1933	NAVY	vs	MERCER (4-3-2)	25	6	**W**
10/14/1933	NAVY	@	Pittsburgh (8-1)	6	34	**L**
10/21/1933	NAVY	vs	VIRGINIA (2-6-2)	13	7	**W**
10/28/1933	NAVY	@	Pennsylvania (2-4-1)	13	0	**W**
11/4/1933	NAVY	vs	NOTRE DAME (3-5-1)	7	0	**W**
11/11/1933	NAVY	@	Columbia (8-1)	7	14	**L**
11/18/1933	NAVY	@	Princeton (9-0)	0	13	**L**
11/25/1933	NAVY	vs	ARMY (9-1)	7	12	**L**
Coach: Rip Miller			**Season Record >>**	90	86	**5-4**

Schedule Source: Steve's Football Bible LLC

Selected game(s) highlights

Army {@ Franklin Field – Philadelphia, PA}

Army scored a pair of first-half touchdowns and held on for a 12-7 win over a feisty Rip Miller-coached Navy club. The win was Army's ninth in as many games, and a Dec. 2 victory over 2-5-1 Notre Dame would all but guarantee the Cadets the 1933 national title. However, the Fighting Irish spoiled these hopes by handing Army a 13-12 setback.

For the first time since 1916, Army scored in the opening quarter against Navy. Paul Johnson took Bill Clark's punt and returned it 81 yards for the touchdown. But the extra point was blocked, which enabled Navy to take a 7-6 lead when Red Baumberger galloped 38 yards to the Cadet end zone. Nonetheless, Army's Jack Buckler, whose extra point was blocked on his team's first score, raced 25 yards for the winning touchdown in the second half.

1934 Navy Midshipmen

In their first season under head coach Tom Hamilton, the Midshipmen compiled an 8–1 record and outscored their opponents by a combined score of 138 to 70. Team Captain was Dick Burns. Fred Borries {RB} was selected as a consensus All-American.

The annual Army–Navy Game was played on December 1 at Franklin Field in Philadelphia, PA. Navy won 3-0.

Home games were played Thompson Field

9/29/1934	NAVY	vs	WILLIAM & MARY (2-6)	20	7	W
10/6/1934	NAVY	vs	VIRGINIA (3-6)	21	6	W
10/13/1934	NAVY	vs	MARYLAND (7-3)	16	13	W
10/20/1934	NAVY	@	Columbia (7-1)	18	7	W
10/27/1934	NAVY	@	Pennsylvania (4-4)	17	0	W
11/3/1934	NAVY	vs	WASHINGTON & LEE (7-3)	26	0	W
11/10/1934	NAVY	vs	Notre Dame (6-3)	10	6	W
11/17/1934	NAVY	vs	PITTSBURGH (8-1)	7	31	L
12/1/1934	NAVY	vs	ARMY (7-3)	3	0	W
Coach: Tom Hamilton			**Season Record >>**	138	70	8-1

Schedule Source: Steve's Football Bible LLC

Selected game(s) highlights

Army {@ Franklin Field – Philadelphia, PA}

Despite the driving rainstorm at Franklin Field, Navy kicker Slade Cutter's 28 yard field goal ended an 11-game drought, as the Midshipmen's 3-0 win marked their first triumph over Army since 1921.

Nothing indicates the treacherous weather conditions better than the final statistics. Army and Navy combined to record five first downs and 132 yards of total offense between them. Collectively, they also completed three-of-eight passes and punted 25 times.

1935 Navy Midshipmen

In their second season under head coach Tom Hamilton, the Midshipmen compiled a 5–4 record and outscored their opponents by a combined score of 136 to 89. Team Captain was Louis Robertshaw.

The annual Army–Navy Game was played on November 30 at Franklin Field in Philadelphia, PA. Army won 28-6.

Home games were played Thompson Field

9/28/1935	NAVY	vs	WILLIAM & MARY (3-4-3)	30	0	W
10/5/1935	NAVY	vs	MERCER (4-5)	27	0	W
10/10/1935	NAVY	vs	VIRGINIA (1-5-4)	26	7	W
10/19/1935	NAVY	@	Yale (6-3)	6	7	L
10/26/1935	NAVY	vs	NOTRE DAME (7-1-1)	0	14	L
11/2/1935	NAVY	@	Princeton (9-0)	0	26	L
11/9/1935	NAVY	@	Pennsylvania (4-4)	13	0	W
11/16/1935	NAVY	vs	COLUMBIA (4-4-1)	28	7	W
11/30/1935	NAVY	vs	ARMY (6-2-1)	6	28	L
Coach: Tom Hamilton			**Season Record >>**	136	89	5-4

Schedule Source: Steve's Football Bible LLC

Selected game(s) highlights

Army {@ Franklin Field – Philadelphia, PA}

The 1935 matchup was a tale of two halves. In the first two quarters, Army piled up 303 yards of total offense, holding Navy to just 37. Yet, in the second half, the Midshipmen had more than eight times the total offense than that of the Cadets — 259 yards to 31 for Army. Despite these similarities, there was also one visible difference. Army scored four times in its half, while the Midshipmen were unable to reach the end zone. Final score: Army 28, Navy 6.

Quarterback Monk Meyer had 35- and 40 yard touchdown passes in the opening half, while Whitey Grove added an 80 yard touchdown run on a reverse. Sneed Schmidt's four yard touchdown plunge in the fourth quarter was the only offensive highlight in the Midshipmen's season finale.

1936 Navy Midshipmen

In their third season under head coach Tom Hamilton, the Midshipmen compiled a 6–3 record and outscored their opponents by a combined score of 115 to 74. Team Captain was Rivers Morrell

They finished the season ranked 18th in the first year of the AP Poll. The annual Army–Navy Game was played on November 28 at Franklin Field in Philadelphia, PA. Navy won 7-0.

FINAL RANK: #18 AP

Home games were played Thompson Field

9/26/1936	NAVY		vs		WILLIAM & MARY (1-8)	18	6	W
10/3/1936	NAVY		vs		DAVIDSON (5-4)	19	6	W
10/10/1936	NAVY		vs		VIRGINIA (2-7)	35	14	W
10/17/1936	NAVY		vs		YALE (7-1)	7	12	L
10/24/1936	NAVY		@		Princeton (4-2-2)	0	7	L
10/31/1936	NAVY		@	#20	Pennsylvania (7-1)	6	16	L
11/7/1936	NAVY		vs	#13	NOTRE DAME (6-2-1)	3	0	W
11/14/1936	NAVY		@		Harvard (3-4-1)	20	13	W
11/28/1936	NAVY		vs		ARMY (6-3)	7	0	W
Coach: Tom Hamilton					**Season Record >>**	115	74	**6-3**

Schedule Source: Steve's Football Bible LLC

Selected game(s) highlights

Princeton

Navy and Princeton aimed comeback shots at each other today before a crowd of 45,000 at Palmer Stadium. The midshipmen sought their first victory over the Tiger Princeton won, 7 0. Shortly after the kickoff the Navy launched a drive that carried 52 yards before losing the ball on downs on Princeton's 17. For the rest of the period, Navy, with Ingram doing most of the lugging, displayed a lot more confidence and punch than the Tigers. Jack White broke up one sailor thrust by intercepting an Ingram pass on the Tiger 37 yard line. Jack White ran Fike's kickoff 81 yards to Navy's 15. The Tiger attack bogged down, and Navy took the ball when Sandbach's fourth down pass to Hail left the bail a yard of the needed distance on Navy's 6. White then returned Schmidt's punt 26 yards to Navy's 15 and Sandbach, on the second play, dashed 13 yards to tally, Sandbach also place-kicked the point.

Army {@ Municipal Stadium – Philadelphia, PA}

To meet the supreme ticket demand, the 1936 game was moved from 88,000-seat Franklin Field to 102,000-seat Municipal Stadium. Despite driving deep into Navy territory in the first half, Army was unable to capitalize, as John Schmidt's three yard touchdown run in the fourth quarter was all Navy needed for a 7-0 win over the Cadets.

Following the series' first scoreless opening half since 1930, the third quarter was even less exciting. Army fumbled the football away on three of its next-four possessions, while the Midshipmen were unable to reach the Cadet end zone on three possessions. However, Navy was able to take advantage of a Monk Meyer fumble in the fourth quarter. Aided by a pass interference call against the Cadets' Jim Craig, Schmidt scored his touchdown with two minutes left.

1937 Navy Midshipmen

In their first season under head coach Hank Hardwick, the Midshipmen compiled a 4–4–1 record and outscored their opponents by a combined score of 150 to 74. Team Captain was Ray Dubois.

The annual Army–Navy Game was played on November 27 at Franklin Field in Philadelphia, PA. Army won 6-0.

Home games were played Thompson Field

9/25/1937	NAVY	vs	WILLIAM & MARY (4-5)	45	0	**W**
10/2/1937	NAVY	vs	THE CITADEL (7-4)	32	0	**W**
10/9/1937	NAVY	vs	VIRGINIA (2-7)	40	13	**W**
10/16/1937	NAVY	vs	HARVARD (5-2-1)	0	0	**T**
10/23/1937	NAVY	@	Notre Dame (6-2-1)	7	9	**L**
10/30/1937	NAVY	@	Pennsylvania (2-5-1)	7	14	**L**
11/6/1937	NAVY	vs	COLUMBIA (2-5-2)	13	6	**W**
11/20/1937	NAVY	@	Princeton (4-4)	6	26	**L**
11/27/1937	NAVY	vs	ARMY (7-2)	0	6	**L**
Coach: Hank Hardwick			**Season Record >>**	150	74	**4-4-1**

Schedule Source: Steve's Football Bible LLC

Selected game(s) highlights

Princeton

The Princeton supporters in the crowd of 48,000 had turned out as much for the annual show put on by the Middies as for any other reason. They didn't expect their team to win. But, after that opening touchdown, scored in the first three minutes of play, they stayed in their seats and stayed there until a Princeton interception halted Navy's last, gambling passing attack. It was Bob Hinchman who set the first scoring drive under way. He started it from the Tiger 34 with a 11 yard end run, finished it with a 13 yard pass to Jack Daniel which the latter toted another 41 yards for the touchdown. The sophomore halfbacks pass also put the Tigers in position for their third score, made by Fullback Ashby Harper a fake reverse.

Army {@ Franklin Field – Philadelphia, PA}

In a game that saw the two teams punt a combined 32 times, Army's Jim Craig managed to score on a three yard touchdown run to give his team a 6-0 victory.

Craig's run capped off a 44 yard scoring drive highlighted by a 19 yard pass from Woody Wilson to Jim Schwenk. The teams had a combined 255 yards of total offense, as Craig was the game's highest rusher with 47 yards on 20 carries.

1938 Navy Midshipmen

In their second season under head coach Hank Hardwick, the Midshipmen compiled a 4–3–2 record and outscored their opponents by a combined score of 126 to 60. Team Captain was Lucien Powell.

The annual Army–Navy Game was played on November 26 at Franklin Field in Philadelphia, PA. Army won 14-7.

Home games were played Thompson Field

9/24/1938	NAVY		vs		WILLIAM & MARY (3-7)	26	0	**W**
10/1/1938	NAVY		vs		VMI (6-1-4)	26	0	**W**
10/8/1938	NAVY		vs		VIRGINIA (4-4-1)	33	0	**W**
10/15/1938	NAVY		@		Yale (2-6)	7	9	**L**
10/22/1938	NAVY		vs		PRINCETON (3-4-1)	13	13	**T**
10/29/1938	NAVY		@		Pennsylvania (3-2-3)	0	0	**T**
11/5/1938	NAVY		vs	#4	NOTRE DAME (8-1)	0	15	**L**
11/12/1938	NAVY		@		Columbia (3-6)	14	9	**W**
11/26/1938	NAVY		vs		ARMY (8-2)	7	14	**L**
Coach: Hank Harwick					**Season Record >>**	126	60	**4-3-2**

Schedule Source: Steve's Football Bible LLC

Selected game(s) highlights

Army {@ Franklin Field – Philadelphia, PA}

In front of 102,000 fans, the largest crowd to see a sporting event in 1938, Woody Wilson scored on a one yard touchdown run in the third quarter to help Army to a 14-6 win over Navy.

Army's Charley Long brought the Cadet faithful to their feet in the first quarter when he returned Lem Cooke's punt 79 yards for a touchdown. Navy drove deep into Army territory on each of its next two possessions, only to be stopped once on downs and once on a Wilson interception. However, Cooke tied the score with a one yard touchdown run before halftime.

Navy opened the third quarter poised to take the lead, but Emmette Wood fumbled on the Cadet 17 yard line. Army more than capitalized on this miscue, driving the length of the field to take the lead, and eventually the win, on Wilson's touchdown.

1939 Navy Midshipmen

In their first season under head coach Swede Larson, the Midshipmen compiled a 3–5–1 record and were outscored by their opponents by a combined score of 107 to 88. Team Captain was Allen Bergner.

The annual Army–Navy Game was played on December 2 at Franklin Field in Philadelphia, PA. Navy won 10-0.

Home games were played Thompson Field

9/30/1939	NAVY	VS		WILLIAM & MARY (6-2-1)	31	6	**W**
10/7/1939	NAVY	VS		VIRGINIA (5-4)	14	12	**W**
10/14/1939	NAVY	VS		DARTMOUTH (5-3-1)	0	0	**T**
10/21/1939	NAVY	VS	#2	Notre Dame (7-2)	7	14	**L**
10/28/1939	NAVY	VS		CLEMSON (9-1)	7	15	**L**
11/4/1939	NAVY	@		Pennsylvania (4-4)	6	13	**L**
11/11/1939	NAVY	VS		COLUMBIA (2-4-2)	13	19	**L**
11/25/1939	NAVY	@		Princeton (7-1)	0	28	**L**
12/2/1939	NAVY	VS		ARMY (3-4-2)	10	0	**W**
Coach: Swede Larson				**Season Record >>**	**88**	**107**	**3-5-1**

Schedule Source: Steve's Football Bible LLC

Selected game(s) highlights

COLUMBIA

Refusing to acknowledge defeat even though the tides of fortune ran swiftly against them, Columbia's dauntless band of football warriors today performed something of a miracle in Thompson's Stadium on the Severn. With the game tied at 13-13 heading into the 4th quarter, Columbia's Jack Naylor led a drive that started at the Lions own 18 yard line, Naylor threw a 22 yard touchdown pass to Augie De Augustine for the winning score.

Princeton

A long passing attack that baffled their opponents enabled the Princeton Tigers to close a successful season with a 28 to 0 victory over Navy before 35,000 spectators in Palmer Stadium today. Three tremendous tosses to Howie Stanley, Princeton end, brought the same number of touchdowns in the first half, and another series of passes set the ball up for Ed Rose to plunge across from the one-foot mark toward the close of the contest.

Army {@ Franklin Field – Philadelphia, PA}

When Emory "Swede" Larson took over the Navy program in 1939, no one had to define the magnitude of the Army-Navy rivalry to him. A three-year letter winner (1919-21), Larson had played on three teams victorious over the Cadets. In fact, Larson arranged to have Billy VIII, Navy's mascot, wear the same blanket that adorned the 1921 goat. This superstition must have paid off, as the Midshipmen shut out Army, 10-0.

Navy scored on its opening drive, as Ulmont Whitehead booted a 33 yard field goal between the uprights to give the Midshipmen a 3-0 lead. Halfback Dick Shafer added a 22 yard touchdown run in the last quarter, as Navy utilized six Army turnovers to finish 3-5-1 on the season.

1940 Navy Midshipmen

In their second season under head coach Swede Larson, the Midshipmen compiled a 6–2–1 record and outscored their opponents by a combined score of 106 to 46. Team Captain was Dick Foster.

The annual Army–Navy Game was played on November 30 at Franklin Field in Philadelphia, PA. Navy won 14-0.

Home games were played Thompson Field

9/28/1940	NAVY		vs		WILLIAM & MARY (6-2-1)	19	7	W
10/5/1940	NAVY		vs		CINCINNATI	14	0	W
10/12/1940	NAVY		@		Princeton (5-2-1)	12	6	W
10/19/1940	NAVY		vs		DRAKE (4-5)	19	0	W
10/26/1940	NAVY		@		Yale (1-7)	21	0	W
11/2/1940	NAVY	#14	@	#15	Pennsylvania (6-1-1)	0	20	L
11/9/1940	NAVY		vs	#7	NOTRE DAME (7-2)	7	13	L
11/16/1940	NAVY		@		Columbia (5-2-2)	0	0	T
11/30/1940	NAVY		vs		ARMY (1-7-1)	14	0	W
Coach: Swede Larson					**Season Record >>**	**106**	**46**	**6-2-1**

Schedule Source: Steve's Football Bible LLC

Selected game(s) highlights

Princeton

Navy drove 70 yards and then ten yards in quick succession for touchdowns in the third period today to come from behind and beat Princeton, 12-6, before a crowd of 40,000. Princeton scored in the opening period after a 57 yard march. Navy's first drove 70 yards to a touchdown. Lenz, Cameron and Busik ripped Princeton's line, moving to the 3. Busik was stopped twice, but, on third down, heaved to Zoeller in the end zone for the score. Shortly thereafter, Navy drove 80 yards for another touchdown. Clark climaxed the drive with a 9 yard end run.

Army {@ Franklin Field – Philadelphia, PA}

Navy celebrated the 50th anniversary of the Army-Navy game with a solid, all-around effort, resulting in a 14-0 triumph.

Navy scored on its first drive, as Bill Busik went the final two yards for the touchdown to make it 7-0. The Midshipmen covered 54 yards in 12 plays, with Busik accounting for 50 of those 54 yards. Although the Army offense could muster just 107 yards of total offense on the afternoon, the Cadet defense held Navy without a point on its next two drives, which were halted deep in Army territory. However, the Midshipmen tallied their final score in the third quarter when Howie Clark tossed a nine yard touchdown pass to Everett Malcolm.

1941 Navy Midshipmen

In their third season under head coach Swede Larson, the Midshipmen compiled a 7–1–1 record, shut out five opponents, and outscored all opponents by a combined score of 192 to 34. Team Captain was Dick Foster. In the annual Army–Navy Game, the Midshipmen beat the Cadets for the third straight year, and finished the season ranked No. 10 in the final AP Poll. Back Bill Busik and tackle Bill Chewning were selected by the Associated Press as first-team players on the 1941 All-Eastern football team. Tackle Gene Flathmann was named to the second team.

FINAL RANK: #10 AP
Home games were played Thompson Field

9/27/1941	NAVY		vs		WILLIAM & MARY (8-2)	34	0	W
10/4/1941	NAVY		vs		WEST VIRGINIA (4-6)	40	0	W
10/11/1941	NAVY		vs		LAFAYETTE	41	2	W
10/18/1941	NAVY	#7	vs		CORNELL (5-3)	14	0	W
10/25/1941	NAVY	#5	@		Harvard (5-2-1)	0	0	T
11/1/1941	NAVY	#11	@	#8	Pennsylvania (7-1)	13	6	W
11/8/1941	NAVY	#6	vs	#7	NOTRE DAME (8-0-1)	13	20	L
11/22/1941	NAVY	#12	@		Princeton (2-6)	23	0	W
11/29/1941	NAVY	#11	vs		ARMY (5-3-1)	14	6	W
Coach: Swede Larson					**Season Record >>**	192	34	7-1-1

Schedule Source: Steve's Football Bible LLC

Selected game(s) highlights

#8 Pennsylvania

A relentless Navy football squad, brandishing power in waterproof perfection as it slammed gallant Penn to defeat, completed "Black Saturday" on the local grid front as 74,000 rain-soaked spectators huddled to the bitter finish yesterday in Franklin Field. By a score of 13 to 6, much more convincing than it sounds as the Middies came on and on in endless relays and dominated throughout. Driving surely through the downpour, Navy scored first in the opening period. Bill Busik hurled a 12 yard pass to Sammy Boothe in Penn's end zone as the quarter waned. Navy notched its second marker as the second half began. It was Midshipman Howard Clark who personally conducted the second touchdown across Penn's goal.

#7 NOTRE DAME {@ Memorial Stadium – Baltimore, MD}

In a thrill packed game marked by brilliant forward passing, free scoring and great punting, Notre Dame's gridiron warriors defeated Navy before 64,793 fans yesterday afternoon in Baltimore Stadium. The score was 20 to 13, the greatest number of points amassed in a battle between these teams in the fifteen year old series. It was a bitterly fought contest from start to finish and marked the first defeat of the Midshipmen this season. It was Angelo Bertelli's deadly right arm that brought about another Notre Dame triumph over the Navy. Navy again had the edge in some of the statistics, the Middies having 15 first downs, against 11 for the Irish. The Middies also gained greater yardage in rushing, 125 yards to 68, but the payoff was in the air where Notre Dame showed its mastery. The victor made 216 yards through its sensational air attack, against 10 for Navy.

Army {@ Franklin Field – Philadelphia, PA}

As a Naval Academy player from 1919-21, Swede Larson never lost to Army. And in his first-two years as head coach, his teams shut out the Cadets by a combined score of 24-0. But prior to the 1941 Army-Navy contest, the Marine major was informed he was being sent to the Naval War College in Newport, R.I. immediately after the football season. As you can imagine, he wanted nothing more than a final victory over Army, which is why he was less than pleased when his club trailed West Point, 6-0, at halftime. Challenging his team to win its last battle on the football field, the Midshipmen answered the call in the second half. Bill Busik's effective running and passing set up touchdowns by Phil Hurt and Howie Clark, which led to a 14-6 Navy win.

1942 Navy Midshipmen

In their first season under head coach John Whelchel (pictured at right), the Midshipmen compiled a 5–4 record, shut out five opponents and outscored all opponents by a combined score of 82 to 58. Team Captain was Alan Cameron.

The annual Army–Navy Game was played on November 28 at Franklin Field in Philadelphia, PA. Navy won 14-0.

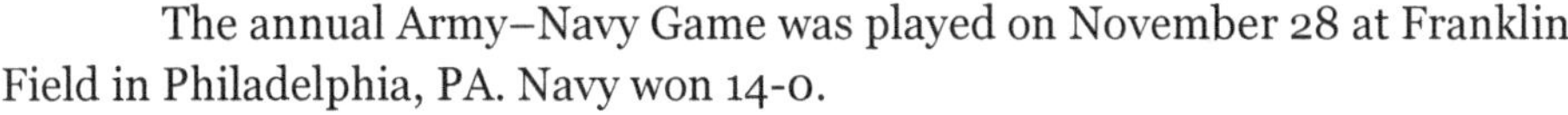

Home games were played Thompson Field

9/26/1942	NAVY	**vs**		WILLIAM & MARY (9-1-1)	0	3	**L**
10/3/1942	NAVY	**vs**		VIRGINIA (2-6-1)	35	0	**W**
10/10/1942	NAVY	**@**		Princeton (3-5-1)	0	10	**L**
10/17/1942	NAVY	**vs**		YALE (5-3)	13	6	**W**
10/24/1942	NAVY	**vs**	#6	GEORGIA TECH (9-2)	0	21	**L**
10/31/1942	NAVY	**vs**	#4	Notre Dame (7-2-2)	0	9	**L**
11/7/1942	NAVY	**@**	#9	Pennsylvania (5-3-1)	7	0	**W**
11/14/1942	NAVY	**vs**		COLUMBIA (3-6)	13	9	**W**
11/28/1942	NAVY	**vs**		ARMY (6-3)	14	0	**W**
Coach: Billy Whelchel				**Season Record >>**	82	58	**5-4**

Schedule Source: Steve's Football Bible LLC

Selected game(s) highlights

Princeton {@ Yankee Stadium – Bronx, NY}

Princeton, a decided underdog before their battle with the Naval Academy, outfought the heavier Midshipmen to gain a 10-0 victory before about 25,000 at Yankee Stadium yesterday. The first freshman to play with a Tiger team since '08, George Franke, scored the touchdown on the first play of the second period, and Bob Sandbach, after kicking the extra point, place-kicked a field goal in the waning minutes of the final quarter.

ARMY

To conserve transportation resources due to World War II, the Army-Navy game was moved to Annapolis in 1942 and West Point for 1943. This meant the West Point Corp of Cadets, except for two cheerleaders, would not be permitted to attend the game, nor would anyone else outside a 10-mile radius of the Maryland state capital. Thus, half of the Brigade of Midshipmen would serve as the Army cheering section, while the other half would root for the Mids. As it turns out, the Cadets would need much more help than this, as Navy turned back Army, 14-0.

Backup halfback Joe Sullivan opened the scoring with a short touchdown run in the second quarter. Hillis Hume set up the other touchdown with an interception deep in Cadet territory midway through the third stanza. Hal Hamberg proceeded to hit Ben Martin with an 18 yard scoring strike. Hume clinched the win with another interception of Army quarterback Doug Kenna at the Navy seven yard line.

1943 Navy Midshipmen {Lambert Trophy}

In their second season under head coach John Whelchel, the Midshipmen compiled an 8–1 record, shut out three opponents and outscored all opponents by a combined score of 237 to 80. Team Captain was Albert Channell. Navy was ranked No. 4 in the final AP Poll. During the season, the Midshipmen beat #5 ranked Duke, #5 ranked Pennsylvania and #7 ranked Army, 13-0. Their only loss was to #1 ranked and eventual National Champion Notre Dame. Don Whitmire {OL} was selected as a consensus All-American.

After the season, Navy was awarded the Lambert Trophy as the best College Football team in the East.

FINAL RANK: #4 AP

Home games were played Thompson Field

Date	Team	Rank		Opp Rank	Opponent			W/L
9/25/1943	NAVY		vs		NORTH CAROLINA Pre-Flight (2-4-1)	31	0	W
10/2/1943	NAVY		vs		CORNELL (6-4)	46	7	W
10/9/1943	NAVY	#4	vs	#5	DUKE (8-1)	14	13	W
10/16/1943	NAVY	#3	vs		PENN STATE (5-3-1)	14	6	W
10/23/1943	NAVY	#3	vs		GEORGIA TECH (8-3)	28	14	W
10/30/1943	NAVY	#3	vs	#1	Notre Dame (9-1)	6	33	L
11/6/1943	NAVY	#7	@	#5	Pennsylvania (6-2-1)	24	7	W
11/13/1943	NAVY	#3	@		Columbia (0-8)	61	0	W
11/27/1943	NAVY	#6	@	#7	ARMY (7-2-1)	13	0	W
Coach: Billy Whelchel					Season Record >>	237	80	8-1

Schedule Source: Steve's Football Bible LLC

Selected game(s) highlights

#5 DUKE

Hal Hamberg threw TD passes in the second quarter and some good fortune to knock off #5 Duke, 14-13. Duke scored on the final play to make it 14-13. Bob Gantt stepped up for the extra point but the Navy line broke through and blocked the kick.

#1 Notre Dame {Municipal Stadium – Cleveland, OH}

A crowd estimated to be well over 80,000 flocked to Municipal Stadium. It was Navy's first road game of the year, as its prior five games were in Annapolis or Baltimore. Angelo Bertelli threw for three TD passes and scored on a run, and the Fighting Irish pulled away for a 33-6 win. A 13-6 game at half, Bertelli hit end John Yonaker on a fourth-and-goal from the 2 to start the third quarter. Miller later scored on a three yard run to effectively seal the win. Notre Dame ran for 323 yards in its vaunted 'T' formation.

#7 Army

For the first time in 50 years, West Point, N.Y. played host to an Army-Navy game. The Midshipmen were less than gracious guests on the field, however, scoring two touchdowns in the second half of a 13-0 triumph.

In the first half, Army got inside the Navy 40 yard line three times but failed to reach the end zone. Navy finally cracked the scoreboard midway through the third quarter when Bob Jenkins capped a 42 yard drive with a one yard touchdown run. Jim Pettit then contributed two of the game's biggest plays, one on each side of the ball. His one yard touchdown run stretched the

lead to 13-0, and he halted an Army drive at the Navy 24 when he intercepted Doug Kenna's pass.

1944 Navy Midshipmen

In their first season under head coach Oscar Hagberg, the Midshipmen compiled a 6–3 record, shut out three opponents and outscored all opponents by a combined score of 236 to 88. Team Captain was Ben Chase. Navy was ranked No. 4 in the final AP Poll. Chase {OL}, Bob Jenkins {RB} and Don Whitmire {OL} were selected as consensus All-Americans.

The annual Army–Navy Game was played on December 2 at Municipal Stadium in Baltimore, MD; Army won 23-7.

FINAL RANK: #4 AP							
Home games were played Thompson Field							
9/30/1944	NAVY		vs		NORTH CAROLINA Pre-Flight	14	21	L
10/7/1944	NAVY		vs		PENN STATE (6-3)	55	14	W
10/14/1944	NAVY	#6	vs		DUKE (6-4)	7	0	W
10/21/1944	NAVY	#9	@	#8	Georgia Tech (8-3)	15	17	L
10/28/1944	NAVY	#12	@	#7	Pennsylvania (5-3)	26	0	W
11/4/1944	NAVY	#6	vs	#2	NOTRE DAME (8-2)	32	13	W
11/11/1944	NAVY	#3	vs		CORNELL (5-4)	48	0	W
11/18/1944	NAVY	#3	vs	#14	PURDUE (5-5)	32	0	W
12/2/1944	NAVY	#2	vs	#1	ARMY (9-0)	7	23	L
Coach: Oscar Hagberg					**Season Record >>**	236	88	6-3

Schedule Source: Steve's Football Bible LLC

Selected game(s) highlights

#7 Pennsylvania

Navy power ground Penn into its first football defeat of the campaign before 73,000 fans here today, 26 to 0. The boys sent by Penn to do a man's job were not equal to the Midshipmen on the ground or in the air, and defensively could not stop the harnessed strength of the Annapolis attack. Bob Jenkins, Bill Barron and Clyde Scott carried the ball for most of the important Navy gains. Scott scored a touchdown in the first quarter, and added another in the third, both on line bucks. Barron tallied twice.

#2 NOTRE DAME {@ Memorial Stadium – Baltimore, MD}

Before 63,000 astonished people in Baltimore's largest athletic plant, the 1944 edition of Annapolis football power ran through and around an outclassed Irish line to the tune of 32 to 13. This was the greatest number of points that any Navy team in 18 attempts, ever scored against any Notre Dame team. The Navy pounced early to score twelve points in the first quarter and kept the scoring kettle boiling by notching three more touchdowns before the afternoon was over.

#1 ARMY {@ Memorial Stadium, Baltimore, MD} {#1 vs #2 Game of the Century}

With the country at war and the dominance of the service academies over the rest of college football, the 1944 Army vs. Navy game was one of the most anticipated matchups in the history of the rivalry. The battle on the gridiron that resulted became the stuff of legend.

As the days ticked down in 1944 for the 46th edition of the Army vs. Navy annual gridiron engagement, the success of the two squads that season had propelled public interest to a fever pitch unparalleled in the series. Breathless media declared the matchup of the #1 Cadets and the #2 Midshipmen the de facto national championship, and the interest of the public at large seemed to cement that sentiment. As the Dec. 2 Army vs. Navy game approached, the two were the best in the land by a wide margin. For the Cadets, that marked a dramatic change from the recent past.

On Dec. 2, 1944, a sold-out crowd of 66,659 gathered in Municipal Stadium on a frigid but clear Saturday afternoon to see the much-anticipated contest. The cold temperatures were exacerbated by a brisk wind that blew through the stadium the entire game. The Navy contingent arrived on boats sailed across Chesapeake Bay, and the Army party was carried on troopships escorted by Navy destroyers.

Despite a series of turnovers, neither team could capitalize on the opportunities. Navy finally managed a first down in the final minutes of the first quarter but relied on a Statue of Liberty pass to do it. Several plays later, they were forced to punt again. Army began to gain momentum in the second quarter when the Cadets' offensive line began opening holes for the tandem of Blanchard and Davis. Army rolled 66 yards on six plays and scored on a 24 yard touchdown run by Dale Hall. Army led 7-0 – the first time the Cadets had done so in six years – and that was where the score stood at the intermission. The first half proved costly to Navy. The Midshipmen's standout former Crimson Tide players, Whitmire and Jenkins, were forced out of the game due to injuries. The depletion to the defense would prove critical in the final 30 minutes of play.

In the third quarter, Army blocked a Navy punt and scored a safety when kicker Jack Hansen was downed in the end zone after recovering the ball. The Midshipmen defense stiffened after the kickoff, and a string of tackles for loss and penalties quickly had the Cadets facing third and 47. Navy's offense picked up where the defense had left off and went on a 73 yard touchdown drive. Army stopped the Midshipmen once
on the goal line but Clyde "Smackover" Scott then smashed it across for the score on the second attempt. As the third period ended it was Army 9, Navy 7, and it remained anybody's ball game.

The Midshipmen started the fourth quarter driving for the score that would give them the lead, but Army's Davis intercepted a pass and took it to midfield. The Cadets turned to Blanchard, giving him the ball eight consecutive times on a scoring drive that covered 52 yards. Army 16, Navy 7. The Midshipmen were forced to punt their next possession, and the Cadets got the ball back on their own 32 yard line. Four plays later, Glen Davis dashed 50 yards for the final touchdown of the game. A few minutes later, the final whistle sounded, and Army had finally beaten its archrival, 23-7. Despite throwing five interceptions and fumbling the ball three times, Army kept control of the contest from start to finish. The Cadets outgained the Midshipmen 181-71 on the ground, and Navy was only able to complete 14 of 24 passes for 98 yards.

1945 Navy Midshipmen

In their second season under head coach Oscar Hagberg, the Midshipmen compiled a 7–1–1 record, shut out three opponents and outscored all opponents by a combined score of 220 to 65. Team Captain was Dick Duden. Navy was ranked No. 3 in the final AP Poll. Dick Duden {E} was selected as a consensus All-American.

The annual Army–Navy Game was played on December 1 at Municipal Stadium in Philadelphia, PA. Army won 32-13.

FINAL RANK: #3 AP
Home games were played Thompson Field

9/29/1945	NAVY		vs		VILLANOVA (4-4)	49	0	W
10/6/1945	NAVY		@		Duke (6-2)	21	0	W
10/13/1945	NAVY	#2	vs		PENN STATE (5-3)	28	0	W
10/20/1945	NAVY	#2	vs		GEORGIA TECH (4-6)	20	6	W
10/27/1945	NAVY	#3	@	#7	Pennsylvania (6-2)	14	7	W
11/3/1945	NAVY	#3	vs	#2	Notre Dame (7-2-1)	6	6	T
11/10/1945	NAVY	#4	vs	#7	MICHIGAN (7-3)	33	7	W
11/17/1945	NAVY	#2	vs		WISCONSIN (3-4-2)	36	7	W
12/1/1945	NAVY	#2	vs	#1	ARMY (9-0)	13	32	L
Coach: Oscar Hagberg					**Season Record >>**	**220**	**65**	**7-1-1**

Schedule Source: Steve's Football Bible LLC

Selected game(s) highlights

#7 MICHIGAN

Michigan lost to a #4-ranked Navy team by a 33 to 7 score. The game was played at Baltimore Stadium in front of a crowd of 59,114 spectators. Michigan's only touchdown was scored by Jack Weisenburger on a two yard run in the second quarter, with George Chiames kicking the point after touchdown. Navy intercepted four Michigan passes and outgained the Wolverines on the ground, 235 rushing yards to 68.

#2 Notre Dame {Municipal Stadium - Cleveland, Ohio}

Notre Dame and Navy met in Cleveland's Municipal Stadium, November 2, before a throng of 82,000 rabid football fans. Both teams entered the game undefeated and left, after 60 minutes of spine-tingling football, with the same status. After the Irish had rolled over the Middies throughout the first half to lead 6 to 0, Clyde 'Smackover" Scott intercepted a Notre Dame pass in the third quarter and ran to a touchdown that left the game in a 6 to 6 deadlock. Behind that score lies football drama. The play that will be a topic of football conversation for many years occurred in the final minute of play when Captain Frank Dancewicz passed to Phil Colella near the Navy goal line. The Rochester, Pennsylvania, freshman drove for the goal but as he did so, Tony Minisi of Navy grabbed him around the neck, hurtling him out of bounds six inches shy of the game-winning touchdown. Colella's feet got into the end zone, but the ball didn't. Notre Dame had time for two tries for a touchdown, but both failed as the gun sounded ending the game. Most observers agreed with the officials that Colella did not score but there are those, too, who are certain he did. The game is over, the score permanently tied, but the discussion will go on. Despite the ultimate-thrilling final minute of the game, the first 59 were anything but dull. The Irish took the opening kickoff and drove deep into Navy territory after a first play pass from Dancewicz to Bob Skoglund clicked for 43 yards. But Navy stiffened and turned back the Irish surge. Late in the opening period, Frank Ruggerio intercepted a Navy pass, carrying it back to the Navy 34. Ruggerio and Elmer Angsman drove to the 11 and Colella went to the 5 from which point Ruggerio smashed through for the touchdown. Stan Krivik's try for point was blocked. Notre Dame continued to dominate play for the remainder of the game save for the moment when Scott raced off with that intercepted pass to give Navy it's only tally of the day. Notre Dame's line played valiant, determined ball all afternoon, stopping Navy second-half drives deep in their own territory several times. Prior to Notre Dame's final thrust that nearly won the game, Dancewicz and Colella succeeded in grounding four straight Navy passes to take the ball on downs on their 40. George Ratterman came in for Dancewicz only to be thrown for a 12 yard loss by Dick Scott, Navy center. Ratterman then went back to pass again, this time connecting with Bill Leonard who had outraced the Middies' secondary. Leonard, handicapped by a leg injury, was caught from behind on the Navy 18 after a gain of 54 yards on the play. The next play was the Dancewicz to Colella pass. The rest of the game is now history. Navy wouldn't be beaten but it was Notre Dame's game from every angle save the score. The Irish ran up 12 first downs to 8 for the midshipmen, rushed for 146 yards and passed for 116 while Navy had a net rushing gain of 34 yards, and passing 55. This was the one Notre Dame wanted to win—and almost did. The Fighting Irish lived up to their name in every sense of the word.

#1 ARMY {@ Municipal Stadium, Philadelphia, PA} {#1 vs #2 Game of the Century}

Because of the war America had just won, the 1945 Army-Navy game might have been one of the most celebratory sporting events in the country's history. A crowd of 102,000, including President Harry S. Truman, packed Municipal Stadium in Philadelphia, which is now the site of a trio of professional ballparks in south Philly: the Wells Fargo Center, Citizens Bank Park, and Lincoln Financial Field, which continues to house Army-Navy games regularly. What might have been the best-ever Navy team battled this incredible Army team to a draw for three quarters. The Midshipmen proved resilient and became the first team all year to score on Army's first team.

The problem: Those three even quarters were the last three. Army had already taken a 20-0 lead in the first 15 minutes. The Cadets took the opening kickoff and took seven plays to set up a Blanchard touchdown. Then Blanchard scored again. Then Davis went 51 yards. From that point forward, Navy outscored the Cadets, 13-12. And that was an achievement. They got to within 20-7 and 26-13, but they couldn't get any closer.

1946 Navy Midshipmen

With the return of Tom Hamilton, head coach from 1936 to 1938, the Midshipmen compiled a 1–8 record and were outscored by their opponents by a combined score of 186 to 105. Team Captain was Leon Bramlett.

The annual Army–Navy Game was played on November 30 at Municipal Stadium in Philadelphia, PA. Army won 21-18.

Home games were played Thompson Field

9/28/1946	NAVY	vs		VILLANOVA (6-4)	7	0	**W**
10/5/1946	NAVY	@		Columbia (6-3)	14	23	**L**
10/12/1946	NAVY	vs		DUKE (4-5)	6	21	**L**
10/19/1946	NAVY	vs		NORTH CAROLINA (8-2-1)	14	21	**L**
10/26/1946	NAVY	@	#6	Pennsylvania (6-2)	19	32	**L**
11/2/1946	NAVY	vs	#2	NOTRE DAME (8-0-1)	0	28	**L**
11/9/1946	NAVY	@	#8	Georgia Tech (9-2)	20	28	**L**
11/16/1946	NAVY	vs		PENN STATE (6-2)	7	12	**L**
11/30/1946	NAVY	vs	#1	ARMY (9-0-1)	18	21	**L**
Coach: Tom Hamilton				**Season Record >>**	**105**	**186**	**1-8**

Schedule Source: Steve's Football Bible LLC

Selected game(s) highlights

Columbia

It seems that the floating Navy is not the only one that has retrogressed this year. Navy's football team, a wartime titan, couldn't keep pace with Columbia's power and deception at sun-soaked Baker Field yesterday, and an SRO crowd of 35,000 sent out waves of cheers to salute a 23-14 Lion triumph. It marked the first time since '39 that the Middies' were beaten by the Lions.

#6 Pennsylvania

Anthony Minisi scored three touchdowns and passed seven yards to a fourth as Penn played 30 minutes of football to smash the U. S. Naval Academy, 32-19. The Quakers racked up five touchdowns and two extra points in the first half, then stopped. Penn chalked up 20 points almost before the Middles had a chance to get into the game. Burly Chuck Bednarik intercepted a Navy pass, ran it back 28 yards and at 7:51 of the first period.

#1 ARMY {@ Municipal Stadium, Philadelphia, PA}

Gen. Dwight D. Eisenhower and Admiral Chester Nimitz were at the game, both giving up their seats for veterans who were wounded in World War II. More than 100,000 fans showed up, and IRS investigators were scattered outside the stadium to tax those who were re-selling the $3 tickets for nearly 20 times face value.

Army was a 28 point favorite, but they were quite fortunate to hold on for a win against a Navy team that was coming in on a 7 game losing streak. The story of this game was perhaps President Truman's bad juju. He sat on Navy's side for the first half, which was dominated by Army, and he sat on Army's side for the 2nd half, when Navy came back and nearly won. In the opening quarter, Navy advanced a pair of ventures into Army territory, but Army end Barney Poole caused a fumble to end the second advance, tackle Art Gerometta recovering at the Army 37. Army drove to a touchdown from there in 4 plays, quarterback Arnold Tucker hitting halfback Glenn Davis for a 46 yard bomb, and Davis scoring from 13 yards out. Undaunted, Navy responded with an 81 yard drive, including passes of 11 and 32 yards, that ended early in the 2nd quarter with a touchdown. The extra point try was blocked, so Army still led 7-6. Army responded to Navy's response in kind: an 81 yard touchdown drive that featured Glenn Davis bursting up the middle for the last 52 yards on one run. An interception soon gave Army the ball at the Navy 38, and 3 plays later, they scored again, Davis hitting Blanchard for a 26 yard touchdown pass. Army led 21-6 at the half, and at this point, all seemed right with the world. But the 2nd half was a completely different story, not only from the first half, but from every game Army had played for the previous 3 seasons. It seemed completely inexplicable, but Army found themselves with little to no gas left in the tank in this 2nd half, and they barely coasted over the finish line of this season on fumes.

Army opened the 3rd quarter with a drive that was stopped at the Navy 31, where Glenn Davis' punt went awry and only traveled 9 yards. Navy drove 78 yards for a touchdown from there, the drive was kept alive by a pass interference penalty. Late in the 3rd quarter, Army went for it on 4th and 1 from their own 35, and Blanchard was stopped short. Navy drove the short field from there, scoring the touchdown early in the 4th quarter on 4th and 3 with a lateral and touchdown pass. Suddenly it was a game, 21-18, the difference being 3 missed extra points by Navy. Army returned the ensuing kickoff to their 32 and moved to the Navy 39 on a 29 yard run by Glenn Davis, but then Davis threw a long pass that was intercepted. Navy launched one last drive deep into Army territory in the game's waning minutes. They picked up 20 yards on a 4th down fullback run that carried to the Army 3 yard line with about 1:30 left. Tackle Goble Bryant and end Hank Foldberg stopped the fullback on the next play, and the other end, Barney Poole, stopped him on the next. A delay of game penalty set the ball back, and Navy's next run was halted at the Army 5. Navy sent in a substitute with 7 seconds left to stop the clock for one more play, but fans were swarming the field at this point (as pictured above: you can see the players still inside the 10 yard line), and the officials never saw the sub, so Navy was unable to get off that last play. Army was off the hook. Except really, they weren't.

A 21-18 win over a 1-8 team, with that team knocking on the goal line at game's end, was just not going to cut it when Notre Dame had been perfect in their games. Navy had a startling 20 first downs to Army's 8, though Navy barely outgained Army 299 yards to 291.

1947 Navy Midshipmen

In its fifth non-consecutive season under head coach Tom Hamilton, the team compiled a 1–7–1 record and was outscored by a total of 165 to 86. Team Captain was Dick Scott.

The annual Army–Navy Game was played on November 29 at Municipal Stadium in Philadelphia, PA. Army won 21-0.

Home games were played Thompson Field

9/27/1947	NAVY	@		California (9-1)	7	14	L
10/4/1947	NAVY	vs		COLUMBIA (7-2)	6	13	L
10/11/1947	NAVY	vs	#13	DUKE (4-3-2)	14	14	**T**
10/18/1947	NAVY	@		Cornell (4-5)	38	19	W
10/25/1947	NAVY	@	#8	Pennsylvania (7-0-1)	0	21	L
11/1/1947	NAVY	vs	#1	Notre Dame (9-0)	0	27	L
11/8/1947	NAVY	vs		GEORGIA TECH (10-1)	14	16	L
11/15/1947	NAVY	vs	#8	PENN STATE (9-0-1)	7	20	L
11/29/1947	NAVY	vs	#12	ARMY (5-2-2)	0	21	L
Coach: Tom Hamilton				**Season Record >>**	86	165	**1-7-1**

Schedule Source: Steve's Football Bible LLC

Selected game(s) highlights

California

A fighting Navy football team went down to 14-7 defeat this afternoon before an audience of 80,000, which filled every nook and cranny of the big bowl. Favored by 2 to 1 odds, the Middies just didn't have the manpower to stand up to the crushing pressure applied by a resurgent pack of Golden Bears. The Middies held the upper hand through the first half until, with only seconds to go, Cal's quarterback, Bob Celeri, dropped back to pass, found his receivers covered and ran the ball 22 yards for a touchdown. Following a scoreless third period, the Bears got possession in their own territory. On third down, Jackie Jensen, Cal's big fullback, Jackie Jensen found a hole inside right tackle. He plunged through, recovered his footing in the Navy secondary, and sprinted 64 yards to cross the goal line standing up.

Cornell

Navy made its first invasion of Ithaca a triumphant procession yesterday as the Middies coordinated air and land power to defeat a stubborn but out matched Cornell team. A record Cornell crowd of 35,500, shedding coats and wraps in the unseasonable 82 degree temperature, saw the more potent Middies, leading by only five points going into the closing quarter, finally draw away from the tenacious Big Red with two game clinching fourth period touchdowns. Jim Wills converted the try for the extra point after five Middie touchdowns and booted a 20 yard field goal with only 3 seconds remaining in the first period to give the Sailors a 17-13 advantage at half time.

#12 ARMY {@ Municipal Stadium, Philadelphia, PA}

In front of 103,000 fans, including President Harry S. Truman, Army scored one touchdown in each of the first-three quarters to cruise to a 21-0 victory over Navy. A Bill Hawkins fumble led to Army's first touchdown, as Bill Kellum caught an 18 yard touchdown pass from quarterback Elwyn Rowan. Navy drove right back down the field on the next possession, but turned the ball over on downs inside the Army 10 yard line. On Army's first play from scrimmage, Rowan went around the end and down the field 92 yards for the go-ahead score. He finished the afternoon with 148 yards rushing.

1948 Navy Midshipmen

In their first season under head coach George Sauer (pictured at right), the Midshipmen compiled a 0–8–1 record and were outscored by their opponents by a combined score of 227 to 77. Team Captain were Pete Williams and Scott Emerson. The annual Army–Navy Game was played on November 27 at Municipal Stadium in Philadelphia, PA. The game ended in a 21-21 tie.

Home games were played Thompson Field

9/25/1948	NAVY	vs		CALIFORNIA (10-1)	7	21	L
10/2/1948	NAVY	vs		CORNELL (8-1)	7	13	L
10/9/1948	NAVY	@		Duke (4-3-2)	7	28	L
10/16/1948	NAVY	vs	#12	MISSOURI (8-3)	14	35	L
10/23/1948	NAVY	@	#7	Pennsylvania (5-3)	14	20	L
10/30/1948	NAVY	vs	#2	NOTRE DAME (9-0-1)	7	41	L
11/6/1948	NAVY	@	#2	Michigan (9-0)	0	35	L
11/13/1948	NAVY	@		Columbia (4-5)	0	13	L
11/27/1948	NAVY	vs	#3	ARMY (8-0-1)	21	21	T
Coach: George Sauer				**Season Record >>**	77	227	0-8-1

Schedule Source: Steve's Football Bible LLC

Selected game(s) highlights

CORNELL

An alert Cornell football team defeated Navy yesterday in the Stadium by a score of 13 to 7. It was the fifth meeting of the two institutions, and the victory the first for the Big Red eleven in the series. Cornell outplayed a jittery Navy team practically throughout the contest scoring twice in the second period to account for all its points. Navy was blanked until the last period, when a series of forward passes and a lateral from Bobby Home to Billy Earl put the Midshipmen in scoring range. Bill Hawkins took the ball across the Cornell goal to save the Midshipman from a shutout. Cornell displayed surprising strength, but the real downfall of the Middies was caused by their inability to produce a sustained ground attack and failure to hold forward passes.

#7 Pennsylvania

Navy came mighty close to upsetting Penn here this afternoon before a capacity audience of 75,000 at Franklin Field. The much-mussed middies surprised by holding the heavily favored Quakers to a 20-14 score. Penn had to go right through to the last period before getting the winning touchdown when Rhoads raced around the ends on successive plays for a first down on the 20. Bagnell made 14 through the middle to the 6. From there he dashed over, again skirting Navy's right flank.

#2 Michigan

Michigan defeated Navy, 35–0, in front of a sellout crowd at Michigan Stadium. Michigan scored in the first quarter on a one yard run by Chuck Ortmann. Tom Peterson extended Michigan's lead with a touchdown run in the second quarter. Michigan added two touchdowns in the third quarter on a run by Wally Teninga and an 18 yard touchdown pass from Bob Van Summern to Dick Rifenburg. Michigan's recovered three Navy fumbles and intercepted two passes, one by Dick Kempthorn and the other by Dan Dworsky.

#3 ARMY {@ Municipal Stadium, Philadelphia, PA}

Considering Army entered the 1948 season finale with an 8-0 mark, as opposed to Navy's 0-8 record, it should not be a surprise that the Cadets were a 20-point favorite. Yet, the Midshipmen proved the oddsmakers wrong by battling Army to a 21-21 tie. Navy quarterback Reaves Baysinger opened the scoring with a two yard touchdown run midway through the first quarter. However, short touchdown runs by Rudolph Cosentino and Harold Shultz enabled the Cadets to take a 14-7 lead at the half. Navy responded with a one yard Bill Hawkins touchdown run to tie the game at 14 in the third quarter. Army then took its second lead of the game when quarterback Arnold Galiffa scored on a 10 yard bootleg. Finally, Hawkins preserved the tie with clutch plays on both sides of the ball. He followed a one yard touchdown run by knocking away a Galiffa pass on fourth down to end the game.

1949 Navy Midshipmen

In their second season under head coach George Sauer, the Midshipmen compiled a 3–5–1 record and were outscored by their opponents by a combined score of 238 to 151. Team Captain was Phil Ryan.

The annual Army–Navy Game was played on November 26 at Municipal Stadium in Philadelphia, PA. Army won 38-0.

Home games were played Thompson Field

9/24/1949	NAVY		@		Usc (5-3-1)	20	42	L
10/1/1949	NAVY		vs		PRINCETON (6-3)	28	7	W
10/8/1949	NAVY		vs	#14	DUKE (6-3)	28	14	W
10/15/1949	NAVY	#18	@		Wisconsin (5-3-1)	13	48	L
10/22/1949	NAVY		@	#14	Pennsylvania (4-4)	7	28	L
10/29/1949	NAVY		vs	#1	NOTRE DAME (10-0)	0	40	L
11/5/1949	NAVY		@		Tulane (7-2-1)	21	21	T
11/12/1949	NAVY		vs		COLUMBIA (2-7)	34	0	W
11/26/1949	NAVY		vs	#4	ARMY (9-0)	0	38	L
Coach: George Sauer					**Season Record >>**	151	238	3-5-1

Schedule Source: Steve's Football Bible LLC

Selected game(s) highlights

PRINCETON

A spirited Navy football team defeated Princeton. 28 to 7, Thompson Field. It was Navy's first gridiron triumph in 16 starts, ending a victory famine that started midway of the 1947 season after the Midshipmen defeated Cornell. A balmy Indian summer afternoon brought out an announced crowd of 36.736. The Midshipmen scored two touchdowns in the first quarter, and once each in the third and fourth. Princeton tallied its lone touchdown in the second period. Navy scored in 8 plays for its initial score and followed with a 61 yard advance on 9 plays for the second touchdown. Forward passes figured in the game clinching Navy touchdowns in the third and fourth quarters. A forward pass, Zastrow to Andresen, culminated a 63 yard march in the third period, and a toss from Zastrow to Hauff was the finishing touch to a 63 yard march by the Midshipmen in the final quarter.

#14 Pennsylvania

Flashing power and precision that had been missing most of the season, unbeaten Penn smashed to a 14-0 halftime lead over Navy in their traditional clash before 66,125 at Franklin Field. Red Bagnall tore off a 74 yard punt return for a first-period touchdown and Ray Dooney capped a 50 yard march in the next period with a blast through the middle for the final three yards. Penn won, 28-7.

#4 ARMY {@ Municipal Stadium, Philadelphia, PA}

If Navy had any questions about Army's No. 4 national ranking in 1949, the Cadets erased those doubts with a 38-0 trouncing of the Midshipmen in the 50th meeting between the two academies. The statistics certainly told the story on this afternoon — Army had 27 first downs compared to eight for Navy, not to mention a 459-107 advantage in total offensive yardage. The Mids advanced no further than the Army 47 yard line, as Cadet Fullback Gil Stephenson gained 127 yards on 26 attempts.

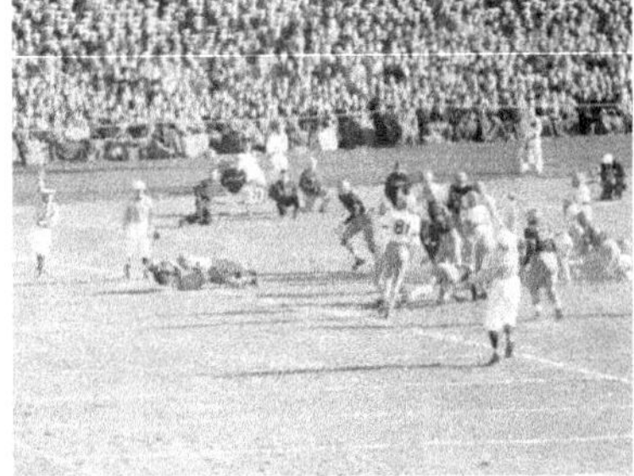

1950 Navy Midshipmen

In their first season under head coach Eddie Erdelatz (pictured at right), the Midshipmen compiled a 3–6 record and were outscored by their opponents by a combined score of 176 to 122. Team Captain was Tom Bakke.

The annual Army–Navy Game was played on December 2 at Municipal Stadium in Philadelphia, PA. Navy won 14-2.

Home games were played Thompson Field

9/30/1950	NAVY		@		Maryland (7-2-1)	21	35	L
10/7/1950	NAVY		vs		NORTHWESTERN (6-3)	0	22	L
10/14/1950	NAVY		@		Princeton (9-0)	14	20	L
10/21/1950	NAVY		vs		USC (2-5-2)	27	14	W
10/28/1950	NAVY		@		Pennsylvania (6-3)	7	30	L
11/4/1950	NAVY		vs		NOTRE DAME (4-4-1)	10	19	L
11/11/1950	NAVY		vs		TULANE (6-2-1)	0	27	L
11/18/1950	NAVY		@		Columbia (4-5)	29	7	W
12/2/1950	NAVY		vs	#2	ARMY (8-1)	14	2	W
Coach: Eddie Erdelatz					**Season Record >>**	122	176	3-6

Schedule Source: Steve's Football Bible LLC

Selected game(s) highlights

Maryland {Byrd Stadium - College Park, Maryland}

The series resumed in 1950 after Georgetown unexpectedly canceled a scheduled game with Navy. Maryland agreed to fill in for Georgetown and hosted the Academy for the Byrd Stadium dedication game in front of a then Washington area-record crowd of 43,836 fans. The two teams last met in 1934, and since that time the Terrapins had hired head coach Jim Tatum. Tatum, an innovator of the split-T offense, had brought consistent success to Maryland in the intervening years. Fearing a renewal of post-game mischief, the Midshipmen attending the match were given strict orders: "Behave like gentlemen and go straight home after the Maryland–Navy football game in College Park tomorrow. No midshipmen will enter the goal post activity or other altercation following the game." Newspapers predicted that Navy would win the 1950 game due to the inexperience of the Maryland quarterbacks, who were led by 19-year-old sophomore Jack Scarbath.

A week before, Scarbath had his first start in a 27–7 loss to Georgia, but he would later become one of Maryland's greatest quarterbacks and the 1952 Heisman Trophy runner-up. In the first quarter against Navy, Scarbath scored on a quarterback keeper. Before the half, he completed passes to ends Stan Karnash and Pete Augsburger for 44- and 59 yard touchdowns. In the third quarter, the Midshipmen responded with a score of their own. In the final period, Maryland end Elmer Wingate returned an interception 34 yards for another touchdown. Then, 54 seconds later, end Lew Weidensaul recovered a Midshipmen fumble, which allowed Ed Modzelewski to rush five yards for the final score by the Terrapins. Navy scored twice more, but Maryland held on to win, 35–21.

Pennsylvania

Mighty Pennsylvania, which is either mighty good or mighty lucky, was pushed all over Franklin Field by Navy during most of the first half this afternoon yet carried a strong 17-7 lead to its locker-room at intermission. Greatly outgained by the Middies, who had clicked off 10 first downs before they got their first, the Penns went for the "big play", scoring on a 61 yarder and again on a bite of 36. Then, after Navy had plowed for its tedious TD, the Quakers added a 24 yard field goal by Herb Agoos to establish the 10-point halftime spread before some 60,000. Penn won, 30-7.

#2 ARMY {@ Municipal Stadium, Philadelphia, PA}

Mighty Army was riding a 27-game unbeaten streak (including two ties) extending from November 1947. They were ranked second nationally, much to the chagrin of veteran Coach Red Blaik, who asserted their claim to the top spot to any sportscaster within earshot. Meantime, Navy had not won the Army-Navy classic since 1943 (1948 was a tie) and had lost their 1949 meeting 38-0. Navy had since accumulated a lackluster 2-6 record during the 1950 season under first-year Coach Eddie Erdelatz. It is not surprising Army was favored by three touchdowns, but somehow the Navy team and Brigade of Midshipmen failed to get the word. Eddie Erdelatz took over the helm of the Midshipmen football program. Although his team struggled to a 3-6 record, the rookie head coach became well acquainted with the magnitude of the Army-Navy rivalry, as his Mids stunned the No. 2 Cadets, 14-2. Navy scored both of its touchdowns in the second half. The first came on a seven yard run by quarterback Bob "Zug" Zastrow. Later, Zastrow found end Jim Baldinger in the end zone for a 30 yard score and a 14-0 lead. Baldinger and Zastrow may have stolen the headlines, but the true heroes were the Navy defensive players. The high-powered Cadet offense managed just one first down and three paltry yards of offense in the first half, and the second half wasn't much better. Army advanced inside Navy's 20 yard line seven times in the third and fourth quarters but came away with nothing to show for it.

1951 Navy Midshipmen

The team was led by second-year head coach Eddie Erdelatz. The Midshipmen compiled a 2–6–1 record and were outscored by their opponents by a combined score of 155 to 132. Team Captain was Frank Hauff.

The annual Army–Navy Game was played on December 1 at Municipal Stadium in Philadelphia, PA. Navy won 42-7.

Home games were played Thompson Field

9/29/1951	NAVY		@		Yale (2-5-2)	7	7	**T**
10/6/1951	NAVY		vs		PRINCETON (9-0)	20	24	L
10/13/1951	NAVY		@		Rice (5-5)	14	21	L
10/20/1951	NAVY		@		NORTHWESTERN (5-4)	7	16	L
10/27/1951	NAVY		@		Pennsylvania (5-4)	0	14	L
11/3/1951	NAVY		vs	#13	NOTRE DAME (7-2-1)	0	19	L
11/10/1951	NAVY		vs		Maryland (10-0)	21	40	L
11/17/1951	NAVY		@		Columbia (5-3)	21	7	W
12/1/1951	NAVY		vs		ARMY (2-7)	42	7	W
Coach: Eddie Erdelatz					**Season Record >>**	**132**	**155**	**2-6-1**

Schedule Source: Steve's Football Bible LLC

Selected game(s) highlights

Maryland {@ Memorial Stadium – Baltimore, MD}

Early in the first quarter, Navy's Frank Brady returned a punt 100 yards for a touchdown and gave the Midshipmen a 7-0 lead, marking the only time during the entire 1951 season that Maryland trailed an opponent in a game. Scarbath connected with receivers on 16 of 34 pass attempts for 285 passing yards and two interceptions. Ed Modzelewski and Paul Weidensaul each scored touchdowns as the Terrapins prevailed, 40-21.

ARMY {@ Municipal Stadium, Philadelphia, PA}

For the first time in series history, the Army-Navy game would be shown on live television. However, this was hardly a "made for TV" special, as both the Midshipmen and Cadets entered the annual grudge match with losing records for the first time ever. Nonetheless, Navy ended its season on a much more pleasant note with a 42-7 victory.

Ironically, the game's biggest play was significant in more ways than one. Trailing 14-7, Army was driving to tie the score. On third-and-goal from the Navy six, Freddie Meyers' pass was intercepted by Navy's John Raster who returned it 101 yards for a touchdown. This took what could have been a 14-14 game and made it a 21-7 Navy lead.

1952 Navy Midshipmen

The team was led by third-year head coach Eddie Erdelatz. They were invited to the 1953 Orange Bowl but refused the bid. The Midshipmen compiled a 6-2-1 record and outscored their opponents by a combined score of 147 to 75. Team Captain was John Gurski. **John Weaver set a Navy single game record with 4 interceptions vs Columbia.** The annual Army–Navy Game was played on November 29 at Municipal Stadium in Philadelphia, PA. Navy won 7-0.

FINAL RANK: #17 UPI

Home games were played Thompson Field

9/27/1952	NAVY		vs		YALE (7-2)	31	0	W	
10/4/1952	NAVY		@		Cornell (2-7)	31	7	W	
10/11/1952	NAVY	#17	vs		WILLIAM & MARY (4-5)	14	0	W	
10/18/1952	NAVY	#20	@		Maryland (7-2)	7	38	L	
10/25/1952	NAVY		@		Pennsylvania (4-3-2)	7	7	T	
11/1/1952	NAVY		vs	#13	NOTRE DAME (7-2-1)	6	17	L	
11/8/1952	NAVY		@		Duke (8-2)	16	6	W	
11/15/1952	NAVY		vs		COLUMBIA (2-6-1)	28	0	W	*-Weaver 4 INT's
11/29/1952	NAVY		vs		ARMY (4-4-1)	7	0	W	
Coach: Eddie Erdelatz					Season Record >>	147	75	6-2-1	

Schedule Source: Steve's Football Bible LLC
***-Single game record**

Selected game(s) highlights

YALE

Navy threw an explosive offense and an even better defense at Yale at Thompson Field and came through with a 31-to-0 football victory, its first opening day triumph since 1946. Scrapping the T-formation they had used through six straight losing seasons, the Middies switched to a blend of the Notre Dame box and the split-T to pile up 254 yards rushing and 102 passing. The defense did an even better job. With Captain John Gurski the only regular back from last year's defensive line, the Middies held Yale to only 6 yards rushing and permitted the Ivy Leaguers to pass midfield just once, in the second quarter when they drove, to the 16. A crowd estimated at 25.000 was on hand to watch the Middies win by the biggest margin in the 51-year-old rivalry between the two teams.

Pennsylvania

Navy held unbeaten Penn to a 7-7 deadlock before 66,000 at Franklin Field as Pennsylvania wasted one scoring chance after another. Navy made good on a 94 yard power and pass parade, engineered by an ex-Jayvee quarterback, Steve Schoderbek. This third period scoring drive matched the Quakers' first-period touchdown and enabled the men of Annapolis to register a moral victory. Eight times Penn had the ball inside the Navy 15 but managed to hit paydirt only once, a Middie fumble paving the way for a short-range scoring buck by Don Zimmer. The Navy tally came on a 33 yard pass play from Schoderbek to fullback Fred Franco.

ARMY {@ Municipal Stadium, Philadelphia, PA}

When a team gains three times as much total offensive yardage as its opponent, as Navy (323) did against Army (106) in 1952, one would think the score would be much loftier than 7-0. However, factor in the 13 turnovers committed by both teams, and the picture becomes much clearer. The 13 miscues, seven by Army and six by the Midshipmen, tied the series record set in 1950. Halfback Phil Monahan was the only player to reach the end zone when he popped over from the two yard line. Navy advanced inside Army's 35 yard line eight more times but came away with nothing to show for it.

1953 Navy Midshipmen

They began the season ranked 13th in the pre-season AP Poll. The team was led by fourth-year head coach Eddie Erdelatz. Team Captain was Dick Olson. The Midshipmen compiled a 4–3-2 record and outscored their opponents by a combined score of 186 to 99.

The annual Army–Navy Game was played on November 28 at Municipal Stadium in Philadelphia, PA. Army won 20-7.

George Welsh led the team in passing with 489 yards and threw 4 touchdown passes. Joe Gattuso led the team in rushing with 412 yards. Ron Beagle led the team in receptions with 14 for 146 yards.

Home games were played Thompson Field

9/26/1953	NAVY	#13	vs		WILLIAM & MARY (5-4-1)	6	6	**T**
10/3/1953	NAVY		vs		DARTMOUTH (2-7)	55	7	**W**
10/10/1953	NAVY		vs		CORNELL (4-3-2)	26	6	**W**
10/17/1953	NAVY	#14	@		Princeton (5-4)	65	7	**W**
10/24/1953	NAVY	#10	@		Pennsylvania (3-5-1)	6	9	**L**
10/31/1953	NAVY	#20	@	#1	Notre Dame (9-0-1)	7	38	**L**
11/7/1953	NAVY		vs		DUKE (7-2-1)	0	0	**T**
11/14/1953	NAVY		@		Columbia (4-5)	14	6	**W**
11/28/1953	NAVY		vs	#18	ARMY (7-1-1)	7	20	**L**
Coach: Eddie Erdelatz					**Season Record >>**	186	99	**4-3-2**

Schedule Source: Steve's Football Bible LLC

Selected game(s) highlights

Pennsylvania

Pennsylvania's, self-styled suicide squad almost committed hari-kari before 52,210 in Franklin Field, but quarterback Ed Gramigna's 25 yard field goal with but 59 seconds to go gave George Hunger's harassed Quakers an upset 9-6 victory and knocked heralded Navy from the list of unbeaten college teams.

#18 ARMY {@ Municipal Stadium, Philadelphia, PA}

The 1953 Army-Navy game was full of surprises. Navy elected to receive the opening kickoff, but the Cadets recovered their own onsides kick. This set the stage for sophomore fullback Pat Uebel, whose three touchdowns, including a 70 yard punt return, propelled Army past Navy, 20-7.

After Uebel's five yard touchdown run made it 7-0, Navy had the chance to tie the score late in the first quarter. The Midshipmen drove to the Army six yard line, but George Welsh's pass was intercepted in the end zone. Navy avoided the shutout when Jack Garrow scored on an eight yard run with 44 seconds left on the clock.

1954 Navy Midshipmen {Lambert Trophy}

The team was led by fifth-year head coach Eddie Erdelatz, and they acquired the nickname "Team Named Desire" during the press conference following the 25–0 road shutout of Stanford, when Erdelatz said, "Every man on this team is full of desire." The Midshipmen compiled an 8-2 record and outscored their opponents by a combined score of 304 to 73. Team Captain was Phil Monahan. Ron Beagle {E} was selected as a consensus All-American.

After defeating #5 Army 27-20 in Philadelphia, the Midshipmen were ranked fifth in both final polls, released in late November, and played in their first bowl game in 31 years. Navy shut out #6 Ole Miss 21–0 in the Sugar Bowl in New Orleans on New Year's Day.

George Welsh led the team in passing with 603 yards and threw 8 touchdown passes. Joe Gattuso led the team in rushing with 636 yards. Earle Smith led the team in receptions with 15 for 195 yards.

FINAL RANK: #5 AP, #5 UPI

Home games were played Thompson Field

Date	Rank			Opponent	TV	PF	PA	W/L	
9/25/1954		vs		WILLIAM & MARY (4-4-2)		27	0	W	
10/2/1954		@		Dartmouth (3-6)		42	7	W	
10/9/1954	#19	@		Stanford (4-6)		25	0	W	
10/16/1954	#9	@		Pittsburgh (4-5)		19	21	L	
10/23/1954		@		Pennsylvania (0-9)		52	6	W	
10/30/1954	#15	vs	#6	NOTRE DAME (9-1)		0	6	L	
11/6/1954	#19	vs		DUKE (8-2-1)		40	7	W	
11/13/1954	#10	vs		COLUMBIA (1-8)		51	6	W	
11/27/1954	#6	vs		ARMY (7-2)		27	20	W	
1/1/1955	#5	vs		Mississippi (9-2)	ABC	21	0	W	Sugar Bowl
Coach: Eddie Erdelatz				Season Record >>		304	73	8-2	

Schedule Source: Steve's Football Bible LLC

Selected game(s) highlights

Pennsylvania

It was "Anchors Aweigh" with a vengeance at Franklin Field yesterday. Releasing all the fury stored up from the frustrations and disappointments of eight previous visits. Navy's Football team steamrollered Penn, 52-6, for the most decisive victory in the 67 year old history of this traditional rivalry. A throng of 41,228, including the Brigade of Midshipmen from the Naval Academy, was treated to the most impressive display of gridiron power and finesse seen here this season as the Annapolis eleven whipped the Red and Blue for the first time since 1945 and romped to its fourth victory.

#6 NOTRE DAME {@ Memorial Stadium – Baltimore, MD}

Notre Dame racked up their fourth victory of the year before 60,000 people at Memorial Stadium by outlasting the Navy 6-0 on the rain saturated turf of Municipal Stadium. Irish Quarterback Ralph Guglielmi, flashing All-American form, threw a touchdown pass to Jim Morse and recovered a Navy fumble in his own end zone to personally thwart the Middie's hope for their first victory over a Notre Dame squad in ten years.

ARMY {@ Municipal Stadium, Philadelphia, PA}

With each team boasting an offense ranked among the top three in the nation, the 1954 Army-Navy game certainly lived up to its billing. The lead was exchanged several times before the No. 6 Midshipmen, "The Team Named Desire," posted a 27-20 victory over the No. 5 Cadets. Down 14-6 midway through the first half, Army roared back to take a 20-14 lead. The Cadets' Don Holleder recovered Dick Guest's fumble at the Navy three yard line, and Pat Uebel slammed it home from there to cut the lead to 14-13 after the extra point. A little more than a minute later, quarterback Pete Vann hit Bob Kyarsky with a swing pass, and the swift halfback raced 42 yards for the go-ahead score. After battling back to take the lead, Army spoiled its fortune by attempting an onsides kick that was unsuccessful. Quarterback George Welsh and his teammates took over at midfield, and six plays later, they led 21-20 after Welsh's five yard run and John Weaver's extra point.

Navy opened the second half by driving to Army's nine yard line, only to fumble. Fortunately for Eddie Erdelatz's club, the Cadets were forced to punt on their ensuing possession. Navy made the most of this opportunity, as an Earle Smith five yard touchdown run made it 27-20. The Midshipmen preserved the victory with a dramatic goal-line stand midway through the fourth quarter and held Army at midfield to end the game.

1955 SUGAR BOWL

The game featured the fifth-ranked Navy Midshipmen and the sixth-ranked Ole Miss Rebels. Running back Joe Gattuso scored on a 3 yard touchdown run as Navy took a 7–0 lead in the first quarter. The second quarter had no scoring. In the third quarter, Navy quarterback George Welsh threw a 16 yard touchdown pass to halfback Jack Weaver, as Navy took command with a 14–0 lead. Gattuso scored on a 1 yard touchdown run, his second of the game, as Navy built a 21–0 lead. With no more scoring, Navy held on to win. With two rushing touchdowns, Gattuso was named the game's MVP.

1955 Navy Midshipmen

Navy began the season ranked No. 8 in the pre-season AP Poll. The team was led by sixth-year head coach Eddie Erdelatz. Team Captain was Phil Monahan. The Midshipmen compiled a 6–2–1 record and outscored their opponents by a combined score of 188 to 56. Ron Beagle {E} was selected as a consensus All-American. George Welsh finished 3rd in the Heisman Trophy voting.

The annual Army–Navy Game was played on November 26 at Municipal Stadium in Philadelphia, PA. Army won 14-6.

Ned Oldham led the team in rushing with 404 yards. Jim Owen led the team in receptions with 19 for 236 yards.

FINAL RANK: #18 AP, #20 UPI
Home games were played Thompson Field

9/24/1955	NAVY	#9	vs		WILLIAM & MARY (1-7-1)	7	0	W
10/1/1955	NAVY	#15	@		South Carolina (3-6)	26	0	W
10/8/1955	NAVY	#12	vs		PITTSBURGH (7-4)	21	0	W
10/15/1955	NAVY	#8	@		Penn State (5-4)	34	14	W
10/22/1955	NAVY	#4	@		Pennsylvania (0-9)	33	0	W
10/29/1955	NAVY	#4	@	#9	Notre Dame (8-2)	7	21	L
11/5/1955	NAVY	#9	vs		DUKE (7-2-1)	7	7	T
11/12/1955	NAVY	#13	@		Columbia (1-8)	47	0	W
11/26/1955	NAVY	#11	vs		ARMY (6-3)	6	14	L
Coach: Eddie Erdelatz					**Season Record >>**	188	56	**6-2-1**

Schedule Source: Steve's Football Bible LLC

Selected game(s) highlights

Pennsylvania

Unbeaten Navy kept its best man on the bench but still rolled to a 33-to-0 victory over Penn today. In place of George Welsh, the nation's total offense leader, Coach Eddie Erdelatz installed Thomas Patrick Forrestal, a sophomore who made the varsity four days ago, at quarterback. He started and played half of the game with the third and fourth' string men sharing the other half. The victory was the ninth straight for Navy and its fifth this year without a loss. Forrestal proved he could run the Academy team by directing three of the five touchdown drives. He set up the first with a 32 yard pass to End Ronnie Beagle, scored the second on a two yard buck and passed ten yards to Beagle for the third. He completed five of 13 tosses for 65 yards. Penn got past the Navy 45 only once and that was after a fumble recovery on the Navy 25.

ARMY {@ Municipal Stadium, Philadelphia, PA}

Although he failed to complete either one of his pass attempts, Army quarterback Don Holleder efficiently directed his team past Navy, 14-6. Navy jumped out to a 6-0 lead, thanks to quarterback George Welsh's one yard touchdown run. However, Army's one-two rushing combination of Pat Uebel and Peter Lash wore down the Midshipmen, as both Cadets managed a touchdown in the second half. Thus, despite posting more first downs (19) and more total offensive yards (330) than Army, Navy could not reach the end zone in the second half.

1956 Navy Midshipmen

The team was led by seventh-year head coach Eddie Erdelatz. Team Captain was Earle Smith. The Midshipmen compiled a 6–1-2 record and outscored their opponents by a combined score of 207 to 76.

The annual Army–Navy Game was played on November 27 at Municipal Stadium in Philadelphia, PA. The game ended in a 7-7 tie.

Tom Forrestal led the team in passing with 808 yards and threw 5 touchdown passes. Ned Oldham led the team in rushing with 393 yards. Earle Smith led the team in receptions with 14. Oldham led with 237 receiving yards. Oldham led the team in scoring with 42 points.

FINAL RANK: #16 AP, #19 UPI
Home games were played Thompson Field

9/29/1956	NAVY		vs	WILLIAM & MARY (0-9-1)	39	14	W
10/6/1956	NAVY		@	Cornell (1-8)	14	0	W
10/13/1956	NAVY		@	Tulane (6-4)	6	21	L
10/20/1956	NAVY		vs	CINCINNATI (4-5)	13	7	W
10/27/1956	NAVY		@	Pennsylvania (4-5)	54	6	W
11/3/1956	NAVY		vs	NOTRE DAME (2-8)	33	7	W
11/10/1956	NAVY	#12	@	Duke (5-4-1)	7	7	T
11/17/1956	NAVY	#15	vs	VIRGINIA (3-7)	34	7	W
12/1/1956	NAVY	#13	vs	ARMY (5-3-1)	7	7	T
Coach: Eddie Erdelatz				**Season Record >>**	207	76	6-1-2

Schedule Source: Steve's Football Bible LLC

Selected game(s) highlights

NOTRE DAME {@ Memorial Stadium – Baltimore, MD}

The Fighting Irish tumbled for the fourth consecutive Saturday at the feet of an injury free, determined and aggressive Navy eleven before some 60,000 drenched spectators in Baltimore Stadium. This game, another in the nation's longest continuous intersectional series, saw Notre Dame strive valiantly in the mud and rain to end their losing ways, and through outmanned, battle on even terms for two quarters. But the Midshipmen, driven by a victory hunger which had gone unsatisfied for eleven straight years against Irish teams, unmercifully ripped off three touchdowns in the third Period and added another as insurance in the fourth to coast to a 33-7 win. Navy's stout defense had little trouble stopping the Irish ground attack as was clearly indicated by the fact that Notre Dame's total rushing offense amounted to only 50 yards. The Middies, on the other hand, payed little heed to the soft turf and rammed the Irish line for 231 yards and added another 122 on 10 pass completions in 16 attempts.

ARMY {@ Municipal Stadium, Philadelphia, PA}

Considering there were nine turnovers between the two teams, it was rather appropriate that the two touchdowns scored in the 1956 game were the result of opponent miscues. In the third quarter, Army's David Bourland intercepted Tom Forrestal's pass and returned it 26 yards to set up Bob Kyasky's four yard touchdown run and a 7-0 lead. In the fourth quarter, one of Army's eight fumbles led to a one yard touchdown run by Rick Dagampat.

1957 Navy Midshipmen {Lambert Trophy}

Led by eighth-year head coach Eddie Erdelatz, the Midshipmen shut out #10 Army 14–0 to end the regular season at 8–1–1; they were ranked fifth in the final polls, released in early December. Team Captain was Ned Oldham.

In December, Navy won its third Lambert Trophy, an award for the season's best college football team in the East. The Middies had previously won the award in 1943 and 1954. Navy and the small-college winner of the Lambert Cup, Lehigh, were lauded as proof that a university could field a competitive football team without compromising its academic standards. Favored by a point, Navy won the Cotton Bowl 20–7 over eighth-ranked Rice on New Year's Day.

Tom Forrestal led the team in passing with 1,270 yards. Harry Hurst led the team in rushing with 634 yards. Ned Oldham led with 7 rushing touchdowns. Pete Jokanovich led the team in receptions with 32 for 386 yards. Hurst led the team in scoring with 48 points. **Forrestal set a Navy single game record with 4 touchdown passes vs Pennsylvania.**

FINAL RANK: #5 AP, #6 UPI

Home games were played Thompson Field

9/21/1957	**#12**	@		Boston College (7-2)		46	6	**W**	
9/28/1957	**#5**	vs		WILLIAM & MARY (4-6)		33	6	**W**	
10/5/1957	**#6**	@		North Carolina (6-4)		7	13	**L**	
10/12/1957		@		California (1-9)		21	6	**W**	
10/19/1957	**#15**	vs		GEORGIA (3-7)		27	14	**W**	
10/26/1957	**#16**	@		Pennsylvania (3-6)		35	7	**W**	*-Forrestal 4 pass TD
11/2/1957	**#16**	@	#5	Notre Dame (7-3)		20	6	**W**	
11/9/1957	**#7**	vs	#16	DUKE (6-3-2)		6	6	**T**	
11/16/1957	**#9**	vs		GEORGE WASHINGTON (2-7)		52	0	**W**	
11/30/1957	**#8**	vs	#10	ARMY (7-2)		14	0	**W**	
1/1/1958	**#8**	vs	#9	**Rice (7-4)**	CBS	20	7	**W**	**Cotton Bowl**
Coach: Eddie Erdelatz				**Season Record >>**		**281**	**71**	**9-1-1**	

Schedule Source: Steve's Football Bible LLC
***-Single game record {Hurst 3 TD receptions}**

Selected game(s) highlights

Boston College

Navy crushed Boston College 46 to 6 today as the Midshipmen launched their football season spurred by Quarterback Tom Forrestal and Captain Ned Oldham. Forrestal completed seven of 10 passes for 143 yards and two touchdowns in the first 17 minutes of the contest as Boston College dedicated its new Campus stadium before a capacity crowd of 28,000. Oldham contributed two touchdowns and three extra points as well as vital yard age on marches. Navy scored the first two times it had possession. The Sailors moved 61 and 73 yards, respectively, as Oldham ran the final yard on one and Forrestal tossed a 5 yard running pass to End Wayne McKee for the other. Navy struck for two more scores before half and three after intermission. Boston College scored 12 seconds after the second period began on a 93 yard scoring pass play from Quarterback Don Allard to Halfback Tom Joe Sullivan.

GEORGE WASHINGTON

Navy crushed George Washington at Thompson Field. 52 to 0, before an estimated 10,000. Eight players scored the eight touchdowns and if the Sailors had a deficiency, it was in making extra points. They connected on only four of eight and one of those had to be run over. The Middie first unit, with Halfback Ned Oldham and Tackle Tony Anthony held out to rest for the big one against Army November 30, played just nine minutes. Navy had a 7-0 lead before three minutes had gone by, added two more touchdowns for a 19-0 bulge at halftime and slammed over five more scores after intermission. Bob Carrell, speedy third-team halfback, turned in the most exciting run of the day, a 55 yard punt return for the final touchdown. Dick Zemhrzuskl, a No, 2 halfback, had a longer run, 60 yards, but was hauled down on the G.W. 16.

#10 ARMY {@ Municipal Stadium, Philadelphia, PA}

Just as running back Ned Oldham was a two-time Naval Academy debate champion, the Midshipmen's 14-0 win over Army left little doubt coach Eddie Erdelatz's club was among the top five teams in the nation. Navy followed its Army shutout with a 20-7 win over Rice in the Cotton Bowl. This placed the Mids No. 5 nationally with a 9-1-1 mark. While Oldham scampered 44 yards for his second touchdown of the day, the Navy defense slowed Army to just 136 total yards. The Cadets entered the game averaging better than 400 yards per game rushing and passing. Defensive guard Bob Caldwell and defensive back Tom Forrestal preserved the shutout with clutch fourth-quarter plays. Caldwell recovered a fourth-quarter fumble at the Navy nine yard line, and Forrestal picked off a pass in the end zone.

1958 COTTON BOWL CLASSIC

The game matched the independent and fifth-ranked Navy Midshipmen and the #8 Rice Owls of the Southwest Conference (SWC). Slightly favored, Navy won 20–7. Rice never recovered after Navy led 13–0 at halftime on touchdown runs by Joe Tranchini and Harry Hurst. Team captain Ned Oldham added another early in the third quarter to give Navy a commanding 20–0 lead. Ken Williams—stepfather of pro wrestler Steve Austin—caught a touchdown pass from Frank Ryan to narrow the lead to 13, but Rice never seriously threatened from that point on. Navy outgained Rice on ground by 222 yards to 137 as the Owls committed six turnovers. Forrestal and Ryan both had 13 completions, which set a Cotton Bowl record.

1958 Navy Midshipmen

Navy began the season ranked 7th in the pre-season AP Poll. The team was led by ninth-year head coach Eddie Erdelatz. Team Captain was Dick Dagampat. The Midshipmen compiled a 6–1–2 record and outscored their opponents by a combined score of 212 to 134.

The annual Army–Navy Game was played on November 29 at Municipal Stadium in Philadelphia, PA. Army won 22-6.

Joe Tranchini led the team in passing with 837 yards and threw 10 touchdown passes. Joe Matalavage led the team in rushing with 271 yards and 4 rushing touchdowns. Joe Bellino led the team in receptions with 19 for 240 yards. Bellino and Matalavage led the team in scoring with 30 points.

Home games were played Thompson Field

9/27/1958	NAVY	#12	vs		WILLIAM & MARY (2-6-1)	14	0	**W**
10/4/1958	NAVY	#15	@		Boston U. (4-5)	28	14	**W**
10/11/1958	NAVY	#12	@	#14	Michigan (2-6-1)	20	14	**W**
10/18/1958	NAVY	#6	vs		TULANE (3-7)	6	14	**L**
10/25/1958	NAVY	#18	@		Pennsylvania (4-5)	50	8	**W**
11/1/1958	NAVY	#15	vs		NOTRE DAME (6-4)	20	40	**L**
11/8/1958	NAVY		vs		Maryland (4-6)	40	14	**W**
11/15/1958	NAVY		@		George Washington (3-5)	28	8	**W**
11/29/1958	NAVY		vs	#5	ARMY (8-0-1)	6	22	**L**
Coach: Eddie Erdelatz					**Season Record >>**	**212**	**134**	**6-3**

Schedule Source: Steve's Football Bible LLC

Selected game(s) highlights

NOTRE DAME {@ Memorial Stadium – Baltimore, MD}

A dazzling display of offensive power coupled with a crippling defense enabled Notre Dame to smother the Naval Academy, 40-20. The Middies, in their bid to win three consecutive games from the Irish, were never in the game as the Irish pounded six touchdowns into the Navy end zone to run up the highest score in nine years. Navy then threw a scare into the Irish with a fine display of ball handling. Stickles boot was taken by Dagampat on the eight yard stripe. Dagampat moved to the left sideline and handed off to Bellino on the 16. The Irish defenses were caught unaware as Bellino sped down the near sideline for six points, untouched by an Irish defender. Navy struck back with a swift pass play when Bellino slipped behind the Notre Dame secondary and took a Tranchini pass all the way for a score. Bellino then ran for two conversion points and a 34-14 score. Navy took over on their own 24 with about five minutes left and passed their way to a score. Maxfield tossed to Dick Zembrznski for the TD. The try for points was stopped and the Irish won, 40-20.

#5 ARMY {@ Municipal Stadium, Philadelphia, PA}

All-America running back Pete Dawkins took the opening kickoff and raced down the sideline. But when he cut back, he collided with teammate Bill Rowe, popping the ball loose. Navy recovered on the Army 40 yard line, and Joe Bellino later scored the first touchdown of the game on a three yard run. Nonetheless, the Cadets had the last laugh, capping West Point's undefeated season with a 22-6 victory over Navy. Bob Anderson scored Army's first touchdown just before halftime on a one yard run and added another short score at the start of the final quarter. Trailing 14-6, Navy was driving down the field with two minutes remaining. But Don Usury picked off Joe Tranchini's pass and returned it 38 yards for a touchdown. The Cadets finished the year 8-0-1, as Dawkins captured the Heisman Trophy. The Midshipmen closed the year at 6-3.

1959 Navy Midshipmen

The team was led by first-year head coach Wayne Hardin (pictured at right). Team Captain was Dick Dagampat. The Midshipmen compiled a 5–4-1 record and outscored their opponents by a combined score of 199 to 166. The annual Army–Navy Game was played on November 28 at Municipal Stadium in Philadelphia, PA. Navy won 43-12.

Jim Maxfield led the team in passing with 711 yards. Joe Bellino led the team in rushing with 564 yards and 7 rushing touchdowns. Dick Pariseau led the team in receptions with 20 for 228 yards.

Home games were played at Navy-Marine Corps Stadium

9/19/1959	NAVY		@		Boston College (5-4)	24	8	**W**
9/26/1959	NAVY	**#13**	**vs**		WILLIAM & MARY (4-6)	29	2	**W**
10/3/1959	NAVY	**#15**	@		Smu (5-4-1)	7	20	**L**
10/10/1959	NAVY		**vs**	#12	SYRACUSE (11-0)	6	32	**L**
10/16/1959	NAVY		@		Miami (6-4)	8	23	**L**
10/24/1959	NAVY		@		Pennsylvania (7-1-1)	22	22	**T**
10/31/1959	NAVY		@		Notre Dame (5-5)	22	25	**L**
11/7/1959	NAVY		**vs**		Maryland (5-5)	22	14	**W**
11/14/1959	NAVY		**vs**		GEORGE WASHINGTON (1-8)	16	8	**W**
11/28/1959	NAVY		**vs**		ARMY (4-4-1)	43	12	**W**
Coach: Wayne Hardin					**Season Record >>**	199	166	**5-4-1**

Schedule Source: Steve's Football Bible LLC

Selected game(s) highlights

#12 SYRACUSE {@ Foreman Field – Norfolk, VA}

Syracuse intercepted four Navy passes and overpowered the Midshipmen on the ground to gain an easy 32-6 victory in the 13th annual Shrine Oyster Bowl in front of 31,750 spectators. Art Baker intercepted a Joe Tranchini pass and returned it 96 yards for a touchdown for the Orangemen. Baker added a 13 yard touchdown run.

NOTRE DAME {@ Memorial Stadium – Baltimore, MD}

A 43 yard field goal by Monty Stickles furnished a melodramatic ending as Notre Dame defeated Navy 25-22, before 58,652 mesmerized people in Notre Dame Stadium. Stickles completed his kick despite a 15 yard penalty for "coaching from the bench" that set the ball back to the 33. The penalty was caused by junior manager Bob McCuthan who ran onto the field with the kicking tee before Don White had a chance to inform the officials. Nevertheless, Stickles booted the ball neatly between the posts with 32 seconds left in the game.

GEORGE WASHINGTON

George Washington University, a 27-point underdog, held Navy in check for better than half of their football game here today, but then Joe Bellino, broke loose to spark the Middies to a 16-to-8 triumph. More than four minutes of the third quarter had ticked off the big Navy-Marine Corps Memorial Stadium clock before the 5-foot-8 Bellino grabbed a pass from Quarterback Joe Tranchini and shot 20 yards into the end zone for the first score of the contest. Thrilling an estimated 14.000 fans, Bellino bounced off three G. W. tacklers as he tore down the sidelines to the score which culminated a 47 yard Navy march. Navy Fullback Joe Matalavage bulldozed over from the 3 to put the Middies out of reach. Greg Mather booted a field goal from the 19 yard stripe for Navy's final three points and a 16-0 advantage

ARMY {@ Municipal Stadium, Philadelphia, PA}

Compiling 405 yards of total offense, Navy rolled to a 43-12 victory over Army. Joe Bellino's 113 yards and three touchdowns on 25 carries led a Midshipmen ground game that finished the afternoon with 288 yards. Joe Tranchini added a pair of short rushing scores as the Mids posted 23 first downs compared to 13 for Army. Despite the statistical difference, Navy held a slim 21-12 lead at the intermission. However, the Midshipmen added three "insurance" touchdowns in the second half. Bellino reached the end zone for the third time in the game, while Tranchini tallied his second touchdown and Roland Brandquist closed the scoring with a one yard run of his own.

1960 Navy Midshipmen {Lambert Trophy}

Led by head coach Wayne Hardin, the Midshipmen finished the season with nine wins and an appearance in the Orange Bowl. The Midshipmen were Lambert Trophy co-champions with undefeated Yale. Senior halfback Joe Bellino was awarded the Heisman Trophy and the Maxwell Award. Bellino was selected as a consensus All-American. Team Captain was Joe Matalavage. The offense scored 262 points while the defense allowed 103 points.

Navy upset third-ranked Washington in Seattle, which vaulted them up eleven places in the rankings, to sixth. They played Air Force for the first time this season, a 35–3 win in mid-October in Baltimore as Bellino scored three touchdowns and made an interception, all in the first half. The annual Army–Navy Game was played on November 26 at Municipal Stadium in Philadelphia, PA. Navy won 17-12.

Hal Spooner led the team in passing with 805 yards and threw 8 touchdown passes. Bellino led the team in rushing with 834 yards. Jim Luper led the team in receptions with 22 for 307 yards. Bellino lead the team in scoring with 18 points.

FINAL RANK: #4 AP, #6 UPI

Home games were played at Navy-Marine Corps Stadium

9/17/1960		@		Boston College (3-6-1)		22	7	W	
9/24/1960		vs		VILLANOVA (2-8)		41	7	W	
10/1/1960	#17	@	#3	Washington (10-1)		15	14	W	
10/8/1960	#6	vs		SMU (0-9-1)		26	7	W	
10/15/1960	#5	vs		AIR FORCE (4-6)		35	3	W	
10/22/1960	#4	@		Pennsylvania (3-6)		27	0	W	
10/29/1960	#4	vs		NOTRE DAME (2-8)		14	7	W	
11/5/1960	#4	@	#15	Duke (8-3)		10	19	L	
11/12/1960	#8	vs		VIRGINIA (0-10)		41	6	W	
11/26/1960	#7	vs		ARMY (6-3-1)		17	12	W	
1/2/1961	**#4**	**vs**	**#5**	**Missouri (10-1)**	**CBS**	**14**	**21**	**L**	**Orange Bowl**
Coach: Wayne Hardin				**Season Record >>**		**262**	**103**	**9-2**	

Schedule Source: Steve's Football Bible LLC

Selected game(s) highlights

NOTRE DAME {@ Municipal Stadium – Philadelphia, PA}

Navy's Middies scored twice on runs by their All-America candidate Joe Bellino to edge Notre Dame's desperately battling Irish, 14-7, on this dark afternoon in the Friendly City. After returning the opening kickoff from Navy's nine to the 19, Bellino swept right end on the first play from scrimmage for a 43 yard gain to Notre Dame's 38. After a one yard gain through the middle of the line by Joe Matalavage, Navy's captain and fullback, Bellino raced for another 18 on a power slice over the left side. Matalavage then hit for seven yards to the 12. On the next play, Bellino took advantage of a crushing block by John Hewitt to sprint 12 yards around right end for the score. End Greg Mather's conversion was good, and the Middies led 7-0 with only 3:03 of the first period gone. With Bellino and Matalavage alternating as ball carriers. Navy slugged its way to Notre Dame's 21. Dietz then threw to end Jim Luper for a first down on the three. Bellino smashed up the middle for two and a half yards on the next play from scrimmage, and then hurdled the piled up lines for the winning six points. Mather converted to make the final score 14-7.

ARMY {@ Municipal Stadium, Philadelphia, PA}

Army was not unhappy to see Joe Bellino graduate from the Naval Academy, as the star running back clinched the 1960 Heisman Trophy with an impressive all-around performance against the Cadets in the 1960 regular-season finale. He touched the ball 25 times and accounted for 192 yards. He gained 85 yards on 20 carries, caught two passes for 16 yards, returned two kickoffs for 46 yards and intercepted one pass and returned it 45 yards. All this equaled a 17-12 Midshipmen triumph. Despite Bellino's exploits, Navy nearly squandered a 17-0 halftime advantage. A pair of Al Rushatz touchdown runs made it 17-12, and Army drove down to the Navy 32 yard line with 1:50 remaining. But quarterback Frank Blanda's desperation pass was intercepted, by none other than Bellino.

1961 ORANGE BOWL CLASSIC

The game matched the fifth-ranked Missouri Tigers of the Big Eight Conference, who defeated the #4 Navy Midshipmen, 21–14. Navy jumped to a 6–0 lead with a 98 yard fumble return for a touchdown. But Missouri answered when Norm Beal intercepted Navy's Hal Spooner, rumbling down the sideline for a 90 yard return, giving Missouri a 7–6 advantage. They then drove 80 yards for a second touchdown and led 14–6 at halftime.

Missouri's defense shut down the Midshipmen's running game, including Heisman Trophy winner Joe Bellino, forcing Navy to pass. But Missouri continued to run the ball, grinding it out for 223 rushing yards. After a scoreless third quarter, Missouri drove down 64 yards and capitalized with a 1 yard run from quarterback Ronnie Taylor. Taylor, who went 1 for 6 passing, threw for only five total yards. Down 21–6, Bellino caught a 27 yard pass from Spooner, and then made the two point conversion, cutting the lead to 21–14. Missouri held on for the win. President-elect John F. Kennedy attended the game.

1961 Navy Midshipmen

The team was led by third-year head coach Wayne Hardin. Team Captain was John Hewitt. The Midshipmen compiled a 7-3 record and outscored their opponents by a combined score of 201 to 136. The annual Army–Navy Game was played on December 12 at Municipal Stadium in Philadelphia, PA. Navy won 13-7.

Ron Klemick led the team in passing with 1,035 yards and threw 6 touchdown passes. John Sai led the team in rushing with 472 yards and 6 rushing touchdowns. Jim Stewart led the team in receptions with 23 for 498 yards. Sai led the team in scoring with 36 points.

Home games were played at Navy-Marine Corps Stadium

9/23/1961	NAVY	@	#7	Penn State (8-3)	10	20	L
9/30/1961	NAVY	vs		WILLIAM & MARY (1-9)	44	6	W
10/6/1961	NAVY	@		Miami (7-4)	17	6	W
10/14/1961	NAVY	@		Cornell (3-6)	31	7	W
10/20/1961	NAVY	@		Detroit Mercy (5-4)	37	19	W
10/28/1961	NAVY	@		Pittsburgh (3-7)	14	28	L
11/4/1961	NAVY	@		Notre Dame (5-5)	13	10	W
11/11/1961	NAVY	vs		DUKE (7-3)	9	30	L
11/18/1961	NAVY	vs		VIRGINIA (4-6)	13	3	W
12/2/1961	NAVY	vs		ARMY (6-4)	13	7	W
Coach: Wayne Hardin				**Season Record >>**	**201**	**136**	**7-3**

Schedule Source: Steve's Football Bible LLC

Selected game(s) highlights

Detroit Mercy

Jerry Gross completed 24 of 44 passes for 278 yards and three touchdowns, all scored by Larry Vargo. It wasn't enough. Navy's arsenal was too deep, too varied and the Middies rammed over three fourth-period touchdowns to dump the University of Detroit, 37-19, before 31,279 fans at Tiger Stadium. Gross, who played beat the clock at the end of the first half in the old Bobby Layne manner, brought the Titans back from a 13-0 second period deficit to a 19-16 lead at the end of the third quarter. Navy's Ron Klemick passed 25 yards to Carl Fink for a 23-19 lead with 4:42 gone in the period. The Middies moved 61 yards in six plays, with Klemick throwing to end Gary Kellner 25 yards for the touchdown. The next time the Middies got the ball they went in again, with Bob Orlosky scoring on a five yard spurt.

ARMY {@ Municipal Stadium, Philadelphia, PA}

Navy may have lost its season opener when it dropped a 20-10 decision to Penn State, but it closed the year in fine fashion with a 13-7 win over Army. Greg Mather, who caught four passes for 36 yards, punted five times for 167 yards and hit 27- and 29 yard field goals, turned in a fine all-around performance. His 27 yarder gave the Mids a 3-0 lead, which they took into the locker room at halftime. Army took the lead early in the third quarter when it went 76 yards in six plays, capped by Al Rushatz's one yard touchdown run. Following an exchange of punts, Navy backup quarterback Bob Hecht took the team 51 yards for the go-ahead score, a 13 yard run by Bill Ulrich. Mather tacked on his second field goal in the fourth quarter to become the first Navy player to score in three series games.

1962 Navy Midshipmen

The team was led by fourth year head coach Wayne Hardin. Team Captain was Steve Hoy. The Midshipmen compiled a 5-5 record and outscored their opponents by a combined score of 184 to 174. The annual Army–Navy Game was played on December 1 at Municipal Stadium in Philadelphia, PA. Navy won 34-14.

Roger Staubach led the team in passing with 966 yards and threw 7 touchdown passes. Pat Donnelly led the team in rushing with 338 yards. Staubach led with 7 rushing touchdowns. Jim Stewart led the team in receptions with 24 for 399 yards. Staubach led the team in scoring with 42 points.

Home games were played at Navy-Marine Corps Stadium

9/22/1962	NAVY	@	#9	Penn State (9-2)	7	41	L
9/29/1962	NAVY	vs		WILLIAM & MARY (4-5-1)	20	16	W
10/6/1962	NAVY	@		Minnesota (6-2-1)	0	21	L
10/13/1962	NAVY	vs		CORNELL (4-5)	41	0	W
10/20/1962	NAVY	@		Boston College (8-2)	26	6	W
10/27/1962	NAVY	vs		PITTSBURGH (5-5)	32	9	W
11/3/1962	NAVY	vs		NOTRE DAME (5-5)	12	20	L
11/10/1962	NAVY	@		Syracuse (5-5)	6	34	L
11/17/1962	NAVY	@	#2	Usc (11-0)	6	13	L
12/1/1962	NAVY	vs		ARMY (6-4)	34	14	W
Coach: Wayne Hardin				**Season Record >>**	**184**	**174**	**5-5**

Schedule Source: Steve's Football Bible LLC

Selected game(s) highlights

Boston College

Quarterback Roger Staubach and fullback Pat Donnelly a pair of precocious sophomores, played a part in all but one touchdown as Navy overcame an early 6-to-0 deficit to defeat Boston College, 26 to 6. A sellout crowd of 25.200 fans at Alumni Stadium watched Staubach repeat his brilliant performance of a week ago against Cornell. Staubach tossed touchdown passes of 13 and 22 yards to end Jim Campbell and Donnelly, respectively. Donnelly also scampered five yards in the third quarter for a touchdown to snap a 6-6 tie and give Navy the lead for good. Second-string fullback Nick Markoff scored the Middies' other touchdown on a six yard run in the fourth quarter

NOTRE DAME {@ Municipal Stadium, Philadelphia, PA}

First half action saw Notre Dame take complete command of Philadelphia Stadium's slick, muddy field, but Navy retaliated in the third quarter; capitalizing on breaks and their running game, they pulled in front, 12-7. But no sooner had the scoreboard registered the lead margin, when Daryl Lamonica struck a surprised Denny Phillips with a 45 yard touchdown pass, giving Notre Dame the deciding points in a very wet and welcome win. Navy made up for its offensive void of the first half on the passing of Roger Staubach and the running of Bob Teall in the third quarter. Twice Teall ran a delayed trap for gains of 12 and 19 yards deep into Irish territory. John Sai climaxed the offensive plot with a 4 yard touchdown run. Lamonica fumbled on the first play of the fourth quarter. Navy recovered and Staubach merely flopped over the goal and even though the two pointer failed again. Navy led 12-7.

#2 Usc

USC held on for a sloppy 13-6 win over Navy at home, they moved to #1. USC gave up 5 turnovers against Navy, the first at their own 23 in the opening quarter, which led to Navy quarterback Roger Staubach's 18 yard touchdown run and a 6-0 Navy lead. In the 2nd quarter, USC quarterback Pete Beathard hit Hal Bledsoe for 3 passes totaling 59 yards, the last going for a touchdown, and in the 3rd quarter Willie Brown scored a 56 yard touchdown on a reverse, making the 13-6 final score. Navy wasn't done, pushing the ball to the Southern Cal 1 yard line in the 4th quarter, but they fumbled the ball away there.

ARMY {@ Municipal Stadium, Philadelphia, PA}

Enjoying a fine sophomore season, Navy quarterback Roger Staubach stepped into the national spotlight when he completed a series-record 10-of-12 passes in Navy's 34-14 victory over Army. The Midshipmen rode the momentum of an early lead, as Army was held deep in its own territory on the game's opening series and was forced to punt. The snap sailed over Army punter Dick Peterson's head and out of the end zone for a safety, giving Navy a 2-0 lead. This advantage was extended by six points when Staubach hit Neil Henderson for a 12 yard score. Staubach tacked on a 21 yard touchdown run midway through the second quarter for a 15-0 lead. Although Army scored just before the half to make it 15-6, Navy scored touchdowns on consecutive possessions to take a commanding 28-6 lead. Staubach hooked up with fullback Nick Markoff for a 65 yard touchdown and later added a two yard touchdown himself.

1963 Navy Midshipmen {Lambert Trophy}

Led by fifth-year head coach Wayne Hardin, the Midshipmen finished the year with an overall record of 9–2 and a loss against Texas in the Cotton Bowl Classic. Team Captain was tom Lynch.

Quarterback Roger Staubach won the Heisman Trophy and the Maxwell Award while leading the Midshipmen to a 9–1 regular season record and a final ranking of No. 2 in the nation. Staubach was selected as a consensus All-American. He led Navy to victory over their annual rivalry with Notre Dame, which would be the Midshipmen's last win over Notre Dame until 2007. In the Crab Bowl Classic, Navy defeated Maryland by a score of 42–7. There was talk of cancelling the 1963 Army-Navy game in the aftermath of the assassination of President John F. Kennedy, but his widow, Jacqueline, insisted that the game should be played. No. 2 Navy accepted an invitation to play in the 1964 Cotton Bowl Classic versus No. 1 Texas, the second No. 1 versus No. 2 bowl game in college football history. Roger Staubach led the team in passing with 1,702 yards and threw 7 touchdowns passes. Pat Donnelly led the team in rushing with 615 yards. Staubach and John Sai led with 9 rushing touchdowns. Ed Orr led the team in receptions with 34 for 433 yards. John Sai led the team in scoring with 60 points.

FINAL RANK: #2 AP, #2 UPI

Home games were played at Navy-Marine Corps Stadium

9/21/1963	#9	@		West Virginia (4-6)		51	7	W	
9/28/1963	#5	vs		WILLIAM & MARY (4-6)		28	0	W	
10/5/1963	#6	@		Michigan (3-4-2)		26	13	W	
10/11/1963	#4	@		Smu (4-7)		28	32	L	
10/19/1963	#10	vs		VMI (3-5-2)		21	12	W	
10/26/1963	#10	vs	#3	PITTSBURGH (9-1)		24	12	W	
11/2/1963	#4	@		Notre Dame (2-7)		35	14	W	
11/9/1963	#4	vs		MARYLAND (3-7)		42	7	W	
11/16/1963	#2	@		Duke (5-4-1)		38	25	W	
12/7/1963	#2	vs		ARMY (7-3)		21	15	W	
1/1/1964	#2	vs	#1	**Texas (11-0)**	CBS	6	28	L	**Cotton Bowl**
Coach: Wayne Hardin				**Season Record >>**		320	165	9-2	

Schedule Source: Steve's Football Bible LLC

Selected game(s) highlights

Michigan

Michigan lost to Navy by a 26–13 score before a crowd of 55,877 at Michigan Stadium. Navy, led by junior quarterback Roger Staubach, was ranked No. 6 in the AP poll. Staubach broke his own Navy single-game record with 307 yards of total offense. He completed 14 of 16 passes for 237 yards and two touchdowns and ran for 70 yards and one touchdown. Michigan quarterback Bob Timberlake was again sidelined; Frosty Evashevski started in his place, and Bob Chandler took over in the second half. Chandler completed nine of ten passes for 138 yards and two touchdowns in a comeback that fell short.

SMU {Cotton Bowl Stadium - Dallas, Texas}

Navy played in the Cotton Bowl twice in the 1963 season. The first time was against SMU on a Friday night at the Texas State Fair, the night before Oklahoma met Texas. The Mustangs would finish 4-7, but on this night, they shocked Staubach, who was at less than full strength - - he dislocated his shoulder at least twice during the game. With the help of some extremely dubious officiating (the refs were suspended after a review of their shoddy work) and flanker Ed Orr's drop of a sure TD pass in the final ticks, Navy was upset 32-28.

Notre Dame

At Notre Dame Stadium, 59,362 homecoming spectators watched in horror as Navy scored four second-half touchdowns to defeat Notre Dame, 35-14. Pat Donnelly scored two touchdowns and rushed for 127 yards in 14 carries — an average of nine yards per try — and Gary Kellner also scored twice, it was quarterback Roger Staubach who detonated the Navy offense. Staubach rolled out around left end to the three as the quarter ended. On the opening play of the second quarter, Staubach rolled out to his right and the Notre Dame defenders, alert for the run, neglected right end Gary Kellner; Staubach hit him with a perfect end zone pass. Fred Marlin converted. Navy halfback John Sai returned the second half opening kickoff back to the 30, and Staubach again jogged onto the field. Nine plays, three and one-half minutes, and three passes later Navy has its second touchdown, on a Staubach pass to Donnelly. Late in the third period. Navy's Ed Orr ran a punt back to the Navy 44. Eight plays later the Middies scored. This time Donnelly did most of the work himself: he covered 47 of the 56 yards to the goal line in five carries — including runs of 20 and 21 yards. John Sai scored from the two. Thirty seconds later Navy scored again. On Notre Dame's first play from scrimmage, Frank Budka was hit just as he released a screen pass intended for Bill Wolski. Kellner intercepted the pass on the dead run and continued to the end zone untouched. The conversion was successful, and Navy led 28-7 with twenty-two minutes left to play.

ARMY {@ Municipal Stadium, Philadelphia, PA}

In a contest that had been postponed one week due to the assassination of President John F. Kennedy, Navy held on for a 21-15 victory over the Cadets.

Halfback Pat Donnelly's three touchdowns gave the Mids a commanding 21-7 lead four minutes into the fourth quarter. Yet, as usual, the next 11 minutes would be plenty interesting. Army took the ensuing kickoff and drove 52 yards in nine plays (all running plays), with quarterback Rollie Stichweh taking it in from the one yard line. Stichweh scored the two point conversion himself, and Navy's lead was cut to 21-15 at the 6:19 mark. Not only did Stichweh score the touchdown and extra points, but he then recovered the onsides kick at the Navy 49 yard line. The Cadets drove to the Navy four yard line, where on third-and-goal, Stichweh handed off to Ken Waldrop, who was tackled by a horde of Midshipmen defenders in a pile. Stuck at the bottom of the pile, Waldrop was unable to get back to the Army huddle before time ran out.

1964 COTTON BOWL CLASSIC

The game was a de facto national championship game; the top-ranked and undefeated Texas Longhorns, champions of the Southwest Conference, defeated the #2 Navy Midshipmen, 28–6. Two touchdown catches by Phil Harris from Duke Carlisle and a Carlisle touchdown run gave the Longhorns a 21–0 lead at halftime. Another touchdown run by fullback Harold Philipp increased the lead to 28–0 after three quarters. The Midshipmen finally scored on a two yard touchdown run by Staubach (who went 22 for 34 for 228 yards), which ended the scoring at 28–6. While the two teams had near even passing yards and near even first downs (18-16), Navy had 29 rushes go for -14 yards while Texas' 43 rushes for 168 yards led to two touchdowns as the Longhorns clinched an undisputed national championship, their first ever. Several Cotton Bowl records were set.

1964 Navy Midshipmen

The team was led by sixth year head coach Wayne Hardin. Team Captain was Fred Marlin. The Midshipmen compiled a 3-6-1 record and were outscored by their opponents by a combined score of 185 to 140. The annual Army–Navy Game was played on November 28 at JFK Memorial Stadium in Philadelphia, PA. Army won 11-8.

Roger Staubach led the team in passing with 1,131 yards and threw 4 touchdown passes. Kip Paskewich led the team in rushing with 363 yards and 5 rushing touchdowns. Ed Orr led the team in receptions with 31 for 299 yards. Paskewich led the team in scoring with 30 points.

Home games were played at Navy-Marine Corps Stadium

9/19/1964	NAVY	**#10**	@		Penn State (6-4)	21	8	**W**
9/26/1964	NAVY	**#10**	vs		WILLIAM & MARY (4-6)	35	6	**W**
10/3/1964	NAVY	**#6**	@	#8	Michigan (9-1)	0	21	**L**
10/9/1964	NAVY		vs		Georgia Tech (7-3)	0	17	**L**
10/17/1964	NAVY		@		California (3-7)	13	27	**L**
10/24/1964	NAVY		@		Pittsburgh (3-5-2)	14	14	**T**
10/31/1964	NAVY		vs	#2	NOTRE DAME (9-1)	0	40	**L**
11/7/1964	NAVY		@		Maryland (5-5)	22	27	**L**
11/14/1964	NAVY		vs		DUKE (4-5-1)	27	14	**W**
11/28/1964	NAVY		vs		ARMY (4-6)	8	11	**L**
Coach: Wayne Hardin					**Season Record >>**	**140**	**185**	**3-6-1**

Schedule Source: Steve's Football Bible LLC

Selected game(s) highlights

#8 Michigan

Michigan defeated Navy 21–0. Navy came into the game ranked No. 5 in the country. The game was marked by 11 turnovers, six by Navy and five by Michigan. Navy quarterbacks threw three interceptions, including two thrown by 1963 Heisman Trophy winner Roger Staubach. Staubach completed 16 of 30 passes for 166 yards. Staubach was eventually forced from the game, limping after being knocked to the turf by Michigan defensive tackle Bill Yearby. The game broke a 20-game streak during which the Midshipmen had not been shut out under Staubach. The New York Times wrote that the Wolverines "brought Roger Staubach, the heroic middie quarterback, back into focus as an ordinary mortal." Michigan wingback Carl Ward rushed for 74 yards on 18 carries and scored two of Michigan's three touchdowns. Fullback Dave Fisher scored Michigan's final touchdown in the third quarter.

Maryland {"Middle Finger incident"}

Before the 1964 game, Maryland supporters stole the Navy mascot, Bill the Goat, but what happened in the game itself was far more controversial. Terrapin players said they would seek revenge against Navy for roughing up Darryl Hill in 1963. Roger Staubach, Navy's Heisman Trophy quarterback, said that "it was not a friendly game ... Jerry [Fishman] did not have friendliness in his eyes. He had an extra mean streak that day." After a punt return, Fishman was penalized for a hard hit that injured receiver Skip Orr directly in front of the Navy stands, intensifying the ever-present heckling from the crowd. In response, Fishman approached the Brigade of Midshipmen section and raised an extended middle finger. After Fishman was penalized again for a late hit on Staubach, Fishman gave the obscene gesture for a second time. High-ranking Navy officers noticed Fishman's middle finger and became incensed. Staubach later said that Fishman "told the fans he thought Maryland was number one and got his fingers wrong." Due to Fishman's actions, Academy officials allowed their contractual obligation to the series to lapse after the 1965 game. Years later, Bud Thalman, Navy sports information director at the time, said the incident had taken place "when there was still some level of sportsmanship in athletes ... It was so out of character it was stunning. There was no inclination from Navy to seek out a renewal. That untoward act of sportsmanship created a bad taste among people."

Navy head coach Wayne Hardin called Fishman's act "a disgrace to college football." Maryland's head coach, Tom Nugent, had a different opinion and said, "Both teams appeared to be just a bunch of red-blooded guys trying to kill each other." The game itself was closely contested. Staubach completed 25 passes, but also threw two interceptions. Late in the fourth quarter, Navy took the lead, 22–21. With less than three minutes remaining, the Midshipmen kicked off and halfback Ken Ambrusko fielded the ball from the Terrapins' end zone. Ambrusko returned it 101 yards for a touchdown, and Maryland won the game, 27–22.

ARMY {@ JFK Memorial Stadium, Philadelphia, PA}

Barry Nickerson's 24 yard field goal helped Army snap a five-game losing streak to Navy with an 11-8 triumph. The Cadet defense made quite a statement on the opening series, as defensive guard Charlie Stowers sacked Navy's Roger Staubach for a safety less than a minute into the game. Army built upon its lead midway through the second quarter when quarterback Rollie Stichweh hit tight end Sam Champi with a five yard touchdown pass. Navy tied the game just before the half when halfback Tom Leiser went up and over from the Army one yard line. A scrambling Staubach found end Phil Norton for the two point conversion. When Nickerson hit the game-winning field goal early in the fourth quarter, it marked Army's first field goal against Navy in 33 years. On its final drive, Navy faced a fourth-and-36 from its own 47, and Staubach's pass fell incomplete.

1965 Navy Midshipmen

The team was led by first-year head coach Bill Elias. Team Captain was Bob Wittenberg. The Midshipmen compiled a 4-4-2 record and were outscored by their opponents by a combined score of 129 to 128. The annual Army–Navy Game was played on November 27 at JFK Memorial Stadium in Philadelphia, PA. The game ended in a 7-7 tie.

John Cartwright led the team in passing with 935 yards and threw 6 touchdown passes. Terry Murray led the team in rushing with 391 yards and 4 rushing touchdowns. Phil Norton led the team in receptions with 35 for 429 yards. Murray led the team in scoring with 30 points.

Home games were played at Navy-Marine Corps Stadium

9/18/1965	NAVY	vs		SYRACUSE (7-3)	6	14	L
9/25/1965	NAVY	@		Stanford (6-3-1)	7	7	**T**
10/2/1965	NAVY	@		Oklahoma (3-7)	10	0	W
10/9/1965	NAVY	vs		WILLIAM & MARY (6-4)	42	14	W
10/16/1965	NAVY	vs		PITTSBURGH (3-7)	12	0	W
10/23/1965	NAVY	@		Georgia Tech (7-3-1)	16	37	L
10/30/1965	NAVY	@	#4	Notre Dame (7-2-1)	3	29	L
11/6/1965	NAVY	vs		MARYLAND (4-6)	19	7	W
11/13/1965	NAVY	@		Penn State (5-5)	6	14	L
11/27/1965	NAVY	vs		ARMY (4-5-1)	7	7	**T**
Coach: Bill Elias				**Season Record >>**	128	129	**4-4-2**

Schedule Source: Steve's Football Bible LLC

Selected game(s) highlights

Oklahoma

In the only meeting between these two teams, the Naval Academy traveled to Norman to play the Sooners in front of over 56,000 spectators. The Midshipmen opened a 10-0 halftime lead and that was all it needed to defeat Oklahoma. The Midshipmen dominated both sides of the football as they amassed 376 yards of total offense while holding the Sooners to 83 total yards.

ARMY {@ JFK Memorial Stadium, Philadelphia, PA}

With each team mustering just one first down in the second half, the 1965 Army-Navy tilt struggled to a 7-7 tie. The game jumped out to an exciting start, as Sonny Stowers' 25 yard touchdown run gave Army a 7-0 lead. Quarterback John Cartwright got the Midshipmen on the board with an eight yard touchdown pass to Terry Murray just before intermission. The 353 yards of total offense between the two teams represented the series' lowest total since 1939 (321). This was also the sixth tie in 66 Army-Navy games and the first since 1956 (also by the score of 7-7).

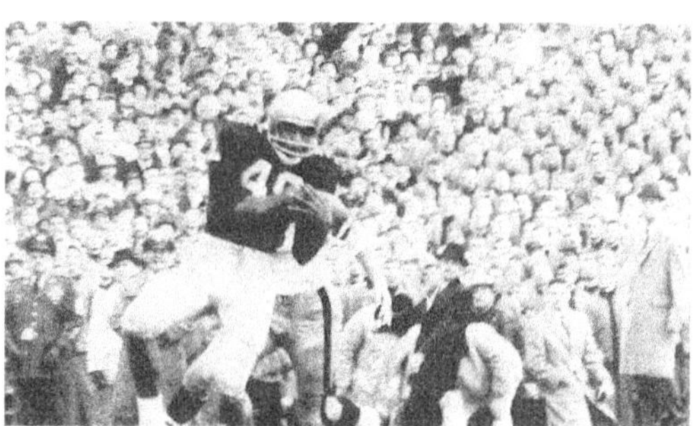

Calvin Huey (pictured at right) became the first Black player to play for Navy in the Army-Navy game.

1966 Navy Midshipmen

The team was led by second year head coach Bill Elias. Team Captain was Don Downing. The Midshipmen compiled a 4-6 record and were outscored by their opponents by a combined score of 152 to 147. The annual Army–Navy Game was played on November 26 at JFK Memorial Stadium in Philadelphia, PA. Army won 20-7.

John Cartwright led the team in passing with 1,146 yards and threw 10 touchdown passes. Terry Murray led the team in rushing with 663 yards. Rob Taylor led the team in receptions with 55 for 727 yards and 4 TD receptions. Murray led the team in scoring with 36 points.

Home games were played at Navy-Marine Corps Stadium

9/17/1966	NAVY		vs		BOSTON COLLEGE (4-6)	27	7	W
9/24/1966	NAVY		@		Smu (8-3)	3	21	L
10/1/1966	NAVY		@		AIR FORCE (4-6)	7	15	L
10/8/1966	NAVY		@		Syracuse (8-3)	14	28	L
10/15/1966	NAVY		@		Pittsburgh (1-9)	24	7	W
10/22/1966	NAVY		vs		WILLIAM & MARY (5-4-1)	21	0	W
10/29/1966	NAVY		vs	#1	NOTRE DAME (9-0-1)	7	31	L
11/5/1966	NAVY		vs		DUKE (5-5)	7	9	L
11/12/1966	NAVY		@		Vanderbilt (1-9)	30	14	W
11/26/1966	NAVY		vs		ARMY (8-2)	7	20	L
Coach: Bill Elias					**Season Record >>**	147	152	4-6

Schedule Source: Steve's Football Bible LLC

Selected game(s) highlights

#1 NOTRE DAME {@ JFK Memorial Stadium – Philadelphia, PA}

Navy a defensive going-over in a 31-7 load of action at John F. Kennedy Stadium. Johnny Pergine put on a one-man show while picking off three Navy passes. In the fourth period, with the Irish leading, 24-0, the Sailors ganged up on substitute punter Bob Gladieux. Heading the charge was six-footer Jim Goebel who deflected the ball back to the goal line, where Jon Bergner, another six-footer, fell on it for the score. Dave Church then place-kicked the extra point. For the Irish, Terry Hanratty went over for two touchdowns. Larry Conjar and Gladieux scored once each after Joe Azarro started the point production with a 42 yard field goal in the first period. He also kicked the four extra points.

ARMY {@ JFK Memorial Stadium, Philadelphia, PA}

Keyed by a pair of Steve Lindell touchdown passes in the fourth quarter, Army capped off its best season (8-2) since 1958 with a 20-7 win over Navy. Sophomore Charlie Jarvis opened the scoring with a 49 yard touchdown run in the first quarter. Lindell's extra point gave the Cadets a 7-0 lead. Under the efficient direction of quarterback John Cartwright, Navy tied the score at seven when Cartwright and Rob Taylor hooked up on a seven yard touchdown pass. The Midshipmen had three opportunities to take the lead in the third quarter but were unable to convert on any of them. The first drive stalled on the Army 47, Cartwright was intercepted inside the Army 20 yard line and John Church's 42 yard field goal attempt was blocked. Lindell then worked his fourth-quarter magic to ensure Army's victory.

1967 Navy Midshipmen

The team was led by third year head coach Bill Elias. Team Captain was Bill Dow. The Midshipmen compiled a 5-4-1 record and were outscored by their opponents by a combined score of 253 to 205. The annual Army–Navy Game was played on December 2 at JFK Memorial Stadium in Philadelphia, PA. Navy won 19--14.

John Cartwright led the team in passing with 1,537 yards and threw 9 touchdown passes. Jeri Balsey led the team in rushing with 559 yards. Cartwright led with 6 rushing touchdowns. **Rob Taylor led the team in receptions with 61, a Navy single season record, for 818 yards, a single season record,** and 6 TD receptions. **Taylor also set single game records for receptions with 10** in three separate games, vs Vanderbilt, William & Mary and Penn State. **Taylor also set the single game record with 179 yards** vs Vanderbilt. Cartwright and Taylor led the team in scoring with 36 points.

Home games were played at Navy-Marine Corps Stadium

9/23/1967		vs		PENN STATE (8-2-1)	23	22	W	*-Taylor 10 receptions
9/30/1967		@		Rice (4-6)	7	21	L	
10/7/1967		@		Michigan (4-6)	26	21	W	
10/14/1967		vs		SYRACUSE (8-2)	27	14	W	
10/21/1967		vs		WILLIAM & MARY (5-4-1)	16	27	L	*-Taylor 10 receptions
10/28/1967		@		Pittsburgh (1-9)	22	21	W	
11/4/1967		@	#10	Notre Dame (8-2)	14	43	L	
11/11/1967		vs		DUKE (4-6)	16	35	L	
11/18/1967		vs		VANDERBILT (2-7-1)	35	35	T	*-Taylor 10 receptions
12/2/1967		vs		ARMY (8-2)	19	14	W	*-Clark 10 receptions
Coach: Bill Elias				**Season Record >>**	**205**	**253**	**5-4-1**	

Schedule Source: Steve's Football Bible LLC
***-Single game record**

Selected game(s) highlights

Michigan

Michigan lost to Navy, 26–21, before a crowd of 72,361 at Michigan Stadium. Michigan halfback Ron Johnson rushed for 270 yards, including touchdown runs of 62 and 72 yards. Johnson's effort broke the Michigan single-game rushing record of 216 yards set in 1943 by Bill Daley. Navy took a 17-14 lead into halftime on a Balsy 3 yard run and a Rob Taylor 15 yard touchdown pass from John Cartwright. John Church kicked two field goals and Terry Murray scored the winning touchdown on a 25 yard run in the 4th quarter.

WILLIAM & MARY

William & Mary football pulled off one of the great football upsets on Oct. 21, 1967, when it defeated the Naval Academy 27-16. Ranked sixth nationally and No. 1 in the East. A three-touchdown barrage in the final quarter brought the Tribe from behind for a 27-16 decision. It was W&M's first win over Navy since 1942. Down 16-0 midway through the third quarter, William and Mary struck back on the passing of Dan Darragh, scoring four touchdowns within 14 minutes to scuttle a team that had been labeled best in the East. A Darragh to Steve Slotnick pass play that covered 51 yards shoved the Indians in front with 3:05 to go, and when Terry Morton drove two yards into the end zone less than a minute and a half later to provide the clincher, a stunned crowd of 19,542 began moving towards the exits. Navy had been a 21-point favorite. For more than 40 minutes, Navy seemed to have matters well in hand. William and Mary's most serious scoring bid had been a thrust that reached the Middie 36 late in the first half, and when Rick Bayer swiped a Darragh pass for the second time and returned it 48 yards for a touchdown 9:41 into the third period, the rest seemed highly predictable.

#10 Notre Dame

Navy kicked away an early scoring opportunity, then kicked away the game as powerful Notre Dame annihilated the frustrated Midshipmen, 43 to 14, in Notre Dame Stadium. Navy scored both its T.D.'s in the second half on short runs by quarterback John Cartwright. Notre Dame stormed to 30 first downs against 12 for Navy. The Irish racked up 313 yards on the ground while compiling a total offense of 509 yards, more than double Navy's mark.

ARMY {@ JFK Memorial Stadium, Philadelphia, PA}

After operating all season from the T-formation, Navy switched to the I-formation for the annual Army contest. It helped the Midshipmen jump out to a 17-point lead and hold on for a 19-14 victory. The Army defense entered the season finale allowing a mere eight points per game but surrendered twice that many by halftime. Touchdown runs by Dan Pike and Jeri Balsly sandwiched a 29 yard John Church field goal to give the Midshipmen a 17-0 lead. Navy stretched the lead to 19-0 in the third quarter when Bill Dow tackled Army punter Nick Kurilko in the end zone for a safety. To energize his struggling offense, Army Coach Tom Cahill inserted quarterback Jim O'Toole into the game. O'Toole led the Cadets into the end zone on two-straight occasions, including a 52 yard scoring strike to end Gary Steele. Army was driving to take the lead when Charlie Jarvis fumbled on the Navy 23 yard line with four minutes remaining. The Midshipmen then ran out the clock to preserve the five-point triumph.

1968 Navy Midshipmen

The team was led by fourth year head coach Bill Elias. Team Captain was Mike Clark. The Midshipmen compiled a 2-8 record and were outscored by their opponents by a combined score of 303 to 136. The annual Army–Navy Game was played on November 30 at JFK Memorial Stadium in Philadelphia, PA. Army won 21—14.

Mike McNallen led the team in passing with 1,342 yards and threw 6 touchdown passes. Dan Pike led the team in rushing with 500 yards. Pike and McNallen led with 4 rushing touchdowns and led in scoring with 24 points. Bill Newton led the team in receptions with 29 for 358 yards.

Home games were played at Navy-Marine Corps Stadium

9/21/1968	NAVY		@	#10	Penn State (11-0)		6	31	L
9/28/1968	NAVY		vs		BOSTON COLLEGE (6-3)		15	49	L
10/5/1968	NAVY		@		Michigan (8-2)		9	32	L
10/12/1968	NAVY		vs		Air Force (7-3)		20	26	L
10/19/1968	NAVY		vs		PITTSBURGH (1-9)		17	16	W
10/26/1968	NAVY		vs		VIRGINIA (7-3)		0	24	L
11/2/1968	NAVY		vs	#12	NOTRE DAME (7-2-1)		14	45	L
11/9/1968	NAVY		@		Georgia Tech (4-6)		35	15	W
11/16/1968	NAVY		@		Syracuse (6-4)		6	44	L
11/30/1968	NAVY		vs		ARMY (7-3)	ABC	14	21	L
Coach: Bill Elias					**Season Record >>**		**136**	**303**	**2-8**

Schedule Source: Steve's Football Bible LLC

Selected game(s) highlights

Michigan

Michigan defeated Navy by a 32 to 9 score in front of a crowd of 56,501 spectators at Michigan Stadium. Ron Johnson gained 121 yards on 22 carries. Michigan's five touchdowns were scored as follows: two yard run by Johnson in the second quarter; three yard run by Dennis Brown in the second quarter; 19 yard pass from Brown to Jim Mandich in the second quarter; 39 yard run by Johnson in the third quarter; and one yard run by Greg Harrison in the fourth quarter. George Hoey returned a punt 63 yards to set up Johnson's first touchdown and returned another punt 36 yards to set up Brown's touchdown pass to Mandich. Hoey also intercepted two Navy passes, returning one of them 48 yards. Tim Killian kicked two out of five extra point attempts and missed a field goal attempt. Navy did not score its lone touchdown until 30 seconds remained in the game, while Michigan's reserves were on the field. Michigan gained 185 rushing yard and 175 passing yards in the game. Navy gained 92 rushing yards and 247 passing yards

ARMY {@ JFK Memorial Stadium, Philadelphia, PA}

Leading by a touchdown midway through the third quarter, Army faced a third-and-eight at its own 35 yard line. Army quarterback Steve Lindell dropped back to pass, only to be hit by defensive end Mike Lettieri. Defensive tackle Tom LaForce caught the fluttering football and raced 36 yards for the tying touchdown. However, backup quarterback Jim O'Toole came on to engineer the game-winning drive late in the third quarter, as running back Charlie Jarvis scored his third touchdown of the day. Early in the fourth quarter, it appeared as if the Midshipmen were poised to take the lead again, driving 63 yards to set up a fourth-and-five at the Cadet 12 yard line. Mike McNallen completed the pass to Mike Clark, but he was stopped two yards short of the first down and Army held on for a 21-14 victory.

1969 Navy Midshipmen

Navy was led by first-year head coach Rick Forzano. Team Captains were Dan Pike and Jeff Kristich. The Midshipmen compiled a 1-9 record and were outscored by their opponents by a combined score of 307 to 98. The annual Army– Navy Game was played on November 29 at JFK Memorial Stadium in Philadelphia, PA. Army won 27-0.

Mike McNallen led the team in passing with 1,312 yards and threw 4 touchdown passes. Dan Pike led the team in rushing with 329 yards. Mick Barr led the team in receptions with 19. Karl Schwelm led with 316 receiving yards. Ron Marchetti led the team in scoring with 24 points.

Home games were played at Navy-Marine Corps Stadium

9/20/1969	NAVY		vs	#3	PENN STATE (11-0)	22	45	L
9/27/1969	NAVY		@		Boston College (5-4)	14	21	L
10/4/1969	NAVY		@	#4	Texas (11-0)	17	56	L
10/11/1969	NAVY		@		Pittsburgh (4-6)	19	46	L
10/18/1969	NAVY		@		Rutgers (6-3)	6	20	L
10/25/1969	NAVY		vs		VIRGINIA (3-7)	10	0	W
11/1/1969	NAVY		@	#10	Notre Dame (8-2-1)	0	47	L
11/7/1969	NAVY		@		Miami (4-6)	10	30	L
11/15/1969	NAVY		vs		SYRACUSE (5-5)	0	15	L
11/29/1969	NAVY		vs		ARMY (4-5-1)	0	27	L
Coach: Rick Forzano					**Season Record >>**	**98**	**307**	**1-9**

Schedule Source: Steve's Football Bible LLC

Selected game(s) highlights

Rutgers

Rutgers, led by sophomore tailback Larry Robertson, sent Navy down to its fifth straight defeat of the season today, 20 to 6, before 27,000 fans in Rutgers Stadium. Robertson, a first-time starter, responded with three touchdowns and gained 161 yards on 34 carries. Robertson scored on a 14 yard run, a 14 yard pass from quarterback Rich Policastro and a 30 yard run. Navy's only score came in the final 56 seconds of play. Mike McNallen, one of the top passers in the nation entering the contest, completed only 10 of 41 passes for 135 yards and the Navy ground attack managed only 69 yards against the tough Rutgers defense.

ARMY {@ JFK Memorial Stadium, Philadelphia, PA}

The new power-I offense installed by Army coach Tom Cahill overwhelmed the Navy defense in the 1969 matchup. Tailback Lynn Moore carried the football 40 times for 206 yards as the Cadets rolled over the Midshipmen, 27-0. While the Army offense was certainly productive, the efforts of the Cadet defense did not go unnoticed. Navy appeared to be on its way to a touchdown just before halftime, but John Bremner picked off quarterback Mike McNallen's pass at the Army 23 yard line. Finally, Navy was inside the Army one yard line late in the fourth quarter, but a dramatic goal-line stand preserved Army's first series shutout in 20 years.

1970 Navy Midshipmen

Navy was led by second year head coach Rick Forzano. Team Captain was Bill McKinney. The Midshipmen compiled a 2-9 record and were outscored by their opponents by a combined score of 327 to 131. The annual Army–Navy Game was played on November 28 at JFK Memorial Stadium in Philadelphia, PA. Navy won 11-7.

Mike McNallen led the team in passing with 1,342 yards and threw 3 touchdown passes. Andy Pease led the team in rushing with 399 yards. Mick Barr led the team in receptions with 34. Karl Schwelm led with 501 receiving yards. Pease led the team in scoring with 18 points. **Mark Schickner tied a single game record with 4 interceptions vs Army.**

Home games were played at Navy-Marine Corps Stadium

9/12/1970	NAVY		vs		COLGATE (5-6)	48	22	W	
9/19/1970	NAVY		@	#7	Penn State (7-3)	7	55	L	
9/26/1970	NAVY		vs		BOSTON COLLEGE (8-2)	14	28	L	
10/3/1970	NAVY		@		Washington (6-4)	7	56	L	
10/10/1970	NAVY		vs		PITTSBURGH (5-5)	8	10	L	
10/17/1970	NAVY		vs	#7	AIR FORCE (9-3)	3	26	L	
10/24/1970	NAVY		@		Syracuse (6-4)	8	23	L	
10/31/1970	NAVY		vs	#3	NOTRE DAME (10-1)	7	56	L	
11/7/1970	NAVY		@		Georgia Tech (9-3)	8	30	L	
11/14/1970	NAVY		vs		VILLANOVA (9-2)	10	14	L	
11/28/1970	NAVY		vs		ARMY (1-9-1)	11	7	W	*-Schickner 4 INT's
Coach: Rick Forzano					**Season Record >>**	131	327	2-9	

Schedule Source: Steve's Football Bible LLC
***-Single game record**

Selected game(s) highlights

#3 NOTRE DAME

Joe Theismann guided the Irish to win number six and a 56-7 thrashing of the Naval Academy. Darryl Dewan, playing for a shaken up Ed Gulyas, carried the ball six times for thirty yards and a touchdown as the Irish drew first blood on an eighty yard march after the opening kickoff. The Irish defensive unit shut the Middies off for the rest of the afternoon. Thirteen times the defense forced the Middies to turn the ball over and seven of those times the offense drove the ball over Navy's goal line. By the final gun the Irish had piled up 408 rushing yards and six rushing TD's.

ARMY {@ JFK Memorial Stadium, Philadelphia, PA}

Entering the 1970 season finale, Navy had given up 32 points per game. Yet, it was the Midshipmen defense that came up big in an 11-7 win over Army. Navy defensive back Mark Schickner, who did not even play football the previous fall, intercepted a series-record four passes to preserve the Mids' second win of the year. His last interception was particularly valuable because it came on the Navy 12 yard line with less than a minute to play. The game remained scoreless until the third quarter when Dick Atha and Joe Albano connected on a 42 yard touchdown pass. Navy's Joe Elfein quickly erased that advantage with a 40 yard touchdown run which, combined with a two-point conversion pass from Mike McNallen to Karl Schwelm, gave Navy an 8-7 lead. Roger Lanning then iced the win with a 33 yard field goal in the fourth quarter.

1971 Navy Midshipmen

Navy was led by third year head coach Rick Forzano. Team Captain was Rick Porterfield. The Midshipmen compiled a 3-8 record and were outscored by their opponents by a combined score of 331 to 146. The annual Army–Navy Game was played on November 27 at JFK Memorial Stadium in Philadelphia, PA. Army won 24-23. Fred Stuvek led the team in passing with 1,125 yards and threw 6 touchdown passes. Dan Howard led the team in rushing with 411 yards. Larry Van Loan led the team in receptions with 41 for 589 yards. Andy Pease led the team in scoring with 24 points.

Home games were played at Navy-Marine Corps Stadium

9/11/1971	NAVY		@		Virginia (3-8)	10	6	W
9/18/1971	NAVY	vs		#14	PENN STATE (11-1)	3	56	L
9/25/1971	NAVY		@		Boston College (9-2)	6	49	L
10/2/1971	NAVY		@	#2	Michigan (11-1)	0	46	L
10/9/1971	NAVY		@		Pittsburgh (3-8)	35	36	L
10/15/1971	NAVY		@		Miami (4-7)	16	31	L
10/23/1971	NAVY	vs		#19	DUKE (6-5)	15	14	W
10/30/1971	NAVY		@	#12	Notre Dame (8-2)	0	21	L
11/6/1971	NAVY		@		Georgia Tech (6-6)	21	34	L
11/13/1971	NAVY	vs			SYRACUSE (5-5-1)	17	14	W
11/27/1971	NAVY	vs			ARMY (6-4)	23	24	L
Coach: Rick Forzano					**Season Record >>**	**146**	**331**	**3-8**

Schedule Source: Steve's Football Bible LLC

Selected game(s) highlights

#2 Michigan

Michigan defeated Navy, 46–0, in front of 68,168 spectators in Michigan Stadium. The game marked the first time since 1948 that a Michigan football team had shut out three consecutive opponents. Michigan's running backs scored five rushing touchdowns, two by Alan Walker and one each by Billy Taylor, Harry Banks, and Fritz Seyferth. With 76 rushing yards, Taylor passed Tom Harmon and moved into second place among Michigan's career rushing leaders. Ed Shuttlesworth also ran for a two-point conversion in the second quarter. Kevin Casey started his fourth game at quarterback and completed only one pass for eight yards, as Tom Slade, Larry Cipa and Jack McBride replaced him after the first quarter and jointly completed eight of 13 passes for 145 yards. Cipa threw a 49 yard touchdown pass to Mike Oldham with three minutes remaining in the game. Dana Coin converted five points after touchdown and kicked a field goal. Michigan out-gained Navy by 428 yards to 71 yards.

ARMY {@ JFK Memorial Stadium, Philadelphia, PA}

In typical Army-Navy fashion, the 1971 contest went right down to the wire. This time, however, it was the Cadets who came out on top, 24-23. This marked the first one-point game in series history. Army had jumped out to a 16-0 first-quarter lead, thanks to two Bob Hines touchdowns and a 42 yard field goal by James Barclay (only Army's second series field goal in the last 40 years). By the third quarter, however, the Midshipmen had reached the end zone three times themselves, as a 12 yard Freddie Stuvek-to-Steve Ogden pass gave the Midshipmen a 21-16 lead. Army quarterback Kingsley Fink opened the fourth quarter with a five yard touchdown pass to Ed Francis to help the Cadets regain the lead, 24-21. On the ensuing drive, Navy began a seven-minute drive that was brought to a halt when Stuvek's fourth-down pass was intercepted at the Army four yard line. The Midshipmen regained possession at the Army 39 with less than two minutes to go. Stuvek drove his offense to the seven yard line and appeared to pick up six more yards on an option pitch to George Perry, but officials ruled that Stuvek's knee was down before he gave up the football. Navy turned the ball back over on downs, and Army punter Ron Dahnof ran off the final eight seconds in the end zone, giving Navy a safety, but Army the win.

1972 Navy Midshipmen

Navy was led by fourth year head coach Rick Forzano. Team Captain was Jim Garban. The Midshipmen compiled a 4-7 record and were outscored by their opponents by a combined score of 257 to 181. The annual Army–Navy Game was played on December 2 at JFK Memorial Stadium in Philadelphia, PA. Army won 23-15.

Al Glenny led the team in passing with 1,091 yards and threw 7 touchdown passes. Cleveland Cooper led the team in rushing with 1,046 yards. Dan Howard led with 6 rushing touchdowns. Bert Calland led the team in receptions with 61 for 650 yards. Howard led the team in scoring with 42 points.

Home games were played at Navy-Marine Corps Stadium

9/16/1972	NAVY	vs		WILLIAM & MARY (5-6)	13	9	W
9/23/1972	NAVY	@	#11	Penn State (10-2)	10	21	L
9/30/1972	NAVY	vs		BOSTON COLLEGE (4-7)	27	20	W
10/7/1972	NAVY	@	#5	Michigan (10-1)	7	35	L
10/14/1972	NAVY	@		Syracuse (5-6)	14	30	L
10/21/1972	NAVY	@	#16	Air Force (6-4)	21	17	W
10/28/1972	NAVY	vs		DUKE (5-6)	16	17	L
11/4/1972	NAVY	vs	#12	NOTRE DAME (8-3)	23	42	L
11/11/1972	NAVY	vs		PITTSBURGH (1-10)	28	13	W
11/18/1972	NAVY	@		Georgia Tech (7-4-1)	7	30	L
12/2/1972	NAVY	vs		ARMY (6-4)	15	23	L
Coach: Rick Forzano				**Season Record >>**	181	257	4-7

Schedule Source: Steve's Football Bible LLC

Selected game(s) highlights

#5 Michigan

Michigan defeated Navy, 35–7, in front of a crowd of 81,131 at Michigan Stadium. Quarterback Dennis Franklin ran six yards around the left end for the first touchdown in the second quarter. Michigan scored 28 points in the third quarter. The quarter began with Navy's Ike Owens fumbling the opening kickoff after being hit by defensive end Mark Jacoby. Franklin then threw a nine-yard touchdown pass to Bo Rather. Four minutes later, Dave Brown scored on an 83 yard punt return for touchdown, tying a Michigan school record. Chuck Heater scored next on a 13 yard run around left end on an option pitchout from Franklin. Michigan scored its fourth touchdown of the third quarter on a 10 yard touchdown pass from Franklin to Paul Seal. Mike Lantry successfully converted five of five extra points. Michigan led 35-0 at the end of the third quarter, but Navy scored a late touchdown on a short pass.

#16 Air Force

Dan Howard took a pitchout and ran yards around left end to score with 31 seconds left today, giving Navy a 21-17 upset football victory over Air Force Academy. It was the Falcons' first defeat of the season. Navy had moved ahead in the third period on a 30-yard scoring pass play from Glenny to his tight end, Steve Ogden. Air Force rallied with 6:36 to play on a 60-yard touchdown pass play from Rich Haynie to Bob Farr that made the score 17-14. Then Navy took the ball on its 20 and drove to the Air Force 5, with Howard carrying six times. Al Glenny pitched the ball to Howard, and he cut inside two tacklers to score the winning touchdown.

#12 NOTRE DAME

Starting with Gary Diminick's 84-yard kickoff return for a touchdown, Notre Dame ran roughshod over Navy. Navy was at the mercy of an Irish offense which, running both inside and outside with ease and passing infrequently but successfully, built up a 35-0 halftime lead. Notre Dame powered for 282 yards on the ground in the first half and amassed a total of 526 yards rushing by the end of the game.

ARMY {@ JFK Memorial Stadium, Philadelphia, PA}

Army and Navy may be well known for their respective efficient, ball-control offenses, but it was a defensive play that keyed Army's 23-15 win in 1972. Army sheared Navy's lead to 12-7 early in the third quarter, thanks to a 43 yard touchdown dash by Bob Hines. Navy drove right back down the field on the ensuing possession, only to stall on the Army 12 yard line. Roger Lanning came on to try a 29 yard field goal, only to have it blocked by the Cadets' Tim Pfister. Scot Beaty retrieved the loose ball and raced 84 yards with the go-ahead touchdown. A Bruce Simpson 21 yard touchdown run extended the lead to 20-12, and Jim Barclay's 23 yard field goal iced the win. Despite the loss, running back Cleveland Cooper etched his name into the Navy record book. His 135 yards on 26 attempts gave him 1,006 yards for the year, the first Midshipmen player to reach this plateau.

1973 Navy Midshipmen {Commander-in-Chief Trophy}

Navy was led by first-year head coach George Welsh (pictured at right). Team Captain was Charlie Miletich. The Midshipmen compiled a 4-7 record and were outscored by their opponents by a combined score of 232 to 221. The annual Army–Navy Game was played on December 1 at JFK Memorial Stadium in Philadelphia, PA. Navy won 51-0.

Al Glenny led the team in passing with 1,295 yards and threw 9 touchdown passes. Cleveland Copper led the team in rushing with 898 yards and 12 rushing touchdowns. Larry Van Loan led the team in receptions with 33 for 542 yards and 4 TD receptions. Coper led the team in scoring with 72 points.

Home games were played at Navy-Marine Corps Stadium

9/15/1973	NAVY	@		VMI (3-8)	37	6	W
9/22/1973	NAVY	vs	#7	PENN STATE (12-0)	0	39	L
9/29/1973	NAVY	@	#4	Michigan (10-0-1)	0	14	L
10/6/1973	NAVY	@		Boston College (7-4)	7	44	L
10/13/1973	NAVY	vs		SYRACUSE (2-9)	23	14	W
10/20/1973	NAVY	vs		AIR FORCE (6-4)	42	6	W
10/27/1973	NAVY	@		Pittsburgh (6-5-1)	17	22	L
11/3/1973	NAVY	@	#5	Notre Dame (11-0)	7	44	L
11/10/1973	NAVY	@		Tulane (9-3)	15	17	L
11/17/1973	NAVY	vs		Georgia Tech (5-6)	22	26	L
12/1/1973	NAVY	vs		ARMY (0-10)	51	0	W
Coach: George Welsh				**Season Record >>**	**221**	**232**	**4-7**

Schedule Source: Steve's Football Bible LLC

Selected game(s) highlights

#4 Michigan

Michigan defeated Navy, 14-0, in front of a Band Day crowd of 88,042 at Michigan Stadium. Michigan's two touchdowns were scored by Chuck Heater on an eight yard run in the first quarter and Ed Shuttlesworth on a one yard run in the third quarter. Navy completed 17 of 30 passes for 173 yards and three interceptions, with a touchdown pass being deflected at the last second by Dave Brown. Navy outgained Michigan with 320 yard of total offense to 285 for Michigan. Michigan completed only one pass for four yards on three attempts.

#5 Notre Dame

Notre Dame amassed 540 yards total offense, including 447 rushing. The Irish defense, top ranked statistically among major college teams, allowed Navy only 195. The Middies managed their only touchdown on a 25-yard pass from Al Glenny to Larry Van Loan early in the fourth quarter following a fumbled punt. Notre Dame put the game out of reach with a pair of touchdowns less than two minutes apart early in the third quarter. An interception by Greg Collins and a diving 18-yard catch by Pete Demrnerle positioned Clements 1-yard scoring run. A fumble recovery deep in navy territory helped extend the margin to 28-0.

ARMY {@ JFK Memorial Stadium, Philadelphia, PA}

A 31-point second quarter fueled the most lopsided victory in series history, as Navy routed Army, 51-0. This bettered the 38-0 win the Cadets posted over the Midshipmen in 1949. In addition, for the first time in series history, a team had two players rush for 100 yards in the same game. Ed Gilmore's 123 yards on 15 carries paced an offense that piled up 460 total yards, while Cleveland Cooper added 102 yards. Of course, it didn't hurt matters that Army turned the ball over five times.

1974 Navy Midshipmen

Navy was led by second year head coach George Welsh. Team Captains were Cliff Collier and Tim Harden. The Midshipmen compiled a 4-7 record and were outscored by their opponents by a combined score of 229 to 131. The annual Army–Navy Game was played on November 30 at JFK Memorial Stadium in Philadelphia, PA. Navy won 19-0.

Phil Poirier led the team in passing with 656 yards. Cleveland Cooper led the team in rushing with 638 yards. Robin Ameen led the team in receptions with 26 for 403 yards. Bob Jackson led the team in scoring with 24 points.

Home games were played at Navy-Marine Corps Stadium

9/14/1974	NAVY		vs		VIRGINIA (4-7)	35	28	W
9/21/1974	NAVY		@	#8	Penn State (10-2)	7	6	W
9/28/1974	NAVY		@	#5	Michigan (10-1)	0	52	L
10/5/1974	NAVY		vs		BOSTON COLLEGE (8-3)	0	37	L
10/12/1974	NAVY		@		Syracuse (2-9)	9	17	L
10/19/1974	NAVY		@		Air Force (2-9)	16	19	L
10/26/1974	NAVY		vs		PITTSBURGH (7-4)	11	13	L
11/2/1974	NAVY		vs	#7	NOTRE DAME (10-2)	6	14	L
11/9/1974	NAVY		vs		THE CITADEL (4-7)	28	21	W
11/16/1974	NAVY		@		Georgia Tech (6-5)	0	22	L
11/30/1974	NAVY		vs		ARMY (3-8)	19	0	W
Coach: George Welsh					**Season Record >>**	131	229	4-7

Schedule Source: Steve's Football Bible LLC

Selected game(s) highlights

#8 Penn State

The Nittany Lions were ranked #8, just off the magical 1973 season that featured an undefeated record and Heisman trophy for John Cappelletti. Then the rain came, and with it, the fumbles. Penn State would finish the day with five of them, allowing Navy to hold on to the slimmest of margins all day. The Nittany Lions would rush for 267 yards and out-first-down Navy 20-6. But between the fumbles and Chris Bahr's four missed field goals--one as time ran out--doomed Penn State as Navy recorded a remarkable 7-6 upset victory.

#5 Michigan

Michigan defeated George Welsh's Navy Midshipmen by a 52-0 score. The game was played at Michigan Stadium before a crowd of 104,232, which included thousands of high school band students participating in the annual band day celebration. Michigan's backs dominated, rushing for 340 yards and six touchdowns on 67 carries. Gordon Bell rushed for 57 yards and three touchdowns on nine carries, Chuck Heater gained 61 yards and two on 13 carries, and Rob Lytle rushed for 101 yards and a touchdown on 15 carries. Dennis Franklin completed five of six passes for 85 yards, including a 29 yard touchdown pass to Jim Smith in the third quarter. Mike Lantry kicked a 31 yard field goal and converted all seven extra points.

BOSTON COLLEGE

Keith Garnette scored three touchdowns and Mike Esposito rambled for 154 yards to lead Boston College to a surprisingly easy 38-to-0 football victory over punchless Navy. The Middies, who have not scored a touchdown in the last 10 quarters, were once again victimized by their own mistakes and penalties. A Navy fumble and an interception handed Boston College two touchdowns in the first quarter and the Eagles drove 68 yards for another touchdown in the opening quarter for a 20-to-0 lead. Then, Navy committed almost every mistake possible to comeback. Penalties repeatedly nullified substantial Middie gains. While the offense was sputtering under quarterbacks Phil Poierer, Mike Yeager and Mike

Rohan, the defense was no match for the hard-running Barnette and Esposito, who led the Eagles to 274 yards rushing.

Air Force

After falling behind 3-0, the Falcons responded with two Dave Lawson field goals to take the lead, 6-3. Navy forged ahead on a 1 yard Kevin Sullivan pass to Phil Poirier and a Bob Jackson 6 yard run. Trailing 16-6 one play into the 4th quarter, Ken Wood started the Air Force comeback with a 1 yard touchdown run. Dave Lawson kicked a 34 yard field goal tie the game with 2:08 left in the game. Air Force got the ball back with little time left, but marched down the field and Lawson came through again, kicking a game winning 31 yard field with 8 seconds left, to give the Falcons a 19-16 victory.

#7 Notre Dame {JFK Stadium - Philadelphia, Pennsylvania}

The 14–6 win over Navy was a turning point in Notre Dame Football history; on the flight back from Philadelphia, a weary Ara Parseghian decided he would leave football. He had important family considerations and constant pressure; the fun was gone. The fighting Irish probably played down to the Middies. Goodman fumbled a punt early in the game and Navy kicked a field goal. They added another in the second half for a 6-0 lead. The only decent Fighting Irish drive to that point ended in a missed field goal. The defense turned it up, forced a punt, and Goodman took it back to their 28. Surviving a bad snap at the five, Clements found Demmerle for a touchdown. Randy Harrison made an interception and returned it 40 yards for a touchdown. It was an ugly win, and Clements had his worst day, 5 of 22 with two interceptions.

ARMY {@ JFK Memorial Stadium, Philadelphia, PA}

With President Gerald Ford among the 83,000 fans in attendance, Navy posted its second-straight shutout over Army, 19-0. The Midshipmen once again jumped out to a quick start, as the defense held the Cadets deep in their own territory. Dave Hoopengardner's punt fell at the Army 34 yard line, and Navy quickly went to work. Under the direction of freshman quarterback Mike Roban, the first plebe to start at quarterback for the Midshipmen against Army, Navy managed a 45 yard field goal from Steve Dykes. Bob Jackson added two short touchdown runs, and Navy led 17-0 at halftime. It was time for the Midshipmen defense to shine in the second half, as it stopped Army on a fourth-and-four from the Navy nine yard line on the first drive of the third quarter. Defensive end Tim Harden recorded a safety midway through the third period when he sacked Army quarterback Scott Gillogly in the end zone. Offensively, Cleveland Cooper became the first player in series history to rush for at least 100 yards in three games. He finished his career with 362 yards on 69 carries versus the Cadets.

1975 Navy Midshipmen {Commander-in-Chief Trophy}

Navy was led by third year head coach George Welsh. Team Captains were Chet Moeller and Steve Barilic. The Midshipmen compiled a 7-4 record and outscored their opponents by a combined score of 227 to 125. The annual Army–Navy Game was played on November 29 at JFK Memorial Stadium in Philadelphia, PA. Navy won 30-6. Navy won the Commander-In-Chief Trophy. Moeller {DB} was selected as a consensus All-American.

Phil Poirier led the team in passing with 729 yards. Bob Jackson led the team with 849 yards. Gerald Goodwin led with 7 rushing touchdowns. Kevin Sullivan led the team in receptions with 19 for 336 yards. Goodwin led the team in scoring with 42 points.

Home games were played at Navy-Marine Corps Stadium

9/13/1975	NAVY	@		Virginia (1-10)	42	14	W
9/20/1975	NAVY	vs		CONNECTICUT	55	7	W
9/27/1975	NAVY	@		Washington (6-5)	13	14	L
10/4/1975	NAVY	vs		AIR FORCE (2-8-1)	17	0	W
10/11/1975	NAVY	vs		SYRACUSE (6-5)	10	6	W
10/18/1975	NAVY	@		Boston College (7-4)	3	17	L
10/25/1975	NAVY	@	#17	Pittsburgh (8-4)	17	0	W
11/1/1975	NAVY	@	#15	Notre Dame (8-3)	10	31	L
11/7/1975	NAVY	@		Miami (2-8)	17	16	W
11/15/1975	NAVY	@		Georgia Tech (7-4)	13	14	L
11/29/1975	NAVY	vs		ARMY (2-9)	30	6	W
Coach: George Welsh				**Season Record >>**	**227**	**125**	**7-4**

Schedule Source: Steve's Football Bible LLC

Selected game(s) highlights

AIR FORCE {RFK Stadium – Washington, DC}

The biggest and fastest Navy football team in many seasons, whipped Air Force, 17-0. Jerry Goodwin was the offensive hero as he ran for 132 yards and scored the first touchdown. John Kurowski and Phil Poirier shared direction of the Middies and each man came through quite well. Kurowski guided Navy to its first touchdown on an 82-yard drive of 12 plays the first time Middies had the ball. He pitched to Goodwin for a 43 yard run on the big play of that drive. Goodwin scampered 10 yards on a wide sweep for the touchdown. Then Poirier called the shots on a 57-yard scoring drive of seven plays in the fourth quarter. The senior quarterback concluded the march by throwing a touch-down pass of 8 yards to his wide receiver, Mike Galpin. In between the touchdowns, Larry Muczynski kicked a 25-yard field goal.

Boston College

Mike Kruczek fired touchdown passes of 15 and 27 yards to flanker Mike Godbolt Saturday night and the Boston College defense stopped three fourth quarter drives to scuttle Navy 17-3. All the Boston College scoring came in the first half as Kruczek completed four of five passes, two for touchdowns, and Fred Steinfort kicked a 48 yard field goal. Navy got no closer than the Eagle 48 in the first two quarters, settling for a fourth quarter 38 yard field goal by Larry Muczyinski. Steinfort opened the scoring with the only points of the first quarter capping an Eagle drive which began on the BC nine following a Navy punt.

#15 Notre Dame

Notre' Dame's heralded defensive corps scored two touchdowns and set up a third enroute to a 31-10 Irish victory. Larry Muczynski.put the middies ahead on a 33 yard field goal. It was the end result of a 44 yard, five play drive. Ross Browner brought his scoring production up to eight points by blocking a punt and pouncing on it in the end zone for an Irish score. Phil Poirer threw a 3 yard TD pass to Kevin

Sullivan to pull the Midshipmen within 17-10. The Irish put the game away in the 4th quarter on a Jeff Weston 53 yard interception return for a touchdown and an Al Hunter 5 yard touchdown run.

ARMY {@ JFK Memorial Stadium, Philadelphia, PA}

Navy nearly pitched its third-straight shutout over Army, but Cadet Quarterback Leamon Hall scored a two yard touchdown late in the fourth quarter to make the final score Navy 30, Army 6. Navy kicker Larry Muczynski opened the scoring with a 27 yard field goal in the first quarter. Bob Jackson then scored a two yard touchdown, and Jeff Hoobler blocked an Army punt that Bob DeStafney returned 42 yards for another score. Muczynski not only converted both extra points, but also added a 31 yard field goal just before halftime to give Navy a 20-0 lead heading into the locker room. Jackson (133 yards) and Gerald Goodwin (117 yards) accounted for 250 of Navy's 305 yards on the ground, as the Midshipmen compiled 325 yards of total offense compared to Army's 206.

1976 Navy Midshipmen

Navy was led by fourth year head coach George Welsh. Team Captains were Jeff Sapp and Kevin Sullivan. The Midshipmen compiled a 4-7 record and were outscored by their opponents by a combined score of 257 to 187. The annual Army–Navy Game was played on November 27 at JFK Memorial Stadium in Philadelphia, PA. Navy won 38-10. Navy won the Commander-In-Chief Trophy.

Bob Lescynski led the team in passing with 1,154 yards and threw 9 touchdown passes. Joe Gattuso led the team in rushing with 591 yards and 7 rushing touchdowns. Dave King led the team in receptions with 27 for 443 yards. Gattuso led the team in scoring with 48 points.

Home games were played at Navy-Marine Corps Stadium

9/11/1976	NAVY	vs		RUTGERS (11-0)	3	13	L	
9/18/1976	NAVY	@		Connecticut	21	3	W	
9/25/1976	NAVY	@	#1	Michigan (10-2)	14	70	L	
10/2/1976	NAVY	vs	#15	BOSTON COLLEGE (8-3)	13	17	L	
10/9/1976	NAVY	@		Air Force (4-7)	3	13	L	
10/16/1976	NAVY	vs		WILLIAM & MARY (7-4)	13	21	L	
10/23/1976	NAVY	vs	#2	PITTSBURGH (12-0)	0	45	L	
10/30/1976	NAVY	vs	#11	NOTRE DAME (9-3)	21	27	L	*-King 10 catch
11/6/1976	NAVY	@		Syracuse (3-8)	27	10	W	
11/13/1976	NAVY	vs		GEORGIA TECH (4-6-1)	34	28	W	
11/27/1976	NAVY	vs		ARMY (5-6)	38	10	W	
Coach: George Welsh				**Season Record >>**	**187**	**257**	**4-7**	

Schedule Source: Steve's Football Bible LLC
***-Single game record {*-King 179 receiving yds}**

Selected game(s) highlights

RUTGERS

Rutgers University overpowered a mistake-prone Naval Academy football team, 13 to 3, yesterday in the season opener for both teams before 17,501 spectators in Navy-Marine Corps Memorial Stadium. The young and inexperienced Midshipmen committed two costly errors, a fumble and a pass interception, each leading to a Rutgers touchdown. Navy, which was losing its first season opener in seven years, took a 3-0 lead in the second period, but that was all the scoring the Middies could muster against a big and mobile Rutgers defense. Rutgers, after recovering a Navy fumble at the Scarlet 38, marched 62 yards in 10 plays for its first score. Quarterback Ben Kosup hit split end Mark Twitty with an 18 yard pass 32 seconds before the end of the first half to give Rutgers a 7-3 lead. In the third period, the Scarlet intercepted a pass by John Kurowski at the Rutgers 33 and moved 67 yards in 14 plays for the second touchdown. Fullback Jeff Greczyn went the final 25 yards on an off-tackle slant for the tally. Navy, which had the ball for only four plays during the third period, twice drove deep into Rutgers territory in the final period but could not score. Early in the fourth quarter the Midshipmen marched to the Rutgers 26 but were driven back to the 42, where they were forced to punt. Late in the final period, Navy moved to a first down at the Scarlet 17 but Kurowski, trying to pass, was tackled for four straight losses and Navy gave up the ball at the Rutgers 36.

#1 Michigan

Michigan defeated Navy by a 70-14 score. The game marked the worst defeat in the history of the Naval Academy's football program. Navy took an early lead on a touchdown by quarterback John Kurowski and led 14-12 halfway through the second quarter. Michigan tied the score with its second safety of the second quarter and outscored 49-0 in the second half to put the game out of reach. Quarterback Rick Leach completed 8 of 12 passes for 179 yards and led the scoring with two rushing touchdowns and two passing touchdowns. A total of nine players scored for the Wolverines.

Air Force

The Air Force defense held Navy to 16 yards passing and scored just enough to beat the Midshipmen, 13-3. Rob Shaw ran 64 yards for a touchdown in the 1st quarter and threw a 13 yard TD pass to Scott Jensen in the 4th quarter to account for the Falcons scoring. The Falcons offense totaled 301 yards on the day.

#2 PITTSBURGH

Tony Dorsett became the leading ground gainer in major-college football history when he carried for 180 yards against Navy and set a varsity career rushing record of 5,206 yards over four seasons at Pittsburgh. Dorsett set the record in spectacular fashion—on a run around left end for 32 yards and his third touchdown of the game. Pitt's fine defense held Navy to only 76 yards on the ground and 30 passing.

ARMY {@ JFK Memorial Stadium, Philadelphia, PA}

Quarterback Bob Leszczynski and running backs Joe Gattuso Jr. and Larry Klawinski accounted for 389 of Navy's 428 yards of total offense, which explains the Midshipmen's 38-10 win. Ironically, Navy's punter Art Ohanian played a key role in his team's first two touchdowns. He placed his first kick inside Army's two yard line, which enabled the Midshipmen to get the ball back near midfield after an impressive outing by the Navy defense. Gattuso capped a six-play, 50 yard drive with a two yard scoring plunge. Late in the first quarter, Ohanian nailed a 51 yard punt inside the Army seven yard line. Leszczynski and wide receiver Phil McConkey closed out the drive with an 11 yard touchdown to give the Midshipmen an advantage they'd never relinquish.

1977 Navy Midshipmen

Navy was led by fifth year head coach George Welsh. Team Captains were Joe Gattuso and Mike Galpin. The Midshipmen compiled a 5-6 record and were outscored by their opponents by a combined score of 230 to 229. The annual Army–Navy Game was played on November 26 at JFK Memorial Stadium in Philadelphia, PA. Army won 17-14.

Bob Lescynski led the team in passing with 1,509 yards and threw 8 touchdown passes. Joe Gattuso led the team in rushing with 1,292 yards and 6 rushing touchdowns. Phil McConkey led the team in receptions with 34 for 596 yards and 4 TD receptions. **John Sturges set a Navy team record with 8 interceptions.** Bob Tata led the team in scoring with 53 points.

Home games were played at Navy-Marine Corps Stadium

9/10/1977	NAVY	vs		THE CITADEL (5-6)	21	2	W
9/17/1977	NAVY	vs		CONNECTICUT	38	7	W
9/24/1977	NAVY	@	#1	Michigan (10-2)	7	14	L
10/1/1977	NAVY	@		Duke (5-6)	16	28	L
10/8/1977	NAVY	vs		AIR FORCE (2-8-1)	10	7	W
10/15/1977	NAVY	@	#17	Pittsburgh (9-2-1)	17	34	L
10/22/1977	NAVY	vs		WILLIAM & MARY (6-5)	42	17	W
10/29/1977	NAVY	@	#5	Notre Dame (11-1)	10	43	L
11/5/1977	NAVY	vs		SYRACUSE (6-5)	34	45	L
11/12/1977	NAVY	vs		GEORGIA TECH (6-5)	20	16	W
11/26/1977	NAVY	vs		ARMY (7-4)	14	17	L
Coach: George Welsh				**Season Record >>**	**229**	**230**	**5-6**

Schedule Source: Steve's Football Bible LLC

Selected game(s) highlights

#1 Michigan

#1 ranked Michigan defeated Navy, 14-7, at Michigan Stadium. Michigan's points were all scored in the second quarter on runs of 13 and 34 yards by running back Harlan Huckleby. Huckleby rushed for 147 yards, and Russell Davis added 93 more, but Navy outgained Michigan by 301 total yards to 277 total yards. Sandy Jones caught a 34 yard touchdown pass from Bob Leszczynski for Navy.

AIR FORCE

The Falcons traveled to Annapolis to play at the Naval Academy on a crisp 58 degree day. In a defensive struggle, the Midshipmen held on for a 10-7 victory. Both teams failed to gain over 200 yards of total offense. Paul Williams caught a 6 yard touchdown pass from Dave Zeibart for the lone Falcon score. Bob Tata kicked a 25 yard field goal with 10 seconds left in the game to give Navy the win.

ARMY {@ JFK Memorial Stadium, Philadelphia, PA}

The two service academies added another epic tale to their series when Army knocked off Navy, 17-14. This was the Cadets' first win in the series since 1972. In typical Army fashion, Coach Homer Smith's club used a ball-control offense to roll up a 17-7 lead at halftime. Nonetheless, Navy battled back with some key offensive plays. It was fourth-and-two on the Army 22 yard line with five minutes left in the third quarter, when John Kurowski rumbled down to the four yard line. Joe Gattuso Jr. slammed into the end zone on the next play, and Bob Tata's point after made it 17-14. The two teams exchanged punts for most of the fourth quarter, as Navy drove down to the Army nine yard line with a little over a minute left. It was fourth-and-two as Navy coach George Welsh dug into his bag of tricks, hoping to catch the Cadets off-guard with a halfback pass. However, Gattuso's throw sailed over the head of wide receiver Phil McConkey, sealing the victory for the Cadets.

1978 Navy Midshipmen {Commander-in-Chief Trophy}

Navy was led by sixth year head coach George Welsh. Team Captains were Phil McConkey and Nick Mygas. The Midshipmen compiled a 9-3 record and outscored their opponents by a combined score of 260 to 130. They played BYU in the inaugural Holiday Bowl and despite being 5 ½ point underdogs, they won 23-16. The annual Army–Navy Game was played on December 2 at JFK Memorial Stadium in Philadelphia, PA. Navy won 28-0.

Bob Lescynski led the team in passing with 1,282 yards and threw 9 touchdown passes. Steve Callahan led the team in rushing with 766 yards and 6 rushing touchdowns. Phil McConkey led the team in receptions with 22 for 532 yards and 6 TD receptions. Fred Reitzel led the team with 5 interceptions. Bob Tata led the team in scoring with 67 points.

Home games were played at Navy-Marine Corps Stadium

9/16/1978		@		Virginia (2-9)	32	0	W	
9/23/1978		@		Connecticut	30	0	W	
9/30/1978		@		Boston College (0-11)	19	8	W	*Tata 4 field goals
10/7/1978		@		Air Force (3-8)	37	8	W	
10/14/1978		vs		DUKE (4-7)	31	8	W	
10/21/1978	#17	vs		WILLIAM & MARY (5-5-1)	9	0	W	
10/28/1978	#18	vs	#15	PITTSBURGH (8-4)	21	11	W	
11/4/1978	#11	vs	#15	NOTRE DAME (9-3)	7	27	L	
11/11/1978	#18	@		Syracuse (3-8)	17	20	L	
11/18/1978		@		Florida State (8-3)	6	38	L	
12/2/1978		vs		ARMY (4-6-1)	28	0	W	
12/22/1978		**vs**		**BYU (9-4)**	**23**	**16**	**W**	**Holiday Bowl**
Coach: George Welsh				**Season Record >>**	**260**	**136**	**9-3**	

Schedule Source: Steve's Football Bible LLC
***-Single game record**

Selected game(s) highlights

Boston College

The Naval Academy defense and kicker Bob Tata took his honor at his word last night as they led the unbeaten Middies to a 19 to 3 football victory over winless and fumble-prone Boston College before 24,112 homecoming spectators. The Navy defense, ranked among the national leaders against the rush, pass and scoring, was superb again, never permitting the Eagles to cross mid-field the entire game. Tata set a Naval Academy record by booting four field goals and added an extra point. Tata kicked field goals of 17, 11, 4t and 41 yards

Air Force

On a sunny, windy day at Falcon Stadium, Air Force welcomed the Midshipmen from the Naval Academy and the Midshipmen ran roughshod over the Falcons, cruising to a 37-8 victory. Bob Tata kicked three field goals and Phil McConkey ran for a 18 yard touchdown and caught a 36 yard touchdown pass from Bob Lesczyinski to lead the Navy attack. Mike Fortson scored the only Air Force touchdown on an 11 yard run. Navy ran for 424 yards while holding Air Force to 47 yards rushing. Steve Callahan ran for 159 yards for the Midshipmen and ran for a touchdown.

#15 NOTRE DAME {@ Cleveland Municipal Stadium – Cleveland, OH}

Navy came into the game undefeated and ranked #11 and hosted #15 Notre Dame before 63,780 fans, boasting the nation's #1 defense. The Fighting Irish wasn't fazed as they raced to a 24-0 halftime lead on the way to a 27-7 thrashing of the Midshipmen. Phil McConkey caught a 13 yard touchdown pass from Bob Powers to avoid the shutout. The Irish rolled up 530 yards of total offense, including 375 yards on the ground.

Syracuse

Jim Goodwill's 13 yard run on a fake punt play kept a Syracuse drive going today, allowing Dave Jacobs to kick a 30-yard field goal with 2:48 remaining and give Syracuse a 20-17 upset over 18th-ranked Navy. Syracuse led by 11 points late in the third period but had to rely on two fourth-quarter field goals by Jacobs to thwart a Navy rally. A freshman running back, Joe Morris, ran for 203 yards in 31 carries against the tough Navy defense. Morris ran 42 yards to score the first Syracuse touchdown. A sophomore quarterback, Tim Wilson, ran 24 yards for a second Syracuse touchdown as the Orangemen built a 14-0 first-period lead. Navy got a 27 yard field goal by Bob Tata and Bob Lefzczynski teamed with Sandy Jones on a 24-yard touchdown pass play to set up Mike Sherlock's 1 yard touchdown run that tied the score at 17 late in the fourth quarter.

Florida State

Jimmy Jordan threw four touchdown passes and Florida State's football team zoomed past Navy 38-6. Early in the second half sophomore nose guard Ron Simmons forced a fumble at the Navy 10 that Florida State recovered, and that opened a door that the injury-riddled Midshipmen could not close. On successive series, Jordan threw touchdown passes of 4, 36 and 51 yards to sophomore Sam Platt - and then one of 23 to Grady King. Navy trailed only 7-6 at halftime until Jordan took over in the 2nd half.

ARMY {@ JFK Memorial Stadium, Philadelphia, PA}

Despite a Nov. 18 loss to Florida State, Navy received word that a win over Army would be enough to earn an invitation to the Dec. 22 Holiday Bowl against Brigham Young. The Midshipmen were more than happy to oblige the bowl officials, blanking the Cadets, 28-0, before upending BYU, 23-16, in San Diego. With the victory, Navy finished 9-3 and ranked 17th in the final United Press International poll. Quarterback Bob Leszczynski and running backs Mike Sherlock and Steve Callahan proved to be more than the Army defense could handle. Leszczynski and Callahan scored the game's first two touchdowns before the duo collectively put the game out of reach with the Midshipmen's third score of the day. Kicker Bob Tata was set to attempt an 18 yard field goal, only to have the snap sail over holder Leszczynski's head. The Navy quarterback quickly retrieved the ball back at the Cadet 40 yard line, scrambled forward 22 yards and fired to a wide open Callahan in the end zone for six more points.

1978 HOLIDAY BOWL

The inaugural Holiday Bowl pitted two teams with local drawing power, the Naval Academy and Brigham Young University. Despite chilly temperatures, the two teams engaged in a hard-hitting battle. Defense dominated the first two quarters. Brent Johnson put the Cougars on the scoreboard first with a 33 yard field goal with 8:26 left in the first quarter. But Navy's Bob Tata boomed a 40 yard field goal to tie the score at 3-3. Jim McMahon sent the Cougars  ahead with a 10 yard pass to Mike Chronister, but Johnson missed the PAT. McMahon ran another in from two yards out in the third period for a 16-3 BYU lead. Navy cut the lead to 16-10 after three quarters and then tied the game on two field goals in the fourth quarter, but it was a 65 yard pass to Phil McConkey that did the Cougars in. Some 52,500 witnessed the game in person. McConkey was named Best Offensive Player and BYU's Tom Enlow won Best Defensive Player honors.

1979 Navy Midshipmen {Commander-in-Chief Trophy}

Navy was led by seventh year head coach George Welsh. Team Captains were Larry Klawinski and Tom Paulk. The Midshipmen compiled a 7-4 record and outscored their opponents by a combined score of 180 to 154. The annual Army–Navy Game was played on December 1 at JFK Memorial Stadium in Philadelphia, PA. Navy won 31-7.

Bob Powers led the team in passing with 983 yards and threw 7 touchdown passes. Eddie Myers led the team in rushing with 651 yards and 5 rushing touchdowns. Dave Dent led the team in receptions with 17 for 269 yards. Steve Fehr led the team in scoring with 38 points.

Home games were played at Navy-Marine Corps Stadium

9/15/1979	NAVY		vs		THE CITADEL (6-5)	26	7	W
9/22/1979	NAVY		vs		CONNECTICUT (3-6-2)	21	10	W
9/29/1979	NAVY		@		Illinois (2-8-1)	13	12	W
10/6/1979	NAVY		vs		AIR FORCE (2-9)	13	9	W
10/13/1979	NAVY		@		William & Mary (4-7)	24	7	W
10/20/1979	NAVY	#20	vs		VIRGINIA (6-5)	17	10	W
10/27/1979	NAVY	#17	@	#12	Pittsburgh (11-1)	7	24	L
11/3/1979	NAVY		@	#13	Notre Dame (7-4)	0	14	L
11/10/1979	NAVY		vs		SYRACUSE (7-5)	14	30	L
11/17/1979	NAVY		@		Georgia Tech (4-6-1)	14	24	L
12/1/1979	NAVY		vs		ARMY (2-8-1)	31	7	W
Coach: George Welsh					**Season Record >>**	180	154	7-4

Schedule Source: Steve's Football Bible LLC

Selected game(s) highlights

AIR FORCE

Steve Callahan scored two touchdowns in the first nine and a half minutes, but the Middies were forced to hang on for the remaining 50 minutes to beat Air Force, 13-9. The game was played before a crowd of 31,109, the second largest to watch a football game at the Navy-Marine Corps Memorial Stadium. This victory was saved when Charles Zingler, a Navy cornerback, broke up two Air Force passes in the end zone in the final 20 seconds. Callahan, who finished with 88 yards in 13 carries, picked up 70 of those yards in the two early touchdown drives by Navy. He ran 50 yards for the first score on Navy's third play of the game. This was a simple burst over the middle and once he was in the secondary, Callahan went untouched by any Falcon defender. Then the junior, who is one of Navy's two top tailbacks, ran over from the Air Force 1 on a pitchout after Navy tried twice to dive over the middle from the 1. This second touchdown ended a 56yard scoring drive that began when Bob Powers, the quarterback, completed his first pass of the game, to Dave Dent for 31 yards.

VIRGINIA

Steve Callahan and Mike Sherlock did not play against Virginia, but Duane Flowers filled in and ran 136 yards with 27 carries, including a 28-yard touchdown run. Virginia tied the Middies, 10-10, on a 50-yard field goal by Wayne Morrison with 3:26 remaining. Bob Powers led an 80-yard drive in six plays and ran the final 6 yards for a touchdown with 2:06 left. Powers completed passes of 25 yards to Greg Papajohn and 24 yards to Dave Dent in that 80yard march.

#12 Pittsburgh

Pittsburgh rallied with three second half touchdowns to beat Navy, 24-7, in the battle for the No. 1 spot among major Eastern football teams. Pittsburgh's Dan Marino finished by throwing for two touchdowns and a total of 227 yards with 22 completions in 30 attempts. Pitt, which committed three turnovers in the first half that stalled drives and led to Navy's only score, kept control of the ball throughout the second half. Navy's total offense was a mere 153 yards although the Middies did manage a 50-yard drive for their touchdown.

#13 Notre Dame

Notre Dame celebrated the 50th anniversary of the dedication of its football stadium on Nov. 3, and the Irish did their part by defeating Navy, 14-0. Vagas Ferguson ran for 155 yards on 34 carries and scored the final Irish touchdown. Rusty Lisch scored from 3 yards out for the Irish final score. Eddie Meyers ended up with 99 yards on 17 carries for the Midshipmen.

ARMY {@ JFK Memorial Stadium, Philadelphia, PA}

The Army defense had no answer for Navy's Eddie Meyers, as the Midshipmen running back gained 279 yards and scored three touchdowns in Navy's 31-7 triumph. The performance capped quite an autumn for the 5-9, 205-pound sophomore who started the season fourth on the Navy depth chart at running back. After starting the season 6-0, the Mids entered the annual battle with the Cadets on a four-game losing streak. Coach George Welsh's club was unable to capitalize on its first possession, but kicker Steve Fehr finished the next possession with a 33 yard field goal to give Navy a 3-0 lead. Navy matched an Army touchdown with two of its own to take a 17-7 lead to the locker room at the half. Meyers added his final two touchdowns midway through the second half to put the contest safely out of reach.

1980 Navy Midshipmen

Navy was led by eighth year head coach George Welsh. Team Captains were Terry Huxel and Frank McCallister. The Midshipmen compiled an 8-4 record and outscored their opponents by a combined score of 226 to 146. They were invited to the Garden State Bowl where they played Houston. The annual Army–Navy Game was played on November 29 at Veterans Stadium in Philadelphia, PA. Navy won 33-6.

Fred Reitzel led the team in passing with 908 yards and threw 7 touchdown passes. Eddie Myers led the team in rushing with 957 yards. Reitzel led with 8 rushing touchdowns. Curt Gainer led the team in receptions with 24 for 340 yards. Elliot Regans led the team with 5 interceptions. Steve Fehr led the team in scoring with 75 points.

Home games were played at Navy-Marine Corps Stadium

9/13/1980	@		Virginia (4-7)	3	6	L	
9/20/1980	vs		KENT STATE (3-8)	31	3	W	
9/27/1980	vs		WILLIAM & MARY (2-9)	45	6	W	
10/4/1980	vs		BOSTON COLLEGE (7-4)	21	0	W	
10/11/1980	@		Air Force (2-9-1)	20	21	L	
10/18/1980	vs		VILLANOVA (6-5)	24	15	W	
10/25/1980	@	#18	Washington (9-3)	24	10	W	
11/1/1980	vs	#3	NOTRE DAME (9-2-1)	0	33	L	
11/8/1980	@		Syracuse (5-6)	6	3	W	
11/15/1980	@		Georgia Tech (1-9-1)	19	8	W	*Fehr 4 field goals
11/29/1980	vs		ARMY (3-7-1)	33	6	W	*Fehr 4 field goals
12/14/1980	**vs**		**Houston (7-5)**	**0**	**35**	**L**	**Garden State Bowl**
Coach: George Welsh			**Season Record >>**	**226**	**146**	**8-4**	

Schedule Source: Steve's Football Bible LLC
***-Single game record**

Selected game(s) highlights

BOSTON COLLEGE

Fullback Kevin Tolbert scored two third quarter touchdowns and Navy's defense held Boston College to 153 total yards to spark the Middies to their third consecutive triumph, a 21-0 shutout over the Eagles.

Air Force

Air Force started the scoring with a Scott Schafer 10 yard touchdown run to give the Falcons a 7-0 lead. The Midshipmen scored the next 13 points for a 13-7 lead early in the 3rd quarter. The Falcons responded with a Scott Schafer 1 yard run for a 14-13 lead. Navy took the lead with just over eight minutes left on a short touchdown run. The Falcons marched down the field and took the lead for good on a Marty Louthan 34 yard touchdown pass to Andy Bark with 1:02 remaining in the game to give Air Force a 21-20 victory.

#3 NOTRE DAME {@ Giants Stadium – East Rutherford, NJ}

The Midshipmen hosted #3 ranked Notre Dame at Giants Stadium. Four different Irish players ran for touchdowns and Harry Oliver kicked two field goals as the Fighting Irish rolled over Navy, 33-0. Jim Stone ran for 211 yards and a touchdown and quarterback Blair Kiel attempted only 8 passes, completing 3 for the Irish.

ARMY {@ Veterans Stadium – Philadelphia, PA}

In rather dominant fashion, Navy regained the series lead for the first time in 58 years, routing Army, 33-6. This was also the first time the Army-Navy game was played at Veterans Stadium. The Midshipmen utilized a balanced attack, as Eddie Meyers' 144 yards on the ground complemented quarterback Fred Reitzel's 138 yards passing. Kicker Steve Fehr was also crucial in Navy's effort, booting four field goals, including a series-record 50 yarder. Once again, turnovers were critical, as the Midshipmen's Travis Wallington recovered Warren Waldorff's fumble at the Navy 15 yard line. Reitzel ran it in from nine yards out, and Fehr's extra point made it 10-0. Navy's defense turned in a stellar effort, limiting Army to 144 yards of total offense. Gerald Walker had one of the Cadets' few offensive highlights with a 26 yard touchdown run.

1980 GARDEN STATE BOWL

After recovering a Navy fumble on their first drive, Houston scored their first of five rushing touchdowns when Terald Clark ran it in from one yard out. After Leo Truss blocked a punt, the Cougars drove 43 yards for their second first-quarter touchdown on a one yard Terry Elston run. Early in the second quarter, Navy had their best scoring opportunity of the afternoon after a Houston turnover. However, Steve Fehr missed a 27 yard field goal and Houston retained their shutout. The Cougars then extended their lead to 28–0 at halftime after touchdown runs of 16 and 26 yards by David Barrett and then Clark. Clark then scored the final points of the game in the third quarter after Clark's third touchdown of the day on a two yard run. For his 163 yards and three touchdowns, Terald Clark was named the MVP of the game.

1981 Navy Midshipmen {Commander-in-Chief Trophy}

Navy was led by ninth year head coach George Welsh. Team Captains were Tim Jordan and Eddie Meyers. The Midshipmen compiled a 7-4-1 record and outscored their opponents by a combined score of 244 to 183. They were invited to the Liberty Bowl where they played Big Ten powerhouse Ohio State and were 14 ½ point underdogs to the Buckeyes. The annual Army–Navy Game was played on November 28 at Veterans Stadium in Philadelphia, PA. the game ended in a 3-3 tie.

Marco Pagnanelli led the team in passing with 1,010 yards. Eddie Myers led the team in rushing with 1,318 yards and 8 rushing touchdowns. Greg Papajohn led the team in receptions with 35 for 517 yards. Jeff Shoemake led the team with 5 interceptions. Steve Fehr led the team in scoring with 76 points.

Home games were played at Navy-Marine Corps Stadium

9/12/1981	vs		THE CITADEL (7-3-1)		17	7	W	
9/19/1981	vs		EASTERN KENTUCKY		24	0	W	
9/26/1981	@	#7	Michigan (9-3)		16	21	L	
10/3/1981	@		Yale (9-1)	ABC	19	23	L	
10/10/1981	vs		AIR FORCE (4-7)		30	13	W	
10/17/1981	@		Boston College (5-6)		25	10	W	*Fehr 4 field goals
10/24/1981	vs		WILLIAM & MARY (5-6)		27	0	W	
10/31/1981	@		Notre Dame (5-6)		0	38	L	
11/7/1981	vs		SYRACUSE (4-6-1)		35	23	W	
11/14/1981	@		Georgia Tech (1-10)		20	14	W	
11/28/1981	vs		ARMY (3-7-1)		3	3	T	
12/30/1981	vs	#15	Ohio State (9-3)	USA	28	31	L	Liberty Bowl
Coach: George Welsh			Season Record >>		244	183	7-4-1	

Schedule Source: Steve's Football Bible LLC
*-Single game record

Selected game(s) highlights

#7 Michigan

In the first quarter, Michigan drove 46 yards on seven plays, with Anthony Carter taking the ball to the 10 yard line on a 22 yard reception. Butch Woolfolk ran four yards for the touchdown. Early in the second quarter, Michigan drove 66 yards on 11 plays, including several passes to Carter and Vince Bean. Quarterback Steve Smith scored on a two yard option run. On Michigan's next drive, Smith was intercepted by Navy's Elliott Reagans, and Anthony Carter sustained a sprained right ankle colliding with Reagans. Carter did not return to the game. Later in the second quarter, Michigan's Tony Jackson fumbled a punt, and Navy recovered at Michigan's 35 yard line. Steve Fehr kicked a 46 yard field goal, and then a 31 yarder with 32 seconds left in the half, to narrow the lead to 14–6 at halftime. Early in the third quarter, Evan Cooper intercepted a Navy pass and returned it to Navy's 34 yard line. Michigan scored on an eight yard touchdown pass from Smith to Vince Bean. Navy responded with a 12-play, 94 yard drive ending with a 22 yard touchdown run by quarterback Marco Pagnanelli on the final play of the third quarter. Navy then drove 66 yards on its next possession, ending with a 45 yard field goal. Late in the fourth quarter, Navy drove 48 yards to Michigan's 22 yard line. With two minutes remaining in the game, Pagnanelli threw to a wide open Troy Mitchell in the end zone, but the pass was overthrown.

Yale

Yale head coach Carmen Cozza called "my biggest win outside of the conference ever," the Elis rallied from a 12-0 deficit to overcome heavily favored Navy, 23-19 yesterday before an estimated crowd of

38,000 at the Yale Bowl. On its first offensive possession, Navy marched 52 yards in eight plays to take a 7-0 lead. Quarterback Marco Pagnanelli capped the drive with a 1 yard keeper off left tackle. Moments later, Navy's Travis Wallington blocked a Yale punt and the Elis' Ken Baer pounced on the loose ball for a safety. Jeff Shoemake returned the ensuing free kick 41 yards to the Yale 26 yard line and Navy was on the move again. Four plays later, kicker Steve Fehr booted a 39 yard field goal. Yale outplayed Navy through the final three quarters. The Elis engineered a 14-play, 45 yard drive midway through the second period and got on the board when Tony Jones kicked a 45 yard field goal, his longest ever. On Yale's next offensive possession, quarterback John Rogari drilled a 15 yard touchdown pass to tight end Tom Kokoska to narrow Navy's margin to 12-9. Following intermission, the Elis struck first when Rogan looped a high floater to split end Curtis Grieve at 12:56 of the 3rd quarter. The Midshipmen came right back, however, when Richard Clouse sprinted 16 yards for the touchdown, one play after Navy had blocked its second punt of the game. Yale scored the winning touchdown with less than four minutes remaining. After forcing Navy to punt from its own end zone. Yale took over at the Midshipmen's 24. This time Rogan did not waste what could well have been Yale's final chance to score. On the first play, Rogan threw his third touchdown pass of the game, again to Grieve in the corner of the end zone.

AIR FORCE

Navy raced to a 17-0 lead in the 2nd quarter and the Falcons never recovered as the Midshipmen rolled to a 30-13 victory in Annapolis. Charlie Heath and John Kershner each had 1 yard touchdown runs for Air Force. Steve Fehr kicked three field goals for Navy and Eddie Meyers rushed for 179 yards and a touchdown. Quarterback Marco Pagnanelli ran for and threw for a touchdown for the Midshipmen.

ARMY {@ Veterans Stadium - Philadelphia, PA}

If one game ever defined a rivalry, then the 1981 Army-Navy contest speaks volumes about the competition between the Midshipmen and the Cadets. Already bound for a Liberty Bowl appearance against Ohio State, Navy entered the afternoon with a 7-3 record. Army, on the other hand, had struggled to a 3-7 ledger. Despite the fact George Welsh's club entered the game as a 19-point favorite, the Mids escaped Philadelphia with a 3-3 tie against West Point. The Cadets' offense may have struggled all afternoon, but punter Joe Sartiano was there to kick it out of a hole. He averaged 57.6 yards on his five punts, with a long kick of 79 yards. Veteran kicker Steve Fehr put Navy on the scoreboard first with a 42 yard field goal at the end of the second quarter. Army's Dave Aucoin responded with a field goal in the third quarter, but he missed on a 55 yard attempt as time expired that would have given the Cadets the win.

1981 LIBERTY BOWL

Ohio State, scoring a pair of second half touchdowns, rallied to defeat an underdog Navy football team, 31 to 28, in the 23rd Liberty Bowl game before 43,216 spectators in Liberty Bowl Memorial Stadium last night. The Buckeyes, favored by 14 points, fell behind the fired up Middies early in the third quarter when George Herlong blocked a Karl Edwards punt and Ken Olson grabbed the loose ball at the OSU 11 yard line and ran it into the end zone to give Navy a 20-17 lead. Then Ohio State came roaring back. After a poor Steve Fehr punt gave the Big Ten Conference co-champs the ball at the Navy 37, the Buckeyes took nine plays to get the TD with tailback Jimmy Gayle capping the march by scoring from 2 yards out. The extra point conversion gave OSU a 24-20 lead. An interception of a Marco Pagnanelli pass by Buckeye safety Kelvin Bell gave OSU the ball at the Navy 26 early in the final quarter. Ohio State boosted its margin to 31-20 five plays later as quarterback Art Schlichter hit wide receiver Cedric Anderson with a 9 yard touchdown pass. Navy wasn't finished, however. After an OSU punt rolled dead at the Navy 3 with 5 minutes 25 seconds remaining, the Middies moved 97 yards in 14 plays with Pagnanelli hitting tight end Greg Papajohn with a 1 yard scoring pass on fourth and goal with 8 seconds remaining. Pagnanelli then threw to Papajohn, who made a one-handed circus catch at the side of the end zone for a 2-point conversion, and the score was 31-28. The Middies tried an onside kick, but OSU recovered at the Navy 46 and ran out the final 7 seconds. Tailback Eddie Meyers, Navy's all-time rushing leader, was named the game's most valuable player after gaining 116 yards on 30 carries. Pagnanelli completed 16 of 27 passes for 202 yards and two touchdowns.

1982 Navy Midshipmen

Navy was led by first-year head coach Gary Tranquill. Team Captains were Dennis McCall and Travis Wallington. The Midshipmen compiled a 6-5 record and outscored their opponents by a combined score of 230 to 196. The annual Army–Navy Game was played on December 4 at Veterans Stadium in Philadelphia, PA. Navy won the game 24-7.

Marco Pagnanelli led the team in passing with 1,133 yards and threw 7 touchdown passes. Napoleon McCallum led the team in rushing with 739 yards and 5 rushing touchdowns. Bill Cebak led the team in receptions with 26 for 415 yards. Brian Cianella led the team with 4 interceptions. Steve Young led the team in scoring with 36 points. **Andy Ponseigo set a Navy team record with 169 tackles.**

Home games were played at Navy-Marine Corps Stadium

9/11/1982	NAVY	vs		VIRGINIA (2-9)	30	16	W
9/18/1982	NAVY	@	#9	Arkansas (9-2-1)	17	29	L
9/25/1982	NAVY	vs		BOSTON COLLEGE (8-3-1)	0	31	L
10/2/1982	NAVY	@		Duke (6-5)	27	21	W
10/9/1982	NAVY	@		Air Force (8-5)	21	24	L
10/16/1982	NAVY	vs		WILLIAM & MARY (3-8)	39	3	W
10/23/1982	NAVY	vs		THE CITADEL	28	3	W
10/30/1982	NAVY	vs		NOTRE DAME (6-4-1)	10	27	L
11/6/1982	NAVY	@		Syracuse (2-9)	20	18	W
11/13/1982	NAVY	@		South Carolina (4-7)	14	17	L
12/4/1982	NAVY	vs		ARMY (4-7)	24	7	W
Coach: George Tranquill				**Season Record >>**	**230**	**196**	**6-5**

Schedule Source: Steve's Football Bible LLC

Selected game(s) highlights

BOSTON COLLEGE

Doug Flutie passed for 279 yards and three touchdowns today as Boston College beat Navy, 31-0. Against the Midshipmen, Flutie threw his fifth, sixth and seventh scoring passes of the season. The first went to Scott Nizolek, his tight end, and the next two to Brian Brennan, a nimble wide receiver. For Navy, Marco Pagnanelli completed 18 of 36 passes for 144 yards. Three were intercepted, and he was sacked four times. McCallum gained 42 yards rushing, and he also managed to run for 145 yards on returns of punts and kickoffs.

NOTRE DAME {@ Giants Stadium – East Rutherford, NJ}

Blair Kiel threw his first two touchdown passes of the season on the way to a 27-10 victory over Navy at Giants Stadium. Kiel completed 18 of 34 passes for 220 yards, threw six consecutive completions on an eight-play drive of 80 yards en route to the first touchdown and set a Notre Dame record of 34 attempts in a game without an interception. Yet the Notre Dame defense, with six interceptions, once again was the steadying influence that shut off Navy's passing game at critical moments and set up two Notre Dame touchdowns. Dave Duerson, one of the best safetymen in Irish history, made three of the interceptions as Notre Dame stole four of Tom Tarquinio's passes in the third period alone. Tarquinio, who tossed a touchdown pass and a 2-point conversion pass after Notre Dame got a 27-2 lead, started in place of Marco Pagnanelli.

ARMY {@ Veterans Stadium - Philadelphia, PA}

Navy turned two first-half Army turnovers into 10 points to fuel a 24-7 win. The game was played under the most ideal weather conditions in series history — clear skies and 70 degrees. Despite the sunny skies, Army's afternoon suddenly turned cloudy when the Midshipmen's Rick Pagel recovered Dee Bryant's fumbled punt at the Cadet eight yard line early in the first quarter. Napoleon McCallum punched the ball in from two yards out, and Todd Solomon's conversion gave Navy a quick 7-0 lead. The Mids stretched this advantage to 10-0 when Solomon followed Brian Cianella's interception with a 25 yard field goal shortly thereafter. Army cut the lead to 10-7 in the second quarter when Mike Staver recovered Rich Clouse's fumble at the Navy 15 yard line. Laughlin took it in from three yards out to cut the lead to 10-7. In the third quarter, a pair of McCallum punt returns set up a one yard James Scannell touchdown run and a 17 yard touchdown pass from Ricky Williamson to split end Bill Cebak.

1983 Navy Midshipmen

Navy was led by second year head coach Gary Tranquill. Team Captains were Jeff Johnson and Andy Ponsiego. The Midshipmen compiled a 3-8 record and were outscored by their opponents by a combined score of 272 to 202. The annual Army–Navy Game was played on November 27 at The Rose Bowl Stadium in Pasadena, CA; Navy won the game 42-13. Napoleon McCallum was selected as a consensus All-American.

Rich Williamson led the team in passing with 1,394 yards and threw 8 touchdown passes. Napoleon McCallum led the team in rushing with 1,587 yards and 10 rushing touchdowns. Marc Stevens led the team in receptions with 41 for 483 yards. Steve Brady and Andy Ponseigo tied for the team lead with 5 interceptions. McCallum led the team in scoring with 66 points.

Home games were played at Navy-Marine Corps Stadium

9/10/1983	NAVY	@		Virginia (6-5)		16	27	L
9/17/1983	NAVY	@		Mississippi State (3-8)		10	38	L
9/24/1983	NAVY	vs		LEHIGH		30	0	W
10/1/1983	NAVY	@	#18	Washington (8-4)		10	27	L
10/8/1983	NAVY	vs		AIR FORCE (10-2)		17	44	L
10/15/1983	NAVY	@		Princeton		37	29	W
10/22/1983	NAVY	vs		PITTSBURGH (8-3-1)		14	21	L
10/29/1983	NAVY	@	#19	Notre Dame (7-5)		12	28	L
11/5/1983	NAVY	vs		SYRACUSE (6-5)		7	14	L
11/12/1983	NAVY	@		South Carolina (5-6)		7	31	L
11/25/1983	NAVY	vs		ARMY (2-9)	ABC	42	13	W
Coach: George Tranquill				**Season Record >>**		**202**	**272**	**3-8**

Schedule Source: Steve's Football Bible LLC

Selected game(s) highlights

LEHIGH

Navy's sputtering offense came to life in the second half and the Midshipmen rolled to a 30-0 victory over Lehigh before 23,000 Navy-Marine Corps Memorial Stadium spectators. The Midshipmen got a stellar performance from their defense, which limited Lehigh to 13 yards rushing and 110 passing, and shut out the Engineers for the first time in 68 games. After bumbling and fumbling to a 3-0 first-half lead, Navy's offense, directed by quarterback Rick Williamson and paced by tailback Napoleon McCallum he gained 146 yards on 29 carries and scored a touchdown tallied two touchdowns in each of the final two quarters. Williamson completed 16 of 32 passes for 180 yards and two touchdowns, a 16 yard scoring strike to Ken Heine and a 13 yarder to Greg Brand. Tailback Rich Clouse scored the other touchdown on a 2 yard run. The Middie offense rolled up 391 yards, 211 rushing.

AIR FORCE

Trailing 10-7 early in the 2nd quarter, Marty Louthan took over and rushed for 4 touchdowns and passed for 130 yards, leading Air Force to a 44-17 victory over the Midshipmen. Mike Brown rushed for 136 yards as the Falcons rolled up 340 yards on the ground. Napoleon McCallum rushed for 211 yards for Navy, highlighted by a 60 yard touchdown run.

Princeton

The game was not nearly as close or thrilling as the 37-29 final score would indicate. Navy allowed Princeton to come back from a 28-7 halftime deficit. The real difference was Navy's Napoleon McCallum - who galloped for 235 yards on 37 carries and who simply dominated the game in the first half when he tied an NCAA record for most carries in one half (32) while netting 213 yards and scoring three touchdowns in those first 30 minutes.

ARMY {@ Rose Bowl Stadium, Pasadena, CA}

With three touchdowns in the first four minutes of the game, Navy rolled to a 42-13 victory over Army at the Rose Bowl. Other than a trip to Chicago in 1926, the Cadets and Midshipmen had never met farther west than Baltimore. However, Rolfe Arnhym, West Point Class of '53 and then Executive Vice President of the Pasadena Chamber of Commerce, helped arrange for the 1983 contest to be played in California.

Navy used a trick play to catch Army off-guard on the opening kickoff, and the Cadets never regained their balance. Craig Stopa's opening kick went to Navy star Napoleon McCallum, who handed it off to return mate Eric Wallace. Wallace then went 95 yards for the game's first touchdown. McCallum added a 14 yard touchdown scamper, and linebacker Steve Brady's 65 yard interception return made it 21-0 just 3:50 into the game. McCallum's 182 yards on 30 carries accounted for a lion's share of the Midshipmen's 296 yards on the ground.

ARMY {@ Rose Bowl Stadium, Pasadena, CA}

1984 Navy Midshipmen

Navy was led by third year head coach Gary Tranquill. Team Captains were Mark Stevens and Eric Rutherford. The Midshipmen compiled a 4-6-1 record and were outscored by their opponents by a combined score of 254 to 240. The annual Army–Navy Game was played on December 1 at Veterans Stadium in Philadelphia, PA. Army won the game 28-11. Bill Byrne led the team in passing with 1,425 yards and threw 11 touchdown passes. Rich Clouse led the team in rushing with 557 yards. Chris Weiler led the team in receptions with 44 for 711 yards and 6 TD receptions. Marc Firlie led the team with 5 interceptions. Todd Solomon led the team in scoring with 65 points.

Home games were played at Navy-Marine Corps Stadium

9/15/1984	@		North Carolina (5-5-1)		33	30	W	
9/22/1984	vs		VIRGINIA (8-2-2)		9	21	L	
9/29/1984	@		Arkansas (7-4-1)		10	33	L	
10/6/1984	@		Air Force (8-4)		22	29	L	
10/13/1984	vs		LEHIGH		31	14	W	*Heine 3 TD catch
10/20/1984	vs		PRINCETON		41	3	W	
10/27/1984	@		Pittsburgh (3-7-1)		28	28	T	
11/3/1984	vs		NOTRE DAME (7-5)	ESPN	17	18	L	
11/10/1984	@		Syracuse (6-5)		0	29	L	
11/17/1984	vs	#2	SOUTH CAROLINA (10-2)		38	21	W	
12/1/1984	vs		ARMY (8-3-1)		11	28	L	
Coach: George Tranquill			**Season Record >>**		**240**	**254**	**4-6-1**	

Schedule Source: Steve's Football Bible LLC
***-Single game record**

Selected game(s) highlights

Air Force

Eric Wallace returned the opening kickoff 97 yards for a touchdown to give Navy an early 7-0 lead. Air Force responded with a Bart Weiss 4 yard touchdown run and a Jody Simmons 47 yard touchdown to give the Falcons a 14-7 lead. After two Navy field goals, Pat Evans scored on a 35 yard run for a 21-13 Air Force lead. Navy rallied to take a 22-21 lead into the 4th quarter. Evans scored from 1 yard out and Weiss ran in the 2 point conversion to give Air Force a 29-22 victory over the Midshipmen. Both Weiss and Simmons rushed for over 100 yards as the Falcons totaled 333 yards on the ground.

LEHIGH

Quarterback Bill Byrne passed for three scores and ran for a fourth and Ken Heine tied a school record with three touchdown catches yesterday as Navy beat Lehigh, 31-14. Byrne completed a pair of touchdown passes in the first half, but his play was erratic, and he connected on only seven of 14 passes for 98 yards. He came back in the second half to hit six of seven for 91 yards.

Notre Dame {Giants Stadium - East Rutherford, New Jersey}

Eighteen seconds remained when John Carney kicked a 44 yard field goal today that enabled Notre Dame to overtake Navy, 18-17, at Giants Stadium. But how many seconds remained on the 25-second clock when Carney kicked the ball? Gary Tranquill, the Navy coach, insisted that time had expired, in which case the Irish should have been penalized 5 yards for delay of game. The 25- second clock tracks the time remaining before the next play must be run. Tranquill said he was certain the clock had reached zero. Notre Dame had beaten Navy for the 21st straight time, the longest continuous streak of one team over another in major college football. Navy's last victory over Notre Dame came in 1963, when Roger Staubach was a junior. The referee, William McDonald, said that the field judge, John Daniels, had lost sight of the clock 'for a few seconds because the defense was jumping up and down." "In his opinion," McDonald added, "the clock did not exceed 25 seconds." As Carney's kick sailed true on its course, Tranquill raced onto the field to confront the officials. He was not only upset about the clock; he was also angry that the officials did not call a roughing-the-kicker penalty against Notre Dame after Mark Colby punted to give the Irish the ball for their final drive. The improbable finish, which began when Notre Dame scored a touchdown and 2-point conversion with 2 minutes 17 seconds remaining, was in no way indicative of much of what preceded it. Irish Now 5-4

The Irish, whose record improved to 5-4, turned the ball over six times, on four interceptions and two fumbles and appeared confused at times. Were it not for their splendid running back, the junior Allen Pinkett, who ran 37 times for 169 yards, Irish fans among the 61,795 in attendance would have had little to cheer about. Yet once Navy (3-4-1) had taken a 17-7 lead on a 6 yard touchdown run by the fullback John Berner, a 2 yard scoring pass from the reserve quarterback Joe Lauletta to the regular quarterback, Bill Byrne, and Todd Solomon's 32 yard field goal with 4:02 left, the Irish roared back. Starting from their own 17 yard line, they moved to the 50 in five plays. After Steve Beuerlein was sacked, he completed three straight passes of 29, 15 and 15 yards, to the split end Tim Brown. Brown's third reception gave the Irish a first down at the 1, and Pinkett, who has scored the first touchdown of the game on a 1 yard burst, did it again. The Irish then made good on a 2-point conversion that cut Navy's lead to 17-15, when Beuerlein tossed a pass to Joe Howard in the end zone. Navy got the ball back with 2:15 to go but could gain only a yard and had to punt. At least two Notre Dame Players were close to Colby as he punted. There, the first disputed play developed. After the punt, Colby lay on the ground, injured. As the Irish were waiting to put the ball in play, from their 18 with one minute remaining, Colby was helped off the field with an injured ankle. Beuerlein then ran for 7 yards, passed twice for 25, and after a 5 yard penalty, he connected with Pinkett for a 29 yard pass play that gave the Irish a first down at the Navy 26. Beuerlein then threw out of bounds to stop the clock with 18 seconds left. Rather than risk another turnover, Faust sent in his field goal team.

#2 SOUTH CAROLINA

Navy stunned second-ranked South Carolina today, 38-21, handing the Gamecocks their first loss of the season. The Gamecocks won their first nine games as the surprise team of the season, but the Midshipmen, after building a 14-7 halftime advantage, scored on three consecutive possessions in the third quarter to take a comfortable lead. Their defense prevented a South Carolina comeback, allowing only two late scores. Two Navy touchdowns in the third quarter were set up by interceptions after

the Middie defense had shut down the running game, forcing the Gamecocks to go to the air. In all, Navy intercepted four passes, recovered one fumble and blocked a field-goal attempt. The Middie offense moved the ball consistently. In one stretch of the third and fourth quarters, the Middies scored two touchdowns on passes from Bob Misch to Chris Weiler, and two on short runs by the halfback Mike Smith

ARMY {@ Veterans Stadium – Philadelphia, PA}

Dec. 1, 1984, is a day to remember in Army football history. With a 28-11 victory over Navy, the Cadets advanced to their first-ever postseason bowl, the Cherry Bowl. The wishbone offense installed by head coach Jim Young worked to perfection, as fullback Doug Black and quarterback Nate Sassaman rushed for 155 and 154 yards, respectively. Ironically, both players went over the 1,000 yard single-season rushing mark during the game. Although the halftime score was 14-3, it could have just as easily been 14-14. With five minutes left in the first half, Navy had a second-and-six on the Cadet 10 yard line, but quarterback Bob Misch was sacked on successive plays, forcing kicker Todd Solomon to salvage the drive with a 40 yard field goal. On the next possession, tight end Mark Stevens caught a short pass from Misch and appeared headed for the end zone. However, Army's Kermit McKelvy stripped the ball from Stevens at the five, and safety Doug Pavek fell on the ball in the end zone for a touchback.

1985 Navy Midshipmen

Navy was led by fourth year head coach Gary Tranquill. Team Captains were Napoleon McCallum and Eric Fudge. The Midshipmen compiled a 4-7 record and outscored their opponents by a combined score of 253 to 239. The annual Army–Navy Game was played on December 7 at Veterans Stadium in Philadelphia, PA. Navy won the game 17-7. Napoleon McCallum was selected as a consensus All-American.

Bill Byrne led the team in passing with 1,694 yards and threw 8 touchdown passes. Napoleon McCallum led the team in rushing with 1,327 yards and 14 rushing touchdowns. McCallum led the team in receptions with 44 for 358 yards. McCallum led the team in scoring with 90 points.

Home games were played at Navy-Marine Corps Stadium

9/7/1985		vs		NORTH CAROLINA (5-6)		19	21	L	
9/14/1985		@		Delaware		13	16	L	
9/21/1985		@		Indiana (4-7)		35	38	L	*Hollinger 3 TD catch
9/28/1985		@	#20	Virginia (6-5)		17	13	W	
10/12/1985		vs	#13	AIR FORCE (12-1)		7	24	L	
10/19/1985		vs		LAFAYETTE		56	14	W	
10/26/1985		vs		PITTSBURGH (5-5-1)		21	7	W	
11/2/1985		@		Notre Dame (5-6)	TBS	17	41	L	
11/9/1985		vs		SYRACUSE (7-5)		20	24	L	
11/16/1985		@		South Carolina (5-6)		31	34	L	
12/7/1985		vs		ARMY (9-3)	CBS	17	7	W	
Coach: George Tranquill				**Season Record >>**		**253**	**239**	**4-7**	

Schedule Source: Steve's Football Bible LLC
***-Single game record**

Selected game(s) highlights

#13 AIR FORCE

Air Force Academy was unable to blow the Naval Academy off the football field today, but they had enough to beat their service rivals, 24-7. The gritty Navy defense kept Air Force well below the 45 points it had been averaging this year, and it kept the Middies in contention until the Air Force scored the final touchdown with 6 minutes 40 seconds remaining in the game. Napoleon McCallum gained 67 yards rushing in 15 attempts and 20 yards in 2 pass receptions. He added to his all-round total by running back 3 punts for 27 yards and 1 kickoff for 20. Navy closed the lead to 14-7 in the third quarter with a 15 yard touchdown pass from the Middie quarterback, Bill Byrne, to John Sniffen, a tight end. But the Air Force had too much power, and the Falcons never surrendered the lead. They ended the scoring with a 20 yard field goal by Tom Ruby and a 2 yard run from the wishbone by Randy Jones.

LAFAYETTE

Napoleon McCallum & Co. treated a sun drenched Homecoming Day crowd of 28,402 at the Naval Academy's Memorial Stadium to a 56-14 TKO of Coach Bill Russo's game, but outmanned, troops. McCallum carried 18 times for 95 yards and three TDs as Navy rolled to a 28-7 lead. He finished with 107 on 21 carries.

PITTSBURGH

Napoleon McCallum ran for two touchdowns and rolled up 121 yards in 34 carries Saturday to lead Navy to a 21-7 upset victory over Pittsburgh. Quarterback Bill Byrne ran 1 yard for Navy's third touchdown. Navy took a 14-7 halftime lead and scored on its first possession of the second half to go ahead 21-7. The Middies, led by McCallum's running and pinpoint passing by Byrne, consumed half of the first quarter with an 85-yard drive for a 7-0 lead on McCallum's 1-yard run. McCallum carried eight times during the 16-play march and Byrne completed six of seven passes. Panthers defensive back Teryl Austin returned a punt 74 yards to Navy's 10 and Comgeni hit Lawson with a 3-yard touchdown pass for Pitt's only score. Austin intercepted a Byrne pass at midfield and returned it to Navy's 3 before fumbling. Navy guard Mark Miller recovered the fumble, and the Midshipmen launched a 93-yard drive that McCallum capped on the 12th play with a 6-yard scoring run. Byrne, after being sacked for 14 yards on the first play of the second half, hit Troy Saunders with a 39-yard pass. Saunders then ran for 25 yards on an end-around and Bryne capped the drive by plunging into the end zone from 1 yard out for Navy's final score.

ARMY {@ Veterans Stadium - Philadelphia, PA}

In his final collegiate football game, Napoleon McCallum rushed for 217 yards on 41 carries to lead Navy past Army, 17-7. The Navy senior posted more yards than the entire Army team, who was limited to 192 yards by a stingy Midshipmen defense. Navy took a 7-0 lead when Bob Misch's 13 yard touchdown pass to Troy Saunders finished a 14-play, 73 yard drive. Army's Clarence Jones responded by taking the ensuing kickoff 61 yards to the Navy 36, and then taking the ball into the end zone eight plays later from 10 yards out. Craig Stopa added his 61st-consecutive extra point, which made him the first player to score in four Army-Navy games. Navy's Chuck Smith put the Mids ahead to stay with a five yard touchdown run in the fourth quarter, as the Cadets failed to capitalize on two golden offensive opportunities. They were stopped on downs at the Navy two yard line in the second quarter, and Stopa's 37 yard field goal attempt in the third quarter sailed wide right.

1986 Navy Midshipmen

Navy was led by fifth year head coach Gary Tranquill. Team Captains were Bill Byrne and Vince McBeth. The Midshipmen compiled a 3-8 record and were outscored by their opponents by a combined score of 306 to 238. The annual Army–Navy Game was played on December 6 at Veterans Stadium in Philadelphia, PA. Army won the game 27-7.

Bill Byrne led the team in passing with 1,463 yards and 10 touchdown passes. Chuck Smith led the team in rushing with 933 yards and 10 rushing touchdowns. Tony Hollinger and Mike Ray led the team in receptions with 30. Ray led with 403 receiving yards. Smith led the team in scoring with 72 points.

Home games were played at Navy-Marine Corps Stadium

9/13/1986	NAVY	vs		VIRGINIA (3-8)		20	10	W
9/20/1986	NAVY	@		Indiana (6-6)		29	52	L
9/27/1986	NAVY	vs		LEHIGH		41	0	W
10/4/1986	NAVY	vs		DARTMOUTH		45	0	W
10/11/1986	NAVY	@		Air Force (6-5)		6	40	L
10/18/1986	NAVY	vs		PENNSYLVANIA		26	30	L
10/25/1986	NAVY	@		Pittsburgh (5-5-1)	JPS	14	56	L
11/1/1986	NAVY	vs	#9	NOTRE DAME (5-6)		14	33	L
11/8/1986	NAVY	@	#8	Syracuse (5-6)		22	31	L
11/15/1986	NAVY	vs		DELAWARE		14	27	L
12/6/1986	NAVY	vs		ARMY (6-5)		7	27	L
Coach: George Tranquill				**Season Record >>**		**238**	**306**	**3-8**

Schedule Source: Steve's Football Bible LLC

Selected game(s) highlights

LEHIGH

Chuck Smith put together one of the best days ever by a Navy running back in helping the Midshipmen drill out-manned Lehigh 41-0 at Navy-Marine Memorial Stadium. All Smith did was score four touchdowns (tying a Navy single-game record), rush for 99 yards despite missing the fourth quarter because of a sore shoulder and chalk up 68 yards in pass receptions. Smith's first TD was a 39 yard pass from senior quarterback Bill Byrne, capping a five play, 57 yard drive on Navy's first offensive possession of the game. His second came later in the period, after Middie middle guard Enoch Blazis pounced on quarterback Harris' fumble at the Engineer 21. On the very next play, Smith gathered in a pitchout, scampered right, and into the end zone. Smith added his third TD of the first half late in the second period, as he went left with a pitchout from the 6 yard line. Linebacker Vince McBeth pirated a Harris pass out in the flat midway through the second period and raced it back 57 yards for a then 20-0 edge. The Lehigh offense was generally unable to sustain drives, as Lee Blum mustered 52 yards rushing on 15 carries, and quarterback Jim Harris was 21-for-52 with four interceptions.

DARTMOUTH

The Midshipmen smashed outclassed Dartmouth, 45-0. The Big Green had no defense for quarterback Bill Byrne and tailback Chuck Smith, who led the assault that resulted in 623 yards total offense before a homecoming crowd of 31 ,543 at Navy-Marine Corps Memorial Stadium. Smith gained 182 yards on 26 carries and scored one touchdown. Smith also caught four passes for 28 yards and a touchdown, giving him 210 all-purpose yards.

Air Force

Chris Blasy kicked two field goals to give Air Force a 6-0 lead, then exploded for 21 second quarter points on the way to a 40-6 blowout over the Midshipmen. Marc Munafo scored from 1 yard out, Pat Evans scored from 2 yards out and Tyrone Jeffcoat caught a 30 yard TD pass from James Tomallo as the

Falcons put the game away early. Munafo added a 1 yard TD run and Dee Dowis scored from 1 yard out in the 4th quarter.

PENNSYLVANIA

Penn quarterback Jim Crocicchia tied a school record with four touchdown passes and threw three of them in the final 11 minutes to rally the Quakers from a 20-10 deficit to their first win over a current Division I-A team since they edged Rutgers, 7-6, in 1963. Crocicchia's final TD pass, a 29 yard strike to running back Jim Bruni with 1 minute, 59 seconds left, pushed the Quakers to a 30-20 advantage and made meaningless for Navy a late touchdown by tailback Chuck Smith (34 carries, 123 yards, 2 touchdowns). The clinching touchdown came after Penn tight end Brent Novoselsky, who caught two fourth-quarter TD passes and three in the game, was penalized for moving before the snap.

ARMY {@ Veterans Stadium - Philadelphia, PA}

Army scored on five of its first-eight possessions en route to a 27-7 victory over the Midshipmen. This marked the Cadets' third-most convincing win over Navy, surpassed only by a 38-0 win in 1949 and a 27-0 triumph in 1969. The game certainly lived up to its billing as one of America's purest rivalries, as neither team committed a single penalty. Sophomore Keith Walker put Army on the scoreboard first with a pair of 24 yard field goals. The Cadets gradually cushioned this lead in the second half, thanks in part to a few bounces that went their way. On first-and-10 from the Navy 30, Cadet Quarterback Tory Crawford kept the ball and raced around the end, where he was hit hard at the 20 yard line. The ball popped loose and rolled all the way down to the three yard line, where an alert Benny Wright fell on it. Andy Peterson carried the ball into the end zone two plays later, and Army took a 13-0 lead. Navy took the ensuing kickoff and went 80 yards in 14 plays, with Don Holl plowing through for a three yard touchdown. Ted Fundoukos added the extra point to make it 13-7. Yet, Army tacked on two more scores to provide the final margin.

1987 Navy Midshipmen

Navy was led by first year head coach Elliott Uzelac. Team Captains were Mike Musser and Chuck Smith. The Midshipmen compiled a 2-9 record and were outscored by their opponents by a combined score of 317 to 160. The annual Army–Navy Game was played on December 5 at Veterans Stadium in Philadelphia, PA. Army won the game 17-3.

Alton Grizzard led the team in passing with 490 yards. Grizzard led the team in rushing with 519 yards and 4 rushing touchdowns. Don Hughes led the team in receptions with 13 for 261 yards. Larry Dickinson led the team with 4 interceptions. Ted Fundoukos led the team in scoring with 42 points.

Home games were played at Navy-Marine Corps Stadium

9/12/1987	NAVY	vs		WILLIAM & MARY	12	27	L
9/19/1987	NAVY	vs		LEHIGH	9	24	L
9/26/1987	NAVY	vs		NORTH CAROLINA (5-6)	14	45	L
10/3/1987	NAVY	@		Virginia Tech (2-9)	11	31	L
10/10/1987	NAVY	vs		AIR FORCE (9-4)	13	23	L
10/17/1987	NAVY	@		Pennsylvania	38	28	W
10/24/1987	NAVY	vs		PITTSBURGH (8-4)	6	10	L
10/31/1987	NAVY	@	#1	Notre Dame (8-4)	13	56	L
11/7/1987	NAVY	vs	#13	SYRACUSE (11-0-1)	10	34	L
11/14/1987	NAVY	@		Delaware	31	22	W
12/5/1987	NAVY	vs		ARMY (5-6)	3	17	L
Coach: Elliot Uzelac				**Season Record >>**	160	317	**2-9**

Schedule Source: Steve's Football Bible LLC

Selected game(s) highlights

LEHIGH

The Midshipmen stumbled for the second straight week against a supposedly inferior opponent, losing to Lehigh. 24-9, before a stunned homecoming crowd of 25,047 at Navy-Marine Corps Memorial Stadium. The Midshipmen committed some simple mistakes, such as running into Lehigh punt returner Jim Watson for a 15 yard penalty that set up a second-quarter field goal and not being able to get off a 44 yard field goal attempt in the fourth quarter, when holder John Nobers fumbled a wobbly snap. Navy kicker Frank Schenk added to the Navy problems by missing field-goal attempts of 47 and 41 yards in the first half. Navy drove inside the Lehigh 35 yard line six times without scoring. There were also two fumbles and one interception that stalled promising drives.

AIR FORCE

Navy seemed poised to erase more than a year's worth of frustrating losses. But Air Force scored 13 points in the final nine minutes to pull out a 23-13 victory. Steve Yarbrough kicked field goals of 34 yards and 32 yards and Andy Smith scored on a 23 yard run. The biggest play down the stretch was a 23 yard touchdown run by Air Force fullback Andy Smith with 4:54 left that broke a 13-13 tie. Alton Grizzard became the first freshman to start at quarterback for Navy since 1974. Late in the second quarter, Grizzard directed a 56 yard, 13-play drive that ended with Ted Fundoukos' first-ever collegiate field goal, a 32 yarder. The play put Navy ahead, 3-0, the first time this season the Midshipmen had led.

Pennsylvania

Alton Grizzard gained 225 yards on 23 carries, scored three touchdowns and led the Midshipmen to a 38-28 win over Penn yesterday at Franklin Field. It was Navy's first win of 1987 and broke a 12-game losing streak. It was Uzelac's first win as Navy coach. It was Grizzard's second start ever. Grizzard gained

163 of his yards in the first half and Navy built a 28-7 lead. On Navy's first drive, Grizzard carried five times for 49 yards and scored on a 3 yard run. On Navy's second drive, Grizzard carried twice for 33 yards, and fullback Curtis Brown scored on a 2 yard run. On Navy's third drive, Grizzard carried three times for 27 yards and scored on a 2 yard run. On Navy's fourth drive, Grizzard carried three times for 47 yards, and Brown scored on an 8 yard run.

#1 **Notre Dame**

Anthony Johnson scored four touchdowns to lead No. 9 Notre Dame to a 56-13 rout of outmanned Navy. Johnson rushed 6, 9, 1 and 2 yards for touchdowns to lead the Irish to their 24th consecutive victory over the Midshipmen. Notre Dame scored touchdowns on six consecutive possessions, including all five in the first half, as the Irish raced to a 35-6 lead. Johnson opened the scoring by scrambling six yards for a touchdown to cap Notre Dame's first possession, and Tim Brown finished the first-half onslaught by beating double coverage to catch a pass from substitute quarterback Kent Graham and score on a 51 yard play. Notre Dame gained 406 yards rushing and 224 yards passing.

ARMY {@ Veterans Stadium - Philadelphia, PA}

Mustering just 191 yards of total offense, Navy suffered a 17-3 loss to Army. This marked the first time the Cadets had posted back-to-back victories in the series since 1971-72. Although Army's Mike Mayweather wore down the Midshipmen defense with 119 yards rushing, the only points of the first half came when Cadet Kicker Harold "Bit" Rambusch booted a 40 yard field goal in the first quarter. Army stretched its lead to 10-0 with 11:02 left in the game when Andy Peterson scored on a one yard run. Behind the leadership of quarterback Alton Grizzard, Navy battled back. Ted Fundoukos kicked a 30 yard field goal to cut the lead to 10-3, only to have Army clinch the win on a seven yard run by quarterback Tory Crawford.

1988 Navy Midshipmen

Navy was led by second year head coach Elliott Uzelac. Team Captains were Mark Pimpo and Bert Pangrazio. The Midshipmen compiled a 3-8 record and were outscored by their opponents by a combined score of 274 to 221. Gary McIntosh led the team in passing with 504 yards. Alton Grizzard led the team in rushing with 633 yards and 6 rushing touchdowns. Carl Jordan led the team in receptions with 29 for 511 yards and 4 TD receptions. Ted Fundoukos led the team in scoring with 51 points.

Home games were played at Navy-Marine Corps Stadium

9/3/1988	NAVY	vs		JAMES MADISON	27	14	**W**
9/10/1988	NAVY	vs		DELAWARE	30	3	**W**
9/17/1988	NAVY	vs		TEMPLE (4-7)	7	12	**L**
9/24/1988	NAVY	@		The Citadel	35	42	**L**
10/1/1988	NAVY	vs		YALE	41	7	**W**
10/8/1988	NAVY	@		Air Force (5-7)	24	34	**L**
10/22/1988	NAVY	@		Pittsburgh (6-5)	6	52	**L**
10/29/1988	NAVY	vs	#2	NOTRE DAME (12-0)	7	22	**L**
11/5/1988	NAVY	@	#16	Syracuse (10-2)	21	49	**L**
11/12/1988	NAVY	@		South Carolina (8-4)	8	19	**L**
12/3/1988	NAVY	vs		ARMY (9-3)	15	20	**L**
Coach: Elliot Uzelac				**Season Record >>**	**221**	**274**	**3-8**

Schedule Source: Steve's Football Bible LLC

Selected game(s) highlights

YALE

Gary McIntosh was back, and the Navy offense was rolling yesterday. McIntosh struck quickly In the second quarter, needing only a total of five plays in three straight series to put 21 points on the scoreboard arid lead Navy to a 4 1 -7 rout of Yale before an overflow homecoming crowd of 31,067 at Navy-Marine Corps Memorial Stadium. McIntosh destroyed Yale's hopes in the second quarter with two long touchdown runs and a 32 yard touchdown pass to Carl Jordan. Navy's 410 yards rushing was the fifth highest total for the Midshipmen since 1948.

Air Force

Andy Smith spearheaded the Air Force attack with 161 yards rushing and a 4 yard touchdown run in the 3rd quarter as the Falcons beat the Midshipmen 34-24. Dee Dowis added 125 yards rushing and scored twice, on an 8 yard run and a 45 yard run. The Falcons led 21-10 at halftime on Dowis' touchdowns and Albert Booker's 2 yard touchdown run. Steve Yarbrough kicked two field goals to cap the scoring for the Falcons. Brian Hill led the defense with 18 tackles.

ARMY {@ Veterans Stadium - Philadelphia, PA}

Army captured the Commander-In-Chief's Trophy with a hard-fought 20-15 victory over Navy. According to Bill Cromartie's "Army-Navy Football: The Greatest Rivalry in Sports," Army coach Jim Young was 25-0 when his team passed the ball no more than three times in a game. This strategy certainly worked against the Midshipmen, as West Point quarterback Bryan McWilliams was the game's top rusher with 100 yards on 21 attempts. When he did drop back to pass, however, McWilliams made the most of the opportunity. With a third-and-six on its own 46 yard line and a 13-9 lead midway through the fourth quarter, McWilliams hit Doug Baker for a 17 yard gain to the Midshipmen 37. He later scored from eight yards out to give his team an 11-point cushion at 20-9. Alton Grizzard led Navy on the ensuing drive, completing five-of-nine passes to enable James Bradley to reach the end zone from two yards out. The two-point conversion failed, and Army recovered the onsides kick to preserve the win and knot the all-time series record at 41-41-7.

1989 Navy Midshipmen

Navy was led by third year head coach Elliott Uzelac. Team Captains were James Bradley and Bob Weissenfels. The Midshipmen compiled a 3-8 record and were outscored by their opponents by a combined score of 272 to 145. The annual Army–Navy Game was played on December 9 at Giants Stadium in East Rutherford, NJ. Navy won the game 19-17. Alton Grizzard led the team in passing with 1,109 yards and 4 touchdown passes. Grizzard led the team in rushing with 626 yards. Shane Smith led the team in receptions with 23 for 356 yards. Frank Schenk led the team in scoring with 49 points.

Home games were played at Navy-Marine Corps Stadium

9/16/1989	NAVY	vs		BYU (10-3)		10	31	L
9/23/1989	NAVY	vs		THE CITADEL		10	14	L
9/30/1989	NAVY	@		North Carolina (1-10)		12	7	W
10/7/1989	NAVY	vs	#20	AIR FORCE (8-4-1)		7	35	L
10/14/1989	NAVY	@	#9	Pittsburgh (8-3-1)	JPS	14	31	L
10/21/1989	NAVY	@		Boston College (2-9)		27	24	W
10/28/1989	NAVY	vs		JAMES MADISON		20	24	L
11/4/1989	NAVY	@	#1	Notre Dame (12-1)		0	41	L
11/11/1989	NAVY	vs		SYRACUSE (8-4)		17	38	L
11/18/1989	NAVY	@		Delaware		9	10	L
12/9/1989	NAVY	vs		ARMY (6-5)		19	17	W
Coach: Elliot Uzelac				**Season Record >>**		**145**	**272**	**3-8**

Schedule Source: Steve's Football Bible LLC

Selected game(s) highlights

#20 AIR FORCE

The teams were tied 7-7 after the 1st quarter, then the Air Force turned it up a notch and scored 28 straight points to finish off the Midshipmen for a 35-7 victory. Ron Gray opened the scoring with a 7 yard TD run. Then Greg Johnson and Steve Senn took over. Johnson ran for two touchdowns and Senn caught two touchdown passes from Dee Dowis and the Falcon defense did the rest, holding the Midshipmen without a score the last three quarters. Alton Grizzard ran for 168 yards and a touchdown for the Middies.

#1 Notre Dame

Top-ranked Notre Dame tied a school record today with its 21st consecutive victory, beating Navy, 41-0. The victory was also Notre Dame's first shutout in six years. The Irish beat Navy for the 26th consecutive time since 1963. Notre Dame rushed for 414 yards and 5 touchdowns and held the Midshipmen (2-6) to 67 yards rushing and 99 yards passing.

ARMY {@ Giants Stadium – East Rutherford, NJ}

In the first Army-Navy game played in East Rutherford, N.J., Frank Schenk hit a 32 yard field goal with 11 seconds left to give the Midshipmen a come-from-behind 19-17 win over the Cadets. Navy got on the scoreboard first when Alton Grizzard hit B.J. Mason with a 54 yard touchdown pass. However, a bad snap on the extra point left Navy with a 6-0 lead. Schenk added three points to that advantage with a 38 yard field goal midway through the first quarter. Army's efficient wishbone offense consumed most of the second quarter, as Cal Cass notched a pair of one yard touchdown runs to give the Cadets a 14-9 lead at halftime. Rodney Purifoy's three yard touchdown run midway through the third quarter, followed by Schenk's extra point, put Navy back ahead, 16-14. Yet, Army regained the lead with two minutes to go in the third quarter when Keith Havenstrite nailed a 21 yard field goal. With 5:02 remaining in the game, Navy took over possession on its own 22 yard line. Grizzard and fullback Mike Burns led the Mids down the field, setting the stage for Schenk's game-winning kick.

1990 Navy Midshipmen

Navy was led by first year head coach George Chaump. Team Captains were Alton Grizzard and Bill Bowling. The Midshipmen compiled a 5-6 record and were outscored by their opponents by a combined score of 294 to 209. The annual Army–Navy Game was played on December 8 at Veterans Stadium in Philadelphia, PA. Army won the game 30-20. Alton Grizzard led the team in passing with 1,438 yards and threw 12 touchdown passes. Jason Pace led the team in rushing with 565 yards and 5 rushing touchdowns. Jerry Dawson led the team in receptions with 46 for 649 yards and 5 TD receptions. Bill Yancey led the team with 5 interceptions. Frank Schenk led the team in scoring with 45 points.

Home games were played at Navy-Marine Corps Stadium

9/8/1990	NAVY		vs		RICHMOND	28	17	W	*Dawson 3 TD catch
9/15/1990	NAVY		@	#11	Virginia (8-4)	14	56	L	
9/22/1990	NAVY		vs		VILLANOVA	23	21	W	
9/29/1990	NAVY		vs		BOSTON COLLEGE (4-7)	17	28	L	
10/6/1990	NAVY		@		Air Force (7-5)	7	24	L	
10/13/1990	NAVY		vs		AKRON (3-7-1)	17	13	W	
10/27/1990	NAVY		vs		JAMES MADISON	7	16	L	
11/3/1990	NAVY		vs	#2	NOTRE DAME (9-3)	31	52	L	
11/10/1990	NAVY		@		Toledo (9-2)	14	10	W	
11/17/1990	NAVY		vs		DELAWARE	31	27	W	
12/8/1990	NAVY		vs		ARMY (6-5)	20	30	L	
Coach: George Chaump					**Season Record >>**	**209**	**294**	**5-6**	

Schedule Source: Steve's Football Bible LLC
***-Single game record**

Selected game(s) highlights

Air Force

Joe Wood kicked three field goals, Chris Howard and Rob Perez each scored from 1 yard out as the Falcons dominated the Midshipmen in a 24-7 victory. Air Force only rushed for 235 yards but held Navy to 31 yards rushing. The Air Force defense intercepted 3 Gary McIntosh passes.

#2 NOTRE DAME {@ Giants Stadium – East Rutherford, NJ}

Notre Dame beat Navy for the 27th consecutive time because there was little wrong with the Fighting Irish's offense. The flanker Raghib (Rocket) Ismail did nothing to hurt his Heisman Trophy chances by gaining 223 yards in total offense, 173 of them on six receptions. His final catch, a 54 yard touchdown pass play over the middle that made the score 44-24 with 2:14 left in the game. Ismail electrified the 70,382 in attendance each time he touched the ball. The bulk of the Notre Dame scoring was handled by five backs – Mirer, Rodney Culver, Tony Brooks, Ricky Watters and Jerome Bettis – each of whom ran in one touchdown. Navy had a chance to take the lead late in the first half. Trailing by 10-7, it failed on three attempts inside the 10- yard line and settled for a tying field goal by Frank Schenk.

ARMY {@ Veterans Stadium – Philadelphia, PA}

Navy was unable to stop the vaunted Army rushing attack, as the Cadets used 367 yards on the ground to post a 30-20 win over the Midshipmen. Behind the efficient performances of quarterback Willie MacMillan and tailback Mike Mayweather, Army turned in a 17-0 second-quarter lead. Navy got on the scoreboard before halftime on a six yard touchdown pass from Alton Grizzard to Jerry Dawson, and a Brad Stramanak 45 yard touchdown run in the third quarter made it 17-14. This was as close as the Midshipmen could get, however, as Army kicker Patmon Malcom padded the Cadet advantage with 38- and 25 yard field goals. Army clinched the win by intercepting a Grizzard pass with 6:10 remaining.

1991 Navy Midshipmen

Navy was led by second year head coach George Chaump. Team Captains were B.J. Mason and Byron Ogden. The Midshipmen compiled a 1-10 record and were outscored by their opponents by a combined score of 321 to 160. It was the program's fewest wins in a season since the winless 1948 season. The annual Army–Navy Game was played on December 7 at Veterans Stadium in Philadelphia, PA. Navy won the game 24-3.

Jim Kubiak led the team in passing with 957 yards. Jason Van Matre led the team in rushing with 544 yards. Tom Pritchard led the team in receptions with 35 for 569 yards. Chad Chatlos led the team with 5 interceptions. Brad Stramanak led the team in scoring with 30 points. **Kubiak set the single game record for most passing yards in a game with 406 yards vs Wake Forest.**

Home games were played at Navy-Marine Corps Stadium

9/7/1991	NAVY	vs		BALL STATE (6-5)		10	33	L	
9/14/1991	NAVY	@		Virginia (8-3-1)		10	17	L	
9/21/1991	NAVY	vs		WILLIAM & MARY		21	26	L	
9/28/1991	NAVY	vs		BOWLING GREEN (11-1)		19	22	L	
10/12/1991	NAVY	vs		AIR FORCE (10-3)		6	46	L	
10/19/1991	NAVY	@		Temple (2-9)		14	21	L	
10/26/1991	NAVY	vs		DELAWARE		25	29	L	
11/2/1991	NAVY	@	#5	Notre Dame (10-3)	NBC	0	38	L	
11/9/1991	NAVY	@		Tulane (1-10)		7	34	L	
11/23/1991	NAVY	vs		WAKE FOREST (3-8)		24	52	L	*-Kubiak 406 pass yds
12/7/1991	NAVY	vs		ARMY (4-7)		24	3	W	
Coach: George Chaump				**Season Record >>**		**160**	**321**	**1-10**	

Schedule Source: Steve's Football Bible LLC
***-Single game record**

Selected game(s) highlights

WILLIAM & MARY

William & Mary used the pinpoint passing of quarterback Chris Hakel and two long touchdown plays to defeat Navy, 26-21, today. Hakel completed 15 of 20 passes for 209 yards, including a 67 yarder to tailback Al Williams in the second quarter that put the Indians ahead to stay. Navy led by 7-3 when Williams took a pass from Hakel behind the line of scrimmage, eluded two tacklers around the 40 and outran several Navy defenders to the end zone. On the next possession, tailback Robert Green opened a 17-7 lead for William & Mary with a 79-yard touchdown run. On a reverse to the left, Green broke two tackles at the line of scrimmage and scored behind strong downfield blocking. Navy closed to 26-21 with 1:13 left in the game when defensive back George Chatlos picked a Williams fumble out of the air and returned it 22 yards for a touchdown. But an on-side kick attempt failed when Doug Emey covered the ball at the Navy 48 and the Indians ran out the clock.

WAKE FOREST

Wake Forest sent Navy to the brink of its worst season in 111 years of football as Gleen Hart and George Coghill provided the big plays in the victory. Hart returned an interception 77 yards for a touchdown late in the first half, and Coghill scored on an 86 yard punt return to make it 35-14 early in the third quarter. The Deamon Deacons scored 24 points in the third period to turn a 21-14 halftime lead into a comfortable 45-17 advantage. Navy quarterback Jim Kubiak set school records with 54 passes and 406 yards and was one short of the school mark for completions, which is 37. He threw for 2 touchdowns and had 3 passes intercepted.

ARMY {@ Veterans Stadium – Philadelphia, PA}

On the 50th anniversary of the Japanese attack on Pearl Harbor, Navy posted its only win of the season with a resounding 24-3 triumph over Army. Following Patmon Malcolm's 39 yard field goal, quarterback Jim Kubiak took over, completing 13-of-16 passes for 157 yards. Kubiak and Jason Van Matre were instrumental in Coach George Chaump's offensive scheme. Van Matre would direct the Midshipmen attack up to the opponent's 25 yard line. Van Matre would then shift to tailback to make room for freshman Kubiak as the signal caller. Van Matre and Billy James each added a touchdown on the ground. Defensively, linebacker Byron Ogden led the Mids with 15 tackles.

1992 Navy Midshipmen

Navy was led by third year head coach George Chaump. Team Captains were Chad Chatlos, Eric McGowan and Steve Palmer. The Midshipmen compiled a 1-10 record and were outscored by their opponents by a combined score of 338 to 131. It was the second straight season that Navy won only one game. Jason Van Matre led the team in passing with 955 yards and threw 6 touchdown passes. Van Matre led the team in rushing with 632 yards. Tom Pritchard led the team in receptions with 30 for 404 yards and 4 TD receptions. Chad Chatlos led the team with 4 interceptions. Tim Rogers led the team in scoring with 33 points.

Home games were played at Navy-Marine Corps Stadium

9/12/1992	NAVY		vs	#23	VIRGINIA (7-4)	0	53	L
9/19/1992	NAVY		@		Boston College (8-3-1)	0	28	L
9/26/1992	NAVY		vs		RUTGERS (7-4)	0	40	L
10/3/1992	NAVY		@		North Carolina (9-3)	14	28	L
10/10/1992	NAVY		@		Air Force (7-5)	16	18	L
10/24/1992	NAVY		@		Delaware	21	37	L
10/31/1992	NAVY		vs	#10	NOTRE DAME (10-1-1)	7	38	L
11/7/1992	NAVY		vs		TULANE (2-9)	20	17	W
11/14/1992	NAVY		vs		VANDERBILT (4-7)	7	27	L
11/21/1992	NAVY		@		Rice (6-5)	22	27	L
12/5/1992	NAVY		vs		ARMY (5-6)	24	25	L
Coach: George Chaump					**Season Record >>**	**131**	**338**	**1-10**

Schedule Source: Steve's Football Bible LLC

Selected game(s) highlights

#10 NOTRE DAME {@ Giants Stadium – East Rutherford, NJ}

The Fighting Irish, who had been favored by as many as 38 points, won by 38-7. It was Notre Dame's 29th consecutive victory in the schools' series. Rick Mirer passed for 221 yards and two touchdowns. Notre Dame scored on five of its six possessions in the first half to take a 31-0 lead. Navy's wishbone offense did not advance past midfield until the fourth quarter when Notre Dame's starters were on the sideline. The touchdown came after Dave Shaw, an end, intercepted Kevin McDougal's attempt at an inside screen pass at the Notre Dame 22. On the next play the indefatigable Navy quarterback, Jason Van Matre, finally had some pass protection and he fired the football to wide receiver Tom Pritchard, who broke off a pattern in the back of the Notre Dame end zone. That came with five minutes left to play, and the Irish retorted with their fifth touchdown, on a 47 yard drive. Van Matre carried the ball 26 times for 70 yards and somehow completed 9 of 14 pass attempts for 93 yards.

ARMY {@ Veterans Stadium - Philadelphia, PA}

Patmon Malcolm's 49 yard field goal with 12 seconds left fulfilled the greatest comeback in Army-Navy history, as Army overcame a 17-point deficit to defeat the Midshipmen, 25-24. Entering the game 1-9, Navy jumped out to a 24-7 lead. However, Army came right back with three-straight scores, including a 68 yard touchdown pass from Rick Roper to Gaylord Greene. The Midshipmen led 24-22 with seven minutes left in the fourth quarter when the two teams exchanged punts. The Army defense held the Midshipmen without a first down, forcing Navy to kick into a considerable wind. Army began its final drive on the Navy 33 yard line. Malcolm initially kicked a 44 yard field goal, but a delay of game penalty negated the three points and pushed Army five yards back. Nonetheless, Malcolm nailed the 49 yarder for the win.

1993 Navy Midshipmen

Navy was led by fourth year head coach George Chaump. Team Captains were Jason Van Matre and Javier Zuluaga. The Midshipmen compiled a 4-7 record and were outscored by their opponents by a combined score of 307 to 203. The annual Army–Navy Game was played on December 4 at Giants Stadium in East Rutherford, NJ. Army won the game 16-14. **Jim Kubiak led the team in passing with 2,628 yards, setting a single season record**, while throwing 11 touchdown passes. Jason Van Matre led the team in rushing with 428 yards. Brad Stramanak led with 10 rushing touchdowns. Van Matre led the team in receptions with 59. Damon Dixon led with 620 receiving yards. Stramanak led the team in scoring with 60 points.

Home games were played at Navy-Marine Corps Stadium

9/11/1993	@		Virginia (7-5)		0	38	L	*Dixon 10 catch
9/18/1993	vs		EASTERN ILLINOIS		31	10	W	
9/25/1993	vs		BOWLING GREEN (6-3-2)		27	20	W	
10/2/1993	@		Tulane (3-9)		25	27	L	
10/9/1993	vs		AIR FORCE (4-8)		28	24	W	
10/16/1993	vs		COLGATE		31	3	W	
10/23/1993	@	#20	Louisville (9-3)		0	28	L	
10/30/1993	vs	#2	NOTRE DAME (11-1)	ABC	27	58	L	
11/13/1993	@		Vanderbilt (4-7)		7	41	L	
11/20/1993	vs		SMU (2-7-2)		13	42	L	
12/4/1993	vs		ARMY (6-5)		14	16	L	
Coach: George Chaump			**Season Record >>**		**203**	**307**	**4-7**	

Schedule Source: Steve's Football Bible LLC
***-Single game record**

Selected game(s) highlights

COLGATE

Two blocked kicks and an Interception led to three Navy touchdowns and the Midshipmen ultimately wore down the Division I-AA Red Raiders, 31-3, before 21,780 at Navy-Marine Corps Stadium. The game was less than three minutes old when defensive back Kevin Mattix broke through to block Tom Morelli's punt. Fellow defensive back Robert Green recovered on the Colgate 10 and ran It In for a touchdown. Dave Gwinn converted for a 7-0 lead with only 2 minutes, 11 seconds off the clock. Jim Kubiak found Dixon open in the right corner of the end zone. Gwinn again added the extra point for a 14-0 lead. Kubiak then put together one of his best scoring drives, moving the Midshipmen 70 yards on seven plays before Gwinn kicked a 35 yard field goal Just as the halftime gun sounded. 300-pound tackle Max Lane bolted three yards from the fullback spot to cap an 84 yard march. Lane then tossed the ball into the stands, leading to a 15 yard unsportsmanlike conduct penalty on the ensuing kickoff.

ARMY {@ Giants Stadium – East Rutherford, NJ}

Navy's furious fourth-quarter rally fell just short, as Army escaped with a 16-14 win. Down 16-0 at the start of the fourth quarter, Navy found the Cadet end zone twice within a two-minute span, as quarterback Jim Kubiak scored on a three yard keeper and found tight end Jim Mill for an eight yard score. The Midshipmen were poised to take the lead with four minutes remaining and the ball on their own 20 yard line. Tailback Billy James gained 60 yards on six carries on the drive, which reached the Army three yard line. Fullback Brad Stramanak picked up a yard on first down, and Kubiak spiked the ball on second down. Stramanak struggled to pick up a yard on third down, and freshman kicker Ryan Bucchianeri's 18 yard field goal attempt sailed wide right.

1994 Navy Midshipmen

Navy was led by fifth year head coach George Chaump. Team Captains were Chris Hart and Jim Kubiak. The Midshipmen compiled a 3-8 record and were outscored by their opponents by a combined score of 399 to 188. The annual Army–Navy Game was played on December 3 at Veterans Stadium in Philadelphia, PA. Army won the game 22-20.

Jim Kubiak led the team in passing with 2,388 yards and threw 10 touchdown passes. Monty Williams led the team in rushing with 215 yards and 7 rushing touchdowns. Damon Dixon led the team in receptions with 51 for 556 yards. Williams led the team in scoring with 48 points.

Home games were played at Navy-Marine Corps Stadium

9/3/1994	NAVY	@	San Diego State (4-7)		14	56	L
9/10/1994	NAVY	vs	VIRGINIA (9-3)		10	47	L
9/17/1994	NAVY	@	Bowling Green (9-2)		21	59	L
10/1/1994	NAVY	vs	DUKE (8-4)		14	47	L
10/8/1994	NAVY	@	Air Force (8-4)		21	43	L
10/15/1994	NAVY	vs	LAFAYETTE		7	0	W
10/22/1994	NAVY	vs	LOUISVILLE (6-5)		14	35	L
10/29/1994	NAVY	@	Notre Dame (6-5-1)	NBC	21	58	L
11/5/1994	NAVY	@	Tulane (1-10)		17	15	W
11/19/1994	NAVY	vs	RICE (5-6)		29	17	W
12/3/1994	NAVY	vs	ARMY (4-7)		20	22	L
Coach: George Chaump			**Season Record >>**		**188**	**399**	**3-8**

Schedule Source: Steve's Football Bible LLC

Selected game(s) highlights

LAFAYETTE

The Naval Academy football team broke a 10 game losing streak yesterday, but just barely, holding off Division I-AA Lafayette College, 7-0, before 20,511 at Navy-Marine Corps Memorial Stadium. The Midshipmen accounted for all the scoring with a nine-play, 82 yard drive late in the first quarter, climaxed by freshman tailback Pat McGrew's 13 yard run. Ryan Bucchianeri kicked the extra point. Jim Kubiak completed 17 of 31 passes for 170 yards but was sacked five times for 40 yards.

ARMY {@ Veterans Stadium - Philadelphia, PA}

Once again, Army and Navy showed a penchant for dramatic finishes, as Kurt Heiss' career-best 52 yard field goal with 6:19 left gave the Cadets a 22-20 victory. As usual, the game was exciting from the opening kickoff to the final gun, as the 65,308 fans in attendance saw six lead changes and six plays of more than 40 yards. With its vaunted wishbone attack, Army rolled up 373 yards on the ground against Navy, while Midshipmen quarterback Jim Kubiak riddled the Cadet secondary for 361 yards and two touchdowns. Kubiak's first touchdown pass, a 27 yarder to Damon Dixon, gave Navy a 7-3 lead at the end of the first quarter. After Army regained the lead with a Don Ross one yard touchdown run midway through the second quarter, the Midshipmen came right back on their next possession. On the first play from scrimmage, tailback Michael Jefferson raced 73 yards for a touchdown. Ryan Bucchianeri's extra point gave Navy a 14-10 advantage, which it held through halftime. Heiss' 35 yard field goal brought the Cadets to within one at 14-13 to start the second half. Army then took the lead on its next possession, as Kevin Vaughn's three yard touchdown run made it 19-14. Navy came right back to take a 20-19 lead late in the third quarter, as Kubiak hit tight end Kevin Hickman for a 56 yard touchdown pass. However, the two-point conversion attempt failed, setting the stage for Heiss' game-winning field goal.

1995 Navy Midshipmen

Navy was led by first-year head coach Charlie Weatherbie (pictured at right). Team Captains were Andy Thompson and Garrett Smith. The Midshipmen compiled a 5-6 record and outscored their opponents by a combined score of 223 to 189. The annual Army–Navy Game was played on December 2 at Veterans Stadium in Philadelphia, PA. Army won the game 14-13.

Ben Fay led the team in rushing with 869 yards. Chris Mccoy led the team in rushing with 803 yards and 7 rushing touchdowns. Cory Schemm led the team in receptions with 25. Matt Scornavacchi led with 328 receiving yards. **Sean Andrews tied the single season record with 8 interceptions**. McCoy led the team in scoring with 42 points.

Home games were played at Navy-Marine Corps Stadium

9/9/1995	NAVY	@		Smu (1-10)		33	2	W
9/16/1995	NAVY	@		Rutgers (4-7)		17	27	L
9/23/1995	NAVY	vs		WAKE FOREST (1-10)		7	30	L
9/30/1995	NAVY	@		Duke (3-8)		30	9	W
10/7/1995	NAVY	vs		VIRGINIA TECH (10-2)		0	14	L
10/14/1995	NAVY	vs		AIR FORCE (8-5)		20	30	L
10/21/1995	NAVY	vs		VILLANOVA		20	14	W
11/4/1995	NAVY	@	#8	Notre Dame (9-3)	NBC	17	35	L
11/11/1995	NAVY	vs		DELAWARE		31	7	W
11/18/1995	NAVY	vs		TULANE (2-9)		35	7	W
12/2/1995	NAVY	vs		ARMY (5-5-1)		13	14	L
Coach: Charlie Weatherbee				**Season Record >>**		**223**	**189**	**5-6**

Schedule Source: Steve's Football Bible LLC

Selected game(s) highlights

Rutgers

Navy gave Rutgers all kinds of problems tonight before the Scarlet Knights escaped with a 27-17 victory. The freewheeling first half ended in a 17-17 tie, with each team kicking a field goal in the last 38 seconds. But in the second half, Navy, operating from its unusual wing bone offense with two wide receivers and two slotbacks, gained only 51 yards. It did not get past the Rutgers 28 yard line. The game turned for Rutgers on a defensive play. Charles Woolridge stripped the ball from Navy's quarterback, Chris McCoy. Woolridge recovered on Navy's 26. Three plays later, on an option route, Marco Battaglia outran Navy's strong safety, Joe Speed. Ray Lucas, the Rutgers quarterback, passed to the end zone, and Battaglia outleaped Speed for a 25 yard touchdown. For Navy, McCoy rushed 25 times for 59 yards (that included four sacks) and completed 7 of 13 passes for 124 yards.

AIR FORCE

The Falcons jumped off to a 17-0 lead on a Jake Campbell 32 yard TD reception from Beau Morgan, a Morgan 1 yard touchdown run and a Randy Roberts 21 yard field goal. Brandon Wilkerson scored a third quarter touchdown on a 6 yard run and Nakia Addison scored in the 4th quarter on a 2 yard run as the Air Force left Annapolis with a 30-20 victory over the Midshipmen. Morgan led the way with 113 yards rushing.

VILLANOVA

Ben Fay guided the Midshipmen to a 20-14 homecoming victory over Division I-AA Villanova before 26,726 at Navy-Marine Corps Memorial Stadium. Fay got considerable help from running back Tim Cannada, who amassed 108 yards on 23 carries. Trailing 7-6, Travis Cooley swooped in for a fumble recovery at the 12. A pass interference call on Navy's first play made it first down and goal from the 1. Two plays later Fay spun into the end zone with 4 minutes 53 seconds to play in the third quarter. A false start on the two-point try put Navy back to the 8, and Villanova, sensing a pass, lined up as such for the second attempt. But Fay dropped back three steps and sprinted up the middle. He wasn't touched until he dove into the end zone for a 14-7 lead. Navy got an insurance touchdown with 10:14 to play, with Cannada running seven yards up the middle for a 20-7 lead.

ARMY {@ Veterans Stadium - Philadelphia, PA}

John Conroy's one yard touchdown run with 1:03 left capped a 99 yard drive and gave Army an exciting 14-13 win over Navy. The victory was the Cadets' fourth straight in the series, as those four games were decided by a total of six points. Navy capitalized on an Army turnover on the third play of the game, as Ben Fay found LeBron Butts for a 22 yard touchdown to give the Midshipmen a 7-0 lead. Conroy then tied the game at seven when he scored the first of his two one yard touchdown runs. With the score still tied at halftime, Navy took the second-half kickoff and promptly marched 52 yards in 16 plays. Freshman kicker Tom Vanderhorst, playing in his first collegiate football game, connected on a 39 yard field goal to give Navy a 10-7 lead. The Newnan, Ga., native helped extend that advantage to 13-7 with a 22 yard field goal at the start of the fourth quarter. With a fourth-and-goal at the Army one yard line with 8:26 left, the Midshipmen were poised to score again. However, the pass attempt by Chris McCoy fell incomplete in the end zone, and Army took over on downs en route to the game-winning drive.

1996 Navy Midshipmen

Navy was led by second year head coach Charlie Weatherbie. Team Captains were Clint Bruce and Ben Fay. The Midshipmen compiled a 9-3 record and outscored their opponents by a combined score of 392 to 309. The Midshipmen were invited to the Aloha Bowl where they played California. The annual Army–Navy Game was played on December 7 at Veterans Stadium in Philadelphia, PA. Army won the game 28-24.

Chris McCoy led the team in passing with 759 yards and threw 6 touchdown passes. McCoy led the team in rushing with 1,228 yards and 16 rushing touchdowns. Cory Schemm and Astor Heaven led the team in receptions with 19. Astor led with 396 receiving yards. Rashad Smith led the team with 4 interceptions. McCoy led the team in scoring with 102 points.

Home games were played at Navy-Marine Corps Stadium

9/7/1996	@		Rutgers (2-9)		10	6	W	
9/21/1996	vs		SMU (5-6)		19	17	W	
9/28/1996	@		Boston College (5-7)		38	43	L	
10/5/1996	vs		DUKE (0-11)		64	27	W	
10/12/1996	@		Air Force (6-5)		20	17	W	
10/26/1996	@		Wake Forest (3-8)		47	18	W	
11/2/1996	vs	#19	Notre Dame (8-3)	CBS	27	54	L	
11/9/1996	vs		DELAWARE		30	14	W	
11/16/1996	vs		TULANE (2-9)		35	21	W	
11/23/1996	@		Georgia Tech (5-6)		36	26	W	
12/7/1996	vs	#23	ARMY (10-2)	CBS	24	28	L	
12/25/1996	**vs**		**California (6-6)**	**ABC**	**42**	**38**	**W**	**Aloha Bowl**
Coach: Charlie Weatherbee			**Season Record >>**		**392**	**309**	**9-3**	

Schedule Source: Steve's Football Bible LLC

Selected game(s) highlights

Air Force

The Naval Academy took a 10-7 lead into the 4th quarter and needed the late game heroics of Tom Vanderhorst, who kicked a 25 yard field goal with 9 seconds left to give the Midshipmen a 20-17 victory. Beau Morgan ran for 112 yards and an 11 yard touchdown run in the 1st quarter. Stephen Pipes returned an interception 31 yards for a touchdown in the 4th quarter for a 14-10 Falcon lead. Dallas Thompson kicked a 49 yard field goal to tie the game at 17-17 with 2:11 remaining in the game, only to have the Midshipmen drive down the field to set up Vanderhorst's game winner.

#19 Notre Dame {Croke Park – Dublin, Ireland}

Notre Dame thrashed Navy, 54-27, before 38,651. Valiant attempts by Navy to catch up, after the Irish had taken an early 14-0 lead, were repeatedly followed by Notre Dame touchdown drives. The game's turning point came with less than four minutes left in the first half, when Navy had just scored its first touchdown to pull within 14-7. Chris McCoy then completed a 59 yard pass to Corey Schemm, and the Navy rooters roared in hope. But the play was nullified by a penalty. Before the half ended, Notre Dame received a poor punt and drove 42 yards in three plays, capped by Denson's 33 yard touchdown run.

TULANE

Navy defeated Tulane, 35-21, and the Middie quarterback, Chris McCoy, had a hand in all five touchdowns. He had 44 rushes, a Navy record, good for 214 yards and 3 touchdowns, and he completed 5 of 11 pass attempts for 98 yards and 2 touchdowns. McCoy became the first quarterback and only the fifth Navy player to rush for more than 1,000 yards in a season.

#23 ARMY {@ Veterans Stadium - Philadelphia, PA}

Army stopped Navy eight times inside the 10 yard line during the final four minutes of the game to preserve a 28-24 win over the Midshipmen. With the victory, the Cadets clinched their first Commander-In-Chief's Trophy since 1988 and accepted a bid to the Poulan Weedeater Independence Bowl. Thanks to touchdown runs from quarterback Chris McCoy and fullback Patrick McGrew and a 15 yard McCoy-to-LeBron Butts touchdown pass, the Middies jumped out to a 21-3 second-quarter lead. The Cadets then used a 44 yard touchdown run from Ronnie McAda and a 22 yard J. Parker field goal to head into the locker room down 21-13 at the half. On the second play of the third quarter, Bobby Williams took the pitch from McAda and went 81 yards for a touchdown. However, the two-point conversion failed, and Navy maintained a 21-19 lead. After the Middies missed a 42 yard field goal, Army drove right back down the field and took a 25-21 lead when Demetrius Perry scored from three yards out. Navy's Tom Vanderhorst brought his team within one, 25-24, when he hit a 31 yard field goal to close the third quarter. Although Parker's 20 yard field goal with 6:35 left in the game provided the game's final margin, Navy drove down inside the Cadet 10 yard line on each of its last-two possessions but was unable to score.

1996 ALOHA BOWL

The game started with California cornerback Deltha O'Neal taking the opening kickoff 100 yards for a touchdown, giving the Golden Bears a 6-0 lead, but the extra point was blocked. Navy answered with a 7 yard touchdown run from tailback Tim Canada taking a 7-6 lead with 6:21 remaining in the 1st quarter. The Golden Bears retook the lead just 3 minutes later with a 6 yard touchdown pass from Pat Barnes to Bobby Shaw giving Cal a 13-7 lead. The Midshipmen answered with two scores in the opening 5 minutes of the second stanza giving the Midshipmen a 21-13 lead. Navy scored on touchdown drives of 76 and 95 yards. With 6 minutes to play in the first half, Cal quarterback Pat Barnes found wide receiver Sean Bullard for a 20 yard touchdown pass and found Na'il Benjamin for the two point conversion tying the game at 21. The Cal defense then forced a 3 and out, and 
Deltha O'Neal scored on a 31 yard wide receiver reverse giving the Golden Bears a 28-21 lead. With just 39 seconds in the first half, Navy quarterback Chris McCoy threw a 2 yard touchdown pass tying the game at 28, but Cal answered with a 20 yard Pat Barnes strike to Bobby Shaw, giving Cal a 35-28 lead going into halftime.

The second half featured less scoring. In the third quarter, Ryan Longwell kicked a 41 yard field goal to give Cal a 38-28 lead. In the fourth quarter, with 8 minutes remaining, back-up quarterback Ben Fay forever became a part of Navy Football lore as he came off the bench and led the first of 2 Navy 4th quarter drives first scored on a 3 yard touchdown run making the score 38-35. Cal drove deep into Navy territory but turned it over at the Navy 16 yard line with 3 minutes left. Then with just 1:41 remaining in the game, Fay scored on the game winning 10 yard touchdown run, making the final 42-38 Navy. The game was notable for its offensive output, with both teams putting up 1080 combined yards, an Aloha Bowl record. Navy rolled up 646 yards of total offense in the game. The first half featured 63 points being scored. Wide receiver Cory Schemm broke the bowl game record for receiving yards with 193 in the game.

1997 Navy Midshipmen

Navy was led by third year head coach Charlie Weatherbie. The team Captains were Chris McCoy and Gervy Alota. The Midshipmen compiled a 7-4 record and outscored their opponents by a combined score of 398 to 209. The annual Army–Navy Game was played on December 6 at Veterans Stadium in Philadelphia, PA. Navy won the game 39-7.

Chris McCoy led the team in passing with 1,203 yards and threw 11 touchdown passes. McCoy led the team in rushing with 1,370 yards and 20 rushing touchdowns. Pat McGrew led the team in receptions with 18 for 407 yards. McCoy led the team in scoring with 120 points.

Home games were played at Navy-Marine Corps Stadium

9/5/1997		@		San Diego State (5-7)		31	45	L	
9/13/1997		vs		RUTGERS (0-11)		36	7	W	
9/20/1997		@		Smu (6-5)		46	16	W	
9/27/1997		@		Duke (2-9)	JPS	17	26	L	
10/11/1997		vs	#19	AIR FORCE (10-3)		7	10	L	
10/18/1997		vs		VMI		42	7	W	
11/1/1997		@		Notre Dame (7-6)	NBC	17	21	L	
11/8/1997		vs		TEMPLE (3-8)		49	17	W	
11/15/1997		vs		COLGATE		52	24	W	*McGrew 3 TD catch
11/22/1997		vs		KENT STATE (3-8)		62	29	W	
12/6/1997		vs		ARMY (4-7)		39	7	W	
Coach: Charlie Weatherbee				**Season Record >>**		**398**	**209**	**7-4**	

Schedule Source: Steve's Football Bible LLC
*-Single game record

Selected game(s) highlights

RUTGERS

Chris McCoy accounted for 201 yards and four touchdowns today as Navy overwhelmed Rutgers, 36-7, in the Middies' home opener. McCoy rushed for 83 yards and three touchdowns and threw for 118 yards and a score. Irv Dingle added 113 rushing yards for the Midshipmen. Navy scored two touchdowns in 16 seconds in the first quarter. After McCoy's 2 yard run gave Navy a 7-0 lead with 8 minutes 13 seconds left, Rutgers (0-3) failed to field the kickoff and Navy covered the free ball at the Rutgers 9. McCoy scored on the next play.

#19 AIR FORCE

In another offensively challenged game, the Air Force left Navy-Marine Corps Memorial Stadium with a narrow 10-7 victory over the Midshipmen. Navy took the lead on a Chris McCoy 8 yard touchdown run. The Falcons responded with an Alex Wright 33 yard field goal to trail 7-3 at halftime. In the 3rd quarter, Tim Curry recovered a blocked punt in the end zone and Air Force held on for the victory. Air Force managed 229 yards of total offense while the Midshipmen managed 215 yards of total offense.

Notre Dame

Notre Dame barely escaped a miraculous last-second finish by the Navy football team yesterday and extended its NCAA-record winning streak over the Midshipmen to 34 games, but this 21-17 victory before a stunned crowd of 80,225 deserved several asterisks. A Hail Mary pass with three seconds remaining by Navy quarterback Chris McCoy bounced off the fingertips of safety Deke Cooper near the Irish 25. Slotback Pat McGrew scooped the ball out of the air before it hit the ground and made a mad dash for the end zone. But television replays showed that McGrew juggled the ball out of bounds on the 1 yard line after being nudged by cornerback Allen Rossum. The near-miss on the 69 yard completion only added to the frustration of the Middies, who outplayed heavily favored Notre Dame for almost the entire game, save for a time-consuming 17-play, 93 yard scoring march in the fourth quarter that provided the margin of victory. Co-captain Gervy Alota, who led an inspired Navy defense with 10 tackles and also picked up a first down on a fake punt, summed up his team's bitter emotions. McCoy, who had been hyped as a Heisman Trophy candidate before the season, was impressive running the ball, gaining 147 yards on 23 carries and accounting for both Navy touchdowns on 9- and 2 yard dashes. But the senior co-captain was guilty of throwing three interceptions, and the Irish ultimately converted two of the thefts into touchdowns. The first pick by linebacker Kory Minor on the Navy 29 set up a 14 yard touchdown pass from Ron Powlus to flanker Bobby Brown, tying the game 7-7 after Navy had staged a flawless 61 yard scoring drive on the game's first offensive series.

The lead then seesawed with Navy taking a 10-7 halftime advantage on Tom Vanderhorst's 22 yard field goal. Vanderhorst failed to convert from 33 yards out just before the half, a miss that would prove costly. The Irish rebounded to take a 14-10 lead in the opening minutes of the second half. Junior tailback Autrey Denson (19 carries for 125 yards) circled left end, shook off a tackle by cornerback Gerald Wilson and raced 48 yards to score. But an interception by safety Rashad Smith, who also had a fumble recovery, led to a 48 yard touchdown drive to put the Mids back on top, 17-14, late in the third quarter. They appeared in excellent position to finish the job after a short punt gave them the ball on their own 42. Runs by McCoy and Tim Cannada advanced the ball to the Irish 18. On second down, McCoy barely missed Marty Metcalf with an end-zone pass. And then came the fateful interception. With considerable time to throw, McCoy threw into a crowd and strong safety Benny Guilbeaux stepped in front of wide receiver LeBron Butts to steal the pass in the end zone and return it to the 7.

On the first play of Notre Dame's long winning drive, Denson seemed to lose the ball and safety Kevin Lewis pounced on it on the Irish 7. But the officials ruled Denson was down. After the near-stunning comeback by Navy left the fans in semi-shock, the Mids were berated by Irish supporters for walking through the Notre Dame band.

COLGATE

Navy jumped to a 31 point lead in the first half before allowing Colgate a first down, got a brief scare in the fourth quarter, and then rebounded to a 52-24 victory yesterday before 21,038 at Navy-Marine Corps Memorial Stadium. The Midshipmen, who boosted their record to 5-4, seemed to relax on defense after dominating the Division I-AA Red Raiders in the first half, 335-92 in total yardage. Colgate sophomore quarterback Ryan Vena led a spirited comeback, passing for three touchdowns and running for a two-point conversion to narrow the deficit to 38-24 with 12:52 remaining. But Navy capitalized on a 90 yard kickoff collaboration between senior Pat McGrew and sophomore Matt Nelson to change the momentum. McGrew returned the ball to the 42 and kept his legs churning amid a crowd of' would be tacklers before lateraling to Nelson, who found clear sailing down the right sideline. According to the rule book, Nelson was credited with a 58 yard touchdown return.

ARMY {@ Giants Stadium – East Rutherford, NJ}

With the Navy defense holding Army to just 84 yards of total offense, the Midshipmen rolled to a 39-7 victory over the Cadets in East Rutherford, N.J. The 32-point win was not only Navy's largest margin of triumph over Army since 1973, but it was also the fifth largest for either team in series history. Although Army drove 74 yards in two plays for a game-opening touchdown, quarterback Johnny Goff and Co. managed to gain just 13 yards the rest of the afternoon. Meanwhile, Navy quarterback Chris McCoy directed the Midshipmen to a record-setting day on the ground, gaining 205 yards on 31 carries. Fullback Tim Cannada added a career-high 133 yards on 30 carries, as Navy rolled up 383 yards rushing overall. Midshipmen wide receiver LeBron Butts also set a new series standard with his third career touchdown. Defensively, linebacker Travis Cooley had seven tackles, while defensive tackle David Viger and linebacker Jason Coffey added five stops apiece.

1998 Navy Midshipmen

Navy was led by fourth year head coach Charlie Weatherbie. Team Captains were Jason Wolf and Jason Snider. The Midshipmen compiled a 3-8 record and were outscored by their opponents by a combined score of 376 to 255. The annual Army–Navy Game was played on December 5 at Veterans Stadium in Philadelphia, PA. Army won the game 34-30.

Brian Broadwater led the team in passing with 838 yards and threw 7 touchdown passes. Broadwater led the team in rushing with 679 yards. Irv Dingle led with 6 rushing touchdowns. Ryan Read led the team in receptions with 17 for 433 yards and 6 TD receptions. Tom Vanderhorst led the team in scoring with 45 points.

Home games were played at Navy-Marine Corps Stadium

9/10/1998	NAVY	@		Wake Forest (3-8)	ESPN	14	26	L
9/19/1998	NAVY	vs		KENT STATE (0-11)		38	24	W
9/26/1998	NAVY	@		Tulane (12-0)		24	42	L
10/3/1998	NAVY	vs	#16	WEST VIRGINIA (8-4)		24	45	L
10/10/1998	NAVY	@		Air Force (12-1)		7	49	L
10/17/1998	NAVY	vs		COLGATE		42	35	W
10/24/1998	NAVY	@		Boston College (4-7)		32	31	W
11/7/1998	NAVY	vs		RUTGERS (5-6)		33	36	L
11/14/1998	NAVY	vs	#12	NOTRE DAME (9-3)	CBS	0	30	L
11/21/1998	NAVY	vs		SMU (5-7)		11	24	L
12/5/1998	NAVY	vs		ARMY (3-8)	CBS	30	34	L
Coach: Charlie Weatherbee				**Season Record >>**		255	376	3-8

Schedule Source: Steve's Football Bible LLC

Selected game(s) highlights

Air Force

Cale Bonds ran for two first half touchdowns and the Falcons raced to a 35-0 halftime lead on the way to a 49-7 thrashing of the Midshipmen. Bonds rushed for 167 yards and passed for 194 yards, while throwing two touchdown passes, one to Dylan Newman from 22 yards out and one to Matt Rillos for 46 yards. The Falcons rushed for 342 yards and had 536 yards of total offense. The defense held the Midshipmen to 195 yards of total offense.

COLGATE

Brian Broadwater led the Midshipmen to a dramatic 42-35 victory over Colgate. He rushed for 216 yards and two touchdowns, including his game-winning 61 yard sprint with 61 seconds left. He also completed eight of nine passes for 165 yards and a pair of touchdowns. Trailing the Division I-AA Red Raiders 35-21 at the start of the fourth quarter, Broadwater directed scoring drives of 92, 54 and 9 yards to break Navy's three game losing streak. He produced a 35-35 tie throwing a 54 yard strike to fellow sophomore Ryan Read with 8:56 left. Read caught the ball in stride at the Colgate 20 and won the race to the end zone. But the homecoming crowd of 28,504 had to hold its breath while Colgate staged a last ditch effort to force overtime. Quarterback Ryan Vena (20-for-35, 377 yards, three touchdowns) almost got the job done. Starting from his 20 and battling the clock, he moved the Red Raiders in rapid fashion to a first down at the Navy 15 with 22 seconds left, but Vena threw four straight incompletions and Navy had held on.

Boston College

The Boston College football team suffered their most heartbreaking loss of the season on Saturday, falling to Navy, 32-31, after John Matich's last-second field goal attempt sailed wide left. The

Eagles led 28-10 at one point in the third quarter, but were unable to hold on, as the Midshipmen outscored them, 22--3, in the last 17 minutes of the game.

ARMY {@ Veterans Stadium - Philadelphia, PA}

In the highest-scoring game in Army-Navy history, the Cadets overcame an 11-point third-quarter deficit to upend the Midshipmen, 34-30. The 64 points scored by the two teams surpassed the previous record of 55, set in 1959 and '83. Army has now won the last-five contests at Veterans Stadium by a total of 12 points. Navy jumped out to a 10-0 first-quarter lead when Tim Shubzda kicked a 35 yard field goal and fullback Irv Dingle added a 17 yard scoring run. However, backup quarterback Joe Gerena directed the Cadets' comeback with touchdown runs of 25 and 69 yards, respectively, handing Army a 13-10 advantage at the end of the first quarter. Navy used its aerial attack to regain the lead, as quarterback Brian Broadwater found wide receiver Ryan Read for 49- and 69 yard scoring strikes to give the Midshipmen a 24-19 halftime lead. The 69 yard touchdown pass marked a new series record. The two teams traded touchdowns in the third quarter, but a Navy turnover set the stage for an exciting final stanza. The Midshipmen had the ball first-and-goal on the Army four yard line, but Navy's Matt Harden fumbled the ball into the end zone, where the Cadets' Jason Walker recovered it. Three plays later, fullback Ty Amey ran 70 yards for the game-winning touchdown. Kicker Eric Olsen added a 26 yard field goal late in the game to provide the final margin. Despite the impressive offensive performance by both teams, the game was marred by what took place after Amey's score. A railing collapsed in the Army student section, sending nine Cadets (four West Point students and five military academy prep school students) tumbling 12 feet to the ground.

1999 Navy Midshipmen

Navy was led by fifth year head coach Charlie Weatherbie. The team Captains were Chris McCoy and Gervy Alota. The Midshipmen compiled a 5-7 record and outscored their opponents by a combined score of 326 to 306. The annual Army–Navy Game was played on December 4 at Veterans Stadium in Philadelphia, PA. Navy won the game 19-9.

Brian Broadwater led the team in passing with 806 yards and 4 touchdown passes. Brian Madden led the team in rushing with 879 yards and 9 rushing touchdowns. Matt O'Donnell led the team in receptions with 22 for 347 yards. Tim Shubzda led the team in scoring with 88 points.

Home games were played at Navy-Marine Corps Stadium

9/4/1999		vs	#10	GEORGIA TECH (8-4)	FSN	14	49	L	
9/11/1999		@		Kent State (2-9)		48	28	W	
9/18/1999		vs		BOSTON COLLEGE (8-4)	FSN	10	14	L	
9/25/1999		@		Rice (5-6)		17	20	L	
10/2/1999		@		West Virginia (4-7)		31	28	W	
10/9/1999		vs		AIR FORCE (6-5)		14	19	L	
10/23/1999		vs		AKRON (7-4)		29	35	L	
10/30/1999		@		Notre Dame (5-7)	NBC	24	28	L	
11/6/1999		@		Rutgers (1-10)		34	7	W	
11/13/1999		vs		TULANE (3-8)		45	21	W	
11/20/1999		@		Hawaii (9-4)		41	48	L	
12/4/1999		vs		ARMY (3-8)	CBS	19	9	W	*Shubzda 4 field goals
Coach: Charlie Weatherbee				**Season Record >>**		**326**	**306**	**5-7**	

Schedule Source: Steve's Football Bible LLC
***-Single game record**

Selected game(s) highlights

AIR FORCE

The Midshipmen held a 7-0 halftime lead, but Air Force reeled off 19 straight points in the 2nd half for a 19-14 victory over Navy. Jackson Whiting kicked a 23 yard field goal followed by a Dave Adams 49 yard field goal. Mike Thiessen ran 53 yards for a touchdown and Jeremy Laster ran 1 yard for a touchdown to ice the game for the Falcons. Thiessen rushed for 108 yards to lead the Falcon offense.

Notre Dame

On the brink of exorcising the ghosts of many losses past, the Midshipmen again fell victim to their haunting misfortunes of 1999 yesterday and dropped their 36th consecutive game to Notre Dame, 28-24, before 80,012 sun-splashed fans at Notre Dame Stadium. Navy (2-6) has been accustomed to narrow defeats this season -- this was its fifth by six or fewer points -- but the latest was especially heartbreaking because of the opposition and because of a controversial measurement with 1: 20 remaining that could have iced the Irish for good. Instead, Notre Dame (5-3) marched on to score the winning touchdown with 36 seconds left. The outcome assured that Notre Dame would extend the mastery of the Midshipmen that has existed since Roger Staubach and mates dominated here, 35-14, in 1963. The streak is the longest winning streak by one team over another in NCAA history. Navy led, 24-21, on a 33 yard Tim Shubzda field goal with 5: 56 left in the game when the Irish launched their final possession. At the Navy 37, the Irish faced a fourth-and-10 play and Jarious Jackson passed to Bobby Brown, who twisted and turned while in the grasp of two Midshipmen, trying to squirm for precious bits of yardage. The measurement was close, but the Irish were awarded a first down by mere inches, prolonging the drive. Six plays later, Jackson scrambled and lofted a pass to Jay Johnson near the left sideline. Johnson eluded the tackle attempt of Davede Alexander at the 5 and lunged into the end zone for a 16 yard touchdown with 36 seconds remaining. Had the sticks fallen in Navy's favor, the ball would have turned over to the Midshipmen, and Notre Dame had expended all its timeouts. The Irish overcame 130 yards worth of penalties with a 146 yard rushing game by Julius Jones and a resourceful -- if unartistic -- performance by Jackson. Third nationally in passing efficiency, Jackson was 15-of-33 for 200 yards with two touchdowns and two interceptions

ARMY {@ Veterans Stadium, Philadelphia, PA}

Sophomore quarterback Brian Madden rushed for a career-high 177 yards and one touchdown, while senior kicker Tim Shubzda tied an Army-Navy game record with four field goals to lead Navy over Army, 19-9, in front of a Veterans Stadium record crowd of 70,049. The game was the 100th in the storied rivalry. Madden, who was named the Most Valuable Player of the game by the Philadelphia Sportswriters Association, put Navy on the board first with his two yard touchdown run. It was Navy's only touchdown of the day. Shubzda drilled field goals of 35, 34, 37 and 38 yards, in helping put the Cadets away as the Midshipmen built a 19-3 lead. The Navy defense was sensational all day, holding West Point to just 210 yards of total offense. Gino Marchetti led the way with two fumble recoveries and a forced fumble. John Chavous recorded a team-high tying 10 tackles and intercepted his first career pass, while Daryl Hill also recorded 10 tackles, including two tackles for a loss and a sack. David Ryno, Brad Wimsatt and Chris Lepore had seven tackles apiece. The Midshipmen also got a huge lift from senior punter Tray Calisch, who averaged 50.3 yards per punt over six punts, a Navy record for the Army-Navy game.

2000 Navy Midshipmen

Navy was led by sixth year head coach Charlie Weatherbie. Team Captains were Brian Broadwater and Brad Wimsatt. The Midshipmen compiled a 1-10 record and were outscored by their opponents by a combined score of 391 to 182. The annual Army–Navy Game was played on December 2 at M&T Bank Stadium in Baltimore, MD. It was the first Army-Navy game played in Baltimore since 1944; Navy won the game 30-28.

Brian Broadwater led the team in passing with 858 yards. Raheem Lambert led the team in rushing with 597 yards. Ed Malinowski led with 5 rushing touchdowns. Brandon Rampani led the team in receptions with 22 for 324 yards. Chris Lepore led the team with 5 interceptions. David Hills led the team in scoring with 44 points.

Home games were played at Navy-Marine Corps Stadium

9/2/2000	NAVY	vs		TEMPLE (4-7)		6	17	L
9/16/2000	NAVY	@		Georgia Tech (9-3)		13	40	L
9/23/2000	NAVY	@		Boston College (7-5)		7	48	L
9/30/2000	NAVY	vs	#18	TCU (10-2)	FSN	0	24	L
10/7/2000	NAVY	@		Air Force (9-3)		13	27	L
10/14/2000	NAVY	vs	#20	NOTRE DAME (9-3)	CBS	14	45	L
10/21/2000	NAVY	vs		RUTGERS (3-8)		21	28	L
10/28/2000	NAVY	vs		TOLEDO (10-1)		14	35	L
11/11/2000	NAVY	@		Tulane (6-5)		38	50	L
11/18/2000	NAVY	vs		WAKE FOREST (2-9)		26	49	L
12/2/2000	NAVY	vs		ARMY (1-10)	CBS	30	28	W
Coach: Charlie Weatherbee				**Season Record >>**		182	391	**1-10**

Schedule Source: Steve's Football Bible LLC

Selected game(s) highlights

Air Force

Nate Beard ran for 45 yards and two touchdowns and Air Force forced two fourth-quarter turnovers in a 27-13 victory over Navy. Navy got as close as 17-13 on a 45 yard field goal by David Hills late in the third quarter before Air Force began controlling the clock with fullbacks Beard and Scott Becker. Beard capped a nine-play, 36 yard scoring drive with a 1 yard TD run that gave Air Force a 14-point lead with 7:21 left. The Falcons took a 17-10 lead into the half after David Adams kicked a 38 yard field goal set up by a blocked punt.

#20 NOTRE DAME {@ Florida Citrus Bowl – Orlando, FL}

Notre Dame, ranked #20, beat Navy 45-14 for their 37th straight victory in college football's longest continuous intersectional rivalry. Matt LoVecchio threw for 183 yards and two touchdowns and Tony Driver scored twice on fumble returns for the #20 Irish. LoVecchio threw TD passes of 11 yards to Dan O'Leary and 32 yards to Tony Fisher before being replaced by Gary Godsey, whose 46 yard scoring pass to Jay Johnson finished the rout. Navy avoided a shutout when Ed Malinowski threw fourth-quarter TD passes of 46 yards to Brandon Rampani and 9 yards to Brian Williams.

ARMY {@ M&T Bank Stadium – Baltimore, MD}

The 101st meeting in the storied rivalry between Army and Navy ended with the Midshipmen surviving with a 30-28 victory. The Black Knights scored the first points of the game less than three minutes into the contest on a 65 yard run by Michael Wallace. Navy responded to the challenge by scoring the next 27 points and held a 27-7 lead late in the third quarter. David Hills started the Navy scoring with a 23 yard field goal, followed by a Brian Broadwater 45 yard run towards the end of the first period. Broadwater turned to the air for the next Navy score, connecting on a 32 yard touchdown strike to Brian Williams. Hills closed the first-half scoring with a 32 yard field goal. Navy's defense accounted for the Middies third quarter score as Brad Wimsatt recovered an Army fumble and rumbled three yards into the end zone. Army began its comeback by blocking a Williams punt and returning it six yards for a third-quarter touchdown and closed to 27-21 on a 23 yard touchdown pass from backup quarterback Curtis Zervic to Brian Brueton. Navy managed a little bit of breathing room as Hills drilled a 27 yard field goal with 5:32 left in the game. Army, though, took just 2:48 off the clock in completing a 10-play, 56 yard drive to make the score 30-28 on a 21 yard touchdown pass by Zervic. The Black Knights attempted, and recovered, the onsides kick attempt, but the officials ruled the ball did not go the necessary 10 yards before it was touched by an Army player, thereby turning the ball over to Navy. Hills missed a 43 yard field goal attempt, but Army ran into Hills, giving Navy a first down and the Middies ran out the clock to pick up its only win of the year.

2001 Navy Midshipmen

Navy was led by head coach Charlie Weatherbie in this seventh season for most of the year. He was replaced by Rick Lantz for the last three games of the season. Team Captains were Ed Malinowski and Jake Bowen. The Midshipmen compiled a 0-10 record and were outscored by their opponents by a combined score of 344 to 183. The annual Army–Navy Game was played on December 1 at Veterans Stadium in Philadelphia, PA. Army won the game 26-17.

Brian Madden led the team in passing with 902 yards and threw 4 touchdown passes. Madden led the team in rushing with 905 yards and 8 rushing touchdowns. Jeff Gaddy led the team in receptions with 24 for 365 yards. David Hills led the team in scoring with 61 points.

Home games were played at Navy-Marine Corps Stadium

8/30/2001	NAVY	@		Temple (4-7)		26	45	L
9/8/2001	NAVY	vs	#10	GEORGIA TECH (8-5)	FSN	7	70	L
9/22/2001	NAVY	vs		BOSTON COLLEGE (8-4)		21	38	L
10/6/2001	NAVY	vs		AIR FORCE (6-6)		18	24	L
10/13/2001	NAVY	vs		RICE (8-4)		13	21	L
10/20/2001	NAVY	@		Rutgers (2-9)		17	23	L
10/27/2001	NAVY	@		Toledo (10-2)		20	21	L
11/10/2001	NAVY	vs		TULANE (3-9)		28	42	L
11/17/2001	NAVY	@		Notre Dame (5-6)	NBC	16	34	L
12/1/2001	NAVY	vs		ARMY (3-8)	CBS	17	26	L
Coach: Charlie Weatherbee				**Season Record >>**		**183**	**344**	**0-10**

Schedule Source: Steve's Football Bible LLC

Selected game(s) highlights

AIR FORCE

Keith Boyea ran for a career-high 118 yards and led three long touchdown drives as Air Force beat Navy 24-18. Boyea scored on a 43 yard run in the final seconds of the first quarter, and Air Force also got touchdown runs of 23 yards from Anthony Butler and 14 yards from Leotis Butler. Air Force finished with 293 yards rushing. Navy regained possession with 2:18 left, after an Air Force punt rolled dead at the 9. Madden drove the Mids to near midfield, before a pass off the hands of a Navy receiver was intercepted by Adam Hanes at the Air Force 41.

Toledo

Chester Taylor rushed for a season-high 195 yards and scored two touchdowns to lead Toledo to a 21-20 non-conference victory before a Mid-American Conference record crowd of 36,852 at the Glass Bowl on Saturday. Tavares Bolden chipped in with another strong performance, throwing for 282 yards on 21-of-29 passing. Bolden threw a 13 yard touchdown pass to a wide open Andrew Clarke, putting Toledo ahead 21-17 with 13:20 remaining. Navy pulled to within a point when David Hills kicked a 30 yard field goal. But the Midshipmen could not move the ball on their final possession of the game and punted it away with 2:47 to play. Toledo held on to the ball the rest of the way and claimed the win. Toledo didn't take the lead until the first two minutes of the second half when Taylor scored on a nine yard run that put the Rockets up 14-10. Bolden's 57 yard pass to Danta Greene set up the score. Greene finished with eight receptions for a career-high 117 yards. It was a trick play that put Navy ahead in the third quarter and had the Midshipmen thinking about the upset. Madden threw a lateral to wide receiver Chandler Sims, who then found Tony Lane for a 34 yard touchdown pass that gave Navy a 17-14 lead. Navy struck first when Madden faked a handoff and scampered 12 yards into the end zone. The touchdown capped a 78 yard, eight-play drive. Madden picked up 16 yards while scrambling away from pressure to set up David Hill's 42 yard field goal that put Navy ahead 10-0 early in the second quarter -

the biggest lead the Midshipmen have had all season. Madden finished with 121 rushing yards on 24 carries. Navy had 140 rushing yards in the first half.

ARMY {@ Veterans Stadium, Philadelphia, PA}

Army jumped out to a 13-0 lead on its first-two possessions and never looked back, defeating Navy, 26-17 at Veterans Stadium in front 69,708 spectators. With the loss, Navy finished 0-10, its worst record in school history. The only other Navy teams to go winless were the 1948 squad (0-8-1), the 1883 team (0-1) and the 1879 team (0-0-1). Army set the tone early, stuffing Navy on its first possession and then scoring five plays later on Ardell Daniels' 60-yard touchdown run. Army made it 13-0 on its next possession as Clyde Clark let a sure interception, and possible touchdown, go right through his hands into the arms of Army tight end Brian Bruenton who turned and rumbled 42 yards for a touchdown. The Navy defense settled down after Army's second touchdown, allowing just 197 yards in Army's final-15 possessions after allowing 138 yards on its first-two possessions. Navy, though, was unable to get back into the game as the offense could never get untracked and the special teams made two critical errors that ended any hope of a comeback.

2002 Navy Midshipmen

Navy was led by first year head coach Paul Johnson. Team Captains were Donnie Fricks and Josh Brindel. The Midshipmen compiled a 2-10 record and were outscored by their opponents by a combined score of 436 to 290. The annual Army–Navy Game was played on December 7 at Giants Stadium in East Rutherford, NJ. Navy won the game 58-12.

Craig Candeto led the team in passing with 843 yards and threw 5 touchdown passes. Candeto led the team in rushing with 775 yards and 16 rushing touchdowns. Eric Roberts led the team in receptions with 17 for 429 yards. Candeto led the team in scoring with 96 points.

Home games were played at Navy-Marine Corps Stadium

8/31/2002	NAVY		@		Smu (3-9)		38	7	W
9/7/2002	NAVY		vs	#21	NC STATE (11-3)		19	65	L
9/21/2002	NAVY		vs		NORTHWESTERN (3-9)		40	49	L
9/28/2002	NAVY		vs		DUKE (2-10)		17	43	L
10/5/2002	NAVY		@		Air Force (8-5)		7	48	L
10/12/2002	NAVY		vs		RICE (4-7)		10	17	L
10/19/2002	NAVY		@		Boston College (9-4)		21	46	L
10/26/2002	NAVY		@		Tulane (8-5)		30	51	L
11/9/2002	NAVY		vs	#9	NOTRE DAME (10-3)	CBS	23	30	L
11/16/2002	NAVY		vs		CONNECTICUT (6-6)		0	38	L
11/23/2002	NAVY		@		Wake Forest (7-6)		27	30	L
12/7/2002	NAVY		vs		ARMY (1-11)	CBS	58	12	W
Coach: Paul Johnson					**Season Record >>**		**290**	**436**	**2-10**

Schedule Source: Steve's Football Bible LLC

Selected game(s) highlights

Smu

Craig Candeto ran for 153 yards and three touchdowns to lead the Navy Midshipmen to a 38-7 victory over the Southern Methodist Mustangs. Candeto also connected on 4-of-9 passes for 106 yards for the Midshipmen. SMU got off to a quick start and led 7-0 after John Hampton took a 13-yard pass from Tate Wallis in for a score. Navy proceeded to score the next 38 points of the contest and got started with Eric Roberts' nine-yard touchdown run with 6:20 remaining in the first quarter. Candeto then scored three straight touchdowns, on runs of two and 56 yards, before carrying from one yard out to put Navy ahead 28-7 going into the locker room at the half. Roberts started the scoring in the second half with a one-yard touchdown run, and Eric Rolfs drilled a 30-yard field goal in the fourth quarter.

#9 NOTRE DAME {@ M&T Bank Stadium – Baltimore, MD}

Trailing by eight points against lightly regarded Navy late in Saturday's game, the ninth-ranked Fighting Irish rallied behind Carlyle Holliday. Holiday set up the tying score with a 29 yard completion to Omar Jenkins, then hit a wide-open Jenkins for a 67 yard touchdown with 2:08 remaining to give Notre Dame a 30-23 victory. The Irish, who lost three fumbles against Boston College last week, lost three more against the Midshipmen and fell behind 23-15 in the fourth quarter. Holiday's 29 yarder to Jenkins led to a 1 yard TD run by Rashon Powers-Neal. Holiday then lobbed a pass to an open Arnaz Battle in the corner of the end zone for the 2-point conversion that tied it at 23 with 4:28 remaining. After Notre Dame got the ball back at its 33 with 2:19 left, Jenkins slipped behind the Navy secondary, hauled in a long pass from Holiday and sprinted to the end zone. Notre Dame managed only 68 yards rushing, but Holiday made up for it by throwing for 272 yards.

ARMY {@ Giants Stadium – East Rutherford, NJ}

Quarterback Craig Candeto rushed for 103 yards and a school-record six touchdowns to lead Navy to a 58-12 rout over Army in the 103rd playing of the Army-Navy game. Candeto also threw a 23 yard touchdown pass to Tony Lane, accounting for seven of Navy's eight touchdowns. The 58 points scored by Navy are the most in series history and the 46-point margin of victory is the second largest in series history (Navy won 51-0 in 1973). Navy played a near perfect game, scoring on its first-eight possessions. The Midshipmen did not have a turnover or a penalty and didn't punt until nine minutes left in the game. The Midshipmen rushed for 421 yards and piled up an Army-Navy game record 508 yards of total offense. The defense played equally well, allowing a season-low 241 yards of total offense, including just 56 yards on the ground. Fourteen different Navy players carried the ball. In addition to Candeto, the Midshipmen got big performances from sophomore fullback Michael Brimage, who had 10 carries for 84 yards; Lane, who carried the ball five times for 65 yards and senior fullback Bryce McDonald, who rushed for 63 yards and a touchdown on 10 carries. Candeto completed four of his five pass attempts for 87 yards and one touchdown as four different receivers caught passes.

2003 Navy Midshipmen {Commander-in-Chief Trophy}

Navy was led by second year head coach Paul Johnson. Team Captains were Craig Candeto and Eddie Carthan. The Midshipmen compiled an 8-5 record and outscored their opponents by a combined score of 396 to 283. The Midshipmen were invited to the Houston Bowl where they played Texas Tech from the Big 12 Conference. The annual Army–Navy Game was played on December 6 at Lincoln Financial Field in Philadelphia, PA. Navy won the game 34-6.

Craig Candeto led the team in passing with 1,140 yards and threw 7 touchdown passes. Kyle Eckel led the team in rushing with 1,249 yards. Candeto led with 16 rushing touchdowns. Eric Roberts led the team in receptions with 20 for 493 yards and 5 TD receptions. Candeto leads the team in scoring with 96 points.

Home games were played at Navy-Marine Corps Stadium

8/30/2003	vs		VMI		37	10	W	
9/6/2003	@	#25	Tcu (11-2)		3	17	L	
9/20/2003	vs		EASTERN MICHIGAN (3-9)		39	7	W	
9/27/2003	@		Rutgers (5-7)		27	48	L	
10/4/2003	vs		AIR FORCE (7-5)		28	25	W	
10/11/2003	@		Vanderbilt (2-10)		37	27	W	
10/18/2003	@		Rice (5-7)		38	6	W	
10/25/2003	vs		DELAWARE		17	21	L	
11/1/2003	vs		TULANE (5-7)		35	17	W	
11/8/2003	@		Notre Dame (5-7)	NBC	24	27	L	
11/22/2003	vs		CENTRAL MICHIGAN (3-9)		63	34	W	
12/6/2003	vs		ARMY (0-13)	CBS	34	6	W	
12/30/2003	**vs**		**Texas Tech (8-5)**	**ESPN**	**14**	**38**	**L**	**Houston Bowl**
Coach: Paul Johnson			**Season Record >>**		**396**	**283**	**8-5**	

Schedule Source: Steve's Football Bible LLC

Selected game(s) highlights

AIR FORCE {@ FedEx Field – Washington, DC}

Kyle Eckel ran for a career-high 176 yards and a touchdown, and Craig Candeto accounted for two scores as the Midshipmen thrilled the crowd of 30,623 at FedEx Field by shocking previously unbeaten Air Force 28-25. The teams entered ranked 1-2 in the nation in rushing. The Midshipmen never trailed after scoring two touchdowns in a 48-second span of the second quarter to take a 14-3 lead. Navy went up 21-10 by moving 82 yards in 14 plays on the opening possession of the second half. Air Force got to 21-18 when Brett Walker recovered a fumble by Falcons quarterback Chance Harridge in the end zone with 14:09 remaining and Joe Schieffer ran in the two-point conversion. Navy answered with a 13-play, 71 yard drive in which Eckel gained 55 yards on eight carries. The junior fullback scored from the 4 on a fourth-and-1 giving Navy a 10-point cushion with 7:35 left.

Notre Dame

Notre Dame has struggled so much this season that even a victory over Navy is cause for celebration. D.J. Fitzpatrick kicked a 40 yard field goal as time expired to give Notre Dame a 27-24 victory Saturday, extending the Irish's NCAA record for consecutive wins against one team to 40. The Irish (3-6) haven't had much to celebrate this season after getting off to their worst start since 1963. But the win keeps alive Notre Dame's hopes for finishing the season at .500. It also ended a three-game home losing streak -- just the fifth such streak in school history -- and avoided tying the school record of four straight home loses set in 1960. Kyle Eckel scored on runs of 1 and 5 yards in the second half to give Navy

(6-4) a chance at the upset, but the Midshipmen came up short just as they did last year and in 1999 and 1997. Navy called timeout twice to try to freeze Fitzpatrick, but he made the kick even though safety Josh Smith said he got a hand on it.

Julius Jones ran for 221 yards and two touchdowns in his fourth straight 100 yard rushing game against Navy. His best run of the day came on a 48 yard run around the right end in the first quarter to open the scoring. He also scored on a 12 yard run late in the third quarter to give the Irish a 21-17 lead. Jones became just the fourth Irish back to run for 200 yards twice in one season. Tony Lane, who had a 65 yard TD run, led Navy with 92 yards on 18 carries. Quinn was 14-of-27 passing for 137 yards for the Irish, who had 417 yards total offense to just 284 for Navy. Johnson defended his decision to punt the ball away on fourth-and-5 from the Notre Dame 47 yard line with just over two minutes left.

CENTRAL MICHIGAN

Craig Candeto ran for 150 yards and three touchdowns and Kyle Eckel rushed for 167 yards and two scores as Navy routed Central Michigan, 63-34. The Midshipmen gained 530 yards on the ground – despite possessing the ball for just 23 minutes - and came just two points shy of matching their modern record set against Princeton in 1953. Candeto completed both of his pass attempts to Eric Roberts for 105 yards, including an 86 yard strike that gave Navy the lead for good, 14-7, with 7:57 left in the first quarter. Roberts also ran four times for 93 yards and a score for the Midshipmen, who had five different players accumulate their eight rushing touchdowns. Navy led, 28-7, after one quarter and 42-21 at the break.

ARMY {@ Lincoln Financial Field, Philadelphia, PA}

Kyle Eckel rushed for 152 yards and two touchdowns as Navy rolled to an easy 34-6 victory over Army in front of a Lincoln Financial Field record crowd of 70,844. The victory was the fourth for Navy over Army in the last five meetings and gave the Midshipmen the Commander-In-Chief's Trophy, which is presented annually to the winner of the football competition among the three major service academies — Army, Navy and Air Force—and is named in honor of the President of the United States. Eric Roberts added two touchdowns rushing, while quarterback Craig Candeto rushed for 58 yards and threw for 55. The 58 yards rushing put Candeto over 1,000 yards making him just the 23rd quarterback in NCAA history and second in Navy history to rush for 1,000 yards and throw for 1,000 yards in a single-season. The Navy offense punished the Black Knights for 359 of their 414 yards of total offense on the ground. The Navy defense was just as good, if not better, than the offense as the Midshipmen held the Black Knights to 198 yards of total offense. Bobby McClarin led the way with eight tackles, a pass breakup and the first interception of his career. McClarin's interception came in the third quarer on the Navy six yard line with the Mids nursing a 20-6 lead. Eddie Carthan added eight tackles, including a tackle for a loss, while Eli Sanders chipped in with seven tackles and an interception. Sanders interception also came in the third quarter deep in Navy territory, two plays after a Candeto interception.

2003 HOUSTON BOWL

B.J. Symons completed the most prolific passing season in Division I-A history by throwing for 497 yards and four touchdowns to lead the Red Raiders to a 38-14 victory over Navy in the Houston Bowl. Craig Candeto's 2 yard TD run early in the third quarter pulled Navy within 14-7 against the larger, faster and more highly recruited Red Raiders. Navy did it all with virtually no threat of the pass as Candeto completed just two for 33 yards. The Red Raiders' No. 1 passing offense responded, with Symons leading them back quickly to set up a four yard TD run by Taurean Henderson. Keith Toogood tacked on a 21 yard field goal for a 24-7 lead. Texas Tech's 110th-ranked defense never quite stopped Navy, which rolled up 289 yards rushing, but slowed the Midshipmen enough despite a fourth-quarter scoring plunge by Candeto. Symons poured it on at the end with TD passes to Jarrett Hicks and Mickey Peters.

2004 Navy Midshipmen {Commander-in-Chief Trophy}

The team was led by third-year head coach Paul Johnson. Team Captains were Aaron Polanco and Josh Smith. The Midshipmen finished the regular season with a 9–2 record, the first time since the 1963 season that Navy had won nine or more games in a season. Wins over Army and the Air Force Falcons secured Navy's second consecutive Commander-in-Chief's Trophy. Navy secured a berth in the 2004 Emerald Bowl when the Pacific-10 Conference did not have enough teams to fill its bowl obligations. The other tie-in was with the Mountain West Conference (MWC), and the Midshipmen ended up playing the New Mexico Lobos. They won the game with a score of 34–19, finishing with a 14-minute, 26-play drive that set the record for the longest drive in a college football game. The win gave the Midshipmen a final record of 10–2, the first time since the 1905 season that the Midshipmen finished with ten or more wins.

Aaron Polanco led the team in passing with 1,131 yards and threw 8 touchdown passes. Kyle Eckel led the team in rushing with 1,147 yards. Polanco led with 16 rushing touchdowns. Jason Tomlinson led the team in receptions with 16. Eric Roberts led with 291 receiving yards. Polanco led the team in scoring with 96 points.

FINAL RANK: #24 AP, #24 UPI

Home games were played at Navy-Marine Corps Stadium

9/4/2004		vs	DUKE (2-9)		27	12	W	
9/11/2004		vs	NORTHEASTERN		28	24	W	
9/18/2004		@	Tulsa (4-8)		29	0	W	
9/25/2004		vs	VANDERBILT (2-9)		29	26	W	
9/30/2004		@	Air Force (5-6)	ESPN	24	21	W	
10/16/2004		vs	NOTRE DAME (6-6)	CBS	9	27	L	
10/23/2004		vs	RICE (3-8)		14	13	W	
10/30/2004		vs	DELAWARE		34	20	W	
11/6/2004		@	Tulane (5-6)		10	42	L	
11/20/2004		vs	RUTGERS (4-7)		54	21	W	
12/4/2004		vs	ARMY (2-9)	CBS	42	13	W	
12/30/2004	#24	vs	**New Mexico (7-5)**	espn2	**34**	**19**	**W**	**Emerald Bowl**
Coach: Paul Johnson			**Season Record >>**		**334**	**238**	**10-2**	

Schedule Source: Steve's Football Bible LLC

Selected game(s) highlights

Air Force

Geoff Blumenfeld nailed a 30 yard field goal with four seconds left to lift Navy to a 24-21 victory over Air Force. Shaun Carney, who was replaced by Adam Fitch in the third quarter, returned to hit J.P. Waller on a 38 yard pass between two defenders and Alec Messerall on a 10 yarder to Navy's 19. Carney, who finished with 221 yards, hit Darnell Stephens for a touchdown on the next play and then ran in for the 2-point conversion to tie the game at 14. Navy, which had 22 total yards and no first downs in the third quarter, countered with a 66 yard pass from Aaron Polanco to Marco Nelson on a third-and-2. That set up Kyle Eckel's 3 yard touchdown run on an option right. Air Force came right back down the field behind Carney's passing, tying the game on his 12 yard pass to Waller with 2:21 left. Navy got the ball back at its own 25 yard line and quickly moved down the field. Polanco broke off a 32 yard run up the middle to the Air Force 29 and then Eric Roberts went off left tackle for 13 more. After three runs up the middle, out trotted Blumenfeld, who split the uprights.

RICE

A career day by quarterback Alan Polanco and a missed extra point enabled Navy to beat Rice. Polanco ran for a career-high 179 yards, and the Midshipmen benefited from a botched fourth-quarter conversion in a 14-13 victory. Rice pulled to within one point with 4:41 left on an 11 yard touchdown pass from freshman Joel Armstrong to Ed Bailey, but Brennan Landry missed the extra point and Navy held on.

ARMY {@ Lincoln Financial Field, Philadelphia, PA}

Senior fullback Kyle Eckel rushed for a career-high 179 yards and one touchdown, senior quarterback Aaron Polanco threw for two touchdowns and rushed for another and senior safety Josh Smith came up with a team-high 12 tackles and intercepted a pass returning it 67 yards for a touchdown as Navy dominated Army for the third-consecutive year, 42-13, in front of a sellout crowd of 67,882 that included President George W. Bush at Lincoln Financial Field in Philadelphia. The victory gave Navy the Commander-In-Chief's Trophy, which is presented annually to the winner of the football competition among the three major service academies and is named in honor of the President of the United States, for the second-consecutive year. It is just the second time in school history that Navy has won the trophy two-straight years (1978-79). After a scoreless first quarter, Navy exploded for 28-consecutive points. Polanco got things going with a 10 yard touchdown run with 14:23 remaining in the second quarter and then Eckel, who was named the Philadelphia Sportswriters Most Valuable Player for the second-consecutive year, followed with a 23 yard romp on Navy's next possession. Smith would put the game away on Army's next possession when he intercepted a Zac Dahman pass and returned it 67 yards for a touchdown. Mick Yokitis caught a 12 yard touchdown toss from Polanco with 1:15 left in the half to make it 28-0.

2004 EMERALD BOWL

The game began at 1:35 p.m. PST in rainy conditions that had affected the San Francisco Bay Area for days before the contest. The Lobos scored a touchdown on the game's first drive to take an early lead, but the Midshipmen scored three touchdowns to bring the score to 21–7 early in the second quarter. After the Lobos narrowed that lead to 12 points by the end of the third quarter, the Midshipmen began a long drive which took up much of the fourth quarter. The drive ended with a field goal, which gave Navy a 15-point lead with a 
little over two minutes remaining in the game. On the next drive from the Lobos, the Midshipmen forced a turnover on downs and ran out the clock with their last possession to win the game. Midshipmen players Aaron Polanco and Vaughn Kelley were named the game's offensive and defensive Most Valuable Players, respectively. The win caused the Midshipmen to finish the season with a 10–2 record, their best record since the 1905 season. After the game, the Associated Press College Poll and the USA Today Coaches' Poll ranked the team as the 24th best in the nation.

2005 Navy Midshipmen {Commander-in-Chief Trophy}

Navy was led by fourth year head coach Paul Johnson. Team Captains were Lamar Owens and Jeremy Chase. The Midshipmen compiled an 8-4 record and outscored their opponents by a combined score of 410 to 313. The Midshipmen were invited to the Poinsettia Bowl where they played Colorado State from the Mountain West Conference. The annual Army–Navy Game was played on December 3 at Lincoln Financial Field in Philadelphia, PA. Navy won the game 42-23.

Lamar Owens led the team in passing with 1,299 yards and threw 6 touchdown passes. Owens led the team in rushing with 880 yards and 11 rushing touchdowns. Jason Tomlinson led the team in receptions with 25 for 445 yards. Joey Bullen led the team in scoring with 79 points. **Tyler Tidwell set the single season record for sacks with 10.**

Home games were played at Navy-Marine Corps Stadium

9/3/2005	vs		Maryland (5-6)		20	23	L	
9/10/2005	vs		STANFORD (5-6)		38	41	L	
10/1/2005	@		Duke (1-10)		28	21	W	
10/8/2005	vs		AIR FORCE (4-7)		27	24	W	
10/15/2005	vs		KENT STATE (1-10)		34	31	W	
10/22/2005	@		Rice (1-10)		41	9	W	
10/29/2005	@		Rutgers (7-5)		21	31	L	
11/5/2005	vs		TULANE (2-9)		49	21	W	
11/12/2005	@	#7	Notre Dame (9-3)	NBC	21	42	L	
11/19/2005	vs		TEMPLE (0-11)		38	17	W	
12/3/2005	vs		ARMY (4-7)	CBS	42	23	W	
12/22/2005	**vs**		**Colorado State (6-6)**	**espn2**	**51**	**30**	**W**	**Poinsettia Bowl**
Coach: Paul Johnson			**Season Record >>**		**410**	**313**	**8-4**	

Schedule Source: Steve's Football Bible LLC

Selected game(s) highlights

Maryland {M&T Bank Stadium - Baltimore, Maryland}

The 2005 game was played at the M&T Bank Stadium in Baltimore and attended by 67,809 fans. The game was a close contest marked by costly Maryland turnovers and Navy penalties. A Sam Hollenbach interception helped Navy to end the first quarter with a 14–3 lead. Immediately before halftime, Maryland kicked a field goal, and another third-quarter field goal narrowed the deficit to 14–9.

Both Maryland and Navy rushed for touchdowns and failed to make two point conversions in the final quarter. Maryland took over on their own 18 yard line after the Navy kick, trailing 20–15 with 4:37 left on the clock. Hollenbach then engineered a 12-play, 82 yard drive capped by an 11 yard touchdown pass and a two point conversion. Navy took over with one minute left, and completed a first down on their 33 yard line before an interception sealed the game for the Terps 23–20.

AIR FORCE

Trailing by seven points against Air Force with 3 minutes left, the Midshipmen had gone 24 minutes since their last touchdown, and now they faced a fourth down on their own 29. Lamar Owens ran 2 yards for a first down, and Navy scored 10 points in the final 2½ minutes to pull out a 27-24 victory. Joey Bullen kicked a 46 yard field goal with 0.4 seconds left, capping a stunning comeback before 35,211 rain-soaked, appreciative fans. Three plays after Owens' first-down rush, Reggie Campbell tied it with a 40 yard run with 2:22 to go. Then, after a shanked 9 yard punt by Air Force's Donny Heaton, the Midshipmen moved 7 yards to set up Bullen's game-winner.

ARMY {@ Lincoln Financial Field, Philadelphia, PA}

Senior quarterback Lamar Owens rushed for 99 yards and three touchdowns, while sophomore fullback Adam Ballard rumbled for 192 yards and two touchdowns as Navy trounced Army for the fourth-consecutive year, 42-23, in front of a sold out crowd at Lincoln Financial Field (69,322). The win gives Navy the series lead, 50-49-7, for the first time since 1991. The Navy offense, which scored on six-straight possessions, set two Army-Navy game records as the Mids rushed for 490 yards and ran up 531 yards of total offense on a defense that came in ranked 23rd in the nation. The game turned late in the second quarter with Navy leading 14-10. Rob Caldwell and Keenan Little dropped Army running back Carlton Jones for no gain on a third-and-one play from the Army 40 and forced a West Point punt. The Midshipmen took the ball over at their own 34 yard line with 1:15 left and promptly moved down the field in eight plays with Owens capping the drive off with a one yard dive to make the score 21-10. Army got the ball to start the second half and Caldwell once again stopped Jones for no gain on third and one and forced an Army punt. The Midshipmen moved right down the field, marching 75 yards on seven plays with Ballard putting the nail in Army's coffin with a 28 yard touchdown run. Ballard would later answer an Army touchdown with a 67 yard touchdown run on the first play from scrimmage to make the score 42-17. Reggie Campbell and Marco Nelson didn't let Owens and Ballard have all the fun, as Campbell rushed for 60 yards and a touchdown on three carries, while Nelson rushed for 77 yards on seven carries. Jake Biles led the Navy defense with 13 tackles, while Little and Caldwell recorded 10 tackles each. David Mahoney had three tackles for a loss. Owens was named the Philadelphia Sports Writers Association Most Valuable Player for his efforts, marking the fourth-consecutive year that a Navy player has taken home the honor.

2005 POINSETTIA BOWL

Reggie Campbell's thrilling performance, which included 290 all-purpose yards, led Navy to a 51-30 win over Colorado State in the San Diego Country Credit Union Poinsettia Bowl at Qualcomm Stadium. Campbell had touchdown catches of 55 and 34 yards and scoring runs of 22, 2 and 21 yards. He ran 16 times for 116 yards, caught two passes for 89 yards and returned four kickoffs for 85 yards. Colorado State pulled within 10 late in the third quarter after Dustin Osborn caught touchdown passes of 10 and 20 yards from Justin Holland on consecutive possessions. But Navy came right back, and Campbell caught a 34 yard scoring pass from Owens for a 41-24 lead.

2006 Navy Midshipmen {Commander-in-Chief Trophy}

Navy was led by fifth year head coach Paul Johnson. Team Captains were James Rossi and Rob Caldwell. The Midshipmen compiled a 9-4 record and outscored their opponents by a combined score of 367 to 261. The Midshipmen were invited to the Meineke Car Care Bowl where they played Boston College from the Big East Conference. The annual Army–Navy Game was played on December 2 at Lincoln Financial Field in Philadelphia, PA. Navy won the game 26-14.

Kaipo-Noa Kaheaku-Enhada led the team in passing with 384 yards and threw 5 touchdown passes. Adam Ballard led the team in rushing with 792 yards. Enhada and Brian Hampton led with 10 rushing touchdowns. Jason Tomlinson led the team in receptions with 16. Reggie Campbell led with 244 receiving yards. Matt Harmon led the team in scoring with 61 points.

Home games were played at Navy-Marine Corps Stadium

9/2/2006	vs		EAST CAROLINA (7-6)		28	23	W	
9/9/2006	vs		MASSACHUSETTS		21	20	W	
9/16/2006	@		Stanford (1-11)		37	9	W	
9/23/2006	vs		TULSA (8-5)		23	24	L	
9/30/2006	@		Connecticut (4-8)		41	17	W	
10/7/2006	@		Air Force (4-8)		24	17	W	
10/14/2006	vs	#24	RUTGERS (11-2)		0	34	L	
10/28/2006	vs	#11	NOTRE DAME (10-3)	CBS	14	38	L	
11/4/2006	@		Duke (0-12)		38	13	W	
11/11/2006	@		Eastern Michigan (1-11)		49	21	W	
11/18/2006	vs		TEMPLE (1-11)		42	6	W	
12/2/2006	vs		ARMY (3-9)	CBS	26	14	W	
12/30/2006	**vs**	**#23**	**Boston College (10-3)**	**ESPN**	**24**	**25**	**L**	**Meineke Car Care Bowl**
Coach: Paul Johnson			**Season Record >>**		**367**	**261**	**9-4**	

Schedule Source: Steve's Football Bible LLC

Selected game(s) highlights

Air Force

Air Force, trailing 24-7 midway through the fourth quarter, pulled within a touchdown with 3:06 left and recovered the onside kick. Navy's defense ended the comeback attempt when Rashawn King broke up Shaun Carney's pass to Victor Thompson on a fourth-and-6 at the Navy 47 for the Midshipmen to hold on for a 24-17 victory. The inside-outside rushing attack of Adam Ballard and Brian Hampton helped the Midshipmen methodically move the ball all afternoon. Ballard rushed 134 yards on 27 carries and Hampton contributed 105 yards and two touchdowns. The Midshipmen totaled 317 yards on the ground. Navy all but put the game away with two time-consuming drives that resulted in a 38 yard field goal by Matt Harmon and a 2 yard touchdown run by Hampton. Navy had the ball for more than 13 minutes in the third quarter. The Midshipmen ran 26 plays to Air Force's five.

#11 NOTRE DAME {@ M&T Bank Stadium – Baltimore, MD}

With Saturday's 38-14 win over Navy, Notre Dame extended the longest winning streak against one opponent in I-A history. Brady Quinn accounted for four touchdowns and #11 Notre Dame amassed a season-high 471 yards Saturday in a 38-14 victory over Navy, the Fighting Irish's 43rd consecutive win in the series. With Quinn leading the way, the Irish scored on their first five possessions to take a 31-14 lead. The Irish were then stuffed at the Navy 1 before Quinn completed his marvelous performance with his third touchdown pass. For a while, Navy kept pace with the Irish. Notre Dame led 17-14 in the second quarter and yielded 211 yards rushing before halftime. Navy quarterback Kalpo-Noa Kaheaku-Enhada scored two touchdowns in his first college start and Reggie Campbell ran for 81 yards, but the Midshipmen couldn't mount enough offense to beat Notre Dame.

ARMY {@ Lincoln Financial Field, Philadelphia, PA}

The Navy defense scored nine fourth-quarter points on an interception and safety and set up three more points with a second interception, as Navy blew open a tight game and went on to defeat Army for the fifth-consecutive year, 26-14, in front of a sold-out crowd of 69,943 at Philadelphia's Lincoln Financial Field. The score was tied at seven at the half, but the Midshipmen scored on their first possession of the second half to take the lead for good when senior Jason Tomlinson scored on a 33 yard reverse. The Navy defense took over from there, holding Army to just 59 yards on its first five possessions. Junior nickel back Jeff Deliz picked off his first-career pass on Army's first drive of the fourth quarter, setting up a 35 yard field goal by sophomore Matt Harmon that gave Navy a 17-7 lead. Three plays later, senior Keenan Little picked off a Carson Williams pass and rumbled 40 yards for a touchdown to give the Midshipmen an insurmountable 24-7 lead with 5:22 remaining. The Navy defense, however, was not finished scoring as senior outside linebacker Tyler Tidwell recorded sacks on consecutive plays, the second one in the end zone for a safety. Army scored a meaningless touchdown with two seconds left to cut the final margin to 12. Sophomore fullback Eric Kettani, who entered the game on Navy's first series after junior starter Adam Ballard went out with a broken right leg, led the Midshipmen with 67 yards rushing on 15 carries. Sophomore quarterback Kaipo-Noa Kaheaku-Enhada added 64 yards on 15 carries. Junior slot back Reggie Campbell, who scored Navy's first touchdown of the day on a nine yard touchdown run, carried the ball six times for 26 yards. The Navy defense was led by senior Rob Caldwell, who recorded 11 tackles. Little had seven tackles to go along with his interception, while Tidwell and sophomore Clint Sovie were also in on seven tackles. Tomlinson was named the Philadelphia Sportswriters Association Most Valuable Player.

2006 MEINEKE CAR CARE BOWL

Boston College got on the board first following a 2 yard touchdown run by quarterback Matt Ryan. The extra point failed, and Boston College led 6–0. Navy quarterback, Kaipo-Noa Kaheaku-Enhada, known as a running quarterback, surprised BC by throwing a 31 yard touchdown pass to wide receiver Tyree Barnes, to put Navy on top 7–6. In the second quarter, Navy used its powerful option running attack, and Zerbin Singleton plowed five 
yards for a touchdown to increase Navy's lead to 14–6. Running back Brian Toal answered for Boston College with a 1 yard touchdown run to make it 14–13. Kaheaku-Enhada once again threw a touchdown pass, this one covering 24 yards to Jason Tomlinson to increase Navy's lead to 21–13. With no time left in the half, kicker Steve Aponavicius drilled a 26 yard field goal, to cut the lead to 21–16.

In the third quarter, Navy was poised to score a touchdown, but BC's defense held strong and forced a field goal. Matthew Harmon connected on the 22 yard field goal to extend Navy's lead to 24–16. With 7:36 left in the fourth quarter, Ryan found tight end Ryan Purvis for a 25 yard touchdown pass. The two point conversion attempt failed, and Navy still led 24–22. Navy had the ball, with 1:43 left in the game, and Boston College had no time outs left. On the next play, Reggie Campbell fumbled an option pitch that was recovered by BC's Jo-Lonn Dunbar at the Navy 40 yard line. Ryan threw a 16 yard pass to Ryan Purvis to get BC into field goal range. Steve Aponavicius drilled a 37 yard field goal as time expired to give Boston College the 25–24 win.

2007 Navy Midshipmen {Commander-in-Chief Trophy}

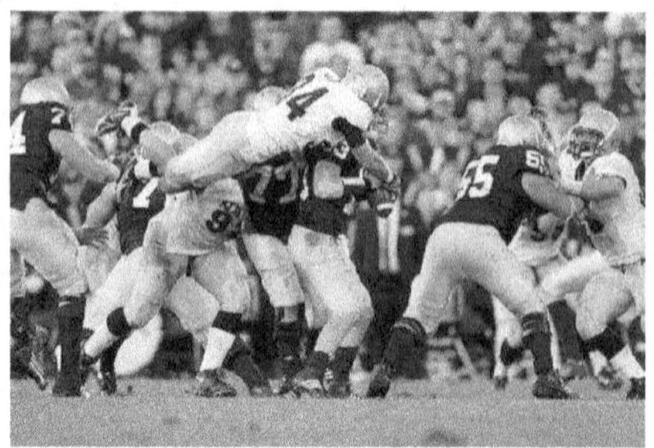

The team was led by sixth year head coach Paul Johnson until he accepted the head coaching position at Georgia Tech prior to the team's final game of the season. Offensive line coach Ken Niumatalolo was first promoted to interim head coach and then named as the team's permanent head coach. Team Captains were Reggie Campbell, Jeff Deliz and Irv Spence. After beginning the season with a 4–4 record through the first eight games, including a loss to Football Championship Subdivision (FCS) foe Delaware, the Midshipmen broke a 43-year losing streak in the Navy–Notre Dame football rivalry in the 2007 Navy vs. Notre Dame football game by winning in triple overtime. The next week, the team became bowl eligible by winning its sixth game of the season in the 2007 Navy vs. North Texas football game, which set a record for the most points scored in a regulation-length FBS college football game. The Midshipmen finished the regular season with an 8–4 record and secured a berth in the 2007 Poinsettia Bowl, which had a single-year tie-in with the USNA. The other tie-in was with the Mountain West Conference (MWC). In a close game that came down to the final seconds, Navy lost the game to the Utah Utes with a score of 35–32.

Kaipo-Noa Kaheaku-Enhada led the team in passing with 952 yards and threw 8 touchdown passes. Eric Kettani led the team in rushing with 880 yards. Enhada led with 12 rushing touchdowns. Reggie Campbell led the team in receptions with 13. Zerbin Singleton led with 263 receiving yards. Ketric Buffin led the team with 4 interceptions. Enhada led the team in scoring with 80 points.

Home games were played at Navy-Marine Corps Stadium

8/31/2007	@		Temple (4-8)	ESPNU	30	19	W	
9/7/2007	@	#15	Rutgers (8-5)	ESPN	24	41	L	
9/15/2007	vs		BALL STATE (7-6)		31	34	L	
9/22/2007	vs		DUKE (1-11)		46	43	W	
9/29/2007	vs		AIR FORCE (9-4)		31	20	W	
10/10/2007	@		Pittsburgh (5-7)	ESPN	48	45	W	
10/20/2007	vs		WAKE FOREST (9-4)		24	44	L	
10/27/2007	vs		DELAWARE		52	59	L	
11/3/2007	@		Notre Dame (3-9)	NBC	46	44	W	
11/10/2007	@		North Texas (2-10)		74	62	W	
11/17/2007	vs		NORTHERN ILLINOIS (2-10)		35	24	W	
12/1/2007	vs		ARMY (3-9)	CBS	38	3	W	
12/20/2007	**vs**		**Utah (9-4)**	**ESPN**	**32**	**35**	**L**	**Poinsettia Bowl**
Coach: Paul Johnson			**Season Record >>**		**511**	**473**	**8-5**	

Schedule Source: Steve's Football Bible LLC

Selected game(s) highlights

AIR FORCE

Playing before a record crowd and with Navy's four-year hold on the Commander-in-Chief's trophy on the line, quarterback Kaipo-Noa Kaheaku-Enhada stepped up with two fourth-quarter touchdown runs, leading the Midshipmen to a 31-20 win over Air Force. Trailing 20-17 early in the fourth quarter, Navy drove 73 yards for the go-ahead touchdown. Kaheaku-Enhada hit O.J. Washington for 53 yards to the Air Force 20. Eric Kettani converted a fourth down at the 11, and then Kaheaku-Enhada scored on fourth down from the 2, giving Navy the lead with 13:01 to play. After an Air Force punt, Kaheaku-Enhada broke loose for 78 yards to put the Midshipmen up 31-20 with 9:18 left. The Falcons outgained the Midshipmen with 474 yards but were held without a score three times inside Navy's 20 yard line. Zerb Singleton rushed for 65 yards, including a 12 yard touchdown, and Kettani had 58 yards for Navy. Reggie Campbell scored Navy's first touchdown on a 37 yard run for a 7-3 lead, and Singleton's run put the Midshipmen ahead 14-10 at the half. Washington had career highs with four catches and 79 yards. Joey Bullen's 29 yard field goal staked Navy to a 17-13 lead before Chad Hall's 5 yard run put Air Force ahead 20-17 late in the third.

Pittsburgh

Joey Bullen kicked a 29 yard field goal in the second overtime and Navy then held as Pitt inexplicably gambled by going for a touchdown on fourth down when a chip-shot field goal would have forced another overtime, and the Midshipmen upset the Panthers 48-45. With Pitt facing fourth-and-goal at the Navy 2, Wannstedt went for the win and freshman Pat Bostick threw too high to tight end Darrell Strong on a fade route in the end zone with Rashawn King in coverage. Navy's Reggie Campbell had three touchdowns, on a 25 yard pass from Kaheaku-Enhada in the first overtime and a 4 yard run and a 10 yard pass play in regulation.

Notre Dame {Midshipmen end the streak}

It's over. After 44 years and three overtimes. Navy finally beat Notre Dame 46-44 in triple overtime on Saturday, ending the Fighting Irish's NCAA-record winning streak against the Midshipmen at 43 games. Navy scored a 46-44 3OT victory over Notre Dame to snap the Fighting Irish's 43-game winning streak against the Midshipmen, the most consecutive victories over one major opponent in  NCAA history. Roger Staubach was quarterback for the Midshipmen in 1963 when they beat Notre Dame 35-14. Since then, the Irish have had their way – that is until Saturday. Seven times during the streak the Midshipmen had chances to win in the fourth quarter only to be thwarted by bad luck, questionable calls or big plays by the Irish. A few times on Saturday it looked as though the win would elude them again. But this time it was the Midshipmen who managed to make the decisive plays. Kaipo-Noa Kaheaku-Enhada threw a 25 yard TD pass to Reggie Campbell on the first play of the third overtime, then found him again for the 2-point conversion.

Notre Dame cut the lead to two on a 5 yard TD run by Travis Thomas. But after a pass interference call gave Notre Dame a second chance at the 2-point conversion, defensive lineman Michael Walsh and linebacker Irv Spencer tackled Thomas well short of the end zone on the final play. For Notre Dame, it was its school-record fifth straight home loss, another low point in a season of lows. Weis said the 43-game winning streak had no meaning to him or the team. Weis said the home losing streak was much more important to the players. It also is the first time the Irish have lost five at home in one season. Notre Dame did have its best game offensively, rushing for 235 yards, nearly doubling their season output, and James Aldridge ran for 125 yards. It wasn't enough. The Irish, who did little to slow Navy's option offense, held the Midshipmen to three-and-out late in the fourth quarter with the score tied at 28. Greg Veteto had the first punt of the game, and Tom Zbikowski returned it 32 yards to the Navy 38. The Irish drove to the 24, but on fourth-and-8 Weis decided to go for it rather than attempt a field goal. Chris Kuhar-Pitters, who earlier returned a fumble 16 yards for a touchdown, sacked Evan Sharpley with 45 seconds left. It was the fourth sack for Navy, which entered the game with five. Notre Dame, which hadn't scored more than 20 points this season, led 21-14 at halftime, the first halftime lead for the Irish. The two teams traded touchdowns most of the day and had just traded missed field goals when Kuhar-Pitters came up with his big play early in the fourth quarter. Sharpley dropped back to pass and was wrapped up by nose guard Nate Frazier and defensive end Michael Walsh knocked the ball loose. Kuhar-Pitters scooped up the loose ball and rumbled into the end zone. Kaheaku-Enhada ran in the 2-point conversion to give the Midshipmen a 28-21 lead. The Irish responded, though, with a touchdown of their own as Thomas went in from 3 yards out with 3:25 remaining to tie it. In the first overtime, Navy's Eric Kettani scored from a yard out and Notre Dame tied it with Duval Kamara's 8 yard touchdown catch.

The teams traded field goals in the second OT. Robert Hughes, whose brother Tony was fatally shot on Tuesday, scored Notre Dame's first touchdown on a 3 yard run. Irish players, some of whom attended the funeral Friday, swarmed Hughes. He ran over to the sideline and got a hug from Weis. Weis said the biggest disappointment for him is the Irish couldn't win the game for Hughes and his family.

North Texas

During the first quarter of the game, the Mean Green led the Midshipmen by as much as 18 points. In the second quarter the teams combined to score 63 points, setting records for most points scored in a quarter and a half. The Midshipmen rallied around a strong rushing offense to take the lead at the beginning of the third quarter, and the Mean Green's offensive momentum sputtered during the second half. Navy held the lead for the remainder of the game.

Although the Mean Green had not scored on its first possession in its previous eight games, the team scored on its opening drive against the Midshipmen when wide receiver Casey Fitzgerald caught a nine yard touchdown pass from quarterback Giovanni Vizza. The Mean Green recovered an onside kick on the ensuing kickoff and scored another touchdown on the following drive. After the Midshipmen kicked a field goal on their first possession, North Texas added another touchdown, giving them a 21–3 lead. Navy scored a touchdown with seven seconds remaining in the quarter. The period ended with the Mean Green ahead, 21–10. After Navy forced North Texas to begin the second quarter with a punt, Midshipmen running back Eric Kettani fumbled the ball on the second play of the next drive and the Mean Green recovered. The next eight possessions – four from each team – resulted in touchdowns. Four of the drives took less than a minute of game time to reach the end zone, and a fifth took barely over a minute. In the final two minutes of the half the Midshipmen forced the Mean Green to punt after three plays, and Navy quarterback Kaipo-Noa Kaheaku-Enhada threw a 47 yard pass to running back Reggie Campbell. The Midshipmen ran for another touchdown on the next play. North Texas got the ball back with seven seconds left in the half but chose not to attempt to score again. At the end of the first half, the Mean Green led the Midshipmen 49–45.

Navy began the third quarter with a 9-play, 60 yard touchdown drive composed completely of runs. This gave them their first lead of the game at 51–49 (the extra point attempt was blocked). On the next North Texas drive, Midshipmen outside linebacker Ram Vela intercepted Giovanni Vizza's pass at the Midshipmen 20 yard line. Three plays later, Navy running back Zerbin Singleton ran 65 yards for another touchdown, making the score 58–49. The Mean Green responded with a 7-play, 59 yard drive, which ended with another Vizza touchdown pass to Casey Fitzgerald. On the next play from scrimmage, Kettani ran 49 yards. Two plays later he ran for another touchdown, bringing the score to 65–56 at the end of the third quarter. The next Mean Green drive ended in another interception, this time by Midshipmen linebacker Matt Wimsatt. After the ensuing drive stalled at midfield, the Midshipmen downed a punt at the North Texas two yard line. Two plays later the Mean Green were called for holding in the end zone, giving Navy a safety. Campbell returned the ensuing free kick for a touchdown, giving the Midshipmen a 74–56 lead. Running back Micah Mosley scored another touchdown for the Mean Green, but their two point conversion attempt failed, leaving them down 74–62. The Mean Green attempted another onside kick, but Navy recovered. One first down was enough to enable the Midshipmen to run out the clock for the win.

ARMY {@ M&T Bank Stadium – Baltimore, MD}

Senior slot back Reggie Campbell piled up 227 all-purpose yards and two touchdowns to lead Navy to a 38-3 victory over Army in front of 71,610 fans at M&T Bank Stadium in Baltimore. The victory was the Midshipmen sixth-straight over Army. Navy broke the game open over the final 7:31 of the second half. Army cut Navy's lead to 7-3 on a 28 yard field goal by Owen Tolson, but Campbell returned the ensuing kickoff 98 yards for a touchdown. The return was the second longest in school history and tied an Army-Navy game record. On Army's first play after the Campbell return, junior defensive end Michael Walsh drilled Army's Wesley McMahand in the backfield, separating the ball from McMahand in the process. Senior linebacker Irv Spencer recovered the fumble at the Army six yard line. Three plays later,

Shun White scored from one yard out to make the score 21-3 with 5:49 left. After the two teams traded punts, the Midshipmen were able to get the ball back one more time after Army threw the ball on third-and-one from its own 36. When the pass sailed out of bounds with 11 seconds to go, it forced the Black Knights to punt to Campbell. Campbell returned the punt 46 yards before being tackled at the Army 34 yard line. With one second left, senior Joey Bullen came on and nailed a 51 yard field goal into a tough wind to give Navy an insurmountable 24-3 lead at the half. The field goal by Bullen was the second longest in school history. The Navy defense pitched a shutout in the second half and the offense picked up 14 more points as Campbell scored on a 12 yard touchdown run and Jarod Bryant scored on a one yard run. Bryant's touchdown was set up by a blocked punt by Bobby Doyle. Navy's defense played its best contest of the year, holding Army to just 217 yards of total offense, including just 100 yards on the ground on 40 carries. Walsh led the way for the Midshipmen with eight tackles, two tackles for a loss and a forced fumble. Ross Pospisil recorded seven stops and a fumble recovery, while Spencer had five tackles, a tackle for a loss, a fumble recovery and two pass break-ups. The Navy rushing attack, which came in averaging a nation's best 357.4 yards per game, was held to just 287 yards on 61 attempts. Senior fullback Adam Ballard rushed for 56 yards on 13 carries, while Zerbin Singleton rushed for 55 yards and a touchdown on five carries. Singleton's touchdown was a 38 yard dash down the right sideline that put Navy up 7-0 in the first quarter. Campbell added 47 yards on five carries. The Midshipmen attempted just five passes, completing two for seven yards.

2007 POINSETTIA BOWL

Both teams' offenses moved the ball down the field effectively during the game's first few drives, but neither team could make it into the end zone, leaving the game scoreless after one quarter. The Utes scored first in the second quarter, and the Midshipmen tied the game at 7–7 on their next drive. Navy added a field goal with 28 seconds left in the half to give the Midshipmen a 10–7 lead at halftime. After the Midshipmen scored another touchdown to increase that lead to 17–7, the Utes scored three unanswered touchdowns to gain a 28–17 lead. The Midshipmen narrowed that lead to three points after scoring another touchdown and two point conversion, and after a series of defensive battles for both teams, the Utes scored again with 1:27 left in the game. Navy scored another touchdown on its next drive to bring the score to 35–32 and recovered an onside kick to retain possession with less than a minute left in the game.
Midshipmen quarterback Kaipo-Noa Kaheaku-Enhada's final pass down field, however, was intercepted, allowing the Utes to run out the remaining seconds and win the game with a final score of 35–32.

2008 Navy Midshipmen {Commander-in-Chief Trophy}

The team was led by first-year head coach Ken Niumatalolo (pictured at right). He was promoted from the offensive line coach before the season, after his predecessor, Paul Johnson, accepted the head coaching position at Georgia Tech. Team Captains were Clint Sovie and Jarod Bryant. The Midshipmen finished the regular season with an 8–4 record to attain bowl eligibility. Navy secured a berth in the inaugural EagleBank Bowl, which had a tie-in with the two independent military academies, the other being Army. The other tie-in was with the Atlantic Coast Conference (ACC). Due to a chaotic and closely contested season in the ACC, in the EagleBank Bowl, Navy ended up playing Wake Forest in a re-match of a regular season game, despite a statement in their contracting disallowing it. Unlike the earlier game, Navy lost the rematch against Wake Forest, 29–19.

Kaipo-Noa Kaheaku-Enhada led the team in passing with 305 yards. Shun White led the team in rushing with 1,092 yards and tied with Ricky Dobbs with 8 rushing touchdowns. Tyree Barnes led the team in receptions with 20 for 400 yards. Matt Harmon led the team in scoring with 95 points. **Shun White set a single game rushing record with 348 yards vs Towson. Matt Harmon set a single season record with 19 field goals.**

Home games were played at Navy-Marine Corps Stadium

8/30/2008	vs		TOWSON	CBSSN	41	13	W	*-White 348 rush yds
9/5/2008	@		Ball State (12-2)	ESPN	23	35	L	
9/13/2008	@		Duke (4-8)	ESPNU	31	41	L	
9/20/2008	vs		RUTGERS (8-5)	CBSSN	23	21	W	
9/27/2008	@	#15	Wake Forest (8-5)	ESPNU	24	17	W	
10/4/2008	@		Air Force (8-5)		33	27	W	*Harmon 4 field goals
10/18/2008	vs	#23	PITTSBURGH (9-4)	CBSSN	21	42	L	
10/25/2008	vs		SMU (1-11)	CBSSN	34	7	W	
11/1/2008	vs		TEMPLE (5-7)	CBSSN	33	27	W	
11/15/2008	vs		NOTRE DAME (7-6)	CBS	21	27	L	
11/25/2008	@		Northern Illinois (6-7)		16	0	W	
12/6/2008	vs		ARMY (3-9)	CBS	34	0	W	
12/20/2008	**vs**		**Wake Forest (8-5)**	**ESPN**	**19**	**29**	**L**	**Eagle Bank Bowl**
Coach: Ken Niumatalolo			**Season Record >>**		**353**	**286**	**8-5**	

Schedule Source: Steve's Football Bible LLC
***-Single game record**

Selected game(s) highlights

#15 Wake Forest

Number 15 Wake Forest committed a season-high six turnovers and Navy turned those miscues into 24 points as the Midshipmen upset the Demon Deacons 24-17 in front of 33,173 fans at BB&T Field. Quarterback Riley Skinner threw a career-high four interceptions, and the Wake Forest offense fumbled the ball two times to account for the six turnovers. Navy dominated the ground game, rushing for 292 yards on 59 carries, while the Deacons rushed for only 43 yards on 31 carries. Navy passed the ball four times in the contest for 51 yards, while Wake passed the ball 40 times, completing 26 of those passes for 270 yards. Eric Kettani ran for 175 yards on 19 carries for Navy. Navy's Ketric Buffin led the team in tackles with seven and had an interception. On the second play from scrimmage, Skinner threw an interception to Ross Pospisil. The Midshipmen took advantage of the Deacon miscue, driving 51 yards on eight plays to take a 7-0 edge. Quarterback Kaipo-Noa Kaheaku-Enhada scored on a four yard run to put Navy ahead with 9:57 remaining in the first quarter. Navy extended its advantage to 14-0 on the first play of the second quarter. The 13-play, 74 yard drive took 7:42 off the clock. Kaheaku-Enhada scored his second touchdown of the day, running into the endzone from three yards out. Skinner threw his career-high fourth interception of the game two plays later. The pass was intercepted by Emmet Merchant at the Midshipmen 25 yard line and returned 12 yards to the 37 yard line. Navy turned the interception into seven points to extend its lead to 24-10. The key play of the drive came on the first play as Kettani rushed up the middle for 57 yards to the Deacon 6 yard line. Jarod Bryant ran the ball into the endzone from four yards out to push the lead to 14 with 3:46 left in the game.

Air Force

The Midshipmen blocked two punts for touchdowns as they beat Air Force for a sixth straight time with a 33-27 win. Blake Carter had a hand in both blocked punts. He scooped up one for a 25 yard touchdown early in the game, and then reached his hand in to block another in the fourth quarter, deflecting it into the end zone, where teammate Bobby Doyle pounced on it. Matt Harmon tied a school record by connecting on four field goals.

NOTRE DAME {@ M&T Bank Stadium – Baltimore, MD}

The Midshipmen trailed 27-7 when Shun White broke loose for a 24 yard touchdown run that seemed as if it would provide little more than window dressing with 1:39 left. Then Navy linebacker Corey Johnson recovered an onside kick at the Notre Dame 41 and the Irish sent their first-team defense back in. It didn't help. Ricky Dobbs completed a 40 yard pass down the sideline to Tyree Barnes, then ran in from a yard out, and it was 27-21 with 1:21 left and another onside kick coming. Navy again took over at the 41. But this time, Dobbs couldn't get the ball downfield. Pat Kuntz's sack keyed the defensive stand, and when Dobbs' final pass sailed high, Notre Dame had held on for the victory.

ARMY {@ Lincoln Financial Field, Philadelphia, PA}

Senior slot back Shun White and senior fullback Eric Kettani combined for 273 yards rushing and three touchdowns, while the Navy defense held the Army offense to 154 yards of total offense as Navy blasted Army for the seventh-straight year, 34-0, in front of a sold-out crowd of 69,144 at Lincoln Financial Field in Philadelphia. It was Navy's first shutout against Army since 1978. Navy jumped out to a 7-0 lead on the third play of the game when White ran 65 yards off an option pitch from quarterback Kaipo-Noa Kaheaku-Enhada. The Midshipmen made it 10-0 on their third drive of the game when Matt Harmon drilled a 23 yard field goal and went up 17-0 right before the half when Kaheaku-Enhada hit White with an 18 yard touchdown pass. Navy put the game away with a methodical drive to open the third quarter, marching 72 yards on 14 plays and taking 7:52 off the clock. Kettani ended the drive with a five yard touchdown run and the rout was on. White was the recipient of the 2008 Philadelphia Sports Congress MVP Award for his efforts. The Navy defense was superb all day, holding the Black Knights to just seven first downs. Fifty of Army's 154 yards of total offense came during mop up time in the fourth quarter. Navy's front three of Nate Frazier, Matt Nechak and Jabaree Tuani dominated the Army offensive line and created havoc all day for the Army offense. Frazier was second on the team in tackles with seven, while recording1.5 tackles for a loss and deflecting a pass. Junior linebacker Ross Pospisil led the Midshipmen with 12 tackles and a forced fumble, while junior outside linebacker Ram Vela had six tackles, a sack and intercepted Army quarterback Chip Bowden's pass and returned it 68 yards for a touchdown. Navy played the game with a heavy heart as it was without the services of senior cornerback Rashawn King who returned home to Raleigh, N.C. on Friday morning to be with his family after the sudden death of his father, Drexel, who suffered a heart attack Thursday night. In memory of Mr. King, the Navy football team wore a sticker on the back of its helmets with the initials DK inside of a black crown.

2008 EAGLE BANK BOWL

Riley Skinner went 11-for-11 and threw the go-ahead touchdown pass to Ben Wooster with 7:52 left, leading Wake Forest to a 29-19 comeback victory over the Midshipmen in the inaugural EagleBank Bowl. The Midshipmen scored the first 17 points in the first meeting, and this time a 50 yard fumble return by Rashawn King helped Navy bolt to a 13-0 lead. Skinner directed Wake Forest to a touchdown in the final minute of the first half and opened the third quarter with a 73 yard drive that ended with a 5 yard run by Josh Adams for a 14-13 lead. Navy went back in front when Kaipo-Noa Kaheaku-Enhada scored on a 2 yard run with 12:30 to go, but Skinner went 4-for-4 for 69 yards in an 80 yard drive that ended with his 8 yard pass to Wooster. Skinner then hit Devon Brown in the back of the end zone for the conversion that made it 22-19. Rich Belton added a 35 yard touchdown run with 54 seconds left.

2009 Navy Midshipmen {Commander-in-Chief Trophy}

The Midshipmen were led by second year head coach Ken Niumatalolo. Team Captains were Osei Asante and Ross Popisil. On November 7, 2009 athletic director Chet Gladchuk announced that Navy had accepted an invitation to play in the Texas Bowl on Thursday, December 31 at Reliant Stadium in Houston, Texas against the Big 12 Conference's Missouri Tigers. This marked the first time that Navy had gone to bowl games in seven straight seasons. Navy won the 2009 Texas Bowl, 35–13 and finished with a record of 10–4. The annual Army–Navy Game was played on December 12 at Lincoln Financial Field in Philadelphia, PA. Navy won the game 17-3. They won the Commander-In-Chief Trophy for the seventh straight season.

Ricky Dobbs led the team in passing with 1,031 yards and threw 6 touchdown passes. Dobbs led the team in rushing with 1,203 yards and 27 rushing touchdowns. Marcus Curry and Bobby Doyle led the team in receptions with 10. Curry led with 287 receiving yards. Wyatt Middleton led the team with 4 interceptions. Dobbs led the team in scoring with 162 points.

Home games were played at Navy-Marine Corps Stadium

9/5/2009	@	#6	Ohio State (11-2)	ESPN	27	31	L	
9/12/2009	vs		LOUISIANA TECH (4-8)	CBSSN	32	14	W	
9/19/2009	@		Pittsburgh (10-3)		14	27	L	
9/26/2009	vs		WESTERN KENTUCKY (0-12)	CBSSN	38	22	W	
10/3/2009	vs		AIR FORCE (8-5)	CBSSN	16	13	W	
10/10/2009	@		Rice (2-10)	CBSSN	63	14	W	
10/17/2009	@		Smu (8-5)		38	35	W	
10/24/2009	vs		WAKE FOREST (5-7)	CBSSN	13	10	W	
10/31/2009	vs		TEMPLE (9-4)	CBSSN	24	27	L	
11/7/2009	@	#21	Notre Dame (6-6)	NBC	23	21	W	
11/14/2009	vs		DELAWARE	CBSSN	35	18	W	
11/28/2009	@		Hawaii (6-7)	ESPNU	17	24	L	
12/12/2009	vs		ARMY (5-7)	CBS	17	3	W	
12/31/2009	vs		Missouri (8-5)	ESPN	35	13	W	Texas Bowl
Coach: Ken Niumatalolo			**Season Record >>**		392	272	10-4	

Schedule Source: Steve's Football Bible LLC

Selected game(s) highlights

AIR FORCE

Navy held the Falcons without an offensive touchdown and used a field goal in overtime by Joe Buckley to pull out a 16-13 victory. After Buckley kicked a 38 yarder to end Navy's first possession in the extra period, Erik Soderberg was wide left from 31 yards for Air Force. The Falcons forced overtime when Soderberg kicked a 39 yard field goal as time expired. The frantic 54 yard drive was extended when Navy's Tony Haberer was called for roughing the passer after Wyatt Middleton intercepted a pass by Tim Jefferson.

SMU {Gerald R. Ford Stadium - Dallas, Texas}

Even though Navy's trademark triple option offense sputtered in the first half, quarterback Ricky Dobbs never lost confidence. Dobbs and Vince Murray each ran for two touchdowns, Joe Buckley kicked a 24 yard, game-winning field goal in overtime and Navy won its fourth straight, beating SMU 38-35 Saturday night. The Midshipmen (5-2) were held to 11 yards in the second quarter as they fell behind 21-7 in front of former President George W. Bush, who handled the honorary coin toss before the game. Behind Dobbs and its powerful ground game, Navy scored on four straight possessions and rushed for 247 yards after halftime. SMU (3-3) forced overtime on Bo Levi Mitchell's 10 yard touchdown pass to Aldrick Robinson with 1:35 left.

The Mustangs had the ball first in overtime and lost a yard on three plays before Matt Szymanski missed a 43 yard field goal. Dobbs carried twice to give Navy a first down on its possession. Then the Midshipmen ran three plays up the middle to center the ball for Buckley, who also hit a 38 yarder to beat Air Force on Oct. 3. Murray rushed for 141 yards and Dobbs added 89 on the ground as Navy won its fifth straight overtime game. Dobbs, who came into the game leading the nation in scoring, has 16 touchdowns this season. After halftime, Murray gained 101 yards on 15 carries. Shawnbrey McNeal rushed for 131 yards, Zach Line scored twice, and Sterling Moore returned a fumble for a touchdown as the Mustangs fell to 1-10 all-time in overtime. Emmanuel Sanders became SMU's all-time leading receiver on a 6 yard catch early in the third quarter. It was his 236th career reception. After going three and out on its first drive of the second half, Navy's offense got on track. Dobbs connected with Greg Jones for 39 yards and then hit Mario Washington for a gain of 13. Three plays later, Murray's 3 yard TD run brought the Midshipmen within 21-14.

Dobbs, who came in leading the nation in scoring, added a 13 yard run to tie the game at 21 with 4:17 remaining in the third. The junior quarterback has scored in all eight of his career starts. After SMU grabbed the lead back on its next drive, Murray broke loose for a 52 yard gain and scored two plays later. Dobbs gave Navy a 35-28 advantage on a 5 yard run with 9:11 left. Navy was the first FBS team in the 11 years not to throw a pass in a game when it beat SMU in 2008. The Midshipmen piled up 404 yards on the ground on 77 attempts in their 34-7 victory. The Midshipmen rushed the ball six straight times the first time they had the ball, capped by Marcus Curry's 31 yard touchdown run. SMU answered on its next possession, tying the game on Line's 3 yard run. The Mustangs scored twice in a 16-second span to take a two-touchdown lead. Line's 6 yard run gave the Mustangs a 14-7 lead with 8:39 left in the first half. On Navy's first play from scrimmage on its next drive, SMU linebacker Pete Fleps forced Dobbs to fumble, and Moore picked up the loose ball and stepped into the end zone for a 1 yard return with 8:23 remaining before halftime.

#21 Notre Dame

Craig Schaefer sacked Jimmy Clausen in the end zone with 60 seconds left Saturday and Navy held on for a 23-21 victory, over the #19 Fighting Irish. Notre Dame scored with 24 seconds left on a 31 yard pass from Jimmy Clausen to Golden Tate to cut the lead to two, but the ensuing onside kick went out of bounds. Ricky Dobbs threw a 52 yard touchdown pass and ran for another and fullback Vince Murray added a 25 yard TD run for Navy to lead the Midshipmen to consecutive wins in South Bend for the first time since 1961 and 1963. Navy outrushed the Irish, 348 yards to 60. Murray ran for 158 yards and a touchdown on 14 carries. Dobbs added 102 yards on 31 carries and completed 2 of 3 for 56 yards.

ARMY {@ Lincoln Financial Field, Philadelphia, PA}

The Navy defense kept Army out of the end zone for the third-consecutive year, while junior quarterback Ricky Dobbs ran for a touchdown and threw for another as the Midshipmen beat the Black Knights for the eighth-consecutive time, 17-3, in front of 69,541 at Lincoln Financial Field in Philadelphia. The win gave Navy the Commander-In-Chief's Trophy for the seventh-straight year. The Navy defense was dominant all day, allowing Army just 187 yards of total offense. Army's only score came in the first quarter when Dobbs was intercepted by Army's Steve Erzinger at the Navy 28, and he returned it 16 yards to the Navy 12. Army could manage just six yards on three plays and had to settle for an Alex Carlton field goal. Navy hurt itself in the first half with missed assignments and penalties, but finally settled down in the third quarter. Dobbs led Navy on an 11-play, 68 yard drive to start the third quarter and capped the drive by hitting a wide open Marcus Curry with a 25 yard touchdown pass to give Navy a 7-3 lead. The Midshipmen made it 10-3 on their next possession, marching 55 yards on 12 plays with Joe Buckley nailing a 36 yard field goal. The Navy defense set up the final score with linebacker Ross Pospisil knocking the ball out of the hands of Army fullback Kingsley Ehie at the Army 32 yard line and outside linebacker

Craig Schaefer picking the ball up and running it down to the Army 12 yard line. Four plays later Dobbs scored from the one, giving him his 24th rushing touchdown of the season, an NCAA record for a quarterback. Dobbs, who was named the Philadelphia Sportswriter's Most Valuable Player, rushed for 113 yards and a touchdown on 33 carries and completed three of his seven pass attempts for 61 yards and a touchdown. Pospisil and Jabaree Tuani led the Navy defense with seven tackles and a tackle for a loss each. Tony Haberer recorded six tackles and a tackle for a loss, while Emmett Merchant (forced fumble, pass broken up), Chase Burge and Schaefer (fumble recovery, pass broken up) had five stops each. Ram Vela had another big day with four tackles, two tackles for a loss, a sack and an interception.

2009 TEXAS BOWL

Missouri struck first with a 58 yard touchdown pass to Danario Alexander, but that would be the best part of the day for Missouri. Despite a fumble by Navy, the Midshipmen defense shut Missouri down, and gave the ball back to Navy QB Ricky Dobbs, who atoned for his fumble on the previous drive with a one yard TD rush, his 25th of the season. Dobbs would fumble again in the end zone, resulting in Missouri having a chance to take the lead before halftime, but Missouri fumbled on the next play, and Dobbs atoned for his fumble once more with a touchdown. Missouri cut it to 14–10 for halftime, but they would not draw any closer. Navy dominated the rest of the game. After halftime, Navy took a 21–10 lead on a Dobbs pass to Bobby Doyle. Missouri QB Blaine Gabbert then threw an interception, and Navy didn't look back. Navy ate up most of the 3rd quarter before a 4th down stop. However, Missouri could only amass a field goal out of a 95 yard drive. Navy won by a final count of 35–13. Ricky Dobbs took Texas Bowl MVP honors.

2010 Navy Midshipmen

The Midshipmen, led by third year head coach Ken Niumatalolo. Team Captains were Ricky Dobbs and Wyatt Middleton. Navy earned an invitation to the 2010 Poinsettia Bowl on November 7. Navy was guaranteed a spot in the game if they became bowl eligible (won 6 games or more) as part of an agreement between the Naval Academy and the Poinsettia Bowl. San Diego State defeated Navy in the Poinsettia Bowl, 35–14. The Midshipmen finished with a record of 9–4. The annual Army–Navy Game was played on December 11 at Lincoln Financial Field in Philadelphia, PA. Navy won the game 31-17.

Ricky Dobbs led the team in passing with 1,527 yards and threw 13 touchdown passes. **Dobbs 13 TD passes set a single season record.** Dobbs led the team in rushing with 967 yards and 14 rushing touchdowns. Greg Jones led the team in receptions with 33 for 662 yards and 5 TD passes. Dobbs led the team in scoring with 88 points.

Home games were played at Navy-Marine Corps Stadium

9/6/2010	vs		Maryland (9-4)	ESPN	14	17	L	
9/11/2010	vs		GEORGIA SOUTHERN	CBSSN	13	7	W	
9/18/2010	@		Louisiana Tech (5-7)		37	23	W	
10/2/2010	@		Air Force (9-4)		6	14	L	
10/9/2010	@		Wake Forest (3-9)		28	27	W	
10/16/2010	vs		SMU (7-7)	CBSSN	28	21	W	
10/23/2010	vs		NOTRE DAME (8-5)	CBS	35	17	W	
10/30/2010	vs		DUKE (3-9)	CBSSN	31	34	L	
11/6/2010	@		East Carolina (6-7)		76	35	W	
11/13/2010	vs		CENTRAL MICHIGAN (3-9)	CBSSN	38	37	W	
11/20/2010	vs		ARKANSAS STATE (4-8)	CBSSN	35	19	W	
12/11/2010	vs		ARMY (7-6)	CBS	31	17	W	
12/23/2010	**vs**		**San Diego State (9-4)**	**ESPN**	**14**	**35**	**L**	**Poinsettia Bowl**
Coach: Ken Niumatalolo			**Season Record >>**		**386**	**303**	**9-4**	

Schedule Source: Steve's Football Bible LLC

Selected game(s) highlights

Maryland {M&T Bank Stadium - Baltimore, Maryland}

The 2010 game would be the first to award the Crab Bowl Trophy to the winner. 69,348 fans turned out to see the game at M&T Bank Stadium in Baltimore, which was considered a home game for Maryland. Navy dominated the game statistically, controlling the ball for nearly 40 minutes and gaining 485 yards.

The Midshipmen also converted 10 of 18 third-down chances. But their errors and failure to convert near the goal line cost them dearly. Navy kicker Joe Buckley missed a 32 yard field goal attempt, quarterback Ricky Dobbs lost a fumble at the Maryland 1 yard line, and Maryland eventually walked away with a 17–14 victory

Air Force

Tim Jefferson ran for two touchdowns, the second set up when freshman Jamil Cooks hurdled a blocker to smother a punt, and Air Force beat Navy 14-6 on for its first win over the Midshipmen since 2002. Navy drove to the Air Force 33 yard line before Jordan Waiwaiole intercepted Ricky Dobbs' third-down pass with 25 seconds left to seal the victory. Navy pulled within 7-6 on Jim Buckley's second field goal, a 32 yarder with 10:58 remaining in the third quarter. Buckley got Navy on the board with a 25 yard field goal midway through the second quarter after Dobbs' third-down run was stopped short.

NOTRE DAME {@ New Meadowlands Stadium – East Rutherford, NJ}

Ricky Dobbs scored three touchdowns, and Alexander Teich ran for 210 yards to lead Navy to its third victory against the Irish in the last four seasons, a 35-17 rout on Saturday at the New Meadowlands Stadium. The Midshipmen ran for 367 yards, the most ever by Navy against Notre Dame, and Teich carried 26 times to become the first fullback in school history to rush for 200 in a game. Teich got rolling with a 54 yard run up the middle, then the fullback made a one-handed grab on a screen pass and vaulted into the end zone for a 31 yard touchdown. David Ruffer kicked a 45 yard field goal for Notre Dame, but Navy came right back with another touchdown drive. Dobbs finished it with a 3 yard score to make it 14-3. Dobbs ran for 90 yards on 20 carries and tied the school record for rushing touchdowns with 43

ARMY {@ Lincoln Financial Field, Philadelphia, PA}

Senior safety Wyatt Middleton's 98 yard fumble return for a touchdown with 1:03 remaining in the second quarter turned what was shaping up to be a close game into a rout as Navy rolled to its ninth win of the year and ninth-straight win over Army, 31-17, at a sold out (69,223) Lincoln Financial Field in Philadelphia. The 98 yard fumble return was the longest in school history and longest in an Army-Navy game. For his heroics, Middleton was named the Philadelphia Sportswriters Most Valuable Player. Navy had jumped out to a 17-0 lead as Joe Bukley nailed a 36 yard field goal and quarterback Ricky Dobbs threw touchdown passes of 77 yards to John Howell and 32 yards to Brandon Turner. The touchdown pass to Howell was the longest pass play in series history. The Midshipmen were in total control of the game midway through the second quarter until a pair of Dobbs turnovers gave Army life. Dobbs fumbled the ball on first down from his own 23 and it was recovered by Army's Josh McNary. Six plays later, Army quarterback Trent Steelman hit Malcolm Brown with a five yard touchdown pass to cut the Navy lead to 17-7. It was Army's first touchdown against the Midshipmen since the fourth quarter of the 2006 game. Three plays later, Dobbs gave the ball back to Army again as he was stripped by McNary and Stephen Anderson recovered the loose ball at the Army 48. The Black Knights methodically moved the ball down the field, taking it 49 yards in 11 plays. On first and goal from the Navy three, Steelman tried to power his way into the end zone, but senior linebacker Tyler Simmons and senior outside linebacker Jerry Hauburger met Steelman at the two yard line and Simmons' knocked the ball from Steelman's hands. The ball popped up in the air and flew right to Middleton who raced 98 yards for the back-breaking touchdown. Army took the opening kickoff of the third quarter and drove 47 yards on 12 plays with Alex Carlton capping the drive with a 42 yard field goal to make the score 24-10. Navy put the game away with a 13-play, 87 yard, 9:03 scoring drive to start the fourth quarter with slot back Gee Gee Greene waltzing in from the 25 to make it 31-10. Dobbs led the Navy offense with 54 yards rushing on 20 carries. He completed six of his 11 passes for 186 yards with two touchdowns and one interception. Slot back Aaron Santiago had two catches for 54 yards, while wide receiver Greg Jones caught two passes for 23 yards. Simmons paced the Navy defense with 13 tackles and two forced fumbles, while sophomore Matt Warrick, making his first-career start, had 13 tackles and a pass break up. Aaron McCauley had 11 stops, a sack and 2.5 tackles for a loss, while Middleton chipped in nine tackles, two fumble recoveries and a pass break up to go with his 98 yard touchdown return.

2010 POINSETTIA BOWL

Ronnie Hillman scored four touchdowns and matched his career best with 228 yards rushing on 28 carries to lead the Aztecs to their first bowl victory since 1969, 35-14 over Navy in the San Diego County Credit Union Poinsettia Bowl. Hillman pulled in a 15 yard scoring pass from Ryan Lindley after a beautifully executed fake. Lindley faked a handoff to Brandon Sullivan into the line, then hid the ball down by his right hip as Navy stood up the fullback at the line. Lindley hit a wide-open Hillman in the right corner of the end zone for a 28-14 lead on the first play of the fourth quarter. The Aztecs outrushed Navy 279-235. SDSU took a 14-0 lead in the first quarter on Hillman's 22 yard TD run and Lindley's 53 yard TD pass to Vincent Brown. Navy pulled to 14-7 on Ricky Dobbs' 30 yard scoring pass to Greg Jones early in the second quarter. Hillman put the Aztecs up by two touchdowns again as he ran untouched 37 yards up the middle with 3:15 before halftime. Navy closed within one score on Dobbs' 1 yard keeper 7 seconds before halftime. SDSU held Navy on the opening drive of the second half, when Dobbs' pass went off Bo Snelson's fingertips in the end zone on fourth-and-goal from the 3.

2011 Navy Midshipmen

The Midshipmen, led by fourth year head coach Ken Niumatalolo. Team Captains were Alexander Teich and Jabaree Tuani. The Midshipmen finished with a record of 5-7. The annual Army–Navy Game was played on December 10 at FedEx Field in Landover, MD; Navy won the game 27-21.

Kriss Proctor led the team in passing with 78 yards and threw 7 touchdown passes. Proctor led the team in rushing with 914 yards and 14 rushing touchdowns. Brandon Turner led the team in receptions with 14 for 300 yards. Proctor led the team in scoring with 84 points.

Home games were played at Navy-Marine Corps Stadium

9/3/2011	NAVY	vs		DELAWARE	CBSSN	40	17	W
9/10/2011	NAVY	@		Western Kentucky (7-5)		40	14	W
9/17/2011	NAVY	@	#11	South Carolina (11-2)	espn2	21	24	L
10/1/2011	NAVY	vs		AIR FORCE (7-6)	CBS	34	35	L
10/8/2011	NAVY	vs		SOUTHERN MISS (12-2)	CBSSN	35	63	L
10/15/2011	NAVY	@		Rutgers (9-4)		20	21	L
10/22/2011	NAVY	vs		EAST CAROLINA (5-7)	CBSSN	35	38	L
10/29/2011	NAVY	@		Notre Dame (8-5)	NBC	14	56	L
11/5/2011	NAVY	vs		TROY (3-9)	CBSSN	42	14	W
11/12/2011	NAVY	@		Smu (8-5)	FSN	24	17	W
11/19/2011	NAVY	@		San Jose State (5-7)		24	27	L
12/10/2011	NAVY	vs		ARMY (3-9)	CBS	27	21	W
Coach: Ken Niumatalolo				**Season Record >>**		356	347	5-7

Schedule Source: Steve's Football Bible LLC

Selected game(s) highlights

AIR FORCE

Tim Jefferson ran for a 1 yard touchdown in overtime and Parker Herrington added the conversion to give Air Force a wild 35-34 victory over Navy. After Air Force blew an 18-point lead in the fourth quarter, Navy's Kriss Proctor ran for a 1 yard touchdown to begin the overtime. But he was penalized for unsportsmanlike conduct, and Jon Teague's long conversion attempt from 35 yards out was blocked by Alex Means. Air Force led 21-3 at halftime and 28-10 with 14:55 left, but Navy used an 18-point run fueled by a successful onside kick to force overtime. Navy closed to 28-26 with 19 seconds left after recovering an onside kick and getting a 5 yard touchdown pass from Proctor to Gee Gee Greene. Needing a 2-point conversion to force overtime, Proctor rolled left and pitched the ball to Alexander Teich, who scooted into the corner of the end zone. Proctor scored three touchdowns and ran for 134 yards, and Teich rushed for 148 yards.

Notre Dame

Michael Floyd and Jonas Gray scored in a span of 1 minute, 59 seconds Saturday, and Notre Dame rolled from there, rebounding from its rough week with a 56-14 thrashing of Navy. The Irish rushed for seven touchdowns, most in 19 years, while limiting Navy to a season-low 229 yards of total offense in the Midshipmen's sixth straight loss. Notre Dame scored on five of its first six possessions, and had two running backs score multiple touchdowns (Gray had three, Cierre Wood had two) for the first time since 2001. Floyd also had two TDs, scoring on a 56 yard catch and a 10 yard lateral for Notre Dame. The Irish defense hounded young quarterback Trey Miller, who was playing in place of the injured Kriss Proctor, all afternoon. Miller finished just 5-of-13 for 33 yards, and Navy could only manage 196 yards on the ground

SMU {Gerald R. Ford Stadium - Dallas, Texas}

{Associated Press} Ken Niumatalolo celebrated on the sideline more than some of his players did late in Saturday's game against SMU. Navy's coach had good reason to be happy. The Midshipmen still have a shot to play in their ninth consecutive bowl game. Quarterback Kriss Proctor rushed for 107 yards and John Howell scored the go-ahead touchdown to keep the Midshipmen -- who didn't complete a pass all game -- in bowl contention with a 24-17 victory over SMU. After SMU got within 24-17 with 3:40 left, the Midshipmen ran out the clock with the help of Gee Gee Greene's 8 yard run on third-and-6. Greene went airborne on the play, which had Niumatalolo jumping up and down on the sideline. Navy (4-6) is guaranteed a spot in the Military Bowl if it can beat San Jose State and Army. Navy rushed for 335 yards in what served as a preview of sorts if the two teams wind up in the Big East. The Midshipmen also beat SMU in 2008 without attempting a pass. On Saturday, Proctor only threw two passes and one of them was intercepted. Zach Line rushed for 135 yards, his eighth 100 yard effort this season, and Cole Beasley scored two touchdowns, including a 2 yard run that got SMU within 24-17. SMU (6-4) lost its third in four games, while Navy has won five straight against SMU and eight of nine overall.

The teams are connected by late coach Frank Ganz and have a trophy in his honor. After playing center and linebacker for Navy from 1957-59, Ganz coached for 38 seasons -- 24 in the NFL and 14 in college, including for Navy and SMU. Navy's Alex Teich rushed for 90 yards and Greene added 67 yards on the ground. SMU scored on its opening drive of the second half, tying the game 10-10 on J.J. McDermott's 7 yard touchdown pass to Beasley. Navy responded on its next drive to take the lead for good. Howell finished off a 78 yard march with a 1 yard run, giving the Midshipmen a 17-10 advantage with 5:17 remaining in the third. SMU had a chance to tie things late in the third when Chris Banjo recovered Matt Aiken's muffed punt at the Navy 25. The Mustangs couldn't take advantage of the miscue and didn't gain a first down on the ensuing possession as McDermott's fourth-down pass was knocked away. After the failed fourth-down attempt, Mike Stukel's 5 yard TD run early in the fourth quarter gave Navy a 24-10 lead. Navy's bid for a bowl appearance took a hit when it lost six in a row before beating Troy last weekend. The Midshipmen need six victories to play in the Military Bowl. Navy scored on its opening drive on Jon Teague's 39 yard field goal. Chris Ferguson intercepted McDermott to set up Navy's first touchdown of the game. Greene capped a 56 yard drive with a 1 yard scoring run to give Navy a 10-0 advantage. SMU drove deep into Navy territory on their final two drives of the first half without scoring a touchdown. David Sperry intercepted McDermott in the end zone with five minutes remaining in the second quarter. After driving to the Navy 11, SMU's drive stalled and Chase Hover kicked a 28 yard field goal on the final play of the half. Former President George W. Bush and wife Laura attended the game and participated in the pregame coin toss with captains from both teams.

ARMY {@ FedEx Field, Landover, MD}

Senior Jon Teague kicked fourth quarter field goals of 23 and 44 yards as Navy defeated Army, 27-21, for a record 10th-consecutive year, in front of a crowd of 80,789 at FedExField that included President Barack Obama and Vice President Joe Biden. Navy jumped out to a 14-0 lead thanks to a pair of Army fumbles. Army's Raymond Maples fumbled a pitch and senior defensive end Jabaree Tuani recovered the ball at the Army 26 on the Black Knights' second possession of the game. Six plays later, senior  quarterback Kriss Proctor scored from the four to give Navy the early advantage. After the two teams traded punts, Army's Jared Hassin was stripped of the ball by Tuani and junior outside linebacker Brye French recovered the ball at the Navy 45. On the first play after the Army fumble, Proctor scrambled for 32 yards down to the Army 23. Six plays after that, Proctor executed a perfect double option on third-and-eight from the 10 pitching to senior fullback Alexander Teich for the touchdown. Army, however, would come right back and cut Navy's lead in half, as quarterback Trent Steelman directed an eight-play, 67 yard drive that was capped off by a 34 yard touchdown run to make the score 14-7. After the Navy offense went three and out, Army was back in business moving 63 yards in seven plays with Malcolm Brown diving over from the three to tie the game at 14 with just 49 seconds left in the first half. Navy took the opening kickoff of the second half and moved 48 yards in five plays to retake the lead at 21-14. After Teich's 48 yard kickoff return put the Navy offense in business at the Army 48, backup fullback Delvin Diggs had back-to-back carries that picked up 18 yards down to the Army 30. Junior slot back Gee Gee Greene ran for 20 more yards on first down and, after a Teich eight yard run down to the two, Proctor scored his second TD of the day. Once again Army would come right back, marching right through the Navy defense in six plays with Steelman hitting Brown with a 25 yard touchdown pass on third-and-seven to tie the game at 21. After a Proctor fumble turned the ball back over to Army at the Navy 45, the Black Knights short circuited their opportunity to take the lead with an illegal block and a delay of game penalty forcing them to punt. The Midshipmen would take advantage of the opportunity by driving 75 yards in 18 plays with Teague capping the drive with a 23 yard field goal to give Navy a three-point lead. The Midshipmen were forced to kick a field goal after lineman Graham Vickers jumped on third-and-goal from the Army 1. The Midshipmen got the ball right back on the ensuing kickoff when freshman Noah Copeland forced Army returner Scott Williams to cough up the ball and Navy freshman Jordan Drake recovered it at the Army 27. Teague would turn the Army miscue into points with a 44 yard field goal to give Navy a 27-21 lead. Army got the ball back and quickly moved down the field and had the ball first-and-10 at the Navy 28 when the Navy defense came up big. After Brown rushed for four yards on first down, Army tried to catch Navy napping by throwing the ball, but Steelman was dropped by junior linebacker Matt Warrick for a loss of five yards. Steelman would pick up four yards on third down as Tra'ves Bush came flying up from the safety position to make the stop and then on fourth down Steelman was sacked for a loss of one by Warrick to give the ball back to the Midshipmen with 4:31 left. The Navy offense was able to clinch the game by burning 4:29 off the clock as the Midshipmen picked up two first downs, including one where they drew Army offside on a fourth-and-one from the Army 48.

2012 Navy Midshipmen {Commander-in-Chief Trophy}

The Midshipmen were led by fifth year head coach Ken Niumatalolo. Team Captains were Brye French and Bo Snelson. They finished the season 8–5 and were invited to the Kraft Fight Hunger Bowl, where they were defeated by Arizona State. The annual Army–Navy Game was played on December 8 at Lincoln Financial Field in Philadelphia, PA. Navy won the game 17-13.

Keenan Reynolds led the team in passing with 898 yards and threw 9 touchdown passes. Gee Gee Greene led the team in rushing with 877 yards. Reynolds led with 10 rushing touchdowns. Brandon Turner led the team in receptions with 22 for 321 yards and 4 TD receptions. Nick Sloan led the team in scoring with 71 points.

Home games were played at Navy-Marine Corps Stadium

9/1/2012	vs	#24	NOTRE DAME	CBS	10	50	L	
9/15/2012	@		Penn State	ABC	7	34	L	
9/22/2012	vs		VMI	CBSSN	41	3	W	
9/29/2012	vs		SAN JOSE STATE	CBSSN	0	12	L	
10/6/2012	@		Air Force	CBS	28	21	W	
10/12/2012	@		Central Michigan	espn2	31	13	W	
10/20/2012	vs		INDIANA	CBSSN	31	30	W	
10/27/2012	@		East Carolina	FSN	56	28	W	
11/3/2012	vs		FLORIDA ATLANTIC	CBSSN	24	17	W	
11/10/2012	@		Troy		31	41	L	
11/17/2012	vs		TEXAS STATE	CBSSN	21	10	W	
12/8/2012	vs		ARMY	CBS	17	13	W	
12/29/2012	**vs**		**Arizona State**	**espn2**	**28**	**62**	**L**	**Kraft Fight Hunger Bowl**
Coach: Ken Niumatalolo			**Season Record >>**		**325**	**334**	**8-5**	

Schedule Source: Steve's Football Bible LLC

Selected game(s) highlights

Air Force

The Midshipmen prevailed in overtime, winning 28-21. Offensive lineman Jake Zuzek scored Navy's decisive touchdown in overtime, recovering a fumble by Keenan Reynolds, giving Navy a 28-21 lead. The Falcons had a chance to respond. Facing a do-or-die 4th-and-6, Connor Dietz threw a pass to Chris Jordan. The pass, however, was broken up by Wes Henderson, sealing Navy's upset win over Air Force. Air Force jumped out to a 7-0 lead in the first quarter, when Connor Dietz connected with Drew Coleman on a 35 yard touchdown pass, capping off a quick four play, 75 yard drive that took just 1:29 off the clock. Navy bounced back in the second quarter, scoring ten unanswered points headed into halftime. Noah Copeland's 5 yard touchdown run gave Navy a 10-7 lead -- Navy's first lead of the game. Cody Getz, who finished the game with 204 yards rushing on 29 carries, put Air Force back on top in the third quarter, when he scampered for a 14 yard touchdown run, giving the Falcons a 14-10 lead. After a Navy field goal, Air Force extended its lead to 21-13, when wide receiver Dontae Strickland threw a 54 yard touchdown pass to Drew Coleman. Navy tied the game up with 6:35 left to go in the game, when Keenan Reynolds ran for a 15 yard touchdown. Copeland ran the ball into the end zone for the two-point conversion, tying the game at 21-21.

INDIANA

A crowd of 33,441 watched the game on Homecoming Day at Navy-Marine Corps Stadium. The Midshipmen freshman quarterback Keenan Reynolds completed a four yard touchdown pass to junior Matt Aiken with just 2:02 left in the game. The Hoosiers outgained Navy 417 to 353 on the day. Indiana went out to a 10-0 lead on a Mitch Ewald 25 yard field goal and a one yard touchdown run by Stephen Houston. Navy got on the scoreboard in the second quarter on a three yard run by Keenan Reynolds, but then Indiana came back to march down the field for a 72 yard drive culminating in a three yard run by D'Angelo Roberts. Later Navy linebacker Jordan Drake made a huge defensive play, intercepting a Coffman pass and returning it 24 yards for a touchdown. Ewald kicked his second field goal from 23 yards at the end of the half to give the Hoosiers a 17-14 lead. In the third, Navy went ahead on a 17 yard run by Darius Staten, but Ewald's third field goal of the game from 30 yards away put Indiana ahead 23-21 after three quarters. Early in the fourth, Indiana marched 80 yards downfield for a score recorded by Tevin Coleman on a three yard run, taking a 30-21 lead. Navy drove down the field and had 1st-and-goal at the Hoosier six yard line, but ground attempts by Noah Copeland and two by Reynolds left the ball on fourth down at the one. Navy coach Ken Niumatalolo called for a field goal, which was converted from 18 yards by freshman Nick Sloan. Indiana led 30-24 with just 5:30 left in the game. With 3rd-and-3 at the four, Reynolds threw to junior Matt Aiken for the tying score. The PAT kick by Sloan gave Navy the 31-30 lead.

ARMY {@ Lincoln Financial Field, Philadelphia, PA}

Freshman quarterback Keenan Reynolds extended Navy's dominance against Army, scoring the winning touchdown late in the fourth quarter in a 17-13 victory in the 113th playing of America's Game. Navy captured its 11th consecutive victory over Army and in doing so won the Commander-in-Chief's Trophy which is awarded to the team with the best record in games among the three service academies. Army and Navy each beat Air Force, putting the prestigious trophy up for grabs in the regular-season finale for the first time since 2005. In front of 69,607 fans and Vice President Joe Biden at Lincoln Financial Field, Navy caught a break when Army missed a late field goal attempt. Reynolds quickly found Brandon Turner down the sideline for a 49 yard gain. Reynolds then escaped a rush and followed with the eight yard touchdown run with 4:41 left in the game. Unlike previous games over the last decade, the Black Knights were in this one until the final drive. Army had driven to the Navy 14 when fullback Larry Dixon fumbled on a sloppy exchange with quarterback Trent Steelman. Junior nose guard Barry Dabney recovered the fumble, and the Midshipmen sideline went wild as the CIC trophy was coming back to the Naval Academy for a record 13th time after a two-year stint at Air Force. Before Navy started its 11-game winning streak, the longest winning streak in a series that started in 1890 was only five games by either team. Late in the third quarter, Army's James Kelly stripped the ball from Reynolds and linebacker Alex Meier recovered to give the Black Knights the ball at Navy's 37. Eric Osteen kicked a 21 yard field goal 10 plays later for a 13-10 lead. Osteen, however, was wide left on a 37 yard attempt with 6:57 left in the game. Navy made them pay on Reynolds' score. The Midshipmen now lead the series 57-49-7. After a scoreless first quarter, Army and Navy swapped rushing TDs in the second. Navy fullback Noah Copeland plowed straight up the middle for a 12 yard score. Trent Steelman matched him with an 11 yarder for his program-tying 17th TD run of the season, then saluted the cadets after the score. Freshman kicker Nick Sloan put Navy up 10-7 with a 31 yard field goal late in the second, but Army answered when Osteen's 41 yarder as the first half expired hit the upright and bounced in to tie the game at 10. Reynolds was named the Philadelphia Sportswriters Most Valuable Player, rushing for 43 yards and a touchdown and completing 10 of his 17 passes for 130 yards. Sophomore fullback Noah Copeland rushed for 99 yards and a touchdown on 22 carries, while senior slot back Gee Gee Greene caught three passes for 23 yards. Junior linebacker Cody Peterson led the Navy defense with a career-high 14 tackles, while senior outside linebacker Keegan Wetzel recorded 11 tackles, 1.5 tackles for a loss and one sack. Senior Matt Warrick was also in on 11 stops, while sophomore outside linebacker Josh Tate, senior linebacker John Michael Nurthen and Dabney all recovered fumbles.

2012 KRAFT FIGHT HUNGER BOWL

The Sun Devils scored the first 21 points of the game in the first quarter, while keeping the Midshipmen scoreless. After Navy scored its first points in the second quarter, Arizona State scored two more touchdowns to bring the score to 34–7 at halftime. The Sun Devils added four more touchdowns in the third quarter, but the only additional points from the Midshipmen came from a 95 yard kickoff return for a touchdown. Navy scored the only two touchdowns of the fourth quarter, ending the game with a score of 62–28. With five tackles and 2.5 sacks, Will Sutton was named the game's most valuable defensive player. Marion Grice, with 159 yards rushing and two touchdowns, was named the game's offensive MVP. Although the Midshipmen led the game in time of possession, Arizona State's offense needed a little under nine minutes of game time to score five touchdowns in the first half and its first nine touchdowns used a total of 13:38.

2013 Navy Midshipmen {Commander-in-Chief Trophy}

The Midshipmen were led by sixth year head coach Ken Niumatalolo. Team Captains were Matt Aiken and Cody Peterson. They finished the season 9-4 and were invited to the Armed Forces Bowl, where they defeated Middle Tennessee State. The annual Army–Navy Game was played on December 8 at Lincoln Financial Field in Philadelphia, PA. Navy won the game 34-7.

Keenan Reynolds led the team in passing with 1,057 yards and threw 8 touchdown passes. Reynolds led the team in rushing with 1,346 yards and **set a new single season record with 31 rushing touchdowns. Reynolds also set a single season record with 39 total touchdowns.** DeBrandon Sanders and Casey Bolena led the team in receptions with 13. Sanders led with 223 receiving yards. Reynolds led the team in scoring with 188 points. **Reynolds set a single game touchdown record with 7 vs San Jose State. Reynolds also set a single game total touchdown record with 8 vs San Jose State.**

Home games were played at Navy-Marine Corps Stadium

Date			Opponent	TV				
9/7/2013	@		Indiana	BTN	41	35	W	
9/14/2013	vs		DELAWARE	CBSSN	51	7	W	
9/28/2013	@		Western Kentucky		7	19	L	
10/5/2013	vs		AIR FORCE	CBS	28	10	W	
10/12/2013	@		Duke		7	35	L	
10/19/2013	@		Toledo		44	45	L	
10/26/2013	vs		PITTSBURGH	CBSSN	24	21	W	
11/2/2013	@	#25	Notre Dame	NBC	34	38	L	
11/9/2013	vs		HAWAII	CBSSN	42	28	W	
11/16/2013	vs		SOUTH ALABAMA	CBSSN	42	14	W	
11/22/2013	@		San Jose State	espn2	58	52	W	*-Reynolds 7 rush TD
12/14/2013	vs		ARMY	CBS	34	7	W	
12/30/2013	**vs**		**Middle Tennessee**	**ESPN**	**24**	**6**	**W**	**Armed Forces Bowl**
Coach: Ken Niumatalolo			**Season Record >>**		**436**	**317**	**9-4**	

Schedule Source: Steve's Football Bible LLC
*-Single game record

Selected game(s) highlights

Indiana

Keenan Reynolds rushed for 127 yards and three touchdowns, Darius Staten added another 106 yards on the ground and the Midshipmen ground out a 41-35 victory at Indiana in their season opener. Navy held an almost two-to-one advantage in possession time and rushed for 444 yards. They committed only five penalties, had no turnovers and wound up with only three negative rushing plays. Reynolds kept the ball on Navy's throwback triple option 32 times. Geoffrey Whiteside ran nine times for 97 yards, and DeBrandon Sanders carried five times for 68 yards. In all, the Midshipmen ran 70 times, averaging 6.3 yards per carry, and never even bobbled the ball on a pitch. Navy threw just five passes with Reynolds completing two for 71 yards.

AIR FORCE

A record crowd of 38,225 filled Navy-Marine Corps Memorial Stadium for this pivotal matchup. Keenan Reynolds ran for 126 yards and three touchdowns, and the Midshipmen rolled to a 28-10 victory. Air Force came in a heavy underdog after losing four straight, but the Falcons were the better team in the first half and went to the locker room with a 10-7 lead. After that, it was all Navy. It began with the opening drive of the third quarter, when the Midshipmen moved 75 yards in eight plays to take a 14-10 lead. Navy's Chris Johnson, who had two fourth-quarter interceptions.

PITTSBURGH

Nick Sloan booted a 30 yard field goal as time expired that gave the Midshipmen a 24-21 victory over the Panthers. Navy finally got into a rhythm in the second half and put together their most impressive drive of the game to take a 14-13 lead with 14:28 left in the game. Reserve fullback Quinton Singleton's 9 yard scoring run capped the 16-play, 91 yard scoring drive that took 8:15 off the clock. The teams traded touchdowns in the fourth quarter before Sloan kicked the game-winner. Trailing 14-13 midway through the fourth quarter, Tom Savage threw a 3 yard touchdown pass to freshman Tyler Boyd to give the Panthers a 19-14 lead. Devin Street then caught a short pass for the 2-point conversion. Navy responded on the ensuing possession and tied the game on a 10-play, 71 yard drive capped by a 2 yard run by quarterback Keenan Reynolds with 3:53 left in the game. The Midshipmen then forced a 3-and-out on the Panthers' next possession and got the ball at Pitt's 49. Navy ran 11 plays to set up Sloan's game-winning kick.

#25 Notre Dame

Notre Dame used a late touchdown by Tarean Folston to land the decisive blow in a wildly entertaining 38-34 win over Navy for the Fighting Irish. The game featured eight lead changes. Navy made one last charge, but on its 70th rush of the day, a reverse on fourth-an-4 was blown up in the backfield, sealing the Notre Dame victory. For Navy, Keenan Reynolds was the doomed hero, rushing 22 times for 53 yards and throwing for 88 yards; he logged four of the Midshipmen's five touchdowns. But on Navy's final drive, his errant toss forced Navy into a third-and-15, and the Midshipmen couldn't convert. The Midshipmen finished with 419 yards total offense and had 27 first downs, the most ever by a Navy team against Notre Dame.

San Jose State

San Jose State quarterback David Fales threw for 440 yards and five touchdowns, but Naval Academy quarterback Keenan Reynolds ran for an NCAA-record seven rushing touchdowns as the Midshipmen defeated the Spartans 58-52 in three overtimes on Friday night in Spartan Stadium. Fales led the Spartans to a touchdown on the final play of regulation, a two yard pass to Kyle Nunn, and with a two-point conversion to Chandler Jones, the game went to overtime at 38-38. Each team scored touchdowns on their first two overtime possessions. With the Spartans facing a third and goal from the three yard line in the third overtime period, Fales threw a pass to the back of the end zone that was intercepted by Navy's Parrish Gaines. It took Navy just one play, a Reynolds 25 yard touchdown dash around the left side for the winning score. Fales connected with eight receivers led by Thomas Tucker who had nine catches for 107 yards and a touchdown. Chandler Jones made seven grabs for 101 yards and a touchdown and Kyle Nunn had two touchdowns and 51 yards. Tucker totaled 278 all-purpose yards with 62 on the ground and a touchdown and 109 yards in kick returns. Navy rushed for 458 yards on 62 carries, 240 by Reynolds on 36 carries. He also completed 4-of-6 for 46 yards and a touchdown. San José State led at the half 16-10, but the teams would go on to score touchdowns on 12 of the next 16 possessions. Navy found the endzone on its first two possessions of the second half, a three yards run by Reynolds and a three yard pass to Darius Staten for a 24-16 lead. The Spartans responded with a seven-play; 77 yard scoring drive capped by a 23 yard Fales to Jones touchdown. The Spartans two-point conversion failed, and the score was 24-22. The Spartans forced a punt on Navy's next possession and then marched 88 yards down the field and scored on a four yard pass from Fales to Tyler Winston. Fales ran in the two-point conversion and the Spartans were back on top 30-24. Navy scored on its next possession to go back in from 31-30 and increased its lead to 38-30 with just 2:38 to play. Fales then led the team the game-tying score as time expired in regulation.

ARMY {@ Lincoln Financial Field, Philadelphia, PA}

Navy quarterback Keenan Reynolds ran for 136 yards and scored three touchdowns (47, 11 and 1 yard) to lead the Midshipmen to a 34-7 victory, their 12th straight in the series. Reynolds scored on runs of 47 yards, 11 yards and 1 yard. The sophomore has 29 rushing touchdowns, breaking the single-season mark for a quarterback previously held by Ricky Dobbs (Navy, 2009) and Collin Klein (Kansas State, 2011), both of whom had 27. Navy won the Commander-In-Chief's Trophy for the second consecutive season and ninth time in 11 years. The trophy is awarded to the service academy with the most victories in games between Navy, Army and Air Force. The Midshipmen haven't lost to Army since 2001 and lead the series 58-49-7. Navy's 12-game run is the longest in the history of the rivalry that began in 1890. Head coach Ken Niumatalolo became the second coach in Navy history to start his coaching career 6-0 against Army, matching Paul Johnson (2002-07). Army fumbled five times and was intercepted once in its fifth straight defeat. The snow that was forecast in the morning hours began during the pregame pageantry that makes this game a one-of-a-kind spectacle. Army quarterback A.J. Schurr fumbled on the first two drives, the second recovered by Navy at its own 38. Following the turnover, Quinton Singleton burst through a hole in the middle and ran 58 yards to the Army 4, setting up a field goal for a 3-0 lead late in the first quarter. Midway through the second period, Noah Copeland ran 39 yards for a touchdown to make it 10-0. With 2:38 left in the half, Reynolds gingerly picked his way through the Army defense on his record-tying touchdown run. Navy went into halftime leading 17-0. In the third quarter, the snow turned to rain and Army quarterback Angel Santiago did his best to make a game of it. After throwing a 29 yard pass to Xavier Moss, the junior quarterback scored on a 4 yard run to get the Black Knights to 17-7. Reynolds answered with an 11-play drive that produced a field goal. Army then failed to convert a fourth-and-3 from its own 42, a futile gamble that all but assured the Black Knights another frustrating loss against their far more successful service academy rivals. Reynolds scored his record-breaking touchdown with 6:22 left, and the conversion pass from wide receiver Brendan Dudeck made it 28-7.

2013 ARMED FORCES BOWL

Navy defeated Middle Tennessee State in the Armed Forces Bowl, overcoming dirty play from their opponents to win 24-6. Navy took the lead early in the first quarter, when quarterback Keenan Reynolds was able to run into the end zone for a three yard score. The two teams then went into field goal mode, with Middle Tennessee State kicking two and Navy kicking one, making the score 10-6 heading into the second half. It was a chippy game, with multiple unsportsmanlike conduct penalties, a targeting ejection, an

ugly incident in which a Blue Raiders player attempted to stick his fingers inside Reynolds' facemask, and a nasty collision just before the end of the first half that left players from both teams down on the field. Much of the dirtiness of the game fell on the side of Middle Tennessee State, which saw Roderic Blunt ejected after two unsportsmanlike penalties. Middle Tennessee State forced two turnovers in the game against a Navy squad that had given the ball away just eight times all season, but the Midshipmen were able to come out on top. In the fourth quarter, Reynolds punched in another touchdown, and third-string safety George Jamison (who replaced the ejected Wave Ryder and the injured Lonnie Richardson, who was knocked out in the collision) intercepted Logan Kilgore's pass on the next drive to seal it. Just a few plays after the interception, DeBrandon Sanders ran 41 yards into the end zone to expand the lead to 24-6.

2014 Navy Midshipmen

The Midshipmen were led by seventh year head coach Ken Niumatalolo. Team Captains were Noah Copeland and Parrish Gaines. This was the final year as an Independent before the school joins the American Athletic Conference. They finished the season 8–5. They were invited to the Poinsettia Bowl where they defeated San Diego State. The annual Army–Navy Game was played on December 13 at M&T Bank Stadium in Baltimore, MD; Navy won the game 17-10.

Keenan Reynolds led the team in passing with 843 yards and threw 6 touchdown passes. Reynolds led the team in rushing with 1,191 yards and 23 rushing touchdowns. Jamir Tillman led the team in receptions with 20 for 386 yards. Reynolds led the team in scoring with 138 points.

Home games were played at Navy-Marine Corps Stadium

8/30/2014	vs	#6	OHIO STATE	CBSSN	17	34	L	
9/6/2014	@		Temple		31	24	W	
9/13/2014	@		Texas State		35	21	W	
9/20/2014	vs		RUTGERS	CBSSN	24	31	L	
9/27/2014	vs		WESTERN KENTUCKY	CBSSN	27	36	L	
10/4/2014	@		Air Force	CBSSN	21	30	L	
10/11/2014	vs		VIRGINIA MILITARY	CBSSN	51	14	W	
10/25/2014	vs		SAN JOSE STATE	CBSSN	41	31	W	
11/1/2014	vs	#10	NOTRE DAME	CBS	39	49	L	
11/15/2014	vs		GEORGIA SOUTHERN	CBSSN	52	19	W	
11/28/2014	@		South Alabama		42	40	W	
12/13/2014	vs		Army	CBS	17	10	W	
12/23/2014	**vs**		**San Diego State**	**ESPN**	**17**	**16**	**W**	**Poinsettia Bowl**
Coach: Ken Niumatalolo			**Season Record >>**		**414**	**355**	**8-5**	

Schedule Source: Steve's Football Bible LLC

Selected game(s) highlights

Air Force

Kale Pearson's short TD pass to Garrett Brown sealed the game with 35 seconds remaining as Air Force held off Navy 30-21. Pearson put Air Force ahead for good on a 3 yard TD pass to Garrett Griffin in the third quarter. But Navy rallied late and pulled to within a field goal. Air Force recovered the onside kick, and Pearson found Brown on fourth-and-2 from the 13 to clinch the win. The Air Force defense did its part, bottling up the nation's top rushing offense in the second half. Navy gained just 36 of its 251 yards on the ground over the final 30 minutes. The Midshipmen entered the contest averaging 358 yards. Navy's Keenan Reynolds had a late TD pass, along with a 10 yard TD run in the second quarter. His run gave him 49 career scores

#10 NOTRE DAME {@ FedEx Field – Landover, MD}

The sixth-ranked Fighting Irish somehow found a way to beat Navy 49-39. Notre Dame blew a 21-point lead, and its youthful defense surrendered 454 yards. Everett Golson became the first player in Notre Dame history to throw for three touchdowns and run for three scores. After Notre Dame ended its first four possessions with touchdowns, the Midshipmen tallied 24 straight points to move ahead 31-28 with 4 minutes left in the third quarter. Golson put Notre Dame back in front with a 3 yard burst into the end zone, and a 25 yard touchdown run by Tarean Folston made it 42-31 with 12:22 remaining. Two missed field goals by the Irish kept Navy's hopes alive. The Midshipmen took advantage by scoring a touchdown and 2-point conversion to close to 42-39 with 4:18 remaining, but the onside kick failed, and Golson wrapped it up with an 8 yard TD run with 1:27 to go.

South Alabama

South Alabama scored 20 points in the fourth quarter — including a pair of touchdowns in the last five-and-a-half minutes — to rally from a 15-point deficit. The Jaguars even were successful twice on the two-point conversion following Jeremé Jones' 10 yard scoring reception with 39 seconds remaining. But penalties were called on both occasions, and when Brendan Clements intercepted South Alabama's final attempt from the 18 yard line to collect the two points and tie the contest it secured a 42-40 non-conference football victory for Navy. Keenan Reynolds' third touchdown of the day extended the Midshipmen's advantage back to 15 points with just over eight minutes remaining in the game, but South Alabama required less than three minutes to reach the end zone again when Brandon Bridge and Shavarez Smith hooked up for a 48 yard touchdown pass. Reynolds posted 119 yards on 10 carries and Noah Copeland finished with 112 on 17, while Chris Swain recorded nine rushes for 64 yards. In all, Navy racked up 388 yards on the ground

ARMY {M&T Bank Stadium - Baltimore, Maryland}

The game was over, and it was time for Navy to celebrate its 13th straight victory over Army. After the Midshipmen stood respectfully for Army's alma mater, defensive ends Paul Quessenberry and Will Anthony along with nose guard Bernard Sarra hoisted Ken Niumatalolo on their shoulders to give the winningest football coach in Navy history a free ride in the wake of a 17-10 triumph. Niumatalolo broke a tie with George Welsh for most wins at Navy. He also became the first to win his first seven games against Army. The streak remained intact because of Navy's unrelenting defense and quarterback Keenan Reynolds' versatility. The Cadets went up 7-0 in stunning fashion, holding Navy to four yards on its first series before Josh Jenkins blocked a punt and Xavier Moss scooped up the ball and sprinted seven yards into the end zone. Navy senior Pablo Beltran never had a punt blocked before that play - it was his 151st kick - and it marked the first time since 2009 that Army scored first against the Midshipmen. It was a horrid first quarter for Navy, which gained 15 yards on three straight three-and-outs. Army maintained the upper hand in the second quarter, but the momentum turned when Cadets quarterback Angel Santiago was stuffed on a fourth-and-1 from the Navy 30 with just over two minutes left. The Midshipmen then turned to a seldom-used weapon - the forward pass - to pull into a tie at the break. Reynolds completed a 39 yard pass to Jamir Tillman to the Army 31 and connected with Ryan Williams-Jenkins for 12 yards before throwing a 9 yard TD pass to Tillman with 18 seconds to go before halftime. Navy opened the third quarter with a 41 yard kickoff return by Williams-Jenkins. That led to a 45 yard field goal by Austin Grebe for a 10-7 lead. Army then wasted a 50 yard drive, moving to the Navy 30 before Daniel Grochowski hooked a field goal try to the left. Reynolds subsequently directed a 12-play march that lasted nearly eight minutes and ended with the 5-foot-11 junior bulling over the goal line for a 10-point cushion. The two teams traded fumbles and a 52 yard field goal by Grochowski made it 17-10 with 1:51 left, but Navy recovered the ensuing onside kick. The 13-game run by Navy is the longest in the history of a series that began in 1890. Before the Midshipmen went on their unprecedented streak, neither team in this storied rivalry had won more than five in a row. Navy leads the series 59-49-7. In the previous 12 games, the Midshipmen outscored Army 400-132 - including 34-7 last year. Although the score in this one was closer, the result was the same. The Cadets haven't defeated the Midshipmen since 2001. First-year coach Jeff Monken became the sixth coach to lose to Navy over that span.

2014 POINSETTIA BOWL

The Navy football team overcame four turnovers and uncharacteristic penalties Tuesday night to outlast San Diego State, 17-16 and close its season with a dramatic triumph in the Poinsettia Bowl at Qualcomm Stadium. The difference was Austin Grebe's 24 yard field goal that gave the Midshipmen the lead for good with 1 minute 27 seconds left. San Diego State had a chance to reclaim the lead with 24 seconds to play, but the Midshipmen were able to celebrate a second straight bowl victory when Donny Hageman missed a 34 yard field goal try. Navy's offense scored on its first drive of the game but sputtered the rest of the first half. The Midshipmen went ahead, 14-13, on Keenan Reynolds's six yard run midway through the third quarter. The 13-play, 92 yard drive was reliant on fullbacks Chris Swain and Noah Copeland, a senior co-captain, combining for 64 yards on four carries. Navy avoided potential disaster shortly thereafter when DeBrandon Sanders called for a fair catch but had the ball bounce off his hands. San Diego State recovered at the Midshipmen 18, but an illegal formation on first down moved the Aztecs back five yards. On third and five, Quinn Kaehler threw out of bounds, and Navy escaped by allowing only a 31 yard field goal from Hageman. Consecutive turnovers to start the fourth quarter could have doomed Navy for good, but the defense was up to the task. After slot back Ryan Williams-Jenkins fumbled on a muffed exchange from Reynolds to give San Diego State possession at Navy's 41, safety George Jamison intercepted Kaehler to end the threat.

2015 Navy Midshipmen {Lambert Trophy + Commander-in-Chief Trophy}

The Midshipmen were led by eighth year head coach Ken Niumatalolo. Team Captains were Keenan Reynolds and Bernard Sarra. The Midshipmen competed as a member of the Western Division of the American Athletic Conference and were first year members of the conference. In their entire football history, this was the first season that Navy did not compete as an Independent. They finished the season 11–2, 7–1 in American Athletic play to finish in a tie for the Western Division title with Houston. However, due to their head to head loss to Houston, they did not represent the Western Division in the American Championship. They were invited to the Military Bowl where they defeated Pittsburgh. The annual Army–Navy Game was played on December 12 at Lincoln Financial Field in Philadelphia, PA. Navy won the game 21-17.

Keenan Reynolds led the team in passing with 1,203 yards and threw 8 touchdown passes. Reynolds led the team in rushing with 1,373 yards and 24 rushing touchdowns. Jamir Tillman led the team in receptions with 29 for 597 yards and 5 TD receptions. Brandon Clements led the team with 4 interceptions. Reynolds led the team in scoring with 144 points.

FINAL RANK: #18 AP, #18 UPI

Home games were played at Navy-Marine Corps Stadium

Date	Rank	vs/@	Opp Rank	Opponent	TV			Result	Notes
9/5/2015		vs		*COLGATE*	CBSSN	48	10	W	
9/19/2015		vs		EAST CAROLINA	CBSSN	45	21	W	
9/26/2015		@		Connecticut	CBSSN	28	18	W	
10/3/2015		vs		*AIR FORCE*	CBSSN	33	11	W	
10/10/2015		@	#15	*Notre Dame*	NBC	24	41	L	
10/24/2015		vs		TULANE	CBSSN	31	14	W	
10/31/2015		vs		SOUTH FLORIDA	CBSSN	29	17	W	
11/7/2015		@	#15	Memphis	espN2	45	20	W	
11/14/2015	#22	vs		SMU	CBSSN	55	14	W	
11/21/2015	#19	@		Tulsa	CBSSN	44	21	W	
11/28/2015	#16	@	#21	Houston	ABC	31	52	L	
12/12/2015	#21	vs		*ARMY*	CBS	21	17	W	
12/28/2015	**#21**	**vs**		**Pittsburgh**	**ESPN**	**44**	**28**	**W**	**Military Bowl**
Coach: Ken Niumatalolo				**Season Record >>**		**478**	**284**	**11-2**	

Schedule Source: Steve's Football Bible LLC

Selected game(s) highlights

AIR FORCE

Keenan Reynolds ran for 117 of his 183 yards in the first half and the Midshipmen took a 33-11 victory over the Falcons. Reynolds completed 4 of 10 passes for 117 yards with a touchdown on a wet, windy day. Chris Swain had a pair of short yardage scores for the Midshipmen. Air Force committed a season-high four turnovers, all in Navy territory. After Navy's Kwazel Bertrand recovered a fumble by Roberts, the Midshipmen went 64 yards to pull ahead 14-0 with 14:47 left in the second quarter. Reynolds threw a 27 yard pass to Thomas Wilson, who fought off two defenders just inside the end zone. Reynolds continued to be the difference-maker, and another 67 yard run gave the Midshipmen the ball at the 1 late in the second quarter. Three plays later, Demond Brown scored on a sweep and Navy led 21-0 at the break. Navy carried that momentum into the second half. On the opening drive, the Midshipmen went 75 yards on 12 plays and boosted the lead to 27-0 on 1 yard run by Swain

#15 Notre Dame

C. J. Prosise scored one play after linebacker Jaylon Smith recovered a fumble by Chris Swain on the Navy 7 and two plays after Devin Butler recovered a fumble by Dishan Romine at the 26 yard line on the opening kickoff of the second half. Prosise finished with three rushing touchdowns as the 15th-ranked Fighting Irish beat the Midshipmen 41-24. Navy had tied the score at 21-21 with 24 seconds left in the first half after fullback Quentin Ezell gashed the Irish for touchdown runs of 45 and 22 yards. But Justin Yoon kicked a 52 yard field goal in the closing seconds of the first half and Prosise put the Irish ahead by 10 points with a 22 yard run following the second fumble. Navy quarterback Keenan Reynolds sat out part of the second quarter and the end of the game after falling awkwardly on his left leg while being tackled. Reynolds finished with 110 yards rushing on 15 carries, but the Irish held him without a rushing touchdown. The loss ended an eight-game winning streak for Navy.

ARMY {@ Lincoln Financial Field, Philadelphia, PA}

With a shot at history at stake, Keenan Reynolds ended his Navy career with a clean sweep against Army. Reynolds rushed for two touchdowns and threw for another score to lead the No. 21 Midshipmen to their 14th straight win over the Black Knights, 21-17, at Lincoln Financial Field. Reynolds' second rushing TD was his 85th career score, the most for any FBS or FCS Division I player (he ended his career with 88). He is the first quarterback in the 116-game series to go 4-0. Head coach Ken Niumatalolo improved to 8-0 against the Black Knights. Army's Daniel Grochowski missed a 29 yard field goal early in the quarter. Chris Carter lost a fumble at the Navy 34 yard that was recovered by linebacker Ted Colburn. Navy had two interceptions - one off a trick play - on two straight drives to preserve the lead. Army's Hail Mary on the final play of the game fell short. Niumatalolo tied former Army coach Earl "Red" Blaik (8-8-2) for most wins in the series. Reynolds showed why he was a late contender for Heisman Trophy consideration. Reynolds, the only player in team history with two 1,000 yard rushing and passing seasons, put the Middies up 21-17 with a 50 yard TD pass to Jamir Tillman late in the third. A three-touchdown favorite, Navy had it tougher than usual in one of the most storied rivalries in college sports. The Middies won the CIC trophy, awarded to the team with the best record in games among the three service academies. Navy beat Air Force 33-11 this season. The Black Knights got a field goal on the game's opening drive and Tyler Campbell scored on a 29 yard run to make it 10-7 in the first. Carter hit Edgar Poe for a 39 yard TD pass with 2:08 left in the half to make it 17-14 and give Army its first halftime lead since 2009. Army had a lead. It just didn't have Reynolds. Reynolds scored on runs of 58 yards and 1 yard to keep Navy in the game, and then used his arm to find Tillman in the third for the lead.

2015 MILITARY BOWL

Pittsburgh started the 2015 Military Bowl presented by Northrop Grumman with a bang, but it was Navy's record-setting quarterback Keenan Reynolds that had the last laugh as the Midshipmen set a school record for most victories in one season. Reynolds capped his tremendous career with one final spectacular game, passing for one touchdown, rushing for three more and setting the NCAA record for most touchdowns scored in a career to earn Most Valuable Player honors as the Midshipmen beat Pitt Panthers, 44-28, before a sellout crowd of 36,352 at Navy-Marine Corps  Memorial Stadium. Quadree Henderson started the game with a 100 yard kickoff return for a touchdown, but Navy scored the next 31 points. Reynolds led the charge with touchdown runs of 1 and 5 yards and an 11 yard touchdown pass to tight end Tyler Carmona for a 21-7 halftime lead. The Midshipmen padded their lead with a 26 yard touchdown run by Demond Brown and Austin Grebe's 35 yard field goal for a 31-7 lead. Pitt pulled within 31-21 late in the third quarter on a pair of scores by the ACC Offensive and Defensive rookies of the year. Nate Peterman threw a 4 yard touchdown pass to Qadree Ollison and Jordan Whitehead returned a fumble 22 yards for a touchdown with 2 minutes 57 seconds left in the third quarter. But Navy converted a pair of fourth downs on its ensuing drive, leading to Toneo Gulley's 15 yard touchdown run. Late in the game, the only thing yet to be settled was whether Reynolds would become the Football Bowl Subdivision's all-time touchdowns leader. He scored on a nine yard run with 4:19 left to make it 44-28 and seal the game. Reynolds finished 9 of 17 passing for 126 yards and rushed for 144 yards on 24 carries.

2016 Navy Midshipmen

The Midshipmen were led by ninth-year head coach Ken Niumatalolo. Team Captains were Daniel Gonzales and Toneo Gulley. The Midshipmen competed as a member of the West Division of the American Athletic Conference. They finished the season 9–5 overall and 7–1 in American Athletic play to be champions of the West Division. They represented the West Division in The American Athletic Championship Game where they lost to Temple. They were invited to the Armed Forces Bowl where they lost to Louisiana Tech. The annual Army–Navy Game was played on December 10 at M&T Bank Stadium in Baltimore, MD; Army won the game 21-17.

Will Worth led the team in passing with 1,357 yards and threw 8 touchdown passes. Worth led the team in rushing with 1,198 yards and 25 rushing touchdowns. Jamir Tillman led the team in receptions with 40 for 631 yards. Worth led the team in scoring with 150 points. **Worth set a single game total offense record with 428 yards vs South Florida.**

Home games were played at Navy-Marine Corps Stadium

9/3/2016		vs		*FORDHAM*	CBSSN	52	16	**W**	
9/10/2016		vs		CONNECTICUT	CBSSN	28	24	**W**	
9/17/2016		@		Tulane		21	14	**W**	
10/1/2016		@		*Air Force*	CBSSN	14	28	**L**	
10/8/2016		vs	#6	HOUSTON	CBSSN	46	40	**W**	
10/22/2016	**#24**	vs		MEMPHIS	CBSSN	42	28	**W**	
10/28/2016	**#22**	@		South Florida	espn2	45	52	**L**	*-Worth 428 total yds
11/5/2016		vs		*Notre Dame*	CBS	28	27	**W**	
11/12/2016		vs		TULSA	CBSSN	42	40	**W**	
11/19/2016		@		East Carolina		66	31	**W**	
11/26/2016		@		Smu	ESPNU	75	31	**W**	
12/3/2016	**#20**	**vs**		**TEMPLE**	**ABC**	**10**	**34**	**L**	**AAC Championship**
12/10/2016	**#25**	vs		*Army*	CBS	17	21	**L**	
12/22/2016	**#25**	**vs**		**Louisiana Tech**	**ESPN**	**45**	**48**	**L**	**Armed Forces Bowl**
Coach: Ken Niumatalolo				**Season Record >>**		**531**	**434**	**9-5**	

Schedule Source: Steve's Football Bible LLC
***-Single game record**

Selected game(s) highlights

Air Force

Weston Steelhammer led a dominating defensive effort, tailback Tim McVey scored twice, including a 62 yard TD catch, and Air Force beat Navy 28-14. Jalen Robinette had five catches for 163 yards for Air Force. His 75 yard TD catch late in the third quarter broke open the game. The Midshipmen averted a shutout on a 6 yard TD run by Shawn White with 8:33 remaining. The first half was ruled by defense with the only score a field goal. Air Force began to pull away in the third quarter when McVey scored on a 1 yard plunge. Robinette soon followed with his TD catch from Nate Romine, who finished 8 of 14 for a career-high 257 yards and two scores.

Notre Dame {EverBank Field – Jacksonville, FL}

Will Worth ran for 175 yards and two touchdowns, his eighth consecutive game with a rushing score, and the Midshipmen beat the Fighting Irish 28-27 Saturday in the nation's longest-running intersectional rivalry. Trailing 28-24 with a little more than 7 minutes to go, Notre Dame opted for a 31 yard field goal instead of trying to convert a fourth-and-4 play at the 14. Navy got the ball and ran out the clock with its triple-option offense. Worth converted two huge fourth-down plays on the final drive, one on a dive play near midfield and another with a pass to Jamir Tillman. Navy finished with 368 yards, including 320 on the ground.

TULSA

Navy quarterback Will Worth ran for 122 yards and scored three touchdowns, and the Midshipmen took control of the American Athletic Conference's West Division with a 42-40 victory over Tulsa. Midshipmen senior Dishan Romine ran for 97 yards on six carries and got his first career touchdown with a 41 yard scamper that provided a 14-10 lead. Romine also had a 48 yard return on the opening kick-off that set up Navy's first touchdown.

Smu

Will Worth accounted for four touchdowns while becoming the first Navy quarterback with more than 100 yards rushing and 100 yards passing in three consecutive games in a 75-31 victory at SMU. Worth ran 15 times for 107 yards and three touchdowns, increasing his FBS-leading total to 25 rushing scores while playing only three quarters. Worth completed 5 of 7 passes for 104 yards and the go-ahead TD just before halftime. After Navy's first lost fumble in five games led to a touchdown that put SMU up 24-21 late in the first half, the Midshipmen responded with 47 unanswered points. Worth's 8 yard TD pass to Jamir Tillman with 6 seconds left in the first half put the Midshipmen ahead to stay. They scored twice in less than a minute right after halftime, on fullback Shawn White's 50 yard run and Justin North's 25 yard interception return.

2016 AAC Championship Game

Phillip Walker threw two touchdown passes, Temple's defense stuffed Navy's running game and the Owls claimed their first American Athletic Conference title with a 34-10 victory. After Temple scored touchdowns on its first three possessions, protecting the 21-0 lead became substantially easier when No. 19 Navy lost standout quarterback Will Worth to a second-quarter ankle injury. After falling behind 24-3 at halftime, the Midshipmen got a 47 yard run from Zach Abey during a drive late in the third quarter that ended with the quarterback scoring from the Temple 1. Temple opened with TD drives of 75, 59 and 70 yards, and the defense quashed a Navy attack that was averaging 61 points over its previous three games.

ARMY {M&T Bank Stadium - Baltimore, Maryland}

Army ended a 14-year run of frustration against the Midshipmen, using a running game and opportunistic defense to carve out a 21-17 victory. With future commander-in-chief Donald Trump looking on, the Black Knights blew a 14-point lead before quarterback Ahmad Bradshaw scored on a 9 yard run with 6:42 left to give Army the win it had been waiting for since 2001. The Black Knights' 14-game losing streak was the longest by either academy in a series that began in 1890. Army now trails 60-50-7 in one of the nation's historic rivalries. Navy was coming off a physical 34-10 loss to Temple in the American Athletic Conference title game and had only one week to prepare for Army with a new quarterback, sophomore Zach Abey, who was making his first college start. Abey ran for two touchdowns but passed for only 89 yards and was intercepted twice. Navy had three turnovers, all in the first half. By halftime, Army led 14-0 and owned a 14-1 advantage in first downs. Andy Davidson lost a fumble on the Black Knights' first possession of the second half and the Midshipmen recovered at the Army 32. A screen pass for 16 yards set up a 1 yard touchdown run by Abey to get Navy to 14-7. Minutes later, the Midshipmen got a field goal after a replay overturned a lost fumble by Abey at the Army 11. A 41 yard touchdown run by Abey gave Navy the lead with 12:42 remaining. But Army wasn't done. The Black Knights put together a 12-play, 80 yard drive that lasted nearly seven minutes and ended with Bradshaw's TD. Bradshaw went 2 for 4 for 35 yards and an interception in Army's first win in Baltimore since 1944. Davidson ran for 87 yards and two first-half scores, and Kell Walker carried 16 times for 94 yards.

2016 ARMED FORCES BOWL

Jonathan Barnes' 32 yard field goal as time expired to give Louisiana Tech the storybook ending it deserved and clinched the Bulldogs' third consecutive bowl championship over No. 25 Navy Friday in the Lockheed Martin Armed Forces Bowl at Amon G. Carter Stadium in Fort Worth, Texas. Tied 45-45 with under four minutes to play, the junior kicker's game-winning field goal capped off a wild back-and-forth affair between the Bulldogs and Midshipmen that ended up coming down to the final three seconds in the fourth quarter. The two teams combined for nearly 1,000 yards Friday night in Fort Worth with the Bulldogs edging the Midshipmen with 497 yards of total offense. Ryan Higgins set new bowl records for completions as the senior ended the night 29-of-40 passing for 409 yards and four touchdowns through the air. Trent Taylor earned Armed Forces Bowl MVP honors with 12 receptions for 233 receiving yards and two touchdowns. The senior receiver broke bowl records for receptions and receiving yards in a game on his way to leading LA Tech to a third straight bowl title. Louisiana Tech's Carlos Henderson showed off his speed against No. 25 Navy on an 82 yard return on the opening kickoff and the Bulldogs never slowed down from that point. Henderson's shifty return set up Ryan Higgins' quarterback keeper for a 7-0 lead for the Bulldogs in what became the fastest touchdown scored in bowl history less than 90 seconds into the game. Henderson ended the night with 266 all-purpose yards with 129 receiving, 137 kick return yards and two touchdown receptions in the victory. On Navy's first offensive possession, the Midshipmen gave Louisiana Tech an early Christmas gift by fumbling the football, which was recovered by Prince Sam to set up Jonathan Barnes' 22 yard field goal to extend LA Tech's lead to 10. Midway through the first, the Midshipmen settled in and forced a LA Tech punt, which set up an 8-play, 55 yard drive by Navy to cut the lead the three with a 3 yard rushing touchdown by quarterback Zach Abey. The Bulldogs responded on the next drive when Higgins had a hand in the second touchdown of the day for LA Tech with a 19 yard touchdown pass to Trent Taylor to put Tech up 17-7 over Navy with just 18 seconds left in the first quarter. Navy had an answer on the first play of the second quarter as Abey completed a 64 yard touchdown pass to Darryl Bonner to cut the Midshipmen's deficit to 17-14. The Midshipmen took their first lead of the game on the next drive thanks to Abey's efforts on the ground after a 30 yard rush, facemask penalty against the Bulldogs and then a 2 yard quarterback keeper gave Navy a 21-17 lead over LA Tech in the second. Later in the first half, the Bulldog offense got its groove back a little bit with a 9-play, 65 yard drive that led to a 3 yard touchdown reception by Henderson to retake the lead over Navy, 24-21, midway through the second quarter of play. After Navy tied it up at 24-24 thanks to a career-long 40 yard field goal by Barrett Moehring, Louisiana Tech answered with a 51 yard touchdown pass from Higgins to Taylor to send the Bulldogs into halftime with a 31-24 lead over the Midshipmen.

Navy opened the second half with a 14-play drive that took more than seven minutes off the clock and spanned 90 yards before knotting the game at 31-31 with a 24 yard rushing touchdown by Chris High. At the beginning of the fourth quarter, LA Tech drove 70 yards down the field on a drive that included a 41 yard reception by Taylor over the middle to set up Boston Scott's 12 yard rushing touchdown to give the Bulldogs a 38-31 lead over Navy. Navy's Chris High tied the game, 38-38, midway through the fourth with a 9 yard  touchdown run, his second of the game, but Carlos Henderson once again took the stage later in the quarter to give Louisiana Tech another lead. With just over four minutes left in the game, Henderson caught his second touchdown of the night, both coming on fade routes on crucial third down conversions, to give the Bulldogs a 7-point lead in the final quarter. Navy responded quickly with the game-tying touchdown, a 30 yard rushing score by Malcolm Perry to knot the game, 45-45, before LA Tech orchestrated a 9-play, 70 yard game-winning drive that took the final 3:40 off the clock.

2017 Navy Midshipmen

The Midshipmen were led by tenth-year head coach Ken Niumatalolo. Team Captains were Darryl Bonner and D.J. Palmore. They finished the season 7–6 overall and 4–4 in AAC play to tie for third place in the West Division. They were invited to the Military Bowl, where they defeated Virginia, 49–7. The annual Army–Navy Game was played on December 9 at Lincoln Financial Field in Philadelphia, PA. Army won the game 14-13.

Zach Abey led the team in passing with 805 yards and threw 7 touchdown passes. Abey led the team in rushing with 1,413 yards and 19 rushing touchdowns. Tyler Carmona led the team in receptions with 14 for 381 yards and 4 TD receptions. Abey led the team in scoring with 120 points.

Home games were played at Navy-Marine Corps Stadium

Date				Opponent	Network				
9/2/2017		@		*Florida Atlantic*	ESPNU	42	19	W	
9/9/2017		vs		TULANE	CBSSN	23	21	W	
9/23/2017		vs		CINCINNATI	CBSSN	42	32	W	
9/30/2017		@		Tulsa	ESPNU	31	21	W	
10/7/2017		vs		*AIR FORCE*	CBSSN	48	45	W	
10/14/2017	#25	@		Memphis	ESPNU	27	30	L	
10/21/2017		vs	#20	CENTRAL FLORIDA	CBSSN	21	31	L	
11/3/2017		@		Temple	ESPN	26	34	L	
11/11/2017		vs		SMU	CBSSN	43	40	W	
11/18/2017		@	#9	*Notre Dame*	NBC	17	24	L	
11/24/2017		@		Houston	ESPN	14	24	L	
12/9/2017		vs		*Army*	CBS	13	14	L	
12/28/2017		**vs**		**Virginia**	**ESPN**	**49**	**7**	**W**	**Military Bowl**
Coach: Ken Niumatalolo				**Season Record >>**		**2344**	**2400**	**7-6**	

Schedule Source: Steve's Football Bible LLC

Selected game(s) highlights

AIR FORCE

Zach Abey threw a 16 yard touchdown pass to Tyler Carmona with 15 seconds left, and the unbeaten Midshipmen defeated Air Force 48-45 Saturday after blowing a 21-point lead in the second half. Arion Worthman threw a 51 yard touchdown pass to Marcus Bennett with 1:53 remaining to put the Falcons up 45-41, Abey moved the Midshipmen 75 yards in 11 plays for the go-ahead score. Air Force amassed 621 yards and Navy accumulated 557, including 471 on the ground. Abey ran for 214 yards and two touchdowns, and Malcolm Perry contributed two long scores. The Midshipmen converted a short punt and two Air Force fumbles into three touchdowns and a 28-10 halftime lead. After a 75 yard quarterback keeper by Abey made it 38-17 in the third quarter, Air Force rallied.

SMU

Malcolm Perry ran for 282 yards with four touchdowns in his first start at quarterback and backup kicker J.R. Osborn hit an 18 yard, game-winning field goal as time expired to give the Midshipmen a 43-40 victory over SMU. SMU quarterback Ben Hicks threw a 29 yard touchdown to Courtland Sutton and then completed another pass to Trey Quinn for a 2-point conversion that tied the game, 40-40, with 3:32 remaining to play. Garret Lewis entered for the injured Perry and handed the ball to fullback Anthony Gargiulo, who managed 50 yards on two carries to the Mustangs' 9 yard line that eventually set up the game-winning kick by Osborn. Gargiulo finished with a career-high 145 yards on 15 carries and had the game's first touchdown on a 4 yard run. Perry gave Navy a 27-11 lead with a 92 yard touchdown scamper in the second quarter-the second longest run in school history.

#9 Notre Dame

Brandon Wimbush threw for 164 yards and two touchdowns and ran for a score as No. 9 Notre Dame rallied in the rain and wind to beat Navy 24-17. The Irish outgained the Midshipmen 327-318, but Navy outrushed Notre Dame 277-163 and had a huge advantage in time of possession, 42:42 to 17:18. Notre Dame didn't secure the victory until there was 1:28 left in the game. After a timeout on a fourth-and-5 at Notre Dame's 25, Quarterback Zach Abey pitched the ball to slotback Darryl Bonner, who passed downfield to wide receiver Tyler Carmona, who was open for a moment. But Carmona slipped on the wet Notre Dame Stadium turf, the pass fell incomplete and Notre Dame twice took a knee to run the clock out.

ARMY {@ Lincoln Financial Field, Philadelphia, PA}

Bennett Moehring narrowly missed a 48 yard field goal in the swirling snow on the final play and Army held off Navy 14-13 to win its first Commander-in-Chief's Trophy since 1996. Army earned its second straight win over Navy following 14 straight losses in the series. Ahmad Bradshaw pushed over the goal line on a quarterback sneak with 5:10 remaining and Blake Wilson kicked the extra point to put Army ahead. Quarterback Malcolm Perry, who ran for 250 yards and a 68 yard score in the second quarter, then led Navy to the Army 31 with 3 seconds left. Navy elected to try a field goal, and after about 10 players used their feet to clear the steady snow during a timeout, Moehring's kick was long enough but drifted barely left. Army cut its deficit in the series to 60-51-7 in a matchup of bowl-bound teams. The Black Knights claimed the Commander-in-Chief's Trophy thanks to an earlier victory over Air Force. In a game that included only three passes - Army completed its lone toss - the Black Knights produced a 13-play, 65 yard to take a late lead. John Trainor tiptoed the sideline for 8 yards one play before Bradshaw's 12th touchdown of the season. Navy took advantage of the ensuing kickoff going out of bounds and moved down the field. Perry dropped a shotgun snap on fourth down at the Army 37 but picked up the ball and ran for a first down. But Navy committed two false start penalties, making the final field goal attempt more difficult. Snow started falling in the late morning on the 29-degree day, leaving a coating on the field. Workers used blowers to uncover the lines and hashmarks during timeouts as a light snow fell throughout. The weather made one of sports' biggest rivalries an even more physical contest. Army's all-white uniforms - a nod to the 10th Mountain Division of World War II - served as almost camouflage in the snow. Perry's shifty 46 yard run to the Navy 11 early in the third quarter put him over 1,000 yards for the season and led to Moehring's second field goal, from 24 yards, to make it 13-7.

2017 MILITARY BOWL

Navy dominated Virginia in the Military Bowl in Annapolis, 49-7. The Midshipmen allowed a 98 yard kickoff return for a touchdown on the first play of the game, then prevented the Cavaliers from doing anything else for the final 59:48. Navy attempted one pass, which fell incomplete. It was the second time this year that Navy won a game without a completion. Navy controlled the ball for 42:00 and out-gained Navy in total, 452 to 175 (5.9 to 3.2 in yards per play). All those Navy yards were rushing, of course, while almost all of UVA's were through the air. Navy put two rushers over 100 yards in QB Malcolm Perry and fullback Chris High. A third rusher, QB Zach Abey, had five touchdowns.

2018 Navy Midshipmen

The Midshipmen were led by eleventh-year head coach Ken Niumatalolo. Team Captains were Anthony Gargiulo and Sean Williams. The Midshipmen finished the season 3–10, the team's worst record since 2002. They went 2–6 in AAC play to tie fifth place in the West Division. The annual Army–Navy Game was played on December 8 at Lincoln Financial Field in Philadelphia, PA. Army won the game 17-10.

Garrett Lewis led the team in passing with 479 yards. Malcolm Perry led the team in rushing with 1,087 yards. Zach Abey led with 14 rushing touchdowns. Taylor Jackson led the team in receptions with 13 for 222 yards. Abey led the team in scoring with 90 points.

Home games were played at Navy-Marine Corps Stadium

9/1/2018	NAVY		@		*Hawaii*	CBSSN	41	59	**L**
9/8/2018	NAVY	**vs**			MEMPHIS	CBSSN	22	21	**W**
9/15/2018	NAVY	**vs**			*LEHIGH*	CBSSN	51	21	**W**
9/22/2018	NAVY		@		Smu		30	31	**L**
10/6/2018	NAVY		@		*Air Force*	CBSSN	7	35	**L**
10/13/2018	NAVY	**vs**			TEMPLE	CBSSN	17	24	**L**
10/20/2018	NAVY	**vs**			HOUSTON	CBSSN	36	49	**L**
10/27/2018	NAVY	**vs**	#3	*Notre Dame*	CBS	22	44	**L**
11/3/2018	NAVY		@		Cincinnati	ESPNU	0	42	**L**
11/10/2018	NAVY		@	#11	Central Florida	espn2	24	35	**L**
11/17/2018	NAVY	**vs**			TULSA	CBSSN	37	29	**W**
11/24/2018	NAVY		@		Tulane	ESPNU	28	29	**L**
12/8/2018	NAVY	**vs**	#23	*Army*	CBS	10	17	**L**
Coach: Ken Niumatalolo				**Season Record >>**		325	436	**3-10**	

Schedule Source: Steve's Football Bible LLC

Selected game(s) highlights

MEMPHIS

The Midshipmen found themselves in a driving rain and trailing Memphis by 12 points in the fourth quarter. Malcolm Perry got Navy within striking distance with a sensational 19 yard run, and backup Zach Abey scored from the 3 with 2:37 left for a 22-21 victory. Perry ran for 166 yards and two touchdowns. The last time the Midshipmen won when trailing by double digits in the fourth quarter was in 2008, against Temple.

Smu

Hunter Thedford caught a 2-point conversion pass in the first overtime on a play that led to several minutes of discussion by officials and a review before it was held up, and the Mustangs beat Navy 31-30 for their first win over the Midshipmen in 20 years. After Ben Hicks threw a 4 yard touchdown pass to James Proche, SMU chose to go for the win. Navy started overtime with a nine-play possession that ended with quarterback Garret Lewis' plunge from inside the 1 yard line. C.J. Williams ran 52 yards for a tying touchdown with 6:19 left in the fourth quarter and led the Midshipmen with 82 of their 349 yards rushing. Navy had that chance to get even because Jarid Ryan returned a blocked PAT kick for a 2-point conversion from several yards deep in the end zone earlier in the fourth.

Air Force

Air Force trailed, 7-0, early in the second quarter, but then scored 35 unanswered points on its way to a resounding 35-7 victory over the Naval Academy at Falcon Stadium. D.J. Hammond ran for three touchdowns and threw another. Joseph Saucier also scored on a 48 yard run for Air Force. Up by seven at halftime, Air Force added two touchdowns in the third quarter with Hammond leading a pair of 75 yard drives that he finished with 5- and 1 yard scoring runs, respectively. He added the 2 yarder early in the fourth quarter on a quarterback draw. Navy struck first on a 2 yard touchdown run early in the second quarter by Garret Lewis.

#3 Notre Dame {@ Qualcomm Stadium – San Diego, CA}

Quarterback Ian Book was remarkably efficient in leading the Fighting Irish to a 44-22 win. Book threw for 330 yards and two touchdowns, and Dexter Williams ran for 142 yards and three scores. Notre Dame used its superior size and talent to take a 27-0 lead just before halftime. While the defense kept Navy's triple option in check, Book kept the Midshipmen off-balance with lots of play-action. He completed 27 of 33 passes, to 10 receivers. He threw one interception. Notre Dame had 584 yards of total offense. Navy finally broke through thanks to some big plays that led to Zach Abey scoring two 1 yard touchdowns in the third quarter. Book was intercepted early in the fourth quarter, setting up a 33 yard touchdown run by Mike Martin.

#22 ARMY {@ Lincoln Financial Field, Philadelphia, PA}

The #22 Black Knights recovered two fumbles in the fourth quarter, Kelvin Hopkins Jr. had two rushing touchdowns and Army beat Navy 17-10 on Saturday to win its third straight game in the series. President Donald Trump attended the 119th game between the rivals and flipped the coin before spending a half on each side in a show of impartiality. With Navy down 10-7, quarterback Zach Abey lost a fumble on fourth-and-12 deep in its own territory. Hopkins would score on a 1 yard run to make it 17-7 and give Army the cushion it needed to win in front of 66,729 fans at Lincoln Financial Field.

2019 Navy Midshipmen {Lambert Trophy + Commander-in-Chief Trophy}

The Midshipmen were led by twelfth year head coach Ken Niumatalolo. Team Captains were Malcolm Perry, Ford Higgins, Paul Carothers and Nizaire Cromartie. The Midshipmen finished the season 11-2 and were invited to the Liberty Bowl to Kansas State from the Big Twelve Conference. The annual Army–Navy Game was played on December 14 at Lincoln Financial Field in Philadelphia, PA. Navy won the game 31-7. Navy won the Lambert Trophy as the East's best team.

Malcolm Perry led the team in passing with 1,084 yards and threw 7 touchdown passes. **Perry rushed for 2,017 yards, setting a new single season record**, and rushed for 21 touchdowns. Mychal Cooper led the team in receptions with 18 for 380 yards. Perry led the team in scoring with 120 points. **Perry set a new single season record for total offense with 3,099 yards.**

FINAL RANK: #20 AP, #20 UPI

Home games were played at Navy-Marine Corps Stadium

8/31/2019		vs		*HOLY CROSS*	CBSSN	45	7	W	
9/14/2019		vs		EAST CAROLINA	CBSSN	42	10	W	
9/26/2019		@		Memphis	ESPN	23	35	L	
10/5/2019		vs		*AIR FORCE*	CBSSN	34	25	W	
10/12/2019		@		Tulsa	ESPNU	45	17	W	
10/19/2019		vs		SOUTH FLORIDA	CBSSN	35	3	W	
10/26/2019		vs		TULANE	CBSSN	41	38	W	
11/1/2019		@		Connecticut	espn2	56	10	W	
11/16/2019		@	#16	*Notre Dame*	NBC	20	52	L	
11/23/2019		vs	#21	SMU	CBSSN	35	28	W	
11/30/2019	#24	@		Houston	espn2	56	41	W	
12/14/2019	#21	vs		*Army*	CBS	31	7	W	
12/31/2019	**#21**	**vs**		**Kansas State**	**ESPN**	**20**	**17**	**W**	**Liberty Bowl**
Coach: Ken Niumatalolo				**Season Record >>**		**483**	**290**	**11-2**	

Schedule Source: Steve's Football Bible LLC

Selected game(s) highlights

AIR FORCE

Malcolm Perry had a 4 yard touchdown run with 23 seconds remaining to give the Midshipmen a stunning 34-25 victory over Air Force on Saturday. The Falcons scored 16 consecutive points in the final quarter and took the lead on a 1 yard run by Taven Birdow with 3:15 left. Perry led an 11-play, 75 yard scoring drive to claim the victory. Tony Brown returned a fumble 8 yards in the closing seconds to round out the scoring. Perry finished with 111 yards on 23 carries with a pair of touchdowns. He also completed 5 of 7 passes for 144 yards.

#16 Notre Dame

Chase Claypool caught four touchdown passes to match a school record and Book threw five for the third time this season as the Irish won their third straight game in No. 16 Notre Dame's 52-20 rout of No. 21 Navy. Claypool had scoring receptions of 7, 47 and 3 yards from Book to give the Irish a 21-0 lead early in the second quarter. Book threw a 70 yard touchdown pass to sophomore Braden Lenzy later in the quarter as Notre Dame took a 38-3 halftime lead and then hit Claypool with a 20 yard scoring pass on their final play of the game together. The loss ended a five-game winning streak for the Midshipmen who entered leading the nation in rushing with 357.9 yards per game. Malcolm Perry rushed 25 times for 117 yards.

#21 SMU

Malcolm Perry scampered 70 yards with just over six minutes remaining to break a tie and Navy beat the Mustangs 35-28. Perry generated 357 yards of total offense. He finished with 195 yards rushing on 38 carries with two touchdowns and completed 9 of 15 passes for 162 yards and another score. CJ Sanders had a 100 yard kickoff return for SMU tied for the longest in the 60-year history of Navy-Marine Corps Memorial Stadium. After trailing 21-10 at the half, the Midshipmen cut into the margin on a 1 yard plunge by Perry and a 25 yard field goal by Bijan Nichols on their first two possessions of the third quarter. Navy forced a pair of three-and-outs to help shift the momentum and its deliberate running attack began to wear down SMU's defenders. As the Mustangs stacked the box, Perry hit Ryan Mitchell with a 13 yard scoring pass, Mitchell's first career touchdown reception. Navy added a two-point conversion to regain the lead at 28-21 with 14:19 left. SMU tied it at 28-all on a 61 yard touchdown pass from Shane Buechele to Rashee Rice. After Perry's long run broke the deadlock, the Midshipmen came up with a huge stop on a fourth-and-4 from their own 12 with 2:36 remaining. The Midshipmen outgained the Mustangs 540 to 344 and dominated with time of possession 39:40 to 20:20.

ARMY {@ Lincoln Financial Field, Philadelphia, PA}

Malcom Perry dominated Saturday afternoon's affair as he led the #23 Midshipmen to a 31-7 win over Army, ending the three game losing streak to their rival. Perry rushed for 304 rushing yards and two touchdowns, and those 304 rushing yards are the most by any player in the 120 game history of The Army-Navy Game. Things started out well for Army as it put together an incredible 18 play, 78 yard touchdown drive that melted 10:41 off the clock in the first quarter ... but that was it. Army managed only 74 yards of offense in the final three quarters. Compare that to Navy, which ran only four plays for eight yards in the first quarter and finished the day with 396 total yards.

2019 LIBERTY BOWL

The 21st ranked Midshipmen won the AutoZone Liberty Bowl on Tuesday by completing a fourth down halfback option pass in the final minute. CJ Williams' 41 yard completion to Chance Warren on fourth-and-3 gave Navy first-and-goal from the 5 yard line. After quarterback Malcolm Perry spiked the ball, Bijan Nichols kicked a 23 yard field goal with two seconds remaining to give Navy a 20-17 victory over Kansas State. Navy outgained Kansas State 421-170 but wasted a couple of opportunities to put the game away. The Midshipmen led 17-10 late in the third quarter when a holding penalty wiped out a 31 yard run by Perry that would have given them first-and-goal at the 2. Navy ended up punting. Nichols then sent his 38 yard field goal attempt wide left with 8:26 left in the game. Kansas State finally got its offense going at that point, as Skylar Thompson connected with Wykeen Gill on a 15 yard completion and a 42 yard pass on back-to-back plays. Those long gains set up Thompson's 1 yard sneak that tied the game with 5:14 left. Then came Navy's dramatic winning drive.

2020 Navy Midshipmen

The Midshipmen were led by thirteenth year head coach Ken Niumatalolo. Team Captains were Billy Honaker, Cameron Kinley and Jackson Perkins. The Midshipmen finished the season 3-7. The annual Army–Navy Game was played on December 12 at Michie Stadium in West Point, NY; Army won the game 15-0.

Dalen Morris led the team in passing with 579 yards. Nelson Smith led the team in rushing with 645 yards and 8 rushing touchdowns. Mark Walker led the team in receptions with 13. Mychal Cooper led the team with 199 receiving yards. Smith led the team in scoring with 48 points.

Home games were played at Navy-Marine Corps Stadium

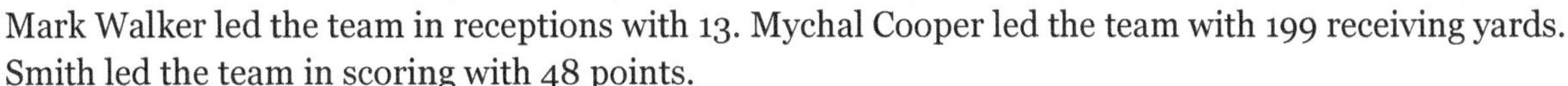

9/7/2020	NAVY		vs		BYU	ESPN	3	55	L
9/19/2020	NAVY		@		Tulane	ABC	27	24	W
9/26/2020	NAVY		vs		TEMPLE		7	40	L
10/3/2020	NAVY		@		Air Force	CBSSN	31	29	W
10/17/2020	NAVY		@		East Carolina	CBSSN	27	23	W
10/24/2020	NAVY		vs		HOUSTON	CBSSN	21	37	L
10/31/2020	NAVY		@	#22	Smu	espn2	37	51	L
11/28/2020	NAVY		vs		MEMPHIS	ESPNU	7	10	L
12/5/2020	NAVY		vs	#22	TULSA	espn2	6	19	L
12/12/2020	NAVY		vs		Army	CBS	0	15	L
Coach: Ken Niumatalolo					**Season Record >>**		166	303	3-7

Schedule Source: Steve's Football Bible LLC

Selected game(s) highlights

Tulane

Cameron Kinley's interception near his own goal line kept Navy's 24-point hole from getting deeper and set the stage for previously benched quarterback Dalen Morris to win back his job by helping the Midshipmen stage a historic rally. Jamale Carothers rushed for 125 yards, Bijan Nichols kicked a 33 yard field goal as time expired, and Navy beat Tulane 27-24 for the largest comeback in school history on Saturday. In the last seven minutes of the third quarter, the Midshipmen scored 16 points on two short Nelson Smith touchdowns and a safety. They tied it on Morris' 32 yard touchdown pass to Mychal Cooper, followed by a 2-point conversion, early in the fourth quarter.

Air Force

Tevye Schuettpelz-Rohl tied a school record with four field goals, Air Force's defense stymied Navy's offense and the Falcons opened their season with a 40-7 win over the Midshipmen. Schuettpelz-Rohl connected from 48, 35, 32 and 40 yards in front of a crowd that consisted only of Air Force cadets given the COVID-19 restrictions. Tyger Goslin had a 73 yard TD toss to Myles Fells in the second quarter. But Navy never completely found its groove on offense. The Midshipmen were held to 90 yards rushing.

#22 Smu

Shane Buechele threw three touchdown passes, Ulysses Bentley IV ran for two scores and No. 22 SMU rebounded from its first loss with a 51-37 victory over Navy and reclaim the Ganz Trophy. Nelson Smith had 55 yards rushing and a touchdown early in the second quarter but finished with 54 for the Midshipmen as SMU controlled the triple-option attack in the second half. The Mustangs slowed Navy's vaunted running game with several big plays in the backfield against the option. SMU finished with 12 tackles for loss. Chance Warren ran for two touchdowns for Navy.

Army {Michie Stadium – West Point, NY}

Tyhier Tyler scored on a 4 yard run early in the fourth quarter, the Army defense stoned Navy with a goal-line stand in the third, and the Black Knights beat their archrival 15-0 at fog-shrouded Michie Stadium. It was the first meeting between the teams at West Point since a 13-0 Navy shutout in 1943. The game was moved to Michie Stadium from Philadelphia because COVID-19 regulations in Pennsylvania would not have allowed the Corps of Cadets and Brigade of Midshipmen to attend. The game turned in the third quarter with Army clinging to a 3-0 lead and on its heels after Arline ripped off a 52 yard run. He was poised to cross the goal line when Cedric Cunningham ran him down and pushed him out of bounds at the 2. When two runs netted nothing, Navy Coach Ken Niumatalolo called timeout. The Army defense then rose to the occasion again, with senior linebacker Jon Rhattigan stopping Arline inches from the goal and West stopping Nelson Smith on fourth down. Army went up 3-0 on Quinn Maretzki's 37 yard field goal early in the second quarter, set up by Tyler's 28 yard completion to Tyrell Robinson, just the second completion of his career. Tyler scored after a Navy turnover, the only one of the game, and Daryan McDonald tacked on a safety late in the fourth when he tackled Navy wide receiver Mark Walker in the end zone on a reverse. Maretzki added a 40 yard field goal.

2021 Navy Midshipmen

The Midshipmen are led by 14th-year head coach Ken Niumatalolo. The
Midshipmen knocked off rival Army to reclaim the Thompson Cup Trophy. For the
second straight season, Navy did not go to a Bowl Game.

Home games were played at Navy-Marine Corps Stadium

9/4/2021	NAVY	vs		*MARSHALL*	CBSSN	7	49	L
9/11/2021	NAVY	vs		*AIR FORCE*	CBS	3	23	L
9/25/2021	NAVY	@		Houston	ESPNU	20	28	L
10/2/2021	NAVY	vs		CENTRAL FLORIDA	CBSSN	34	30	W
10/9/2021	NAVY	vs	#24	SMU	CBSSN	24	31	L
10/14/2021	NAVY	@		Memphis	ESPN	17	35	L
10/23/2021	NAVY	vs	#2	CINCINNATI	espn2	20	27	L
10/29/2021	NAVY	@		Tulsa	espn2	20	17	W
11/6/2021	NAVY	@	#8	*Notre Dame*	NBC	6	34	L
11/20/2021	NAVY	vs		EAST CAROLINA	CBSSN	35	38	L
11/27/2021	NAVY	@		Temple	ESPNU	38	14	W
12/11/2021	NAVY	vs		*Army*	CBS	17	13	W
Coach: Ken Niumatalolo				**Season Record >>**		241	339	4-8

Schedule Source: Steve's Football Bible LLC

Selected game(s) highlights

AIR FORCE

Brad Roberts ran for two touchdowns and Haaziq Daniels added one, and Air Force held the
Midshipmen to one first down before the fourth quarter in a 23-3 victory. This was the earliest meeting in
series history between these teams, scheduled with 9/11 in mind. Roberts ran for a 3-yard TD in the
second quarter, and Daniels scored on a 28-yard run in the final minute of the third. That was plenty of
offense for Air Force on a day the Falcons held Navy without a completed pass through the first three
quarters. Roberts added another touchdown on a 2-yard run in the fourth. Navy finished with only 68
yards of offense.

CENTRAL FLORIDA

Tai Lavatai returned from a two-game injury absence to lead Navy back from a 13 point fourth
quarter deficit and a 34-30 win over Central Florida. With Navy trailing 30-27, Diego Fabot knocked the
ball out of Brandon Johnson's hands after a 20-yard reception and Taylor Robinson recovered at the Navy
47. Eleven plays and over five minutes later, Isaac Ruoss ran in from the 4-yard line to give the
Midshipmen the lead with 3:09 left. UCF quickly went down the field down to the Navy 12, but Robinson,
who dropped a would-be interception two plays earlier, came up with a pick in the end zone on fourth
down with 24 seconds remaining. Bijan Nichols kicked his second field goal and Lavatai, who missed the
previous two games, ran for his second touchdown of the game after Navy entered the fourth quarter
trailing 30-17. Lavatai and Ruoss had 21 carries each as Navy ran for 348 yards led by 85 from Carlinos
Acie. Daniel Taylor recovered a blocked punt in the end zone for a Navy TD in the first half.

#2 CINCINNATI

The unbeaten Bearcats led by 17 at one point, but victory wasn't secure until Arquon
Bush intercepted a pass with 25 seconds left to wrap up a 27-20 victory. Tai Lavatai's 1-yard run made it a
one-score game and Navy recovered an onside kick with 48 seconds left. With the game tied at 10, Navy
was driving and looked poised to use up the remaining time in the second quarter. But after losing yards
on back-to-back plays, the Midshipmen had to try a 51-yard field goal. The kick was blocked, and
Cincinnati's Deshawn Pace nearly ran it back for a touchdown, but he stepped out of bounds with 1 second
left. That was enough time for Alex Bales to kick a 52-yard field goal and give the Bearcats a 13-10 lead.

Jerome Ford's 43-yard touchdown run made it 20-10, and Ridder added a 3-yard TD pass to Josh Whyle later in the third. Navy drove 79 yards in 7:12 and took a 7-0 lead on Lavatai's 2-yard run. The Bearcats quickly tied it on a 31-yard pass from Ridder to Whyle. With Cincinnati down 10-7, Ridder threw an interception deep in Navy territory, but after that the Bearcats scored on their next four possessions.

Tulsa

Tai Lavatai scored a game winning touchdown from the 1 yard line in the fourth quarter and Navy defeated Tulsa 20-17 on Friday night. Lavatai was 0-for-3 passing but gained a career high 64 yards on the ground. The 15-play eight-minute drive in Navy's come from behind win foiled a big night by Tulsa's Anthony Watkins, who scored the Golden Hurricanes first kickoff return for a touchdown in nearly a decade and compiled 178 yards in total offense. Watkins scored a 97-yard kickoff return to open the second half as Tulsa took a 10-3 lead. Late in the first half, Zack Long kicked a 26-yard field goal for a 3-0 lead as Tulsa salvaged points from a five-play drive that began with a Watkins season-long 78-yard rush to the Navy 7-yard line. Bijan Nichols evened the score with a 29-yard field goal for Navy with three seconds left in the first half. After the Watkins kickoff return, Navy scored after two long drives to tie and take the lead. Nichols added a 46-yard field goal for insurance.

#8 Notre Dame

Despite a slow start during which Notre Dame's offense appear to be sleepwalking through a large portion of Saturday's first half against Navy, the Irish stomped off 17 second-quarter points en route to a 34-6 victory over the Midshipmen. Jack Coan delivered the big blow, a 70 yard touchdown pass to Kevin Austin at the end of the first half, and the #8 Fighting Irish shut down Navy's triple-option attack. The touchdown play ended a 5-play, 95-yard scoring drive that took one minute to complete, and it provided a 17-3 halftime lead for the Irish. Kyren Williams ran for 95 yards and two scores as the Irish offense totaled 430 yards. Navy controlled the clock, with 34:33 of possession - but completed just one pass for 18 yards and rushed for 166 yards - 73 on 22 carries by fullback Isaac Ruoss. Navy led 3-0 after the first quarter on the first of two field goals by Bijan Nichols. But the Irish scored 17 points in the second quarter - Jonathan Doerer's tying field goal, Williams' 1-yard TD run and the Coan-to-Austin's touchdown aerial with 50 seconds remaining - for a 17-3 halftime lead.

Temple

Isaac Ruoss ran for two touchdown, Chance Warren had two TD catches and Navy defeated Temple 38-14. The Midshipmen threw just 12 passes for 72 yards but had touchdown tosses from both Tai Lavatai and Xavier Arline. Navy rolled up 219 yards on the ground. Tayvon Ruley and Ra'Von Bonner scored rushing touchdowns of 4 and 1 yards, respectively, for Temple.

ARMY {@ Lincoln Financial Field, Philadelphia, PA}

Quarterback Tai Lavatai ran for two touchdowns and Navy's defense limited Army to 57 second-half yards and a season-low 232 overall in a 17-13 victory Saturday in a game played at the Meadowlands to commemorate the 20th anniversary of the 9/11 terrorist attacks. Navy dominated against bowl-bound Army after giving up an early touchdown. It outgained them 278 yards to 232, including 196-124 on the ground against the nation's No. 2 rushing offense. The Mids held the ball for 34:25 and converted three big plays, including a fourth-down, fake punt in the fourth quarter that wasn't supposed to be a fake punt. Cole Talley added field goals of 31 and 32 yards in helping Army take a 13-7 halftime lead. The Black Knights generated little after that. Navy took over in the second half, taking the kickoff and going 74 yards in 10 plays with Lavatai scoring from 2 yards out. The drive featured a 26-yard run by Chance Warren on fourth-and-4 that got the ball to the 2. It was supposed to be a pass to Lavatai, but Warren saw it wasn't open, so he ran.

2022 Navy Midshipmen

The Midshipmen were led by 15th-year head coach Ken Niumatalolo. Navy finished the season with a 4-8 record and a heartbreaking loss to Army in double overtime, 20-17. For the second straight season, Navy did not go to a Bowl Game. Tai Lavatai led the team in passing with 785 yards and threw 5 touchdown passes. Daba Fofana led the team in rushing with 769 yards and rushed for 6 touchdowns. Jayden Umbarger led the in receiving with 16 receptions for 265 yards. Daniel Davies led the team in scoring with 49 points.

Home games were played at Navy-Marine Corps Stadium

9/3/2022	NAVY	vs		*DELAWARE*	CBSSN	7	14	**L**
9/10/2022	NAVY	vs		MEMPHIS	CBSSN	13	37	**L**
9/24/2022	NAVY	@		East Carolina		23	20	**W**
10/1/2022	NAVY	@		*Air Force*	CBS	10	13	**L**
10/8/2022	NAVY	vs		TULSA	CBSSN	53	21	**W**
10/14/2022	NAVY	@		Smu	ESPN	34	40	**L**
10/22/2022	NAVY	vs		HOUSTON	ESPNU	20	38	**L**
10/29/2022	NAVY	vs		TEMPLE	CBSSN	27	20	**W**
11/5/2022	NAVY	@		Cincinnati	ESPNU	10	20	**L**
11/12/2022	NAVY	vs	#20	*Notre Dame {@ Baltimore}*	ABC	32	35	**L**
11/19/2022	NAVY	@		Central Florida	espn2	17	14	**W**
12/10/2022	NAVY	**vs**		*Army {@ Philadelphia}*	CBS	17	20	**L**
Coach: Ken Niumatalolo				**Season Record >>**		263	292	**4-8**

Schedule Source: Steve's Football Bible LLC

Selected game(s) highlights

East Carolina

Daniel Davies, who came into the game without a field-goal attempt this season, made all three of his tries, including a 36-yarder in the second overtime and Navy beat East Carolina 23-20. The teams exchanged field goals in the first overtime before Davies connected again. Owen Daffer's 37-yard attempt went wide left. East Carolina had the ball in the final minutes, but Tyler Fletcher intercepted Holton Ahlers at the Navy 35 with 25 seconds left to send the game to overtime. The score was 3-3 headed into the fourth quarter when both teams scored two touchdowns apiece. ECU tied the game at 17-all with eight minutes left when a Navy defender tried to jump a route on a short pass but missed and Isaiah Winstead went down the left sideline for a 67-yard score. Right after ECU had taken at 10-3 lead, Tai Lavatai found Vincent Terrell II 15 yards down the middle and Terrell turned it into a 65-yard score with just under 12 minutes left. On the first play after the ensuing kickoff, Eavan Gibbons recovered a fumble at the ECU 25. That turnover turned into a 7-yard TD by Anton Hall Jr. for a 17-10 lead. Ahlers threw a 14-yard TD pass to Ryan Jones for a 10-3 lead to complete an eight-play, 70-yard drive that began when Navy turned the ball over on downs.

Air Force

Haaziq Daniels and the Air Force ground game finally got on track late to help the Falcons hold off Navy 13-10. The option quarterback clinched the win for the Falcons with an 18-yard scamper on third-and-6 in Navy territory, allowing them to run out the clock. This was soon after Matthew Dapore connected on a 22-yard field goal with 4:14 left to give Air Force the lead. Tai Lavatai tied the game at 10-apiece with 10:50 remaining with a 5-yard run on third-and-goal. Lavatai drifted back to pass but when the middle opened, he cruised into the end zone. After Dapore's field goal, Navy went three-and-out. The Falcons raced out to a quick 10-0 lead and rode their defense to a victory in the first leg of the Commander-In-Chief's Trophy. The Falcons got off to a fast start with Daniels completing a long pass to Cormier for a touchdown. It was a pair of first-half fumbles from Daniels that kept Navy within striking distance. The first was with the Falcons deep in Midshipmen territory early in the second quarter. Then, with 34 seconds left in the half and facing third down, Daniels tried to find a receiver downfield but was stripped from behind by Jacob Busic. Navy turned that into a 37-yard field goal to trim Air Force's lead to 10-3 at halftime.

TULSA

Daba Fofana ran for 113 of his 159 yards and three touchdowns in the first half to help Navy cruise to a 53-21 victory over Tulsa. Freshman Nathan Kent broke loose off a reverse for a 70-yard touchdown run late in the first quarter for Navy. It was Kent's first collegiate play. Fofana added scoring runs from 47, 15, and 11 yards in the second quarter as Navy built a 36-14 lead at halftime. Navy rushed 69 times for 455 yards and completed just 2 of 8 passes for 35 yards. Vincent Terrell Jr. added 93 yards rushing and a score. Kent finished with 70 yards.

Smu {Ganz Trophy}

Tanner Mordecai passed for 336 yards and three touchdowns, and he rushed for 74 yards and a score to help SMU beat Navy 40-34. All four of Mordecai's touchdowns went for 20-plus yards. Mordecai raced up the middle for a 60-yard touchdown run to begin SMU's 20-point scoring run in the third quarter. Mordecai also had a short pass to Jordan Kerley, who used two good blocks along the sideline to race for a 33-yard touchdown. Mordecai connected with Roderick Daniels Jr. from 27-yards out for a 40-20 lead midway through the fourth. SMU recovered Navy's onside kick with 2:30 left but went three-and-out before the Midshipmen scored with nine seconds left to cap the scoring. Quarterback Tai Lavatai carried it 25 times for 121 yards and two touchdowns for Navy. Lavatai was 9-of-22 passing for 137 yards with two touchdowns and an interception. Navy's third pass attempt of the game went to Vincent Terrell Jr. for a 24-yard touchdown with 14 seconds left before halftime. Navy opened the second half with a 75-yard drive, ending in Lavatai's 15-yard touchdown run.

TEMPLE

Quarterback Xavier Arline scored on a 23-yard run in overtime and Navy outlasted Temple 27-20. Dashaun Peele then intercepted E.J. Warner in the end zone on fourth-and-11 from the 13 to wrap up the game. Daniel Davies sandwiched two field goals around a 15-yard touchdown run by Daba Fofana to give Navy a 13-0 lead after one quarter. Temple closed to within 13-10 when Layton Jordan forced and recovered a fumble by Arline in the end zone for a touchdown just 1:11 into the third quarter. Anton Hall answered with a 16-yard scoring run and the Midshipmen took a 20-10 lead into the final quarter. Warner hit Amad Anderson Jr. for a 20-yard score and Camden Price kicked a 22-yard field goal with 1:08 left to play to send it to overtime.

#20 Notre Dame {@ Baltimore, MD} {Rip Miller Trophy}

Brady Lenzy reached around a defender with both arms in a sensational display, securing one of four touchdown passes by Drew Pyne before halftime in No. 20 Notre Dame's 35-32 win over Navy on Saturday. Pyne also ran for a touchdown in the first half, and Notre Dame needed all those TDs to hold off the Midshipmen, who came storming back while shutting out the Irish in the second half. Notre Dame blocked a punt for a fifth straight game. Lenzy's catch, however, was the most impressive highlight. Navy's Mbiti Williams Jr. was positioned between Lenzy and the ball on Pyne's deep pass to the goal line, but Lenzy reached around with both hands and controlled the ball, appearing to pin it against Williams' back. Then he pulled it around the cornerback with his right hand to complete the catch. The Irish led 35-13 at halftime before going dormant offensively for the final two quarters. Navy closed to within three with 1:21 remaining, but an unsuccessful onside kick ended the rally. Navy had the ball down 21-13 in the second quarter, but an interception on a trick play gave the Irish possession at the Navy 41. Pyne ran for an 11-yard touchdown moments later, and then the blocked punt by Jack Kiser - Notre Dame's seventh of the season - set up Pyne's 37-yard TD toss to Jayden Thomas. Pyne threw a 5-yard TD pass to Chris Tyree, and then the Midshipmen scored on a 2-yard run by Xavier Arline that made it 21-13. Arline threw a 23-yard touchdown pass to Mark Walker in the fourth, and a 2-point conversion made it 35-24. Then Maasai

Maynor's 20-yard TD pass to Maquel Haywood late in the fourth, along with another 2-point conversion, cut the lead to a field goal.

Army {@ Philadelphia, PA}

The Army Black Knights downed the Navy Midshipmen in a 20-17 double overtime victory on Saturday, the first overtime game in the rivalry's history. With possession in the second overtime, Navy committed a costly turnover when running back Anton Hall Jr. fumbled on the one-yard line. Getting possession back, Army kicker Quinn Maretzki was able to boot a 39-yard field goal to finish it off for the Black Knights. This game was the exact defensive struggle that you would imagine with both familiar foes fighting to impose their will on the other. Navy held onto a 3-0 lead late into the second quarter before a Navy punt block was returned by Jabril Williams for a touchdown to give the Black Knights a 7-3 advantage heading into the half. Hall would turn the game on its head in the third quarter, breaking off a 77-yard touchdown run to put Navy back on top. That surprisingly marked the longest touchdown score in the rivalry's history. With its back against the wall deep into the fourth quarter, Army managed to get into Navy territory to set up a 37-yard field goal by Maretzki to tie the game with 1:53 to go. We were treated to a fireworks show to begin the overtime period. Markel Johnson broke off a 25-yard touchdown run on the first play for Army and Navy immediately followed that up when Xavier Arline hit Marquel Haywood on a wheel route for a touchdown on its first play. Following that was Hall's costly fumble, setting up the game-winning kick for Army.

2023 Navy Midshipmen

The Midshipmen were led by first-year head coach Brian Newberry. Navy finished the season with a 5-7 record and a heartbreaking loss to Army, 17-11. For the fourth straight season, Navy did not go to a Bowl Game.

Passing Yds	Tai Lavatai	701	TD Pass	Tai Lavatai	5
Rushing Yds	Alex Tecza	758	Rush TD	Alex Tecza	5
Receptions	E. Heidenreich/B. Chatman	19	TD Rec.	Eli Heidenreich	4
Receiving Yds	Eli Heidenreich	382	Points	Nathan Kirkwood	34
Interceptions	Rayaun Lee/Dashaun Peele	4	Sacks	Luke Pirris/Justin Reed	4.5

Home games were played at Navy-Marine Corps Stadium

Date				Opponent	TV			
8/26/2023	NAVY	vs	#13	*Notre Dame {@ Dublin}*	ABC	3	42	L
9/9/2023	NAVY	vs		*WAGNER*		24	0	W
9/14/2023	NAVY	@		Memphis	ESPN	24	28	L
9/30/2023	NAVY	vs		SOUTH FLORIDA	CBSSN	30	44	L
10/7/2023	NAVY	vs		NORTH TEXAS	CBSSN	27	24	W
10/14/2023	NAVY	@		Charlotte		14	0	W
10/21/2023	NAVY	vs	#22	*AIR FORCE*	CBS	6	17	L
11/4/2023	NAVY	@		Temple		18	32	L
11/11/2023	NAVY	vs		ALABAMA-BIRMINGHAM	CBSSN	31	6	W
11/18/2023	NAVY	vs		EAST CAROLINA		10	0	W
11/25/2023	NAVY	@	#25	Smu	espn2	14	59	L
12/9/2023	NAVY	vs		*Army {@ Foxborough}*	CBS	11	17	L
Coach: Brian Newberry				**Season Record >>**		212	269	5-7

Schedule Source: Steve's Football Bible LLC

Selected game(s) highlights

#13 Notre Dame

Sam Hartman threw for four touchdowns and the No. 13 Fighting Irish routed Navy 42-3 on Saturday in a season-opening victory in Ireland's capital. Notre Dame scored at will by air and on the ground against the Midshipmen, improving to 3-0 all-time against Navy in Dublin games. Hartman completed 19 of 23 passes for 251 yards. Hartman connected with Jaden Greathouse on two scoring strikes, the second a 20-yard reception that made the score 35-0 early in the third quarter and kept the Irish offense perfect at that point — scoring touchdowns in their first five possessions. After touchdowns runs by Audric Estimé and Jadarian Price, Hartman's first TD pass went to Greathouse, who caught a deep ball at the 5 and took it in for a 35-yard scoring play and a 21-0 lead. Notre Dame's sixth drive ended when new kicker Spencer Shrader missed a 42-yard field goal attempt in the third quarter. Hartman hit Deion Colzie in the flat for a 25-yard touchdown pass that made the score 42-0 early in the fourth quarter.

NORTH TEXAS

Alex Tecza ran for a pair of long touchdowns and Navy held off North Texas 27-24. Tecza had a 39-yard scoring run in the second quarter, and his 21-yarder stretched the Navy lead to 27-17 with 7:07 to play. Ayo Adeyi broke loose on a 47-yard touchdown run that cut the North Texas deficit to a field goal with 5:23 remaining. The Mean Green got the ball back with just under two minutes left at their own 20 but couldn't pick up a first down. Tecza, who averages nearly 73 yards per game, finished with 137 yards rushing on 17 carries. Blake Horvath added 88 yards rushing for Navy (2-3, 1-2 American Athletic Conference), which had 481 yards of offense with 406 on the ground.

EAST CAROLINA

Alex Tecza rushed for the only touchdown and Navy's defense turned in its third shutout this season with a 10-0 victory over East Carolina. It was the first time ECU was shut out in 323 games, going back 26 years to Oct. 4, 1997 at Syracuse. The Midshipmen became the first FBS team to have three shutouts this season. Navy held the Pirates to 189 total yards, intercepted two passes and recovered two fumbles. Navy lost two of its own fumbles, had a field goal blocked and missed another. But Nathan Kirkwood's 27-yard field goal midway through the fourth quarter was more than enough insurance in this game. The field goal came after ECU punter Luke Larsen fumbled, and Adam Walker recovered. The closest ECU came to scoring was a missed 49-yard field-goal attempt in the second quarter. Tecza's 19-yard touchdown came in the first quarter on a two-play possession following quarterback Xavier Arline's 39-yard run. Arline threw for 102 yards and rushed for 68 yards. Tecza rushed for 94 yards on 24 carries. Navy had 276 yards offense.

Army {@ Foxborough, MA}

Army held its ground on a goal-line stand in the final seconds to send Navy mascot Bill the Goat — and Navy superfan Bill, the G.O.A.T. — home disappointed. Army linebacker Kalib Fortner scored on a fourth-quarter strip sack and then helped stuff quarterback Tai Lavatai inches from the end zone with 3 seconds left to lead the Black Knights to a 17-11 victory over Navy on Saturday and win the 124th meeting of the nation's oldest service academies. Bryson Daily ran for 84 yards and threw Army's first touchdown pass against Navy since 2015 to help the Black Knights claim the much-coveted bragging rights for the sixth time in eight tries. Kanye Udoh ran for 88 yards for Army, which also claimed the Commander-in-Chief's Trophy. Lavatai came off the bench in the second quarter and rushed for 74 yards, completing 16 of 26 passes for 176 yards — the most passing yards for a Navy quarterback against Army since 2010. Jayden Umbarger caught six passes for 75 yards and a touchdown that made it 17-9 with 2:47 left. The Black Knights opened a 17-3 lead with less than five minutes to play before Lavatai drove Navy for one score and then took the Midshipmen to the Army 6 in the final minute. He threw two incompletions before hitting Alex Tecza, who was tackled in bounds at the 2. With no timeouts and no opportunity to spike the ball — it was fourth down — Navy scrambled to line up and get the play off. Lavatai surged forward as his whole team pushed, ahead of him and behind, but Army held on; replay confirmed that the ball never crossed the goal line. To kill the remaining 3 seconds, Daily took a shotgun snap, hesitated, and stepped out of the end zone for an intentional safety.

2024 Navy Midshipmen {Commander-in-Chief Trophy}

The Midshipmen were led by Brian Newberry in his second year as the head coach. The Midshipmen finished the regular season with a 9-3 record {7-2 AAC} and were invited to the Armed Forces Bowl in Fort Worth, Texas, where they played Oklahoma from the SEC.

Landon Robinson {DL}, Colin Ramos {LB} and Rayaum Lane {K} were selected to the AAC All-Conference First team.

Passing Yds	Blake Horvath	1,353	TD Pass	Blake Horvath	13
Rushing Yds	Blake Horvath	1,246	Rush TD	Blake Horvath	17
Receptions	Eli Heidenreich	39	TD Rec.	Eli Heidenreich	6
Receiving Yds	Eli Heidenreich	671	Points	Blake Horvath	102
Interceptions	Dashaun Peele	5	Sacks	Justin Reed	6.0

Home games were played at Navy-Marine Corps Stadium

Date				Opponent	TV				
8/31/2024		vs		*BUCKNELL*	CBSSN	49	21	W	
9/7/2024		vs		TEMPLE	CBSSN	38	11	W	
9/21/2024		vs		MEMPHIS	CBSSN	56	44	W	
9/28/2024		@		Alabama-Birmingham	espn2	41	18	W	
10/5/2024		@		*Air Force*	CBS	34	7	W	
10/19/2024	#25	vs		CHARLOTTE	CBSSN	51	17	W	
10/26/2024	#24	vs	#12	*Notre Dame {@ E, Rutherford}*	ABC	14	51	L	
11/2/2024		@		Rice	espn2	10	24	L	
11/9/2024		@		South Florida	espn2	28	7	W	
11/16/2024		vs	#25	TULANE	espn2	0	35	L	
11/29/2024		@		East Carolina	ESPN	34	20	W	
12/14/2024		vs		Army {@ Landover, MD}	CBS	31	13	W	
12/27/2024		vs		**Oklahoma**	**ESPN**	**21**	**20**	**W**	**Armed Forces Bowl**
Coach: Brian Newberry				**Season Record >>**		**407**	**288**	**10-3**	

Schedule Source: Steve's Football Bible LLC

Selected game(s) highlights

MEMPHIS

Blake Horvath complemented two touchdown passes with 211 yards rushing and four scores and Rayuan Lane III had an 86-yard pick-6 in the closing seconds to help unbeaten Navy hold on for a 56-44 victory over Memphis. Memphis took the opening kickoff and marched 65 yards in nine plays with Mario Anderson Jr. scoring on a 7-yard run for a 7-0 lead. Horvath capped a 10-play, 77-yard drive with a 5-yard touchdown run to pull Navy even. Brandon Thomas raced 57 yards for a score with 1:21 left to give the Tigers a 14-7 lead after one quarter. Horvath connected with Eli Heidenreich for a 39-yard touchdown six seconds into the second quarter and Brandon Chatman added a 12-yard touchdown run on the next possession to give the Midshipmen a 21-14 lead. Caden Costa's 29-yard field goal cut the Tigers' deficit to four, but Horvath scored on a 3-yard run with 11 second left to put Navy up 28-17 at halftime. Horvath teamed up with Chatman for a 37-yard score on Navy's first possession of the second half. Memphis answered with Seth Henigan's 37-yard touchdown pass to Roc Taylor the first time the Tigers had the ball. Anderson scored on a 5-yard run with 1:11 remaining, but the Tigers' two-point conversion failed and left them trailing 35-30. Horvath scored on a 7-yard run four seconds into the final quarter and broke free for a 90-yard touchdown on a first-down run to put the Midshipmen up 49-30 with 8:22 left to play. Horvath completed 9 of 12 passes for 192 yards

Air Force

Blake Horvath ran for 115 yards and Eli Heidenreich added 100 yards rushing and receiving, leading Navy to a 34-7 victory over Air Force. Navy won with its usual ground dominance and a defense that allowed only 273 yards. Horvath ran for two touchdowns, Heidenreich added one rushing touchdown and his 51-yard run set up another score in the fourth quarter. Navy had 185 yards rushing in the first half, highlighted by Nathan Kent's 34-yard end-around touchdown on a fourth-down play. Navy led 21-7 at halftime. Air Force scored on a 45-yard pass from Quentin Hayes to Tre Roberson in the second quarter.

#12 Notre Dame {@ East Rutherford, NJ}

Jeremiyah Love ran for 102 yards, two touchdowns and extended his streak of rushing for a TD to eight games as No. 12 Notre Dame took advantage of six turnovers and beat previously unbeaten and No. 24 Navy 51-14. Love scored on runs of 64 and 2 yards and quarterback Riley Leonard ran for a touchdown and threw two more. The Midshipmen lost five fumbles and had six turnovers overall that led to 28 points for the Irish, with Jaylen Sneed recovering a Blake Horvath fumble in the end zone for a touchdown. Horvath scored on a 47-yard run for Navy and finished with 129 yards on 14 carries. Eli Heidenreich scored on a short run for the other touchdown.

Rice

Dean Connors ran for 105 yards and two touchdowns to lead Rice to a 24-10 victory over Navy. Connors scored on a 4-yard run with 9:30 remaining in the first quarter after play resumed following a more than five-hour weather delay. E.J. Warner's 17-yard touchdown pass to Matt Sykes made it 14-0 heading into the second quarter. Connors added a 9-yard touchdown run to stretch the Owls' lead to 24-7 with 2:00 remaining in the third. Blake Horvath threw an interception to Tyson Flowers on Navy's first play from scrimmage but scored on a 9-yard touchdown run midway through the second quarter.

South Florida

The Navy defense held USF to just 60 yards rushing on 25 carries, while the Navy offense ran for 3 touchdowns and threw for another one as the Middies dominated the Bulls from start to finish 28-7 in front of 34,091 fans at Raymond James Stadium in Tampa. The Middies jumped out to a 14-0 lead on the first two possessions of the game. Navy took the opening kickoff and moved 70 yards on four plays with Eli Heidenreich scoring on a 60-yard touchdown run to put the Middies up 7-0. The defense got the ball back for Navy on Kyle Jacob's second interception of the year and the Navy offense promptly moved 79 yards on 13 plays with Brandon Chatman scoring on a beautiful 20-yard touchdown run to make it 14-0. junior striker Kenneth McShan came on a blitz to blast USF quarterback Bryce Archie as he was throwing the ball down the field. Archie's pass ended up short of its intended target and sophomore Ira Oniha picked it off at the Navy 11 and returned the interception 36 yards to the Navy 47 with just 14 seconds left. Two plays later, the Middies led 21-0. Junior fullback Alex Tecza ran up the middle for 15 yards down to the USF 38 and then Horvath hit Tecza with a 38-yard touchdown pass with 2 seconds left to send the Middies into the locker room up 21. Navy made it 28-0 early in the fourth quarter on a 10-yard touchdown run by Blake Horvath. The touchdown was set up by a fake punt that nose guard Landon Robinson took around left end for 34 yards.

Army {@ Landover, MD}

Blake Horvath outplayed Bryson Daily at quarterback, accounting for 311 yards and four touchdowns to help Navy beat No. 19 Army 31-13 on Saturday. Horvath threw for 107 yards and two touchdowns and ran for 204 yards and two TDs. Daily threw a touchdown pass of his own, but he was intercepted three times. Army fell behind 14-0 in the second quarter and never completely recovered. In front of a crowd that included President-elect Donald Trump at the Washington Commanders' home stadium in Landover, Navy took the opening kickoff and drove 65 yards, reaching the end zone on a 1-yard run by Horvath. Daily, who had been intercepted only once all season, had a pass picked off in the second quarter by Dashaun Peele. The Midshipmen took advantage of a short field, going ahead 14-0 on an 18-yard pass from Horvath to Brandon Chatman. Daily answered with a TD pass of his own — 23 yards to Hayden Reed. After a field goal made the score 14-10, Horvath connected with Eli Heidenreich, who broke free up the left sideline for a 52-yard touchdown. Daily missed an open Casey Reynolds in the end zone early in the fourth, and Army settled for a field goal. Navy then faced fourth down near midfield, but Landon Robinson — normally a nose guard — ran 29 yards on a fake punt. Although Robinson fumbled at the end of the play, the Midshipmen were able to recover. Horvath's 1-yard scoring run made it 28-13, and Daily was intercepted twice more before the end of the game.

2024 ARMED FORCES BOWL

Blake Horvath set a Navy record with a 95-yard touchdown run and then scored a go-ahead 6-yarder with 4:34 left as the Midshipmen overcame an early two-touchdown deficit and stopped a late 2-point conversion attempt to beat Oklahoma 21-20 in the Armed Forces Bowl. The Sooners got a 10-yard touchdown pass from Michael Hawkins Jr. to Jake Roberts with six seconds left. They then went for the win, but Hawkins was sacked by Justin Reed on the conversion try. Horvath's record run on a sprint down the middle of the field tied the game at 14 late in third quarter. He then put Navy ahead for the first time on his 6-yard TD run, one play after he converted a fourth-and-3 with a 16-yard pass to Eli Heidenrich. Horvath ran 18 times for 155 yards and completed 7 of 12 passes for 92 yards. Alex Tecza had an 11-yard TD run for the Midshipmen. Oklahoma went up after Gavin Sawchuk's 21-yard TD on the opening drive. It was 14-0 with 5:56 left in the first quarter after Hawkins rolled left, reversed field and got almost to the other side of the field before throwing to Zion Kearney for a 56-yard catch-and-run TD.

2025 Navy Midshipmen {Commander-in-Chief Trophy}

The 2025 Navy Midshipmen football team were led by third-year head coach Brian Newberry. The Midshipmen finished the season with an 11-2 record {7-1 AAC} and were invited to the Liberty Bowl where they played Cincinnati from the Big XII Conference. Navy won the Commander-in-Chief Trophy for the second straight year.

Landon Robinson {DL} was selected as a First Team All-American. Robinson and Rayne Fry {DS} were selected to the First Team All-Conference AAC team. Robinson was named the AAC Defensive Player of the Year.

Passing Yds	Blake Horvath	1,580	TD Pass	Blake Horvath	12
Rushing Yds	Blake Horvath	1,200	Rush TD	Blake Horvath	16
Receptions	Eli Heidenreich	51	TD Rec.	Eli Heidenreich	6
Receiving Yds	Eli Heidenreich	941	Points	Blake Horvath	96
Interceptions	Phillip Hamilton	3	Sacks	Landon Robinson	6.5

Final Rank: AP #23 CP #23

Home games were played at Navy-Marine Corps Stadium

Date	Rank			Opponent	TV			Result	Notes
8/30/2025		vs		*VIRGINIA MILITARY*	CBSSN	52	7	W	
9/6/2025		vs		ALABAMA-BIRMINGHAM	CBSSN	38	24	W	
9/13/2025		@		Tulsa		42	23	W	
9/27/2025		vs		RICE	CBSSN	21	13	W	
10/4/2025		vs		*AIR FORCE*	CBS	34	31	W	*Heidenreich 243 rec. yds
10/11/2025		@		Temple	espn2	32	31	W	
10/25/2025		vs		FLORIDA ATLANTIC	CBSSN	42	32	W	
11/1/2025	#25	@		North Texas	espn2	17	31	L	
11/8/2025		@	#10	*Notre Dame*	NBC	10	49	L	
11/15/2025		vs	#25	SOUTH FLORIDA	espn2	41	38	W	
11/27/2025		@		Memphis	ESPN	28	17	W	
12/13/2025	#23	vs		Army {@ Baltimore}	CBS	17	16	W	
1/2/2026	#22	vs		**Cincinnati**	**ESPN**	**35**	**13**	**W**	**Liberty Bowl**
Coach: Brian Newberry				Season Record >>		409	325	11-2	

Schedule Source: Steve's Football Bible LLC

*-Single game record {Heidenreich 3 TD catch vs Air Force}

Selected game(s) highlights

AIR FORCE

In a record-breaking aerial and ground assault, the Navy Midshipmen defeated the Air Force Falcons, 34–31 at a sold-out Navy-Marine Corps Memorial Stadium in Annapolis. Navy entered the game 4–0 and maintained their perfect start in a back-and-forth thriller that saw the score tied four different times. The decisive moment came late in the fourth quarter. After Air Force tied the game 31–31 on a 53-yard touchdown pass, Navy QB Blake Horvath led an 11-play, 62-yard drive. Facing a 4th-and-1 from the Air Force 12-yard line, a false start forced Navy to settle for a 34-yard Nathan Kirkwood field goal to take a 34–31 lead with 6:47 remaining. The Navy defense then forced a fumble near midfield to ice the game. Horvath threw for 339 yards, and three touchdown passes to Eli Heidenreich, who caught 8 passes for 243 yards. Horvath rushed for 130 yards and rushed for one touchdown.

Temple

The Navy Midshipmen remained unbeaten by defeating the Temple Owls, 32–31 at Lincoln Financial Field in Philadelphia. The game was a classic "tale of two halves" that ended with a gutsy two-point conversion call by Navy head coach Brian Newberry in the final seconds. Temple dominated the first half, physically outmatching Navy and holding a 17–7 lead at the break. The Owls' defense stifled the Midshipmen's triple-option, holding them to just 111 total yards in the first two quarters. However, Navy adjusted in the second half, clawing back into the game through the heroics of quarterback Blake Horvath. The lead changed hands multiple times in a frantic fourth quarter. Temple took a 31–24 lead with just 1:16 remaining after a 1-yard touchdown plunge by Jay Ducker. With no timeouts left, Navy marched 75 yards in just 37 seconds, culminating in a spectacular 51-yard touchdown run by Horvath. Rather than kicking the extra point to tie, Navy went for the win; Horvath found Alex Tecza in the corner of the end zone for a successful two-point conversion with 39 seconds left.

#10 Notre Dame

The No. 10 Notre Dame Fighting Irish delivered a dominant performance to defeat the Navy Midshipmen, 49–10, on a cold and snowy night at a sold-out Notre Dame Stadium. Despite the difficult weather conditions, starting with rain and transitioning to a steady snow, Notre Dame played nearly flawless football. The Irish offense amassed 502 total yards and scored touchdowns on seven of their first nine possessions. Notably, Notre Dame played the entire game without a single penalty, matching a program record last achieved in 1997. Navy, playing without starting quarterback Blake Horvath due to injury, struggled to find a rhythm. While they briefly tied the game 7–7 in the second quarter, they were eventually overwhelmed by Notre Dame's speed and physicality. The Irish blew the game open in the third quarter, outscoring the Midshipmen 21–0 in that frame alone.

#25 SOUTH FLORIDA

The Navy Midshipmen held off a late surge from No. 24 South Florida to win 41–38 in Annapolis. Navy utilized a barrage of explosive plays to take an early command of the game. On just the third play of the afternoon, Alex Tecza ripped off a 76-yard touchdown run to set the tone. By halftime, Navy held a comfortable 24–9 lead, aided by an 82-yard completion from Blake Horvath to Eli Heidenreich. The fourth quarter transformed into a high-scoring track meet. After USF quarterback Byrum Brown scored on a 60-yard dash to pull the Bulls within three, Navy's starting QB Blake Horvath was forced out of the game with an injury. Backup Braxton Woodson stepped in and played the hero, scoring two rushing touchdowns, including a 64-yard sprint, to keep the Bulls at arm's length. USF scored 22 points in the final frame, but Navy recovered a late onside kick to seal the win.

Army {@ Baltimore}

The No. 22 Navy Midshipmen rallied from a nine-point deficit to defeat the Army Black Knights, 17–16, at M&T Bank Stadium in Baltimore. With President Donald Trump in attendance, the Midshipmen secured their second consecutive victory over their rivals and claimed the Commander-in-Chief's Trophy for the second straight year. The 126th meeting between the service academies began as a mirror image, with both teams orchestrating 13-play, 75-yard touchdown drives that ate up over seven minutes each. However, the defenses dominated the middle quarters. Army capitalized on two Navy turnovers to build a 16–7 lead late into the third quarter, fueled by three field goals from Dawson Jones. The game turned in the fourth quarter when Navy safety Phillip Hamilton intercepted an underthrown pass at midfield. Navy marched to the 1-yard line but nearly saw the game slip away when a "tush push" resulted in a fumble; fortunately, Navy's Eli Heidenreich recovered it at the 8-yard line. Facing a 4th-and-goal with the trophy on the line, QB Blake Horvath found Heidenreich on a slant for the game-winning touchdown with 6:32 remaining.

2026 LIBERTY BOWL

The No. 22 Navy Midshipmen capped off a historic season by defeating the Cincinnati Bearcats, 35–13, in the 67th AutoZone Liberty Bowl at Simmons Bank Liberty Stadium in Memphis. The victory secured Navy's 11th win of the season, tying the school record, and marked the first time in program history that the Midshipmen achieved back-to-back 10-win seasons. Played in a steady downpour, the game was a methodical demonstration of Navy's disciplined triple-option and a suffocating defense. Cincinnati entered the game significantly short-handed, missing 18 players due to transfer portal entries and opt-outs, including star quarterback Brendan Sorsby. Navy broke a 7–7 halftime tie with 28 unanswered points in the second half. Quarterback Blake Horvath, named the game's MVP, was the engine of the offense, accounting for three touchdowns. The Navy defense put the exclamation point on the win in the final minutes when linebacker Coleman Cauley recorded a 5-yard "pick-six", the first interception return for a touchdown in Navy's bowl history.